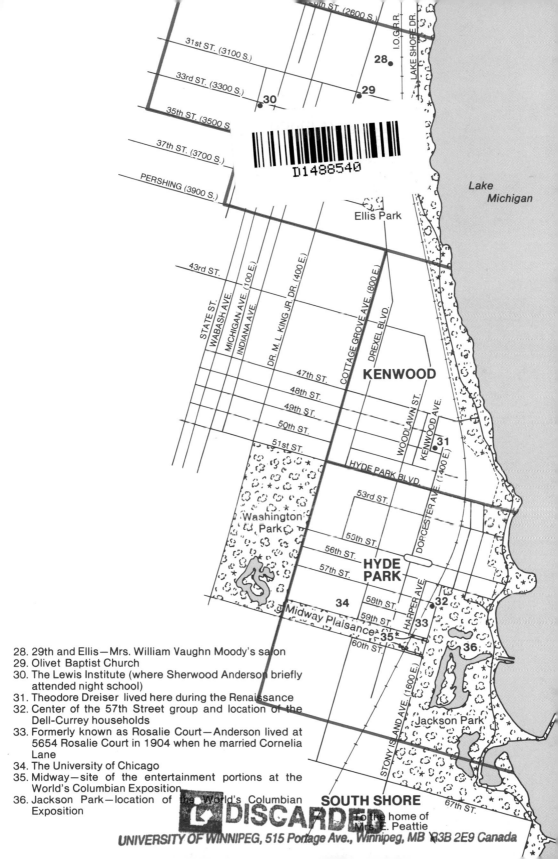

31st ST. (3100 S.)

33rd ST. (3300 S.)

35th ST. (3500 S.)

37th ST. (3700 S.)

PERSHING (3900 S.)

I.O.G.R.R.

LAKE SHORE DR.

28

29

30

Lake Michigan

Ellis Park

43rd ST.

STATE ST.

WABASH AVE.

MICHIGAN AVE. (100 E.)

INDIANA AVE.

DR. M. L. KING JR. DR. (400 E.)

COTTAGE GROVE AVE. (800 E.)

DREXEL BLVD.

47th ST.

KENWOOD

48th ST.

49th ST.

50th ST.

51st ST.

WOODLAWN ST.

KENWOOD AVE. (1400 E.)

31

HYDE PARK BLVD.

53rd ST.

DORCHESTER AVE.

Washington Park

55th ST.

56th ST.

57th ST.

HYDE PARK

HARPER AVE.

34

58th ST.

59th ST.

Midway Plaisance

35

32

33

60th ST.

36

Jackson Park

STONY ISLAND AVE. (1600 E.)

SOUTH SHORE

67th ST.

28. 29th and Ellis—Mrs. William Vaughn Moody's salon
29. Olivet Baptist Church
30. The Lewis Institute (where Sherwood Anderson briefly attended night school)
31. Theodore Dreiser lived here during the Renaissance
32. Center of the 57th Street group and location of the Dell-Currey households
33. Formerly known as Rosalie Court—Anderson lived at 5654 Rosalie Court in 1904 when he married Cornelia Lane
34. The University of Chicago
35. Midway—site of the entertainment portions at the World's Columbian Exposition
36. Jackson Park—location of the World's Columbian Exposition

...the home of Mrs. E. Peattie

A STORYTELLER AND A CITY

Sherwood Anderson (Chicago Historical Society, DN# 9914)

A STORYTELLER AND A CITY

Sherwood Anderson's Chicago

Kenny J. Williams

Northern Illinois University Press
DeKalb, Illinois / 1988

Library Of Congress
Library of Congress Cataloging-in-Publication Data
Williams, Kenny J.
    A storyteller and a city: Sherwood Anderson's Chicago/Kenny J. Williams.
        p.   cm.
    Bibliography: p.
    Includes index.
    ISBN 0-87580-135-8 : $28.50
    1. Anderson, Sherwood, 1878-1941—Homes and haunts—Illinois—
Chicago.   2. Chicago (Ill.) in literature.   3. Chicago (Ill.)—
Description.   4. Literary landmarks—Illinois—Chicago.
5. Authors, American—20th century—Biography.   I. Title.
PS3501.N4Z954   1988
813'.52—dc19
[B]   87-33970
                                                                    CIP

Contents

Sherwood Anderson Chronology   v

PROLOGUE: A STORYTELLER'S CITY

  1 The Legendary Chicago
      and the Real City   5

  2 The City "Triumphant":
      Chicago in Fiction   25

PART ONE: CONFRONTATION

  3 Sam McPherson: An Uncommon
      Portrait of a Chicago Businessman   47

  4 Beaut McGregor: Angry
      Activist in a Disorderly City   89

  5 "Disorderly" Realism   123

PART TWO: RECONCILIATION

  6 "Something Blossomed in
      Chicago": Renaissance Days   145

  7 Songs of the City and Some
      Rooming House People   169

  8 Out of a Town, A City   193

  9 The Metaphoric City   223

EPILOGUE: A STORYTELLER'S MOMENT

  10 Sherwood Anderson's Urban Cycle   259

  Notes   275

  Bibliographic Essay   291

  Index   303

Sherwood Anderson
Chronology

1876   Born in Camden, Ohio, on September 13, to Irwin M. and
        Emma Smith Anderson . . . the third child of seven.

1884   Moved to Clyde, Ohio, with the family . . . briefly attended
        public school while working at so many odd jobs that he
        earned the nickname Jobby . . . became eager to go to Chi-
        cago "to make his mark" in life.

1895   Death of his mother.

1896   Moved to Chicago "to seek his fortune" but worked in a
        North Side factory rolling barrels of apples and stacking
        crates of eggs . . . lived on the West Side . . . first as a
        boarder on Washington Boulevard, then in a tenement with
        his sister and two of his younger brothers . . . attended night
        classes sporadically at Lewis Institute.

1898   Returned to Ohio when his unit of the National Guard was
        activated, as a member of Company I, Sixth Ohio Regiment
        of Volunteer Infantry, he was stationed in the South and saw
        noncombat duty in Cuba.

1899   Company I was retired from national service in May, and An-
        derson went back to Clyde, Ohio . . . attended Wittenburg
        Academy in Springfield, Ohio.

1900   Finished high school at Wittenburg and moved to Chicago
        where he was a copywriter for the Frank B. White Com-
        pany . . . remained with the firm when it became the Long-
        Critchfield Company in 1903 and continued to write for *Agri-
        cultural Advertising*.

1904   Married Cornelia Lane, daughter of an affluent manufacturer from Toledo, Ohio . . . they lived at 5654 Rosalie Court, Chicago, in an area of upwardly mobile young people.

1906   Moved to Cleveland, Ohio, to assume the presidency of United Factories Company, a mail-order firm based in that city.

1907   Moved to Elyria, Ohio, and headed a mail-order paint factory, which became Anderson Manufacturing Company . . . apparently began to consider writing as a serious avocation . . . Robert, the first of his three children, was born.

1908   John, his second child, was born.

1911   Marion, his daughter, was born.

1912   Suffered a "strange illness" in November, later found wandering in Cleveland, reportedly he suffered a breakdown caused by nervous exhaustion, which led him to abandon his business and leave his family.

1913   Returned to Chicago and took a room on 57th Street and once again became a copywriter at Long-Critchfield.

1914   His first short story, "The Rabbit-Pen," appeared in the July issue of *Harper's*.

1915   Was living at 735 Cass Street (now Wabash Avenue) on the Near North Side of Chicago . . . divorced Cornelia Lane Anderson.

1916   Married Tennessee Mitchell . . . *Windy McPherson's Son* published by John Lane . . . many stories set in Winesburg, Ohio, appeared in journals between 1916 and 1918.

1917   *Marching Men* published.

1918   *Mid-American Chants* published . . . lived in New York City for several months.

1919   At the time of the Chicago Race Riot, he was living "on the ground floor of a three-story brick building on Division Street" . . . *Winesburg, Ohio* published, the first book issued in his long relationship with B. W. Huebsch.

1920   His father died . . . lived briefly in Mobile and Fairhope, Ala-
        bama, then moved to Palos Park, a suburb of Chicago . . .
        B. W. Huebsch published *Poor White*.

1921   Traveled to France with his wife as the guest of his friend,
        Paul Rosenfeld . . . met Gertrude Stein, Ezra Pound, James
        Joyce, and Sylvia Beach . . . received the *Dial* prize of $2000
        for his contributions to American literature . . . *The Triumph
        of the Egg* published.

1922   Left Chicago, abandoned his second wife, Tennessee Mitchell
        Anderson, and his advertising job . . . moved to New York
        City and began his association with Elizabeth Prall, who
        managed a bookstore . . . then spent several months in New
        Orleans.

1923   Moved to Reno, Nevada, in February for the sole purpose of
        meeting the residency requirements for divorce . . . *Many
        Marriages* and *Horses and Men* published.

1924   Early in the year, his divorce from Tennessee Mitchell Ander-
        son was granted . . . married Elizabeth Prall, moved to New
        Orleans . . .*A Story Teller's Story* published.

1925   Was on the lecture circuit for several months and traveled ex-
        tensively in the South . . . *Dark Laughter*, his only best seller
        during his lifetime, was published by Horace Liveright, which
        marked the beginning of his relationship with a new pub-
        lisher . . . *The Modern Writer* was published in a limited edi-
        tion by Gelber, Lilienthal, Inc., of San Francisco.

1926   Moved to Troutdale, Virginia, where he built "Ripshin," his
        home near Marion, Virginia . . . *Sherwood Anderson's Notebook*
        and *Tar: A Midwest Childhood* published . . . returned to
        Europe for his second trip, which ended the following year.

1927   Bought the *Smyth County News* and the *Marion Democrat* . . .
        A New Testament was published.

1928   Traveled extensively.

1929   Continued to travel . . . was on the lecture circuit for several
        months . . . *Hello Towns!* published by Liveright . . . *Nearer
        the Grass Roots* and *Alice and the Lost Novel* published by

smaller companies in limited editions . . . marriage to Elizabeth Prall Anderson came to an end with a separation.

1930   *The American Country Fair* published by Random House . . .
        became especially interested in southern factory towns.

1931   *Perhaps Women* was published by Liveright . . . once again
        spent many months on the lecture circuit.

1932   Divorced Elizabeth Prall Anderson . . . went to Amsterdam,
        Holland, to attend a peace conference, "World's Congress
        Against War" . . . *Beyond Desire* published.

1933   Married Eleanor Copenhaver. . . *Death in the Woods* published.

1934   *No Swank* published.

1935   *Puzzled America* published . . . for the next three years
        spent much time traveling in Texas and other southwestern
        communities.

1936   *Kit Brandon* published.

1937   *Plays: Winesburg and Others* published.

1938   Visited Mexico.

1939   Lecture at Olivet College in Olivet, Michigan, resulted in the
        publication of his essay on realism.

1940   *Home Town* published.

1941   Trip to South America interrupted by his death on March 8
        from peritonitis at Colón in the Panama Canal Zone.

1942   Posthumous publication of *Sherwood Anderson's Memoirs*.

A STORYTELLER AND A CITY

PROLOGUE
A Storyteller's City

When you have been sick of [Chicago]
to the very marrow and accepted
it, then at last, walking hopeless,
endless streets—hopeless yourself—
you begin to feel . . . its half-wild
beauty. The beauty of the loose and
undisciplined, unfinished, and
unlimited. Something half wild and
very alive in yourself is there, too.
The city you have dreaded and feared
is like your own soul.

—Memoirs

The Virgin was dead and her son had taken as prophets such men as . . . Emerson and . . . Franklin, the one with his little books in which he set down and saved his acts and impulses, striving to make them all serve definite ends as he saved his pennies and the other preaching the intellectual doctrine of Self-Reliance, Up and Onward. The land was filled with gods but they were new gods and their images—standing on every street of every town and city—were cast in iron and steel. The factory had become America's church and duplicates of it stood everywhere, on almost every street of every city belching black incense into the sky.

—*A Story Teller's Story*

1

The Legendary Chicago
and the Real City

URING THE latter part of the nineteenth century the average
Chicagoan probably knew little about either Benjamin Franklin or Ralph Waldo Emerson and very likely cared less; yet,
practically everybody had been affected by the philosophies of the two
men. Chicago, unabashedly dedicated to worldly success, was a town
that subscribed not only to the twin gospels of hard work and thrift as
precursors to assured achievement but also had an unflinching belief
in the pragmatic aspects of self-reliance. In an existence of less than
sixty-five years, the city was considered the urban center of the
Middle Border. Some boosters actually claimed it had become the
most significant city in the nation. The World's Columbian Exposition
of 1893 left little doubt that Chicago had become an international center. Both foreign and native visitors saw the place as a manifestation
of the forces that had made the United States so dynamic. The fruits
of success could be seen everywhere. Even the obvious urban chaos
had its own strange powers. Truly the city's name, as Henry Blake
Fuller had observed in 1893, was "a shibboleth."

I

As early as the seventeenth century, LaSalle reportedly viewed the
Chicago territory and exclaimed: "This will be the gate of an empire;
this will be the seat of commerce. The typical man who will grow up

here must be an enterprising man. Each day, as he rises, he will exclaim, 'I act, I move, I push.'" Whatever rapture LaSalle felt as he sur-
veyed the swampy land on the shores of Lake Michigan near the
banks of a strange river was not shared by others, and for centuries,
that area of New France was largely ignored.

With the settling of the Northwest Territory after the Revolutionary War, a series of forts were established by the new United States of
America in order to encourage citizens to move westward and to send
a signal to the Indians that the nation meant to protect its own. That
such a fort was established in 1803 in what was to become Chicago
initially did not attract much attention. Named Fort Dearborn and located in an out-of-the-way place, it was considered to be a safe haven
until August 1812. Maybe the men and women living at that particular
military establishment did not think of themselves as distinctive, but
their massacre on August 15 catapulted them into history. Although
John Kinzie's survival later would be used to define the duplicity of
the enterprising man of the new territory, the Fort Dearborn Massacre
provided the source for some late–nineteenth-century romances, in
which the facts of the altercation were overlooked in order to perpetu-
ate the myth of the goodness and helplessness of western pioneers
faced with the cruelty of the Indians.

With the dispersal of many of the region's Indians and with the
opening of the Erie Canal in 1825, easterners used Chicago as a way
station on their treks westward, but many stayed in the community,
which they thought would be America's New Jerusalem. Westerners,
moving toward the cultural and financial center of the United States,
often stopped in Chicago and remained there. In their attempts to go
to the North, southerners—both black and white—traveled the route
that eventually was to become famous as the Illinois Central Railroad.
Several immigrant groups settled in the Chicago territory. For some
the word *Chicago,* generally pronounced "Chee-caw-go," was the
only English word they knew; and they seldom realized that it was
really an Indian word of unknown origin.

Founded in 1833 and incorporated in 1837, at a time when the
Emersonian spirit of freedom and western self-reliance were dominant in the United States, the youngest of the nation's boom towns,
Chicago, early challenged the supremacy of other cities especially
those of the East. Novelist Robert Herrick described the place as
having been created in defiance of nature. Certainly, the growth of
the city and the spectacular rise of the businessman defied all laws of
what had been previously known about urban development. Even

after other sections of the nation, including New England, were bur-
dened by issues of slavery and a mercurial economy, Chicago appeared to be a bastion of the frontier spirit realized in an urban
community.

It soon became difficult to separate the real city from the mythic
product of boosters and historians. From 1849 to 1871, various legends
circulated widely. Some said it was easy to succeed in Chicago because money was plentiful. With just a little ingenuity, so the story
went, one's lot could be improved greatly. Others believed that the
city offered a refuge for those with questionable backgrounds, a belief
substantiated by the practice of seldom recording the lives of the so-
called prominent people prior to their Chicago days. Even a cata-
strophic fire in 1871 did not hinder the I-Will spirit of the new men
and women in the metropolis of the Midwest. Whatever the place of
origin of its citizens, there could be no mistake that Chicago had
become associated with success, freedom, and money—with the
American Dream itself.

One of those dreamers was Sherwood Anderson (1876–1941).
Born in a small Ohio town, he had heard that much money was to be
made in Chicago. Consequently, a belief in the city's legend as well as
a faith in the urban promise lured him to Chicago in 1896. One could
become an immediate success—so the myth of the city maintained.
As a youngster, he had already been called Jobby, because he was
willing to do any chore in order to make money. That he was a hustler
is no denigration. America was built by hustlers; and certainly Chicago, the hustling town, was created by hustlers from Europe, New
England, and midland America. Like others who had cast their fortunes with the city, Anderson overlooked the possibility of failure or
the probability of unfulfilled dreams. The fact that a few had "made
it" was reason enough to keep trying.

For the blasé, modern mind, it is difficult to comprehend the excitement created by Chicago in those days. Historic records reveal the
great expectations of the hordes who left the security of what they
knew in order to venture into this unknown world. Although it may
be said that some arrived looking for a better quality of life, most
were searching for material success. Franklin, the great pragmatist of
American civilization, had demonstrated in his *Autobiography* the ease
with which a person—by following some simplistic directives—could
rise from a lowly position. The Puritan doctrine of success had been
stripped of its religious overtones and popularized by the Emersonian
interpretation of self-reliance. "From rags to riches" had been given

further support by the Horatio Alger stories. People who never had
heard of Franklin, Emerson, or Alger believed fervently that the success formula articulated by each was workable for everybody. The
Chicago entrepreneurs had made the formula seem ordinary. Tales of
prosperity created a general sense of well-being. It was whispered "if
you can't make it in Chicago, you can't make it anywhere."

And so it was that the city lured all who believed in man's victory
against all odds. The urban success stories already had become part of
the folklore of the nineteenth century. Wealthy industrialists, fabu-
lous merchants, and clever financiers basked in the glory of their
worldly progress and looked, with their wives, upon all they sur-
veyed as their own fiefdoms. Chicago's history and extraordinary
growth made it a place with which the rest of the nation—sometimes
begrudgingly—had to reckon.

The development of such cities provoked a great deal of concern
in nineteenth-century America. Moralists tried to insist that the good
life was in some remote way related to beauty and a time-tested ethos.
Romanticists deified nature and had presented the old pioneers, despite the realities of their hardships, as creatures of nature, larger
than life. But gradually the men and women who had tamed the frontier lost their fascination. Increasingly, the great national promise
seemed to be in the developing cities. In fact, Arthur M. Schlesinger,
Sr., observed, "All those impulses and movements which made for a
finer, more human civilization" could be found in the emerging cities
and this included such diverse particulars as "education, literature,
social reform, public hygiene, the use of leisure."[1] There was a growing belief that if the millennium came, the city would be the locus of
much activity because, despite its presumed shortcomings, it provided possibilities unencumbered by historic references, romanticized notions of the land, or unworkable ethical systems.

According to the prevailing tale in Chicago, the American Dream
could become the American Reality. Western bravado, frontier democracy, and American initiative with a strong emphasis upon individualism made the city a place of untold opportunities. Those who
failed in the city were dismissed as misfits who could not cope with
the system of free enterprise—which in Chicago was extremely free.
That the city was built upon the sacrifices and broken dreams of the
downtrodden eluded all but the most perceptive. Chicago clearly was
a city of the present that forgot its past as it worked for the future.

Although the growth of the city was part of a national pattern in

the nineteenth century that led to the development of several outstanding urban centers, it was not long before Chicago proved to be
different from others being established on the frontier. Even in paternalistic nineteenth-century circles, women achieved an independence
not usually associated with urban living; and evidences of the new
business ethic seemed apparent in the metropolis of the Midwest because there were so many examples of the rewards to be gained from
what was politely called a "business sense." The mythic city became
even more legendary when specific successful gambles in railroading,
lumber, and real estate became common knowledge. Stories circulated
about the unbelievably wild capitalistic schemes that made multi-
millionaires out of the most persistent while the city moved headlong
into the mainstream of American civilization. Consequently, it is not
surprising that some of the nation's great fortunes and sensational
rises to power should have originated in Chicago.

The work of Benjamin P. Hutchinson, Samuel W. Allerton, the
Armours, and Gustavus Swift led to the great packinghouse industry,
which until a few years ago was one of the city's major employers.
Thousands of immigrants got their first real knowledge of America in
the stockyards of Chicago. George M. Pullman parlayed his idea of a
palace rail car into the great Pullman Works, which produced the even
greater Pullman Company. McCormick's belief that reaping could be
easier and faster ultimately led not only to the McCormick Reaper
Works but also to the formation of the gigantic combine, the International Harvester Company, which still exists. Detractors charged
that McCormick had stolen the reaper design from a nonaggressive
friend; but Chicago admired McCormick's grit, gall, and push. Only a
few specialists even remember the name of the alleged friend, but
most people know of the McCormick dynasty founded by the shrewd
Cyrus. The Ryersons, Martin and Joseph, discovered a fortune could
be made in lumber. When wood as a building material was no longer
practical, they turned to steel; and together they were instrumental in
the establishment of today's mammoth Inland Steel Company.

Potter Palmer, once a small-time merchant, had the foresight to
abandon the early Lake Street business district and buy the land that
led to the development of State Street, which Chicagoans now call
"the great street." In addition to his general real estate holdings, he
built one of the world's finest hotels which, though no longer controlled by the Palmer fortune, still bears his name. Students of mer-
chandising seldom forget the first Marshall Field whose tomb in

Graceland Cemetery bears simply the two words: *Equity* and *Integrity*. He gave the lady what she wanted and, in so doing, created a personal fortune. Despite the rise of other, and perhaps much better stores, "shopping at Field's" still evokes a sense of the quality much heralded at the turn of the century. The man has faded from the center stage of the city, but his legend lives on in a current slogan of the store: "Marshall Field's *IS* Chicago." Such an overstatement seems acceptable in a place whose history has been predicated upon the use of hyperbole.

There are others whose names are still familiar. Samuel Carson, John T. Pirie, and Robert Scott are better known as Carson, Pirie, Scott and Company. Emmanuel, Solomon, Simon, and Leon Mandel, German immigrants, created Mandel Brothers whose downtown store long was a retailing and architectural landmark. Several years ago, their building at the historic corner of State and Madison Streets was taken over by William Wieboldt's nineteenth-century enterprise. Charles A. Stevens and Montgomery Ward were active in the city's development and stores continue to bear their names. The Morton Salt Company owes its origin to the business acumen of Joy and Mark Morton.

However, there was no monolithic Chicago businessman. From Joseph Medill to Oscar Mayer, names attached to specific products or services became better known, but part of the success of the Chicago experiment undoubtedly was due to the faith of bankers and financiers, such as Lyman Gage, who did not hesitate to invest in the city. Sharing the from-rags-to-riches experience, these men inspired others to believe in the efficacy of the American Dream. Robert Herrick described them as "brave and unselfish, faithful and trusting of the future" then offered the explanation "With the plainest personal habits and tastes, taking no tarnish from the luxury that rose about them, seeking things larger than dollars on their horizon, they made the only aristocracy this country has seen. Their coat of arms bore the legend: 'Integrity and Enterprise.'"[2] While this observation essentially may be true, the early entrepreneurs manipulated people and conditions for gain as well as for satisfaction.

When the city was destroyed in 1871, claims were made that the devastating fire was divine judgment, because God had been angered by the Babylon of the New World. Others viewed the leveling of the city as an ideal opportunity to create a more perfect place. Sermons were delivered about it, and editorials appeared in national publications. Despite the extent of the ruin, there was no question that Chi-

cago would rise again. The determination of the city during this period is often represented by an otherwise undistinguished real estate
agent who posted a sign over his burned-out business which read:
"All gone save wife, children, and energy." With those words Samuel
Kerfoot assured his place in history. But he was not alone in his commitment to the city. Architects, engineers, and builders rushed to
help those businessmen who were determined to stay. Miraculously
the city was rebuilt in less than twenty years, and by 1889 it was insisting that the world be invited to see the restoration.

Nineteenth-century Chicago was a strange place. No one doubted
its fascination with business. LaSalle Street, the hub of midwestern
financial activity, was almost as famous as Wall Street. Yet, the arts
had developed in the midst of this frankly mercantile community
dedicated to economic growth. For example, there was an outstanding architecture, probably one of the area's first artistic responses to
the demands of business. Its fame was worldwide, even though Chicagoans often were ashamed of the starkness of skeleton frame construction, preferring the lavish mansions copied from the palaces and
estates of Europe. The city's cultural institutions could rival those of
older places. There was an art museum and a multitude of private gal-
leries and collections, most of which eventually became part of the
Art Institute of Chicago. Several libraries had been established, and
there was the famous Theodore Thomas Orchestra, forerunner of the
Chicago Symphony. That the city provided an urban laboratory for its
writers should not be surprising. The many newspapers and magazines furnished outlets for those storytellers, journalists, and poets
who were becoming nationally known. Moreover, a number of publishing companies were established in the city and began to challenge
the supremacy of the East. Critics admitted—condescendingly to be
sure—that a regional literature was developing in the Midwest that
could not be ignored.

When the fair opened on May 1, 1893, the problems leading to the
World's Columbian Exposition were forgotten. Chicago proved—if
only for a fleeting moment in the nation's history—that it could produce a perfect city. Exposure to an ideal frequently makes the real
more frightening, and so it was with the Exposition. Some who saw
the display were disturbed not by its magnificence but by its relationship to the actual world. Others were more optimistic. City planners
used this fair as a lesson in the treatment of the major issues of urbanism. They pointed with pride to both the architectural splendor of
the exhibition and to its solution of such mundane necessities as mass

transporation, garbage collection, traffic control, lighting, and police protection. Because it was so spectacular, the fair was called the City Beautiful. Because it promised so much, it was called the New Jerusalem, and there were even a few who dared to call it the City of God. Most people, however, knew it as the White City, a name that originated when its major buildings were sprayed with white paint as a cost- and time-saving device. But, when subsequently bathed in sunlight or by thousands of electric bulbs, these buildings were a display of startling beauty. Clearly, the shimmering Exposition stood in direct contrast to the reality of the Black City, where urban poverty and chaos reigned supreme.

The fair did not dwell on the past in spite of the imitative nature of its architecture. It was a portent of the future, some said. That the dream of the new day could not be sustained was undoubtedly due, at least in part, to the contradictory nature of the Exposition, which was a mass of ambiguities. Its major buildings were phony classical structures that were larger than their erstwhile models. Its architects had rejected the pragmatic buildings of commercial Chicago but, at the same time, had used the girders and beams of that construction. This modern understructure was then molded to look like the temples of ancient Greece and Rome. Whether one wishes to agree with Louis Sullivan's observation that "the damage" of the Exposition would last at least fifty years,[3] after the fair, pseudoclassical structures were erected throughout the nation. Ironically, government buildings and banking institutions were most frequently housed in Greco-Roman temples. The splendor of the classical world rather than the grandeur of the Chicago School of Architecture transformed the Main Streets of America.

The exhibits also contributed to the contradictory nature of the Exposition. They ranged from electric generators reinforcing the powerlessness of man to the World's Congress Auxiliary, a first in international fairs, whose motto Not Things But Men seemed to be the antithesis of the machines and gadgets on display. Even the noted Parliament of Religions in its ecumenical approach seemed ambiguous and unsure of its direction. The various national and state displays provided one type of educational experience while the Midway, ironically the site of the new University of Chicago, with its Ferris wheel and Little Egypt provided a distinctly different one. These two discernible worlds were united by the Fifty-seventh Street shops, the dilapidated remains of which were to figure prominently in the Chicago Renaissance of the early twentieth century. Thus, for those who thought seriously about the Exposition, the entire project offered a strange dichotomy. Like Henry Adams, they "found matter of study to fill a hundred years."[4] However, Chicagoans generally considered 1893 indeed to be the city's *annus mirabilis* and the Exposition to be a fitting expression of the accomplishments of the city. There was such a pervasive sense of optimism that many failed to read the signs of discontent much in evidence throughout the city's brief history. If Chicago were an Eden, the serpent was still in the garden.

The city was vastly overcrowded, and the first extensive slums of the nation already had developed in it. The "huddled masses yearning to breathe free" were herded into dwellings, many of which were unfit for animal habitation. Early, the city showed its inability to cope with the multitude of immigrants teeming into the region in pursuit of the American Dream. There surfaced a strong anti-immigrant attitude that had been smoldering in the city for years. As a further irony, the city that had prided itself on its multiplicity of ethnic groups and on its immigrant origins, that had used these factors to advertise itself as "the most American" city in the days before the Exposition, in less than fifty years, should have become one of the most uncompromising defenders of nativism. The estrangement between the foreign- and native-born citizens was intensified by the widening gap between the haves and the have-nots. There were several strikes and labor disputes before the internationally famous Haymarket Affair of 1886 captured the attention of supporters of human rights in this country as well as in Europe. The reigning power structure and the elite seldom considered the likelihood that the city's pathetically silent majority might protest. But a day of reckoning was to come.

At the close of the Exposition, the depression that had besieged the nation and that barely had been deferred in Chicago caused widespread alarm. The economic problems of the city, as well as the unsolved issues of urbanism, no longer could be ignored, even though municipal corruption, vice, and violence were tolerated in the name of "progress." For those unwilling to understand the deep-seated labor problems and who blamed the situation at the Haymarket on "those anarchists from Europe," the Pullman Strike of 1894 made it clear that capital and labor had reached an impasse. In the eight-year period between the Haymarket Affair and the Pullman Strike, there had been over 500 labor disputes and strikes in the city. At the same time, personal fortunes of the wealthy were increasing at an unbelievable rate. As Chicago was reeling from economic disasters and from its unchecked plunge toward material success, an English clergyman who had come to America to visit the Exposition and who remained "to study" Chicago, William Stead, presented the city stripped of its glamour in his exposé *If Christ Came to Chicago* (1894).

By the end of the nineteeth century, Chicagoans no longer were sure that theirs had been the path to an ideal city. Various reform groups were beginning to see the weaknesses of the commercial structure that had been uncontrolled for years and the muckrakers took delight in disclosing municipal corruption. Their premise that an enlightened and an intelligent electorate could and would make changes did not take into account the power of the political bosses, a power that, by the way, extended well into the twentieth century. Nonetheless, there was a growing concern for the development of a civic conscience. The economic depression illustrated some of the essential weaknesses of the prevailing business ethic. Those who had translated the Darwinian principle of the survival of the fittest to mean that the Chicago businessman was the survivor in a mercantile theory of evolution now began to question whether the law of the jungle should be applied as a law of man.

II

Clearly, Sherwood Anderson, like other migrants to the city, was heir to both the myth and the reality of Chicago. Much had been accomplished, but the city seemed to suggest that there was much more that could be done. In spite of the obvious problems, *success* continued to be the city's watchword and its raison d'être. An expectant air of untold opportunities hovered over the still young and boisterous municipality. On the other hand, real though the legendary city might appear, Sherwood Anderson discovered another Chicago, as did so many others. It was not a place of limitless possibilities but a place of dashed hopes, unrealized dreams, and petty crimes. Describing his initiation into the city of the 1890s in *A Story Teller's Story*, he remembered being "stopped by holdup men who took a few dollars from" him.[5] The commercial buildings might display the tenets of modern design then being promulgated in Chicago and the mansions of the wealthy might exhibit the best of the Beaux Arts tradition, but everywhere, he discovered, there was an urban ugliness that resulted from constructing buildings too quickly with little regard for such niceties as city planning.

Chicago soon educated Sherwood Anderson in the harshness of life in a thriving commercial center, an actuality that replaced the ro-

mantic tales of the industrial world and rendered meaningless the
success stories of the giants of finance, many of whom were still living
and working in Chicago in 1896. Recalling a particular walk "into factory districts [with] long silent streets of grim black walls," he later
raised the question: "Had men but escaped out of the prisons of the
Old World into the more horrid prisons of the New?" Even the rob-
bers in the area who terrorized him were "all too serious about life."
His reflections upon the city led him to consider the groups "not yet
combined" in urban America. Recognizing the importance of the
written and spoken word, he blamed the existence of the melting-pot
theory on "the American writers . . . [who] went on assuming that
the typical American was a transplanted Englishman, an Englishman
who had served his term in the stony purgatory of New England, and
had then escaped out into the happy land, this Heaven, the Middle
West. Here they were all to grow rich and live forever, a happy bliss-
ful existence." And, he raised a cogent question: "Was not all the
world supposed to be watching the great democratic experiment in
government and human happiness they were to conduct so bravely?"
(p. 229). Instead, the city came to mean the juxtaposition of many ethnic groups who shared only the search for the more elusive elements
of success. Surrounded by chaos and hopeful that their dreams would
be fulfilled, these silent optimistic people were early urban victims.

Anderson's first period in Chicago (1896–1898) was one of great
disappointment. His arrival coincided with the city's slow recovery
from its latest economic depression. Jobs were not plentiful, and the
likelihood that he would become an instant business tycoon was remote. He spent long hours rolling barrels of apples and stacking
crates of eggs in a cold storage warehouse on the city's North Side. At
the time, he was living in a crowded boarding house at 708 West
Washington Boulevard. The only positive feature about his living ar-
rangement was that he was surrounded by people from his home
town, all of whom in varying degrees were searching for the same
fruits of urban success. As in a rite of passage, his fellow boarders
joined him in facing the actual and the illusionary Chicago.

He led one life but dreamed of another. Although, by his own
admission, he was a common laborer, he wanted so much more. He
imagined himself "living in one of the big hotels overlooking the lake,
or in a great airy apartment." Instead, by this time, his older sister
and two of his younger brothers had come to Chicago. The four of
them lived in a small tenement apartment. "In the winter the place
was heated by small coal burning stoves. There was a stove pipe, a
long one, fastened to the ceiling with wire that went over [his] bed to

its hole in the wall." Anderson remembered, "The joints of the pipe were always coming loose. Coal soot fell down on my bed and sometimes blackened my face. There were two beds in an adjoining room, my sister in one the two children in the other."[6] In a city that expected its residents to have money, Sherwood Anderson had little. His sense of futility developed as he saw no hope of extricating himself from his situation. And as he walked the crowded streets, he felt more and more alone. The streets of the West Side were filthy and beggars were plentiful. The irony of it all: the poor begging from the poor. But he never forgot that there was another Chicago. "Occasionally, on Sunday afternoons," he said, "I went to walk on Michigan Boulevard . . . , then as now a noble and beautiful street, and there saw beautifully dressed women going along with faultlessly dressed men" (*Memoirs* 1969 ed., 154).

Although he had spent little time in school, Anderson began to realize how important education could be in his "rise" in the world. But attending night school in Chicago was a disaster. By the time he reached his classes at Lewis Institute (which eventually became a part of the Illinois Institute of Technology) and "went into the warm room," he was unable to concentrate. Recalling those days, many years later, in his *Memoirs,* he admitted: "The book was before me but I fell forward on my desk and slept. I was so weary I couldn't keep my eyes open" (1942 ed., 16). Whatever he learned about the industrial and business worlds of the city did not make him sufficiently confident about his chances. Neither was he particularly interested in the artistic community that was becoming more articulate in the aftermath of the World's Columbian Exposition.

The story of his first escape from Chicago is well known. When Company I of the Sixteenth Infantry Regiment of the Ohio National Guard (into which Anderson had enlisted in 1895 for a five-year tour of duty) was called into active service during the Spanish-American War, Anderson returned to Ohio. Entering the army on call for the Spanish-American War, he explained in *A Story Teller's Story* that his enlistment was due to being "broke" and he wished "to avoid going back into a factory." But, he also admitted that his desire to be a "hero" made him return to his village in order to join the military because the townspeople "would want to think I had given up a lucrative position in the city to answer my country's call." Although he had returned on a freight train, "at a station twenty miles from home [he] bought a new suit of clothes, a new hat, neckties, and even a walking stick" (278–79 *passim*). Deliberately, he followed the path of other urban failures who, upon returning to their former homes, refused to acknowledge the reality of the city, preferring instead to contribute to the myth of urban success.

He saw noncombative duty in the South and in Cuba. At the conclusion of his brief military service, he completed his high school education at Wittenberg Academy in Ohio, an experience he continued to remember pleasantly throughout his life. With the events of his first sojourn in Chicago repressed, Anderson returned to the city in 1900 as an advertising solicitor in the early days of the development of the "Madison Avenue" techniques of marketing. He was enthusiastic about the possibilities of being a copywriter, which not only put him on the fringes of the world of business but also permitted him to use his talent with words.

At the turn of the century, although in its embryonic stages, advertising was extremely personal. Much of Anderson's success in this area was based upon his ability to make both his clients and their publics believe in whatever product was being promoted. The single-purposed commitment to buying and selling often meant that shoddy and inferior goods received the same treatment as those that were worthy. Advertising was predicated upon both "the big lie" and the use of middle-class values that emphasized success with its mirage of "the good life." In a particularly telling essay in this regard, Anderson explained the virtue of ready-made clothes to an audience accustomed to home-sewing and hand-me-downs. Voicing little of his later support for the continuation of the individual craftsman, he spoke from the perspective of the manufacturer rather than from that of the consumer or artist. In "The Farmer Wears Clothes,"[7] Anderson appealed to a large untapped market and noted that "some of the big, general advertisers seem to be grasping the fact that the agricultural press is tucked up close to the hardest reading, best living class of people in the world, the American farmer."

From 1900 to 1906, Anderson achieved a degree of financial security, first as an agent in the Chicago office of the Crowell Company then as a copywriter for the Frank B. White Agency, which became the Long-Critchfield Company in 1903. Advertising permitted him to work within the system and gave him an opportunity to support his belief in the efficacy of business. Although he was later to reject these years, he demonstrated his aptitude for advertising and promotional writing. His early work reveals his excitement and interest in the life he had chosen. From all appearances, his success in the city was assured. At last he had found a niche that might lead to the fulfillment of those great expectations about which he had dreamed. Perhaps, he was not yet a tycoon nor an industrialist; but his work was important to the region's financiers, because he understood the need for businessmen to appeal to the largest possible public in order to enlarge their spheres of influence.

His marriage in 1904 to Cornelia Lane, the well-educated daughter of a Toledo businessman, marked a milestone in his "rise" in the world. She had all of the outward manifestations of culture, had traveled extensively, and was liberated enough to allow his growth. They lived on the fashionable South Side of Chicago at 5654 Rosalie Court. He continued to contribute to such popular trade journals as *Agricultural Advertising*. Whatever sense of disillusionment came to mark his views on the debilitating nature of both the city and the American Dream, during his second period in Chicago he was a staunch advocate of the prevailing business optimism. He believed, as did some other novelists of the era, that the wealthy men and women of the city were truly concerned about the betterment of people and institutions. He admired those who had been successful and assumed that they had discovered the road to happiness. He knew that it was only a matter of time before he, too, made his fortune and achieved fame. Consequently, by 1906, when he was firmly convinced that he could apply the lessons learned in Chicago to his own business, he was ready to return to Ohio.

He became associated with the United Factories Company of Cleveland, an early conglomerate designed to capitalize upon the growing popularity of the mail-order business. As the firm's chief executive officer until 1907, Anderson had an opportunity to utilize his talents and penchant for writing advertising copy. The firm, however, had been built upon a shaky foundation, and fortunately for him, he was able to pull out of it in time. He moved his family to Elyria, Ohio, where he began a mail-order paint business. Soon it became the Anderson Manufacturing Company. He joined the right clubs and did enough of the right things—like an early Babbitt—to become a spectacular success in the small town of Elyria. As a minor business magnate, he quickly achieved the external evidences of prosperity. In many ways Anderson now represented the fulfillment of the American myth. The Dream had become a reality for him.

But his career as a businessman was short lived. He discovered that life in the world of commerce brought little personal happiness. He became increasingly doubtful and was agitated by it all. On November 27, 1912, he suffered a breakdown—sometimes referred to as "a strange illness"—that became a significant turning point in his life.

There are as many analyses of the events of this time as there are interpreters of it.[8] Anderson himself later aided in creating an aura of mystery around the entire episode. Yet, his amnesia and illness represented not only a personal declaration of independence and a questioning of those values that had seemed so important but also an escape from the inevitability of business responsibility, routine work, and the demands of family life. This "turning point" clearly indicated his inability to cope with his life as it existed. Thus, his ultimate rejection of the life of business resulted in his denial of the motivating Dream.

To escape to a new life while running away from the old meant that he had to find someplace to go. He chose, once again, Chicago. His biographers sometimes get rhapsodic as they chant reasons for his return to the city, but it was probably as much a matter of convenience as some great call beckoning him to a place of unexplained fascination. He now knew the city well, and his brother Karl, the artist, was there. Consequently, early in 1913 he was back in Chicago. Instead of taking his family with him (which by now included three children), he took the manuscripts that had occupied his attention during "business hours" and in his spare time.

For several months, he lived on Fifty-seventh Street on the city's South Side, the hub of the activities of the group centered around Floyd Dell and his former wife. No longer cherishing dreams of great wealth, he discovered that happiness, which he thought would come with being part of "the system," was not related to money. Certainly, this was not a momentous discovery; yet, when he resumed his career in advertising, the routine of it all seemed antithetical to his own goals. Although his return to his former job was a means of survival, he later was to make much of his search for truth. As he tried to find a rationale for his life, he finally reasoned in both *A Story Teller's Story* and in his *Memoirs* that a life devoted to publicizing various products was not adequate preparation for "a life of truth." He knew the limitations of any procedure designed to sell things without a regard for merit. His recollections of these days display his growing sense of despair. What he came to view as constant lying made him feel unclean.

III

By 1913, both the city and Sherwood Anderson had changed drastically. For each of them, the exuberant idealism of the nineteenth century had been replaced by the harsh realities of the twentieth. In

1896, the year of Anderson's arrival in Chicago, the city, despite its youth, had reached a stage of civic euphoria. Much had happened to prove the city's greatness and the efficacy of its business culture. It was not only a well-known financial center, but also there had been established a loose kinship between aesthetic ideas, institutions, and those who considered themselves "enlightened." The ambiguous nature of the city during this period was apparent. Like Florence of the Medicis, the city's commitment to commerce was matched by exciting work being done in the arts and in literature. The twentieth century, however, witnessed an increasing sense of instability and a greater sense of personal alienation, characteristics of modern life that were to take their toll. The integrity and the unifying force of the institutions as well as the ideas of the past crumbled under the banner of "progress." All of this seemed more obvious as one moved from small towns to large cities. Thus, to move from a village in Ohio to the metropolis of the Middle Border was to be thrust into a new era.

Coping with the city as it had become often was difficult. Nostalgic views of "the good old days" became a typical diversion for some. This was not a desire to return to the physical hardships and discomforts of the past but a means of identifying with a period that did not seem as chaotic or as turbulent as the present. There were still those who regarded Chicago as a place of opportunity. They emphasized the business mystique because, despite the deaths of some of the old pioneers, stories of their conquests and entrepreneurial successes remained alive in the folklore of the city. As a result, many urban dwellers continued their never-ending searches for SUCCESS; however, astute observers of the city realized that the myth of Chicago had delayed the ability of some to deal with urban actuality. Without always realizing it, many Chicagoans were afflicted with a general wave of cynicism, in part due to a delayed recognition of the manifestations of discontent that the nineteenth century had failed to consider in its headlong rush toward success. Then there were the unmistakable signs of the widespread acceptance of scandalous behavior and practices.

By 1913, Charles Yerkes had come, seen, and momentarily conquered—much to the chagrin of the businessmen who were outsmarted by him. And perhaps, if he had not been immortalized in Dreiser's Frank Cowperwood, Yerkes would have remained a minor footnote in the history of a city that had a pantheon of such businessmen. Samuel Insull, however, was another story. By 1913 he had become a force with which both the city and the world had to deal. Legends about him are legion. He was ruthless, but he adapted well to a city built by manipulators. Eventually, the city was rocked by a small-time gangster whose name became a household word and a symbol of his urban community. In the universe of Al Capone, all the egomania of the age was magnified. Furthermore, Capone and his crowd captured the fearful imaginations of America and the world. In even the remotest sections, Chicago became known as the "bang-bang" city. The replacement of Franklin-Emerson-Alger as urban deities by Yerkes-Insull-Capone was as much a leading indicator of the times as any other expression and was almost as ceremonial as a pagan ritual.

Within a twenty-year period, Sherwood Anderson had chosen to live in Chicago on three occasions. His youthful dreams of 1896 gave way in 1900 to a greater sense of reality, but he still believed it possible to cooperate with the dominant structure in order "to get ahead." His nominal rise in the world of advertising led to some false notions and eventually sent him back to Ohio to embark upon a business career. But a small-town manufacturer, no matter how successful, certainly was no Chicago tycoon, and the possible routine of life was no substitute for the imagined excitement of the life of an American businessman.

Although he may not have known all of the particulars of the city's history, Anderson must have been aware of the meteoric rise of Chicago. The city's growth had been accompanied frankly by the belief in money, not for any social value but simply for the sake of getting it (although there were those who convinced themselves that their purposes were altruistic and who made quite a display of philanthropic endeavors). Spending in the city was best described by Thorstein Veblen who, in viewing Chicago's elite, defined "conspicuous consumption" for the nation. Increasingly, however, people were exploited and life itself seemed to become more meaningless. There was no attempt to mask the distinctly commercial goals with the vagueness of the "Protestant ethic" or with the religious premise that related one's "calling" with the degree of visible success achieved. God or His will may have played an integral part in the destiny of seventeeth-century New England, but Chicago reinforced the eighteenth-century deistic idea that man himself could be divine. Whereas the city's creators may have harbored delusions of grandeur, the legends finally admitted that Chicago was a place of amorality, where brute force frequently manifested itself through the evident demoralization and dehumanization of those who worked incessantly for material things.

During the twenties and Anderson's final break with Chicago,

however, the city's importance in the world of letters had been established through the aid of such critics as William Dean Howells and
H. L. Mencken as well as by the acceptance of Chicago writers in the
East. America's reading public, often unfamiliar with basic literary genres, had adopted Fuller's urbanized version of the term *cliff-dwellers*,
viewed the nation's businessmen as "titans" in the sense of Dreiser,
and knew of Sandburg's celebration to the "hog butcher of the world."
Chicago's novelists and poets, rather than its historians and social scientists, had given the rest of the nation a sense of the city.

Ultimately, the saga of Sherwood Anderson in Chicago is in part
the story of a man caught in the midst of a period of transition in urban life, of a man who never quite recovered from his initiation into
the city. His journey from the world of business to the world of art
gave him a perception that few writers ever achieved from first-hand
experiences and observations, but his realization of the significance of
the city as a symbol for American culture was not the result, at least
initially, of systematic study nor analysis. Instead, it evolved from his
personal experiences. By the time, however, that he was beginning to
contemplate and question the meaning of the city, Chicago had already become representative of some powerful forces in human existence. Its builders and destroyers were personifications of elements to
be found in the modern American city. Yet, considering the number
of times he referred to his repudiation of his former life as well as to
his illness of 1912, Anderson seemed to take some delight in establishing the romantic image of the individual who assumes poverty as a
means of counteracting the negative influences of the commercial
world. But, in 1913, his major goal was not the establishment of a legendary Sherwood Anderson but simply coping with his new life, as
he recognized that he probably could do no more than co-exist with
the city.

He joined others who were attempting to define the Chicago experience. *Windy McPherson's Son* (1916) and *Marching Men* (1917) demonstrated the immediate effects of the city upon him. His descriptions
of the city's neighborhoods and architecture, his delineations of urban stereotypes, including the city's businessmen, coupled with his
concern for thwarted dreams and urban corruption are a few indications of the extent to which he had absorbed the facts of Chicago life.
But, he went beyond producing guidebooks to the city or sociological
treatises in fiction.

While the probings of his early novels are articulations of a developing urban artist, much of his latter work, in varying degrees, bears

the stamp of Chicago. For example, *Mid-American Chants* (1918), *Winesburg, Ohio* (1919), *Poor White* (1920), some of the stories in both *The Triumph of the Egg* (1921) and *Horses and Men* (1923) as well as *Many Marriages* (1923) and *Dark Laughter* (1925) illustrate specific facets of his concern by examining the effects of urban nature upon human nature. He derived his definition of the urban from what Chicago was and what it was not. He understood, as had some of his predecessors and followers, that the growth of this particular city was indicative of prevailing patterns in American civilization. Unaffected by the traditionalism of the East or South and stripped of all pretensions, Chicago stood boldy as a powerful city, conditioning those who lived within its corporate boundaries and influencing the perceptions of those for whom the word *Chicago* was a "shibboleth." The times were chaotic, and Anderson joined other writers who were trying to give meaning to the resulting culture, not unlike a similar attempt made in another age by Washington Irving, Ralph Waldo Emerson, and Nathaniel Hawthorne.

As he came to terms with the impact of urban life, Anderson seemed to pass through several stages. In the initial period, when he was convinced that the business world was to be the salvation of the nation, his advertising copy extolled the virtues of the commercial and the urban as *the* American way. But, in Chicago, he learned that this life was not without its victims and disappointments. He saw the obvious conflicts between the actuality of the city and the legends of it that continued to be more meaningful than urban reality. He came to understand the inevitability of the factory systems and industrialism but was not content to accept, without question, a naturalistic view of life. He was convinced that the individual could rise above the constricting forces of the city. Thus, at a given moment in his career, his was a significant urban voice analyzing both the phenomenon of the American city and the effects of urbanism upon a group of characters. Storyteller that he was, Sherwood Anderson embarked upon a narrative quest that was to explore, at least in part, the essence of the city.

You know my city—Chicago
    triumphant—
    factories and marts and the roar
    of machines—horrible, terrible,
    ugly and brutal.

It crushed things down and down.
    Nobody wanted to hurt. They
    didn't want to hurt me or you.
    They were caught themselves . . .

                —"Song of Industrial America"
                    from *Mid-American Chants*

2

The City "Triumphant"

Chicago in Fiction

N MANY ways, Sherwood Anderson's early work was heir apparent to the distinctive urban novel that came out of nineteenth-century Chicago. Why such a novel should have developed is perhaps one of the unanswered questions of American literary history; however, during particular epochs certain cities have captured the spirit and imagination of an entire era and have seemed to become symbolic of an age. Painters, poets, and novelists have contributed to these urban images. Athens, Rome, Paris, London, New York, Charleston, Natchez—their very names evoke responses that include more than the cities ever meant to a single individual. In similar fashion, at a given moment, Chicago became the metaphoric statement for the strengths and weaknesses of American culture. Eastern cities were too bound to Boston and Europe. Western cities were too isolated or too oriented to Spanish and Indian influences. But in Chicago, American business, architecture, and literature came into their own. Thus, to many nineteenth-century Americans, Chicago was not only a place but also an idea. No midwesterner ever thought of The City without thinking of Chicago, and few Americans thought of urban success without pointing with varying degrees of pride to life in Chicago. As Felix Fay of Floyd Dell's 1920 novel, *Moon Calf*, recalls the large map of the United States hanging in the railroad station, he describes it as "the map with a picture of iron roads from all over the Middle West centering in a dark blotch in the corner" which was Chicago.[1] Centuries ago, all roads might have led to Rome, but in modern America

all iron roads led to Chicago. The place was both a beginning and
an end.

The factors that contributed to the growth of the city have been
adequately explored by social scientists, but the independent work of
a group of novelists did more to present the actual and mythic city
to the American public. Ultimately, the legendary city overshadowed
the real one. It was the city "triumphant" rather than the characters
that became the central figure of much of this literature. Although it
was called *the city beautiful,* at least to some, Chicago was "horrible,
terrible, ugly, and brutal." Difficult though it may be to imagine the
impact of the place upon people, such novelists as the Reverend E. P.
Roe, Henry Blake Fuller, Robert Herrick, Frank Norris, Theodore
Dreiser, and a host of other writers have attempted to describe the
encounter between the city and the person as they chronicled the
meeting of their heroes and heroines with the metropolis of the Midwest. In time, the Chicago of fiction was as real as the geographical
location.

Perhaps, if he had written nothing more than *Windy McPherson's
Son* and *Marching Men,* Sherwood Anderson's identification as "a Chicago novelist" would not seem inappropriate. From E. P. Roe in the
1870s to Mark Smith and William Brashler in the 1980s, the novelists of
Chicago have been united in their belief that there is a common rele-
vant description that helps to define the city. They claim it is a place of
strength and great power, built by businessmen and industrialists for
others of their kind. So important are these figures that in effect they
represent the new American cultural heroes, replacing Natty Bumppo
and the pioneers who conquered the wilderness. If these figures begin with the innocence of Adam, they quickly replace it with sophisticated determination to succeed at all costs. Commerce and Industry,
the urban gods demanding absolute loyalty, are the new signs of
progress.

Thus even though novelists might describe specific facets of urban existence or particular sites as well as characters in the city, the
dominant setting clearly is more than just a fictionalized locale. Existing as a dynamic entity, the city has a life of its own; and Chicago's
storytellers have emphasized the city's role in determining the course
of human action. Unlike the romantic determinists who see and
understand the force of physical nature, the urban novelists locate the
power of life not only in human nature but also in the general layout
of the city often characterized by a chaotic approach to its architec-

ture. It was assumed that the ugliness of cities had been caused not only by hurried development and the phenomenal speed of industrial growth but also by erratic residential housing that included the overcrowded multiple-family tenements, apartment buildings for the ordinary, and the spacious mansions for the wealthy. The last became more elaborate and needlessly conspicuous because such houses were the most certain visible manifestations of earthly accomplishment. While the laboring classes were herded into makeshift living quarters, often no better than hovels, the "housing" for factories clearly was (as it still is) better designed and planned. In time, there emerged a distinctive commercial architecture and significant industrial designs.

Not to be overlooked is the important role played by the city's geography. Divided by the Chicago River and its North and South branches, the three "sides" of Chicago are viewed as having distinct characteristics. In time, it was acknowledged that within each section there were various neighborhoods, often distinguished by specific national groups. Many storytellers, especially the later ones, have focused upon certain ethnic centers of power, recognizing them as small towns within the larger city and describing their restaurants, newspapers, local color, and unique character. These writers have realized that the city is not as unified as its name might suggest. Thus, by the middle of the twentieth century, Chicago was defined, for example, by the distinctly different South Sides of James T. Farrell and Richard Wright, by the West Sides of Sherwood Anderson and Meyer Levin (also equally different), and the North Sides of Nelson Algren's Division Street and the Lake Shore Drive neighborhood of Margaret Ayer Barnes and her sister, Janet Ayer Fairbanks. Looming over all of these sections, of course, is the often indefinable Chicago.

Anderson's attitude toward the real city and the mythic one controls the action in his first two published novels, both of which came at a critical point in fictional depictions of the city. In many ways, he was a transitional figure, bridging what had been the focus of the nineteenth-century urban novel while serving in the vanguard of what was to come later in the twentieth century. The concerns of novelists have been marked by certain inescapable patterns. When chambers of commerce assert the beauty of a given city, they usually mean designated showcase areas. To go beyond such sections is to face, according to both the social historians and novelists, a lack of any plan for expansion as well as massive disorder. The determined proliferation of construction had no regard for the integration of the natural setting and surroundings. Emphasis upon meadows and other parts of the romantic landscape changed to the presentation of chaotic city-scapes where pollutants were unchecked and life's calm moments were pierced by all sorts of screaming mechanical devices. In the end, one is trapped in the city not only by physical ugliness but also by unnatural, penetrating sounds.

Chronicles of city life could not avoid emphasizing the sense of urban loneliness ironically reinforced by people who are constantly being herded into groups. They go into the factories at a specified time and come out together. Each shift moving in unison. Life is ulti-mately translated into a sameness that would suggest its being pro-duced by automatons. Many labor-saving devices are created, but in the process the nature of the self-reliant individual is altered to match the modifications taking place in the transformed city. Feeling that one is in control of life is absent. A sense of well-being is traded for an animal existence and necessarily leads either to a rejection of familiar ties on a personal level or to a denial of loyalty to a particular place and its society. As a result, the inevitability of human isolation and loneliness become central elements in the urban experience. Within such a schema, the natural world seldom has a place in urban novels, which record the tales of those characters who have come together in answer to the demands of their understanding of what the city can offer to them.

The pressures of external forces are so great that there generally is a collapse within the individual, and the rise of the city finally chronicles the loss of one's humanity. That some protest novelists tried to reaffirm the need for social programs and other aids to help the less fortunate is as well known as Howells' theory of complicity, but such an agenda has not been an integral part of urban literature. Instead the irony of such philanthropists as a Mr. Dalton of *Native Son*, who might donate games to a community center while maintain-ing their slum buildings, is very apparent. Consequently, an unasked question hangs over the action as an implied litany: "What does it profit a man to gain the whole world and lose his soul?" While there is an underlying spiritual message in Anderson's considerations of ur-ban themes, one of the immediate effects of the city upon him was to reinforce his own concern for the alienation of modern men and women.

If the motivating force of life is a recognizable success in which one's condition is determined by what others can see, then an urban population can be divided simplistically into two groups: those who succeed according to the rules of the place and those who do not. Within this context, businessmen and industrialists form a ruling elite controlling the resources and the people of the community. For a number of years, these men were the central figures of the Chicago novel. Presented as instinctive—albeit lucky—gamblers, they are credited with building the city. Tales of their exploits had become such an integral part of urban folklore that their successes served as an inspiration for those rushing into the city. At the same time, urban novelists reinterpreted the romantic doctrine of self-reliance in more selfish terms and used it to justify a rugged individualism that neither cared about others nor about the effects of "self-reliant" actions upon the totality of society. The concentration of wealth in the hands of a few, while not peculiar to urban life nor even to the American experience, reinforced a sense of inferiority and isolation for nonachievers, primarily for two reasons. The proximity of city dwellers made it impossible to overlook outward signs of accomplishment. Furthermore, the acceptance of the American Dream suggested that the believer subscribed to the idea that human worth was somehow connected to prosperity. But in the city, mitigating circumstances often prevented even the most dedicated from succeeding.

On one level the prevailing sense of inequity is expressed in the very basic conflict between capital and labor—with a capital determined to maintain its advantage at all costs, a capital tempted to explain the lack of labor's accomplishments as inherent in the weakness or redefined moral fiber of the worker. Some even introduced a religious argument to add credence to their points of view. But the employer–employee discord occurred in a setting that touted an achievement predicated upon the ability of people to cooperate with or subordinate themselves to the demands of the place. To fail was to admit that one had neither the strength to persevere nor sufficient will; and the city would not tolerate innate character weaknesses. In time, relations between the weak and the strong became strained, and there was a growing animosity between those who succeeded and those who did not.

As presented both in history and in fiction, the captains of industry and giants of capitalism find joy in the "game" or "battle" as they justify the activities of their lives; but producing comes to have no goal other than continued production. The concept of need is unimportant. It is as if these men are drawn into a pattern and have lost the purpose of life. Anderson reduces this characteristic to the absurd in *Poor White*, when he portrays a Mrs. Woodburn whose every waking moment is devoted to knitting socks. What he says of her is often applicable to the urban entrepreneur. She "sat in a large chair under a lamp and knitted children's stockings. They were . . . for the children of the poor . . . [but] the stockings never left her house. In a large trunk upstairs lay hundreds of pairs knitted during the twenty-five years of her family life." And he concludes that her activity is one of "the trivial by-products of her age's industrial madness."[2]

While they repeatedly have suggested that the city is symbolic of the notion that material success results in spiritual death, the novelists have emphasized in the midst of such grimness that the city has a discernible effect upon young men or women from the outside who have been influenced by tales of life in the city. Although they have been warned about urban pitfalls and have been told that only a few are likely to see their dreams fulfilled, they have chosen to ignore that reality in the belief that they can overcome whatever deterrents exist. The American Dream undergirds their faith in themselves; thus, what happens to the outsider forms the core of a phase of Chicago fiction and creates the central tensions of such narratives. At the same time, there is an element of unexpected optimism in those stories that suggests knowing, understanding, or recognizing the problem of urban life is to solve its more apparent riddles and obvious contradictions.

Inasmuch as Anderson's personal and social relationships were appreciably altered by the activities of the now-famous Chicago Renaissance, one might conceivably be led to view his work as a product of that movement. Without denying the effects of his association with the city's artistic community, his early novels, written before his final return to the city, really are a significant phase of the urban novel that developed in Chicago during the nineteenth century and extended into the early years of the twentieth century. The Chicago novel was far more popular than traditional literary histories might suggest. It had permeated the mainstream of American literature and for the most part followed the formulae developed by Roe, Fuller, Herrick, and Dreiser. The single works of Frank Norris and Hamlin Garland as well as those of such lesser lights as Hobart C. Chatfield-Taylor, Arthur Eddy, I. K. Friedman, Will Payne, Lillian Sommers, Opie Read, George Lorimer, and James Weber Linn—to name a few— might not be impressive individually; yet, when taken together as a subgenre, their work represents a formidable statement of the extent to which the city had become symbolic of the pragmatic business interests of the nation.

In spite of the differences in fictional techniques, major concerns, and literary ideologies as well as character presentations and developments, there is a strange similarity, for example, among Dennis Fleet (*Barriers Burned Away,*), George Ogden (*The Cliff-Dwellers*), Carrie Meeber (*Sister Carrie*), Curtis Jadwin (*The Pit*), Edward Van Harrington (*Memoirs of an American Citizen*), Frank Cowperwood (*The Titan*), Sam McPherson (*Windy McPherson's Son*), and Beaut McGregor (*Marching Men*). These characters view Chicago, as did their historical counterparts, as a place where the desires for personal fortunes could be fulfilled, where success could be achieved. The story of each is a result of the impact of the urban upon the human. It is not surprising that so many of these works display naturalistic elements. The city was indeed overpowering, and the characters were caught in various webs of their own choosing.

Much has been made of the so-called "revolt-from-the-village" movement that inspired writers from midwestern towns to migrate to the city and expose the pettiness of the small community. Their escape *from* the imagined restrictions of their villages was balanced by their travel *to* the mecca of success. Dreiser spoke knowingly of Carrie as "a waif among the forces." He called the city "a magnet" capable of attracting the uninitiated, who feel they could not spend the remainder of their lives stifled by the limited opportunities of their home towns. Even when unstated, "the waif" and "magnet" images become the most graphic means of defining the relationship between the individual and the city. Individuals, standing alone in time, orphaned from history, were convinced that the attractiveness of the city would bode well for them. Clearly, Chicago was the place to be.

Responses to the city were as ambivalent as American civilization itself. A new American character was emerging. Old ideas and former ideals could not adequately explain the direction of the nation's life. Chicago became the symbol for the glorification of material success at the same time that it stood for spiritual death. Integrity, human warmth, and a humane concern for others did not and could not exist in the fictional portraits of the city. The place was so powerful that it conditioned the lives of the rich and poor alike. Lacking a soul, the city forced its godless life upon men and women who had chosen to sacrifice themselves upon the urban altar. After dramatizing the age-old unanswerable query that questioned the efficacy of gaining the world only to lose one's soul, the city implicitly raised the issue of the simultaneous existence of life and death. Within this context, what was success? What was failure? Chicago gave some answers that may have been unsatisfactory to social scientists and theologians who were trying to discover the meaning of the city, but at least these responses provided subject matter for an entire generation of writers who created and contributed to the Chicago novel.

The earliest group of Chicago novelists had determined before other American storytellers that there had to be an acceptance of an entirely different set of standards in order to understand the growth of the city and the role of human beings in an urban environment. They realized that the old standards of morality—good versus evil—no longer could be applicable. Suddenly, the basic principles of religion did not seem quite as important as they had been. They also recognized that the common juxtaposition of the countryside with the evolving industrial centers might make good studies in American romanticism but hardly addressed key issues germane to the growth of American cities, which by their very nature needed more truthful accounts if they were to be presented fairly. Furthermore, agrarianism did not respond to the needs of these people, who not only chose to live in cities but also seemed to thrive in them. The Main Streets of American towns lost their fascination.

As early as 1872, E. P. Roe, in his *Barriers Burned Away*, had created a character in the image of what seemed to be important in Chicago. Unlike the usual fictional businessman, Mr. Ludolph is a German immigrant; however, he is afflicted by the expected mania for making money. A widower with a desirable daughter, "his only object is staying [in the city is] the accumulation of a large fortune."[3] He succeeds in part because the city is a place of opportunity for all and because he is willing to forego any principle in order to succeed. Dennis Fleet, the young hero from a Wisconsin town, is equally determined. "The world was all before him, and Chicago, the young . . . giant city of the West, seemed an El Dorado, where fortune, and perhaps fame, might soon be won. Not only would he place the family beyond want, but surround them with every luxury" (p. 31).

The attempted rise of Dennis provides Roe with the opportunity to portray urban crime, the prevailing business structure with its acceptance of corruption, the developing caste system within the city as well as the community's early religious conflicts. But, the typical optimism that pervades so much of Chicago history is recorded at the end of the novel as Dennis, after the Fire of 1871, sees "the city rise from its ashes in statelier proportions and richer prosperity. With a thrill of exultation he heard the report that some Napoleonic businessmen had already telegraphed for building materials, and were even now excavating the hot ruins" (p. 541). Because the author's didacticism and sentimentality overshadow the very realistic portrait of the ante-fire Chicago, Roe's novel is frequently ignored.

Yet, throughout the latter part of the nineteenth century, *Barriers Burned Away* continued to enjoy a wide circulation and appeared in several editions both in this country and abroad. Although the novel often was used in church groups to prove to young people that religion and business could eventually coexist, it did so by demonstrating the advantages of religious commitment without placing emphasis upon its "other worldly" aspects. In its time, the novel then fulfilled an important role by denying the necessity for businessmen "to sell" all their goods and give to the less fortunate. As in the cases of the New England Puritans, Roe made it clear that making money could be an acceptable ritual. Less than fifty years later, Sherwood Anderson was also to examine the nature of religion in the life of a businessman.

Henry Blake Fuller's *The Cliff-Dwellers* of 1893, which he considered his first "essay in realism," introduces Erastus Brainard, a Yerkes-like figure, as an example of all that is negative about the businessman. Like Roe's Mr. Ludolph, Brainard is extremely selfish, but he thinks less of his family than does Ludolph. Of significance in the portrait of the businessman in the early fiction of Chicago is the dehumanizing aspect of the life of commerce as success becomes more and more attainable. The description of Brainard, for example, with little change could be applicable to many of the men who built Chicago. They might have integrity and be enterprising, but most of them had "never lived for anything but business." Fuller continues his picture: "[Erastus] had never eaten and drunk for anything but business—his family shared his farm-like fare and his primitive hours. He had never built for anything but business. . . . He never dressed for anything but business. . . He wrote about nothing but business—his nearest relative was never more than 'dear sir,' and he himself was never otherwise than 'yours truly'; and he wrote on business letterheads even to his family."[4]

Indicating the strong bond between government and big business, Fuller demonstrates how Brainard's success is predicated upon his control of the city council and state legislature. There is strong evidence to suggest that Fuller's Brainard is a composite of his own grandfather and father, both of whom reflected to the novelist all that was villainous about urban businessmen; but the fact remains that the portrait is one rooted in the history of the city. These sinister musclemen of business, described as a soulless lot, hold both government and citizens as captives.

From the negative portrait of Brainard, Fuller turned in *With the Procession* (1895) to David Marshall, who is more ineffectual than wicked, who has outlived his usefulness, and who is now face to face with a city he does not understand. Vaguely, he realizes that conditions after the Fire of 1871 necessitated certain financial deals and risks if businessmen were to recoup their losses, but he worries about the toll this will take. As David views his older son, he "almost seemed to see the moral fibre of Roger's nature coarsening—perhaps disintegrating—under his very eyes, and he asked himself reproachfully how much this might be due to tasks of his own imposition."[5] Viewing the city as representative of some powerful forces, Fuller observed that despite the World's Columbian Exposition, there was an apparent laissez-faire approach to life. "In this Garden City of ours every man cultivates his own little bed and his neighbor his; but who looks after the paths between?" The lack of concern so characteristic of urban life is made manifest as these "paths between" are viewed as "a kind of No Man's Land, and the weeds of rank iniquity are fast choking them up. The thing to teach the public is this: that the general good is a different thing from the sum of individual goods." Later storytellers have accepted Fuller's observations and often use them as central tenets in the presentation of the mythical city.

> This town of ours labors under one peculiar disadvantage: it is the only great city in the world to which all its citizens have come for the one common, avowed object of making money. There you have its genesis, its growth, its end and object; and there are but few of us who are not attending to that object very strictly. (p. 248)

The interrelationship between the importance of money and a lack of concern for others was incorporated early into the Chicago novel. Even the nobility of philanthropy, Fuller explains, can be reduced by its selfish motivations. Mrs. Bates, one of the central figures in the novel, observes while discussing "the art of giving" with a reluctant David Marshall: "As I have said so many times to Mr. Bates, 'Make it something that people can *see*.'" She continues by pointing out that a contribution of "two or three thousand dollars to the public" in order to reduce "the municipal debt" or clean the streets would be meaningless. People do not relate to abstract debts, and street cleaning "would be forgotten with the coming of the next rainstorm." The obiter dictum of giving, according to Mrs. Bates, is to make it "something solid and something permanent; it must be a building"

(p. 114). The wealthy's sense of noblesse oblige, so much a part of the urban development of the nineteenth century, was often played out in various ways in the fictional studies of the period and usually followed the directives of Mrs. Bates, who is perhaps one of the strongest figures ever created by Fuller. (Howells praised her as one of American fiction's exciting characters.[6]) She is determined, articulate, and not satisfied to be her husband's silent partner. She is committed to a goal in life that mandates she keep up "with the procession" and head it whenever possible.

With the Procession also makes one of the clearest statements regarding the basic conflicts between the old and new businessmen, a conflict that augments the development of dramatic tension in the novel. The reader becomes aware that the David Marshalls, worthy though they may be, have no place in a new America, where speculation and financial combinations have been substituted for the efforts of individual entrepreneurs. Thus, it is fitting that when the novel opens, Marshall has already died; and his story is told through flashbacks. If Belden (the partner Marshall is forced to take in order to save his business after the Fire of 1871) and Roger seem less than admirable, at least they are in the vanguard of American "progress."

Tangential to the development of the businessman as a cultural hero are the unexamined roles played by women in a commercial culture. The Chicago novelists, fully aware of the rising masculine figure, were also mindful that the traditional fictional female was lost in the city. Repeatedly, one notes the frequency with which the businessman is portrayed as having married a traditional woman while seeking the companionship or advice of a strong woman more nearly his intellectual equal. It is often suggested that his rise in the world of commerce is directly due to the influence or the strength of a woman who pushes him forward.

Hamlin Garland's *Rose of Dutcher's Coolly* (1895) balances the story of the innocent seeking refuge in the city as it presents two other "new" women within the urban milieu. Selecting Chicago because it is close to her Wisconsin home and because it had become the accepted belief that the place was sympathetic to freedom-seeking individuals, an emancipated Rose travels to the city "to find" herself. She comes to understand that part of urban adjustment is predicated upon knowing the distinctions between Chicago and Dutcher's Coolly, which she interprets as differences between the city's rhythms and those of the land. As she learns to comprehend her own sexuality, she is aided by Dr. Isabel Herrick, one of the early professional women in fiction, whose feminism does not create such an automaton as the Dr. Prance who appears in Henry James's *The Bostonians* of 1887.

By the end of the century, the urban themes suggested by Roe, Fuller, and Garland had been explored thoroughly and accepted as the major concerns of those interested in rendering the city in fiction. Not surprisingly, writers continued to be fascinated with the inevitable conflict pitting the human against the urban and usually chose to express this in terms of the city's business culture with the financier occupying center stage. Like Fuller's work, Opie Read's *The Colossus* (1893) deals with the idea that the city is a powerful force subduing all but permitting those willing to acknowledge its existence the ability to succeed within its parameters. The price is high as people forfeit not only their humanity but also their souls. A repeated theme in Chicago fiction, it makes the actions and characterizations quite predictable; but this does not necessarily lessen the impact of such stories.

Will Payne's portrayal of a businessman in *The Money Captain* (1898),[7] duplicates the pattern of Erastus Brainard. Totally committed to business, Dexter is fascinated by the "game" of finance and finds it impossible to control his obsession. However, he has little or no interest in human beings. Payne describes his hero as "a shadow, merely a passing, personified figment of the vast stirrings of industry and accumulation of wealth that came out of the country's rich soil" (p. 114). Dexter realizes he is as much a victim of the city as is the worker who is tied to the system. At one point he observes: "A hundred thousand dollars, made as I've made my money and as most men make their money, means a hundred thousand new things to do. So it goes, piling up. The more money I make, the tighter I am tied up" (pp. 216–17).

In *The Gospel of Freedom* (1898), Robert Herrick locates the core of urban problems within the nature of the city, which is defined as an "instance of a successful, contemptuous disregard of nature by man" and which "stands [as] a stupendous piece of blasphemy against nature."[8] John Wilbur, the hero, is spellbound by Chicago and is lulled into believing that the road to power is dependent upon a commitment to the spirit of acquisition. Like Curtis Jadwin of Frank Norris's *The Pit* (1903), he forsakes everything to statisfy his mania. The city to John Wilbur is "like a congenial Alpine air" stimulating "his appetites [because] the strife for advancement summoned all his virility, and the sense of rapid success exhilirated him" (p. 204). Herrick includes a carbon copy of the many Yerkes-inspired figures who people the Chicago business novel. Seen through the eyes of Wilbur's wife, the shadowy Wrightington exhibits all the negative features generally associated with this type of character.

> The great Wrightington! this name hawked about ever since she had known anything of Chicago filled her with a kind of terror. He was an unscrupulous adventurer, who had 'gone broke' several times, yet was always triumphant; a man received nowhere, of no respectable affiliations yet a power to be followed. Many of the respectable element secretly admired his audacity [and] . . . followed his lead. He was brazen, impudent, cynical, and inevitable. Of late the [news]-papers had been frantic over Wrightington . . . they teemed with the usual charges of scandalous corruption and bribery which his transactions periodically aroused. (p. 121)

By 1905 and the publication of his *Memoirs of an American Citizen*, Herrick not only utilized the themes and portraits displayed so prominently in the fictional presentations of the Chicago businessman but also emphasized the inevitability of it all. Edward Van Harrington, the hero, recognizes that "no one . . . ever came to Chicago . . . in those days without a hope in his pockets of landing at the head of the game sometime."[9] Herrick wonders what effect the loss of soul will have on the man of commerce if such a character has money and power. Using the first-person narrator, Herrick has Van Harrington explain himself. His constant self-justifications are indicative of his sense of accomplishment. At one point, he looks over Chicago apologetically and observes, "I, too, was part of this. The thought of my brain, the labour of my body, the will within me, had gone into the making of this world." Seeing all of his possessions ("my plants, my car line, my railroads, my elevators, my lands") arrayed before him, he concludes they are "all good tools in the infinite work of this world." Voicing the usual disclaimer, he reasons: "Conceived for good or for ill, brought into being by fraud and daring—what man could judge their worth. They were done; and mine was the hand. Let another, more perfect, turn them to a larger use; nevertheless, on my labour, on me, he must build" (p. 346).

Between *The Gospel of Freedom* and *Memoirs of an American Citizen*, Herrick probed the effects of the city on various characters. In both *The Web of Life* (1900) and *The Common Lot* (1904), he focused his attention upon the professional man in a materialistic society. In the earlier novel he offered a solution very similar to a conclusion Anderson was to repeat in *Windy McPherson's Son*. The hero, Dr. Howard Sommers, escapes from the city in search of peace, which he eventually finds within himself rather than in a total rejection of the city. Once this is accomplished, his return to the city seems anticlimactic. Jackson Hart, the architect who is the hero of *The Common Lot*, seeks solace in nature after his frantic acceptance of the shoddy standards of commercialism rather than in the uplifting ones of his art; however, before this is effected, his wife blames the city for what her husband has become. "Chicago had moulded him and had left his nature set in a hard crust of prejudice. The great industrial city where he had learned the lesson of life throttled the finer aspiration of men like a remorseless giant, converting its youth into iron-clad beasts of prey answering to one hoarse cry, 'Success, Success, Success!'" [10]

During the period in which Herrick was exploring, often angrily, various facets of Chicago life, Frank Norris's *The Pit* was published in 1903. Fred Lewis Pattee credited Norris with capturing the spirit of the new realism as well as of Chicago. Referring to the Chicago-born novelist as "a voice from California," Pattee claimed that Norris had "precipitated a new period" by being "a voice free from provincial narrowness and a Puritanical intolerance." [11] Floyd Dell thought the novel, despite its shortcomings, was "the best fictional guidebook to Chicago in existence." He felt Norris had "sketched the city in broad, powerful strokes, taking in with his amateur vision aspects of its life that veteran Chicagoans had felt without being able to express. Never, surely, was a city 'done' so well. Better than any book written by a real Chicagoan, he gives us in his novel a sense of Chicago's streets and buildings and business—its localized existence." [12]

Perhaps taking a cue from Fuller, who attempted to use an office building as a metaphoric statement for urban life, and from those Chicago writers who were intent upon giving detailed descriptions of sites within the city, Norris tried to use the Board of Trade Building and its "pit" as well as LaSalle Street as his central symbols. Early in the novel the reader learns that the structure which is the location of grain speculation is "black, grave, monolithic, crouching on its foundations, like a monstrous sphinx with blind eyes, silent, grave,— crouching there without a sound, without sign of life under the night and the drifting veil of rain." [13] It is significant that at the end of the novel, as the central characters leave Chicago in defeat, the Board of Trade Building once again is the focal point. Using the same description he had used in the opening pages of his novel, Norris notes that this is "the last impression" Laura, Curtis Jadwin's wife, has of the city (pp. 420–21).

In spite of his mania for the power that will come if he can corner the wheat market, Curtis Jadwin perhaps is more likable than most of the fictional businessmen. The reader can only detect the extent to which his activities have been demoralizing by viewing the effect he has had on those about him. Laura, who is completely ignorant of his business dealings, becomes bored when he spends so much time in the pit and turns momentarily to another man for attention. The men who work with Curtis Jadwin become more and more dehumanized. But despite Jadwin's clear violation of the laws of nature in trying to corner the market, many readers are saddened by his final defeat.

Arthur J. Eddy's *Ganton and Co.* (1908) did not introduce any new themes to the business novel. It repeatedly emphasized the strength and power of the city in the usual supernatural terms. Its author also agreed that the political structure, a clear ally of business, was corrupt. By this time the novelists had created a fictional formula, which included the idea that the life of business was really "a game," that titans functioned with a single purpose. They worked for money, which in turn gave them more power with which to command more money, and the never-ending circle continued ad infinitum. Although they had families, they paid little attention to them. Their children, either because of overindulgence or neglect, could not cope with life. Thus the weaknesses of the second generation, a popular concept in dynasty novels, became of greater significance in these works because they reinforced the dehumanization of men and women who operate under the aegis of the commercial world. In the final analysis, the estrangement of family members became just one of the prices of success. All-powerful though they were, businessmen, so generations of readers had been convinced, were at the mercy of the city that was a still stronger force.

The first group of Chicago novelists essentially were genteel in outlook. Yet, they were aware before the age of Dreiser that, when mercantilism became dominant, human existence would necessarily assume distinctive characteristics as a response to this artificial life. Although they had general misgivings about the direction of American civilization, such writers as Roe, Fuller, Chatfield-Taylor, Wyatt, Garland, Payne, and Herrick believed that corrections could be made within the system. Some of them were even optimistic or naive enough to think that eventually the business structure would regulate itself. Readers can often detect personal misgivings displayed by these novelists who seldom voiced overt protest. The few utopian works that appeared in the latter part of the nineteenth century also placed much hope in the benefits to be derived from the commercial world when that universe operated for all mankind. For example, such tract-novels as Robert Cowdrey's *A Tramp in Society* (1891), Henry L. Everett's *The People's Program* (1892), and *The Beginning: Romance of Chicago As It Might Be* (1893) by "a small debating club of workingmen" acknowledged that changes needed to be made, but they could not deny the city's phenomenal growth and success. The novels might plead for moral regeneration, but readers did not have to be unduly perceptive to realize that the utopian plans would not yield as much as the existing commercial structure.

The twentieth century saw the rise of stronger elements of protest. Clarence Darrow's *An Eye for an Eye* (1905), Upton Sinclair's *The Jungle* (1906), and Frank Harris's *The Bomb* (1908) added another dimension to the Chicago novel. Both Darrow and Harris examined a judicial system that favored the rich and powerful while appearing to be against the weak and downtrodden. Harris especially was interested in the anti-immigrant attitudes that prevailed during the Haymarket Affair. Sinclair's attack upon the meat-packing industry was a plea for greater understanding of the inhuman conditions that existed in the city for those foreign workers whose faith in the American Dream had led them to Chicago. In all three works, the invidious business world looms as a specter controlling the lives of those whose only sin consists of being poor and not knowing how "to beat the system." The protests of these writers later were perfected and made part of the aesthetic milieu of such midcentury novelists as James T. Farrell, Nelson Algren, and Richard Wright, who shifted the focus from the ruling business and social elites to the pitiful lives of the urban dispossessed.

By 1914, Theodore Dreiser had set the stage for the ultimate portrait of the Chicago businessman and the pervasive nature of the city. Aided by the repetitive work of the preceding novelists, there was a growing acceptance of the fictional studies of the city as the only reality. Fewer and fewer people were concerned about the hard-working men and women who bore little resemblance to a Frank Cowperwood. Introduced in *The Financier* (1912) and hardened by his prison experience, Cowperwood, a thinly-disguised Charles T. Yerkes, reached Chicago at a time when he was as ready for it as the city was for him. In *The Titan* he declared: "Here was life . . . here was a seething city in the making. There was something dynamic in the very air." He later saw the importance of "this singing flame of a city, this all-

America, this poet in chaps and buckskin, this rude, raw Titan, this Burns of a city!"[14] Dreiser continues his novel by presenting a Chicago of power and corruption, where strength is the only marketable commodity.

Accompanying the technological advances leading to the nation's supremacy, there had been a corresponding loss of faith; and the absence of tradition served to emphasize the materialism of the age. Thus, when Sherwood Anderson returned to Chicago in 1913 with his manuscripts that included *Windy McPherson's Son* and *Marching Men*, the general sense of urban optimism had faded. Moreover, between 1896 and 1913, there had evolved a distinct novel with discernible patterns. The "Chicago School of Fiction" received considerable attention not only from Howells and Dell in national publications but also from H. L. Mencken. It was the inconoclastic critic who demonstrated just how widespread was the belief in the city's literary ferment. Less than fifteen years after Howells had made the name of the city "a literary watchword," Mencken praised Chicago for being more "American" and more "national" than some of the older cities and claimed that "all literary movements that have youth in them and a fresh point of view" as well as "the authentic bounce and verve of the country and the true character and philosophy of its people" are products of Chicago, "the most civilized city in America." In rhapsodic fashion, he proclaimed in his celebration of the city, which appeared on October 28, 1917, in the Chicago *Tribune:*

> Find me a writer who is indubitably American and who has some thing new and interesting to say, and who says it with an air, and nine times out of ten . . . he has some sort of connection with the abbatoir by the lake—that he was bred there or got his start there, or passed through there during the days when he was tender.

What he called a "Chicago habit of mind" permeated the work of such writers as "Fuller, Norris, Dreiser, Herrick, Patterson, Anderson, and all other outstanding American writers" that made them "reek of Chicago in every line." Mencken felt that the "Chicago habit of mind" also led to an "originality" that superseded "conformity." His celebration concluded: "I give you Chicago. It is not London-and-Harvard. It is not Paris-and-buttermilk. It is American in every chitling and sparerib, and it is alive from snout to tail."

Three years later, Mencken wrote of Chicago as "The Literary

Capital of the United States" in the London *Nation* (April 17, 1920). Perhaps more tempered than his earlier article, it substantially repeated the same ideas:

> With two exceptions, there is not a single American novelist, a novelist deserving a civilized reader's notice—who has not sprung from the Middle Empire that has Chicago for its capital. It as plainly dominates the energy and aspiration of all that fertile region as Edinburgh dominates Scotland. From Ade to Dreiser nearly all the bright young Indianians have gone to Chicago for a semester or two, and not only Indianians, but also the youngsters of all the other Middle Western States. It has drawn them in from their remote wheat-towns and far-flung railway junctions, and it has given them an impulse that New York simply cannot match—an impulse toward independence, toward honesty, toward a peculiar vividness and *naivete*—in brief, toward the unaffected self-expression that is at the bottom of sound art. New York, when it lures such a recruit eastward, makes a pliant conformist of him, and so ruins him out of hand. . . . But Chicago, however short the time it has him, leads him inevocably [*sic*] through a decisive trial of his talents. Witness Anderson, Dreiser, Masters, Sandburg, and Ade. . . . For originality Chicago has a perennial welcome, and where the welcome is, there the guests are to be found. Go back for twenty or thirty years, and you will scarcely find an American literary movement that did not originate under the shadow of the stockyards.

When one considers the long literary tradition in the city as well as the experimental work produced during the twentieth century, it is no wonder that Mencken could celebrate the city as "the literary capital of the United States," but by that time the major work of the writers about whom he spoke had been completed and many of them had indeed gravitated "eastward."

Retrospectively, one can discover that from E. P. Roe's *Barriers Burned Away* up to, but not including, Fuller's *The Cliff-Dwellers* of 1893, there had been the suggestion—sometimes slight but nonetheless present—that religion or intense morality could offer a viable answer to the problems of urbanism. The reader is told that Dennis Fleet is a "Christian," specifically a Protestant who rejects the "romanism" of his German employer whose religious commitment is maintained although it does not figure prominently in his portrayal. Fleet prevails because his faith is so strong. By the time of *The Cliff-Dwellers*, however, religion no longer is an alternative. The rules and regulations

governing organized society are of little import in determining the
success of a character. An acceptance of what Fuller called "the off
hand Western ways" in *The Cliff-Dwellers* (p. 181) usually preceded
business success in a place where the frontier was still a real factor in
the minds of most settlers.

Fuller made several observations on the city from the viewpoint
of an outsider (usually someone from the East) and, in so doing, characterized many of the major objections to the city. For example, the
emphasis upon size is presented ironically in the statement: "If you
can only be big you don't mind being dirty" (p. 226). And as an east-
erner looks at his brother who has moved to Chicago, Fuller summarizes the effects of the city:

> Winthrop favored his brother with a stare of frank curiosity. Wal-
> worth had spoken with some warmth [about Chicago]; he seemed
> disposed to throw an undue ardor into his defense of his adopted
> home—a city where quality, and where the 'prominent' citizen made
> the 'eminent' citizen a superfluity. Then, too, Winthrop coupled with
> the earnest lines in his brother's forehead a slightly dingy necktie
> under his chin. He observed, moreover, in the polishing of the shoe
> which Walworth, for greater emphasis, was beating on the carpet, a
> neglect of the heel in favor of the toe. And there were several other
> indications of a growing carelessness in dress. (p. 235)

In many ways, then, Chicago represented the urbanization of the
frontier.

When he turned to the creation of fiction, in some respects, Sherwood Anderson followed the genre that had been established by the
novelists of Chicago. His first published works include scenes and
characters from the city as well as a record of his views. Out of this,
Anderson eventually developed an art form that grew out of his urban experience. By so doing, he was able to illustrate the effects of
urbanism upon the evolution of an aesthetic principle. The autobiographical nature of much of what he wrote demonstrated in a tangible
way the truth of his assertion "no man can escape the city." In this he
joined other so-called Chicago novelists, who have chronicled the city
in the process of becoming and also have recognized that nothing can
stem the tide of urban "progress."

Like others who had identified the city as a place where large
crowds gather and people jostle each other on the streets, Sherwood
Anderson was convinced that these moments of contact represent for

many the only means of communication. The concept that there is loneliness in the midst of the crowd is repeated constantly in urban fiction; however, after Sherwood Anderson, the city's novelists tended to restrict their urban visions to particular neighborhoods thereby giving to their characters at least an elementary sense of belonging. Thus, in the midst of the disorderly city, such writers as Farrell, Algren, and Wright suggested that if characters would remain where they "belong" they might have the means to communicate with one another no matter how limited their lives might be.

How well Anderson knew the Chicago novel is not clear even though by his time the genre had become a distinct form within American fiction. Some of its practitioners, such as Floyd Dell, Ben Hecht, and Theodore Dreiser, were to become his acquaintances and allies. His association with Clarence Darrow related to sociopolitical issues, and apparently he thought of E. P. Roe only as a melodramatic novelist with whom, on occasion, he was identified.[15] When he realized that he had "become part of what was for a time called 'The Chicago School' of Writers,"[16] he was referring primarily to the Renaissance group and not to the earlier novelists. In the end, it seems that Chicago helped Anderson sort out his views of urban life. The city might make clear the human tragedy that results from alienation, loneliness, lack of love, and the inability to fulfill one's desires; but, as Anderson was to learn, people cannot run away from themselves nor abandon the search for truth. He became fascinated not only by the chaos but also by the fragmentation and ambiguity of life as he observed it. Isolated though they were from the demands of human warmth, urban dwellers at least were pulled together by the same lures of the city. Whether a literary artist, like a painter, could capture this duality at a given instant became a central question for Anderson. Recording the city's rhythms and capturing a sense of its dissimilar images ultimately conditioned his sense of reality. But before this occurred, through his confrontation with the city, Anderson completed *Windy McPherson's Son* and *Marching Men*.

PART ONE
Confrontation

Fear.

Something huge, not understandable.
Streets thirty miles long, perfectly
flat. Buildings and houses you dream
about in distorted dreams. . . .

I was a raw boy just out of my Ohio
town when I first came to Chicago.
What city man, come out of a small
town, can forget his first hours in the
city, the strangeness and terror of the
tall buildings, the human jam?

—*Memoirs*

The changing, hurrying life of [Chicago] profoundly interested the tall, strong boy from the Iowa village, who had the cold, quick business stroke of the money-maker, combined with an unusually active interest in the problems of life and living. Instinctively he looked upon business as a great game in which many men sat. . . .

—*Windy McPherson's Son*

3

Sam McPherson

An Uncommon Portrait
of a Chicago Businessman

THE SENSE of wonder and feelings of trepidation that travelers faced at the turn of the century have essentially disappeared; but there was a time when the sons and daughters of the Middle Border hastened to the city—believing that Chicago offered a chance for success. Forgetting the broken dreams of the failures, they overlooked the reality of the place and thought "going to Chicago" meant the possibility of new opportunities. Like others of his generation, Sherwood Anderson wanted the good life that he heard could be found in Chicago, but his first period in the city was to make him question the prevailing tales. When he began to write, it is not unusual that reactions to the city should have provided one subject for him.

The ambiguity of his attitude toward the urban experience is reflected in his first two published novels, as he seemed to view the city from both hopeful and adversarial positions. In many ways, *Windy McPherson's Son* (1916) and *Marching Men* (1917) are mirror images of each other. One deals not only with success and its price but also with urban acceptance and survival. The other analyzes urban rejection, rebellion, and disorder. Both see the city as a phenomenon that arouses alarm and passion; yet, each attempts an analytical concern that tries to transpose the sociological into the aesthetic. *Windy McPherson's Son* examines a businessman in the city; *Marching Men* looks at a particular type of professional man in an urban setting. As was customary in the Chicago novel of which they are a part, both, however, utilize not only the geography of the city but also the suggestive theme that the city plays a controling role in the lives of its citizens. But beyond his use of naturalistic elements, there is the beginning of his revision of the currently practiced realism. Consequently, whether Sherwood Anderson's solutions for urban life are viable is not quite as important as the manner in which he used the confrontation between individuals and urban life.

I

Windy McPherson's Son initially repeats the formula of the urban success story popularized by the Chicago novel that preceded Anderson's work. Yet, it introduces themes and motifs while raising questions not usually associated with the city's story. The novel deals with Sam McPherson (the son of the town's ne'er-do-well) who goes to the city after years in Caxton, Iowa, listening to tales of urban travelers and dreaming of his own conquests. Although strong-willed and determined, he is subjected to both the negative and positive influences of Chicago. As he yields to the city's demands, he discovers that the challenges are exhilarating. Marriage to Sue Rainey, a businessman's daughter, ensures his place in a firm but that marriage, predicated upon impractical ideals, soon fails. Sam turns to his business world with a vengeance only to leave it in search of a better life. The novel then shifts from the city to the wandering life of the now nomadic hero. It sets up a contrast between the urban and the rural. When he rejects the city, Windy's son soon discovers that the most effective answer to the questions raised by urban life is to accept not only the place but its limitations with an understanding that the city can never again deny the importance of the individual. In its version of the generally accepted success story, Anderson's narrative makes a notable contribution to the Chicago novel in particular and to urban literature in general.

Since most critics are inclined to begin a study of Sherwood Anderson with *Winesburg, Ohio*, his earlier work is dismissed as an interesting, albeit weak, prelude to his outstanding period as a writer. To accept the undisputed greatness of *Winesburg, Ohio*, however, should not cause deprecations of his work leading up to that collection of tales. Both *Windy McPherson's Son* and *Marching Men* have merit. Taken together, they represent an analysis of the city in fiction somewhat at variance with many other such novels. The commonly held urban myths fade as Anderson thought creatively about the evolution of the city. Hart Crane's apprehension about the apostolic nature of the two novels is well-founded;[1] yet, whatever propaganda exists should not overshadow Anderson's evolving urban vision.

The critical judgments of *Windy McPherson's Son* represent a diversity of opinions. They have become increasingly more negative, but the novel received the attention often accorded first works, while it was both praised and damned for its Chicago connection. Samuel Tait, Jr., claimed that the novel contained "an unmistakable ethical stink," partially explained by Anderson's contact with the literary liberation that came out of Chicago.[2] On the other hand, Llewellyn Jones praised Anderson as a participant in the renaissance movement and considered him to be a follower of Dreiser, Masters, and Sandburg, especially in his treatment of the small midwestern town.[3] Comparing Anderson to other regional writers was not uncommon. Jane Heap complained that Anderson was like Dreiser in producing "only a homily," and she felt he had merely succeeded in the presentation of the ugly.[4] Although Harry Hartwick considered him to be a "Dreiser with the backbone removed,"[5] H. W. Boynton rejected any similarity between Dreiser and Anderson but related *Windy McPherson's Son* to *Spoon River Anthology* in terms of purpose and style.[6] Floyd Dell, who later referred to himself as Anderson's "literary father,"[7] heralded the novel as part of the world of Dostoevsky and the other great Russian realists.[8] Such associations made H. W. Boynton uncomfortable, although he agreed that Anderson's work, which he thought to be a good first effort, seemed to be in the tradition of Russian naturalism with the grimness of Dostoevsky.[9]

In an era when the search for "the great American novel" was still being actively pursued, it was not surprising that some reviewers addressed the nationalistic qualities of the work while others focused on style. The *New York Times Book Review* commented on the true "American-ness" of the work.[10] Yet, in her review in the *Little Review*, Jane Heap observed "Anderson strives too earnestly to create a totally American novel." Occasionally reviewers spoke of the work's poetic qualities.[11] Ben Hecht enthusiastically praised Anderson as "a great new American artist with the poetic vision to write heroically of America,"[12] but Harry Hartwick dismissed Anderson as "a Whitman gone to seed." Gerald Gould discovered that the work was filled with "great amounts of dull prose" with few redeeming features. Occasionally, the novel was "enlivened by worthwhile parts," but, he concluded, Anderson did not have "the ability to give form to the novel."[13]

H. L. Mencken, although allowing that Anderson had written "realistically of [the] rejection of business," was among those who rejected the novel but saw its promise and thought its author possibly would produce something of outstanding quality in the future.[14]

Anderson's obvious manipulation of his characters escaped the critical attention of many early reviewers. Willing to admit the weaknesses of the novel, Paul Schlueter confessed that Sam McPherson is "not quite like" other fictional heroes in American life.[15] Llewellyn Jones found the novel's characters generally stimulating; but William Lyon Phelps thought they were "too detailed and unreal," although he admitted that there was a certain unpolished strength in the work.[16] A year after the novel's appearance, the *Bookman* noted the autobiographical element in it;[17] yet, an earlier critic for the *Times Literary Supplement* accused Anderson of being too imaginative and asserted that a central problem of the novel resulted because the writer was incapable of dealing with "reality."[18]

Two aspects of the novel came under close scrutiny. Most critics noted its conclusion as the work's weakest part. Waldo Frank, a strong Anderson supporter, felt the ending marred an otherwise realistic study.[19] *The North American Review* attributed the ineffectiveness of the last episodes to Anderson's combination of the real business world with the romantic search for self.[20] Writing in the Boston *Evening Transcript,* one D.L.M. suggested that the unbelievable ending was an indication of either a new writer who could not handle his materials or a writer who was attempting to soften the narrative by appealing to the public's desire for "happing endings."[21] Generally, every reviewer noted the obvious "search" that forms a major theme in the novel as an important quest. H. W. Boynton argued that the "old theme of searching for happiness is given fresh American treatment."[22]

Present-day critics pay scant attention to *Windy McPherson's Son,* undoubtedly because of their repeated emphasis upon Anderson's short stories of village life. As a result, important sections of the novel are either overlooked or misread. Representative of current critical judgment is the one so cogently presented by Brom Weber, who asserted that the strength of the novel rests in the first eight chapters, before the Chicago experience, because "many sentences [in this section] are packed with the hum of feeling and have a Biblical cadence." By contrast with Anderson's difficulty in the development of characters and narrative, Weber felt as long as Anderson dealt with Caxton his "imagery and diction were generally . . . free from cliche and stereotype."[23]

Without denying the stylistic characteristics of the opening chapters as cited by Weber, one cannot overlook "the Chicago experience" for it provides the central tension of the novel. By the time of *Windy McPherson's Son*, the Chicago novel (or at least its formula) had become so commonplace that at first glance Anderson's version of the city seems to follow closely the traditional attitudes without introducing any new approaches. Nonetheless, the novelist dared to suggest that the deterministic elements of the city did not have to be as powerful as Herrick, Dreiser, and others had implied. During a period when literary naturalism seemed dominant, he offered another approach to the urban hero, which neither minimized the force of the city nor ignored the power of the human will. Long before detente assumed its political overtones, Anderson suggested it as a method of urban survival.

The novel's examination of the success formula reflects Anderson's concern about the contradictory nature of the national emphasis upon "getting ahead." In two separate letters to Waldo Frank, Anderson addressed the issue and spoke of the significance of the matter in American culture.[24] In March 1917, he wrote that "Americans . . . got a wrong start in life." He continued, "The notion of success in affairs, in love, in our daily life is so ingrained that it is almost impossible to shake it off." Later that year he wrote of the need "to shake off the success disease, to really get over our American mania for 'getting on.'" In wondering "why the desire for success [is] so deep-seated," he rhetorically raised this question with Frank: "Is it because we are neither urban or rural that we have neither the crude sincerity of the Russians or the finished gesture at art and life of the Frenchman?"

Perceptive though his query was at the time, observers of American life realize that from John Smith through Benjamin Franklin and Horatio Alger to modern popular literature, the "fairy-tale" syndrome has been a psychological cornerstone in the nation's culture, even when it has not been believed. Called the American Dream by many for lack of a more precise description, the public has accepted the notion that success, whether earned or bestowed gratuitously, will bring happiness. Even those who cannot believe in the totality of the Dream have often subconsciously assumed the importance of money under such glib retorts as "but we can buy our own form of misery." In *Windy McPherson's Son*, there is some of this glibness; however, despite its many technical flaws, the novel presents a graphic portrait of a Chicago businessman who comes to understand the need to control his destiny. The fact that Sam McPherson was created by a businessman, who knew through personal experience the techniques and the demands of making money in the city, lends an air of verisimilitude to the character not often accorded to such fictional portraits. The unhappiness and personal disquietude that come with the fulfillment of the American Dream are deemed of sufficient magnitude that the hero, like his creator, tries to escape his "successful" life. Yet, if Sam has any illusions of following the biblical directive to sell his goods and give to the poor, these are quickly shattered by what he discovers on his quest.

The novel accepts the historical and stereotypical role of the city as a factor in the developing spirit of the nation. As a symbol of American civilization, Chicago is a pervasive element in Anderson's work. The city as portrayed in *Windy McPherson's Son* is neither particularly beautiful nor ugly, but it is large. Descriptions of it emphasize its territorial limits and necessarily minimize the human elements. In time, Sam understands as he "walks[s] for endless miles through the lighted streets" that from the city he is "getting in a dim way a realisation of the hugeness of life." [25]

In addition to the expected general allusions to crowds, tall buildings, and other manifestations of urban life, the novel transmits a sense of place by specific references to fixed landmarks and recognizable sites. If he accomplished nothing else, Sherwood Anderson demonstrated his knowledge of the city's landscape. There is the presence of such well-known buildings as the Coliseum on Wabash Avenue and the Rookery at 209 S. LaSalle. Identifiable streets (South Water, Dearborn, Van Buren, State, Monroe, Michigan, and LaSalle—to name a few) as well as the Chicago River and Lake Michigan are mentioned. Some important actions take place in Jackson Park as well as in Grant Park. Furthermore, there are allusions to the three "sides" of Chicago, which also are used to chart Sam's rise in the city. As was true of so many of his historic counterparts, Sam first lives on the West Side. When he becomes moderately successful, he moves to the South Side; and when he becomes a Chicago tycoon, he is on the North Side in "a huge stone house . . . near the shores of Lake Michigan" (p. 220). Much of the action, however, takes place in the downtown commercial area.

Anderson begins with the premise that Chicago is not only an accomplished fact but also a powerful place designed for the strong and accepts its corollary that the weak are not tolerated despite any feeble attempts by some to alter the course of human destiny. "Life is a battle in which few men win and many are defeated and in which hate and fear play their part with love and generosity" (p. 227). Essentially, then, *Windy McPherson's Son* is concerned with the evolution of a Chicago businessman and his reaction to success. Following the pattern of Edward Van Harrington and other fictional titans prior to his time, Sam is a product of a small midwestern town who sees "himself going on and on, directing, managing, ruling men. . . . 'I will run factories and banks and maybe mines and railroads,' . . . and his mind leaped forward so that he saw himself, grey, stern and capable, sitting at a broad desk high in a great stone building" (p. 138).

Prior to Anderson's work, two fictional businessmen dominated the literature. Among some of the earlier novelists who wished to believe in the efficacy of the American Dream, the businessman was portrayed as a dashing, romantic, all-caring figure who rose from the people and who really was committed to the good of the community. A pragmatist for whom the "from-rags-to-riches" theme was real, nonetheless he was concerned about the personal elements of business and continued to maintain an active interest in the product as well as in his employees. This figure remained in fiction as the "old" man of business, most commonly seen in the days before the Fire of 1871. The other portrait displayed a dark and sinister, selfish creature who literally consorted with the Prince of Darkness. His love of money as well as his hunger for power made him less than human. Willing to sacrifice everything to realize his goals, he became prominent as business moved from the personal to the impersonal. While both figures are rooted in fact, as the history of Chicago or any large urban area will prove, the historic patterns were obviously far more complex than their fictional counterparts. Anderson, in going beyond a mere revelation of the actuality of this character, reintroduced greater dimensions into the figure as he attempted to analyze the strange dichotomy between man's search for material success and for a fulfillment of self.

Consequently, in some respects, *Windy McPherson's Son* explores the relationship between worldly gains and inner peace. It generally has been assumed, especially in fiction, that the two cannot exist simultaneously. Not only does the issue form the basis of Herrick's *Memoirs of an American Citizen* but also seems to be central to the novel that was developed in Chicago. Whereas earlier novelists raised the question and sought simplistic, moralistic solutions, Anderson examined the biblical parable's query through his portrayal of the efforts of a single businessman's search for the truth of human existence, an important search that becomes the alternative to either blind acceptance or complete rejection of the commercial world. Yet, apparently Anderson could not cope with a central problem implicit in his treatment of the actions of his hero. And, in the end, this destroys some of the effectiveness of the novel.

No matter how admirable it might be, Sam's search seems to beg the question. For example, when Sam turns his back on his material gains to search for truth, the reader (conditioned by the expectations of American civilization) sees more fantasy than reality in his actions. One can understand—and perhaps even applaud—Sam's spectacular rise in the armaments industry despite his use of questionably ethical methods, but ultimately his search for *Truth* in the midst of success appears out of character with the usual perceptions of the real world. Such a search seems highly unlikely in a culture nurtured by dreams of earthly comforts, and many readers are suspicious of any conversion that results in the repudiation of the "things" of this world. As Anderson has presented Sam's actions, the solution given by the novelist is not really the answer to the problem. Sam also discovers this; but in the process, he gains a sense of the humanizing effects of love. Whether or not one trusts Anderson's conclusion is partially dependent upon an acceptance of the validity of Sam's escape from the business world. It is an action that taxes the expectations of the reader.

The story of Sam McPherson, however, does not begin in Chicago. From childhood he has heard tales of the fortunes to be made in the city, and these have provided strong motives for his life. By the time he departs from his hometown, certain tendencies and desires already have been awakened in him. The city, providing opportunities for a development unavailable in his village, is the catalyst permitting the fulfillment of Sam's basic nature. Thus, he indeed is a product of Chicago, and his development from a small-town hustler to a Chicago titan is as much the chronicle of a city as it is the story of Windy McPherson's son. Ultimately, the story explores that code of behavior demanded by the urban environment. Although he deals with several facets of the city, Anderson primarily is concerned with a presentation of the business world in an age of transition. Sam grows to maturity in a Chicago where personal loyalty as a business principle is being replaced by the more impersonal concept of monopolies and combines. As the old order passes away, a new order emerges that is destined to become the base for modern America.

II

Sam's life in Chicago and his reactions to the city are made more understandable through some Caxton figures who are early influences. When Sam McPherson, like the young Sherwood Anderson, displays his sense of business while still a child, John Telfer, the town's resident sophisticate, good-naturedly calls him a "little money grubber" (p. 56) and refers to him as "a little mole" seeking worms underground when he tries for anything that will bring a few pennies. Telfer predicts, "One of these days he will buy the town and put it in his vest pocket" (p. 12). The youngster does indeed work very hard selling papers and doing odd jobs "to increase the totals at the foot of the pages in the yellow bank book" (p. 72). Caxton is highly supportive and "had taken him to its bosom; it had made of him a semi-public character; it had encouraged him in his money-making. . . . When he was a boy, scurrying between the legs of the drunkards in Piety Hollow . . . , there was always some one to speak a word to him of his morals and to shout a cheering word of advice" (pp. 107–108).

Telfer serves primarily as Sam's spiritual father and does a great deal toward the early education of the youth. A man of leisure himself, the sage of Caxton is aware of the "art" of business. In a most telling monologue, he defines the artist simply as "one who hungers and thirsts after perfection, not one who dabs flowers upon plates to choke the gullets of diners." Accordingly, he decrees, "It is the artist who . . . has the divine audacity. Does he not hurl himself into a battle in which is engaged against him all of the accumulated genius of the world?" Turning his attention to the affairs of the day, Telfer explains a businessman as one who "succeeds by outwitting the little minds with which he comes in contact." On the other hand, a "scientist is of more account—he pits his brains against the dull unresponsiveness of inanimate matter and a hundredweight of black iron he makes do the work of a hundred housewives." But, like a businessman, the "artist tests his brains against the greatest brains of all times; he stands upon the peak of life and hurls himself against the world" (pp. 13–14). Commenting on Sam's hustling ability, Telfer observes, "Who says the spirit of the old buccaneers is dead? That boy didn't

understand what I said about art, but he is an artist just the same!"
(p. 17).

Telfer's justification for his own life provides a rationale for Sam's
later search. "I do not paint pictures; I do not write books; yet I am an
artist . . . practising the most difficult of all arts—the art of living.
Here in this western village I stand and fling my challenge to the
world. . . . Make a study of my life . . . [i]t will be a revelation to you"
(p. 14). That Telfer is a man of observation rather than of action seems
inconsequential; but as the novel progresses, one becomes increasingly aware of the contrast between those who observe and those
who participate in "the game of life."

When Sam develops an uncritical admiration for men of means
and, on one occasion, notes the exposure that newspapers give to the
wealthy, Telfer says, "Make money! Cheat! Lie! Be one of the men of
the big world! Get your name up for a modern, high-class American"
(p. 75). Then using the implied moral subtleties between *money* and
the *love of money*, Telfer comments at length upon "money-making" as
"one of the virtues that proves man [is] not a savage." Furthermore,
"money makes life livable. . . . It brings into men's lives beauty and
the love of beauty." The mythmakers of our culture have repeatedly
romanticized victims of poverty. Noting that "writers are fond of telling stories of the crude excesses of great wealth," Telfer muses, "No
doubt the things they tell of do happen. Money, and not the ability
and instinct to make money, is at fault." In his cynical observation, he
raises a question about "the cruder excesses of poverty" and cites
"the drunken men who beat and starve their families, the grim si-
lences of the crowded, unsanitary houses of the poor, the inefficient,
and the defeated." He directs the young Sam to "sit around the
lounging room of the most vapid city rich man's club . . . and then sit
among the workers of a factory at the noon hour" in order to discover
that "virtue . . . is no fonder of poverty than you and I."

Yet, there are certain ambiguities inherent in a money-oriented
society. Before the younger man sets out for Chicago, Telfer asserts,
"No matter what may come in the future, in our day money-making
precedes many virtues that are forever on men's lips . . . [i]t has lifted
him up—not money-making, but the power to make money. . . . It
gives freedom and destroys fear." But he judiciously cautions Sam to
remember that "the man who has merely learned to be industrious,
and who has not acquired that eager hunger and shrewdness that en-
ables him to get on, may build up a strong dextrous body while his
mind is diseased and decaying" (p. 78). Clearly established is the no-

tion that the importance of money-making is partially predicated upon its association with those elements of creativity necessary for growth and development. In his usual iconoclastic fashion, Telfer reminds Sam:

> In books and stories the great men starve in garrets. In real life they are more likely to ride carriages on Fifth Avenue and have country places on the Hudson. Go, see for yourself. Visit the starving genius in his garret. It is a hundred to one that you will find him not only incapable in money getting but also incapable in the very art for which he starves. (p. 79)

Once in the city, Sam becomes aware of the validity of all of Telfer's assertions. In fact, "the stroke that he saw in the hand of the successful business men about him is the stroke also of the master painter, scientist, actor, singer, prize fighter. It was the hand of Whistler, Balzac, Agassiz, and Terry McGovern" (p. 121).

As a youngster, however, Sam's commitment to money is not rooted in the philosophical distinctions made by his mentor. He is motivated by an all-consuming desire to compensate for his family's meager circumstances and for the town's lack of respect for his father. For him, then, the pursuit of money is not an abstract exercise but a necessary reality that will make possible his rise in the world, because throughout his young life—and in spite of any disclaimers he may have heard he has "seen the silent suggestive power of cash" (p. 80).

If John Telfer serves as Sam's spiritual father, Freedom Smith is his practical guide in the world of business. The eloquent good wishes of the former are matched by the pragmatic sense of the latter who sees Sam's potential and strikes a deal with him. Although he has been working since nine years of age, Sam is determined to become a man of means; working for Smith opens new opportunities. Thus, through a series of skillful negotiations, Sam sells his paper route at no loss to himself and becomes a buyer for Freedom Smith. As he begins to make money for Smith, he becomes more restless, feeling his talents would be better served in the city.

By this time, Chicago had already assumed legendary proportions. The people of Caxton think of it as a place to make money. Their views are reinforced, as are Sam's, by the stories that come from traveling salesmen who constantly "talked . . . of the city and of the money to be made there." And it is "from them he got into his nostrils a whiff of the city and, listening to them, he saw the great ways filled with hurrying people, the tall buildings touching the sky, the men running about intent upon money-making, and the clerks going on year after year on small salaries getting nowhere, a part of, and yet not understanding, the impulses and motives of the enterprises that supported them" (pp. 75–76). As Sam continues to dream of success, he realizes that Chicago is really the place for him.

> He conceived of life in the city as a great game in which he believed he could play a sterling part. Had he not in Caxton brought something out of nothing, had he not systematised and monopolised the selling of papers, had he not introduced the vending of popcorn and peanuts from baskets to the Saturday night crowds? Already boys were in his employ, already the totals in the bank book had crept to more than seven hundred dollars. He felt within him a glow of pride at the thought of what he had done and would do. (pp. 75–76)

Eventually, it is Freedom Smith who provides Sam with the chance to go to the city. Freedom "had written to the Chicago firm to whom he sold most of the things he bought, telling of Sam and his ability, and the firm had replied making an offer that Sam thought far beyond anything he might hope for in Caxton" (p. 82). The three years working with Freedom Smith have been good ones. He has learned much, and the experience has taught him

> not to doubt his ability to cope with such business problems as might come his way. He knew that he had become what he wanted to be, a good business man, one of the men who direct and control the affairs in which they are concerned because of a quality in them called Business Sense. He recalled with pleasure the fact that the men of Caxton had stopped calling him a bright boy and now spoke of him as a good business man. (p. 85)

In the meantime, the offer from the Chicago firm coincides with the terminal illness of his mother. With the death of Jane McPherson, there is nothing to bind Sam to Caxton.

While the early chapters of the novel establish the direct connection between the teachings of both John Telfer and Freedom Smith with the development of Sam McPherson, significant on another level is the story of a strained father–son relationship. As much as Sam may have wished it to be otherwise, the title of the novel suggests an unbreakable tie between father and son. Sam is not as independent as his entrepreneurial schemes in Caxton and Chicago indicate. As the progeny of Windy McPherson, Sam is often pitied because of the embarrassing antics of his father.

Throughout the few episodes involving Windy, whether exemplified by his giving more money than the wealthier men when the townspeople attempt to collect subscriptions for a Fourth-of-July celebration (money he can ill afford) or his playing out to its dismal conclusion the lie that he tells about being a great bugler during the Civil War, there is a clear indication the older man needs and strives for attention. To some degree he is successful. When, however, Sam makes it obvious he does not believe the tales of his father, "Windy [roars] with amazement" (p. 29) and proceeds to tell a long story that Sam eventually believes. That the entire Fourth-of-July celebration turns into another fiasco is not surprising. Windy cannot blow the bugle no matter how grand a figure he makes astride the great white horse. But the incident serves to strengthen Sam's resolve "to do" something with his own life. "You may laugh at that fool Windy, but you shall never laugh at Sam McPherson" (p. 33).

In one of his many intrusive comments, Anderson explains Windy as a misunderstood phenomenon of the post–Civil War period. That the character cannot cope realistically with life in Caxton nor understand the meaning of *truth* is as much a result of the times as it is a manifestation of an inherent weakness. Nonetheless, the lessons learned from his father's relationships with others form the foundation of Sam's interactions with his associates; Sam's desire "to prove" himself to others is displayed as he tries to assert his worth throughout his life. In the final analysis, Windy's legacy to Sam is not totally negative. Sam, "a buyer by instinct," becomes increasingly successful in his early business ventures in part because he recognizes "there is a little of Windy McPherson's grotesque pretentiousness in every man and [he] soon learned to look for and to take advantage of it." Anderson observes that Sam "let men talk until they had exaggerated or overstated the value of their goods, then called them sharply to accounts, and before they had recovered from their confusion drove home the bargain" (pp. 81–82). In the moment of Sam's greatest financial coup in Chicago, the reader learns "instead of another Windy McPherson failing to blow his bugle before the waiting crowd, [Sam] was still the man who made good, the man who achieved, the kind of man of whom America boasts before the world" (p. 246).

That Windy's son is able to pursue the American Dream and rise above his limited early life are testimonies to a general optimistic spirit pervading part of the novel and to Anderson's celebration of upward mobility in American life, which eschews an emphasis upon ancestral ties. In fact, Sam is always suspicious of "birthplaces" although "there could be no doubt that people were born." This particular wariness developed because "he had heard his father claim as his birthplace Kentucky, Texas, North Carolina, Louisiana, and Scotland. This thing had left a kind of defect in his mind. To the end of his life when he heard a man tell of the place of his birth he looked up suspiciously, and a shadow of doubt crossed his mind" (p. 28). In spite of Sam's disgust with his father, who seems to be an ineffectual blusterer, Anderson also implicitly presents Sam in Chicago as the effective braggart who rises to prominence at the turn of the century. If "no real sense of [Windy's era] has as yet crept into the pages of a printed book," the same might be said for Sam's period. Thus, Anderson, who calls for a "Thomas Carlyle" to write the story "of our Windy McPhersons" (p. 21), has fulfilled part of that role by telling the tale of Windy's son.

III

Having established a sense of Sam's early relationship with some of the men of Caxton, Anderson proceeds with the story of Sam McPherson in Chicago. It is a repetition of the usual chronicle of a village boy making good in the city through hard work, luck, and marriage to his employer's daughter. Anderson took a popular formula, added his personal knowledge of the business world, and produced an urban hero who seems to fit a traditional pattern. Yet, Anderson departs from some of the earlier city novelists. As he records Sam's response to the inevitable demands of the city, Anderson suggests that (while accepting the power of the urban) Sam is not completely an unwilling pawn moved by some unknowable intractable force. Rather he is a man who selects and elects certain courses of action. Central to his evolution as the head of the McPherson crowd is the simplistic implication that what he becomes is a result of an unfulfilled personal life. One might assume that had his marriage worked out, Sam would have been different, despite the shifts in the structure of American business. At the same time, one cannot ignore the influence of Chicago upon him.

The homelike quality of the West Side boarding house where he first finds lodging makes the urban initiation less traumatic for Sam, but he obviously is different from the other boarders in determination and in strength. That he is to be one of the strong in the tradition of an Edward Van Harrington or a Frank Cowperwood is clear when he is compared to his fellow townspeople, the Pergrins who run the boarding house. They have not as yet become a part of the city nor do they wish to do so. Various members of the family make annual treks back to Caxton, and Anderson describes them as existing "upon foreign soil. Living amid the roar and hustle of Chicago's vast west side, [they] still turned with hungry heart toward the place of the corn" (p. 122). As a result, they have not been influenced by the urban glitter nor by the promise of the good life that the city seems to offer to others.

The city itself provides an education for Sam as he studies the people and spends a great deal of time "walking about town absorbed in his own thoughts and getting impressions" of the sights around him. In fact, his first realization of the scope and diversity of the city, like Anderson's, is developed by these long, lonely walks through Chicago. As he looks at those passing along, Sam sees "them only as so many individuals that might some day test their ability against his own. And if he peered at them closely and marked down face after face in the crowds it was as a sitter in the great game of business that he looked, exercising his mind by imagining this or that one arrayed against him in deals, and planning the method by which he would win in the imaginary struggle" (p. 126). Sam believes that life in Chicago is a game whose primary rule is the getting of money. "In the city where men of wealth and power in affairs rubbed elbows with him in the street cars and walked past him in hotel lobbies as he watched and waited saying to himself, 'I also will be such a one'" (p. 121), Sam is determined to be a winning player.

His fascination with the city is central to his development. He is thrilled by

> the crowds of men and women, boys and girls, clambering aboard the cable cars, massed upon the pavements, forming in groups, the groups breaking and reforming, and the whole making a picture intense, confusing, awe-inspiring. . . . He liked it all; the mass of people, the clerks in their cheap clothing; the old men with young girls on their arms going to dine in restaurants; the young man with a wistful look in his eyes waiting for his sweetheart in the shadow of the towering office building.

And Anderson comments, "The eager straining rush of the whole, seemed no more to him than a kind of gigantic setting for action; action controlled by a few quiet, capable men—of whom he intended to be one—intent upon growth" (pp. 151–52). Sam's tunnel vision is not unusual. In fact, Janet Eberly, one of Anderson's strong but undeveloped women in the novel, bluntly tells Sam on one occasion, "You think you know what's going on in the world. You think you are doing things, you Chicago men of money and action and growth. You are blind, all blind" (p. 157). Yet, it is a blindness that usually afflicts the men of the business novel and helps to create a particular portrait of the city in fiction.

With youthful enthusiasm, Sam begins his business career in the city's South Water Street district, working for a commission firm that is "a partnership, not a corporation, . . . owned by two brothers" (p. 134). Unlike the LaSalle Street of most of the business-oriented novels dealing with Chicago, here "all day the food stuff of a vast city flowed through the narrow streets." The diversity of South Water Street lends a sense of its dynamism to the place and suggests its frequently overlooked importance to the city. Offering one of the few descriptions of that neighborhood in fiction, Anderson notes:

> Blue-shirted, broad-shouldered teamsters from the tops of high piled wagons, bawled at scurrying pedestrians. Upon the sidewalks in boxes, bags, and barrels, lay oranges from Florida and California, figs from Arabia, bananas from Jamaica, nuts from the hills of Spain and the plains of Africa, cabbages from Ohio, beans from Michigan, corn and potatoes from Iowa. In December fur-coated men hurried through the forests of northern Michigan gathering Christmas trees that found their way to warm firesides through the street. And summer and winter a million hens laid the eggs that were gathered there, and the cattle on a thousand hills sent their yellow butter fat packed in tubs and piled upon trucks to add to the confusion. (p. 133)

Although initially he does not understand the full significance of all of these products being assembled in one place, Sam is aware that South Water Street represents money.

It is not long before Sam devises a number of schemes. By seizing every opportunity, within three years, he parlays a sum of thirty-six hundred dollars (not all of which belongs to him) into thirty-six thousand. The prospect of making money gives Sam life and vitality. That this often involves lying, cheating, and stealing does not seem particularly important to him. The end justifies the means, but he is careful that his employers do not catch him. As a one-man secret operation,

> Sam had eggs and apples lying in warehouse against a rise; game, smuggled across the state line from Michigan and Wisconsin, lay frozen in cold storage tagged with his name and ready to be sold at a long profit to hotels and fashionable restaurants; and there were even secret bushels of corn and wheat lying in other warehouses along the Chicago River ready to be thrown on the market at a word from him, or, the margins by which he kept his hold on the stuff not being forthcoming, at a word from a LaSalle Street broker. [Turning deals becomes second nature to him as daily he sees] more clearly the power of cash. (p. 136)

The two brothers for whom Sam works represent the dual aspects of business in the city. Sam is perceptive enough to realize that the older one is "the real master." That he is an ardent church worker adds to the irony of his characterization. The other brother is "a much inferior man," whose New England education is used to display his lack of suitability for life in Chicago. The introduction of the East as producing an ineffectual man of business is a stereotype that did not begin with Anderson, but it is used in the city's fiction to suggest that the dynamics of the place meant Chicago needed "new" men and women who could cope with the demands of the city rather than those who had been subjected to an effete culture and its moral traditions.

Like other businessmen, the young Sam is proud of himself and early learns to explain his actions. The ability to justify amoral behavior is an important element in the perceived philosophy and accepted code of the commercial world. Years later, he could comment that when he worked on South Water Street he "used to sit on a barrel of apples at the edge of the sidewalk thinking how clever [he] was to make more money in one month than the man who raised the apples made in a year" (p. 134). Yet, while devoted to money-making, Sam has misgivings. Even though he has "in him the making of the new, the commanding man of business," Anderson observes there is a "quality in him that made him sit by the window thinking before going" to a good friend "with [an] unfair contract, and the same quality . . . sent him forth night after night to walk alone in the streets when other young men went to the theatres or to walk with girls in the park. He had, in truth, a taste for the lonely hours when thought grows. . . . He had something in him that wanted a chance" (p. 140).

As he foreshadows the impending defection of Sam from the world of business, Anderson also introduces his own sense of the possibility of a business-oriented society based upon the innate goodness of the strong men who are products of the period. He intrudes upon the action to report:

> There may be business men in America who do not get what they can, who simply love power. One sees men here and there in banks, at the heads of great industrial trusts, in factories and in great mercantile houses of whom one would like to think thus. They are the men who one dreams have had an awakening, who have found themselves; they are the men hopeful thinkers try to recall again and again to mind.
>
> To these men America is looking. It is asking them to keep the faith, to stand themselves up against the force of the brute trader, the dollar man, the man who with his one cunning wolf quality of acquisitiveness has too long ruled the business of the nation.
>
> I have said that the sense of equity in Sam fought an unequal battle. He was in business, and young in business, in a day when all America was seized with a blind grappling for gain. The nation was drunk with it, trusts were being formed, mines opened; from the ground spurted oil and gas; railroads creeping westward opened yearly vast empires of new land. To be poor was to be a fool; thought waited, art waited; and men at their firesides gathered their children around them and talked glowingly of men of dollars, holding them up as prophets fit to lead the youth of the young nation. (pp. 139–40)

After three years on South Water Street and through a fortunate set of circumstances as well as through the intervention of a friend in advertising, Sam, marked as a man on the rise, is hired by the distinguished Rainey Arms Company, an old firm in the city. He moves from a company committed to the produce of the world to one that specializes in instruments of destruction and practically completes his own destruction. The firm's offices are in one of the city's "newest and biggest skyscrapers" (p. 143). It is a family-owned business, founded as a result of the work of an inventor and the foresight of a drygoods merchant, who allegedly sold guns to both the Union and Confederate forces during the Civil War. As the present head of the company, the merchant's son rejects that tale and "would have liked to think of the first Rainey as a huge Jove-like god of arms. Like Windy McPherson of Caxton, given a chance, he would have invented a new ancestor" (p. 145). Nonetheless, the family has received millions of dollars from the exploits of the drygoods merchant. By the time of Sam's association with the firm, Colonel Tom and his daughter are the principal owners.

Anderson understands the helplessness of the old businessmen as they face evolving monopolies and financial empires, but Sam knows such men as Colonel Tom Rainey do not belong in the American economic system. Much to his chagrin, however, he discovers "among the department heads . . . a great deal of loyalty and devotion to Colonel Tom." Sam convinces himself that "something [is] wrong. He himself had no such feelings of loyalty although he was willing to give lip service to the resounding talk of the Colonel about the fine old traditions of the company, he could not bring himself to a belief in the idea of conducting a vast business on a system founded upon lip service to traditions, or upon loyalty to an individual" (p. 144). He knows that such business techniques no longer suit the style of the city and concludes that inasmuch as somebody will be destined to lead the company into a new day, he might as well be the person. With no more definite plan than that, he makes himself indispensable to Colonel Tom.

Through a series of maneuvers, Sam's power increases. Soon he is an integral part of the activities of the firm. Using the traditional formula of pitting the old business methods against the new, Anderson makes it clear that Sam is a winner. Not only does he seem to be in control of his destiny but he also dictates the future of others. At this moment in his life, man and city seem to be completely compatible.

> Standing in the offices in LaSalle Street or amid the clang and roar of the shops he tilted up his chin with the same odd little gesture that had attracted the men of Caxton to him when he was a barefoot newsboy and the son of the town drunkard. Through his head went big ambitious projects. "I have in my hand a great tool . . . with it I will pry my way into the place I mean to occupy among the big men of this city and this nation." (p. 150)

Sam realizes what a David Marshall of Fuller's *With the Procession* could not. The times and the city demand a new type of entrepreneur. Just as there is no place for a psychological or physical return to Caxton neither is there room for the old, personal approach to business. One has to become part of the ruthlessness and the manipulation that characterize modern enterprises. And, Sam correctly assesses his era. "It is a time of big things." As might be expected, he can support his actions by claiming he is merely a tool, a naturalistic device consistently used in urban fiction to suggest the power of the environment. Self-justification is a notable trait of these fictional businessmen, and Sam predictably asserts: "What I am doing has to be done and if I do not do it another man will. The Colonel has to go. He will be swept aside. He belongs to something old and outworn. Your socialists, I believe, call it the age of competition" (pp. 242–43).

On the surface the marriage of Sue Rainey and Sam also appears to be repetition of the much-used formula: Small-town boy comes to the city in search of the American Dream and marks his rise in the world by marrying the wealthy daughter of a still wealthier magnate. Although Sam convinces himself that he is proud of Sue's love, the reader understands this love is inextricably tied to the large block of stock she holds in the Rainey Arms Company, just as hers is based upon some idealistic notion of his strength and the "service to mankind" that they will render through the children they will produce. She is portrayed initially as a strong-willed woman. Unlike the elite of the city, who are often content to live and feed on the despair of others, she appears to be different. Sam is impressed by her sense of humaneness, her ideals, and by her willingness to accept him without condescension even though he is a product of a social world alien to hers; but of greater importance is the fact that Sue represents a public recognition of his success.

For a variety of reasons, marriage makes Sam a less efficient businessman and reinforces the incompatibility between husband and wife. The growing sense of alienation between Sue and Sam increases when they do not have the desired children. Sue's friends include a widely assorted group; but whether the college professor or the writer of romantic western tales or the painter, Sam finds them to be a useless lot. All of them, however, idolize his ability to function in the marketplace. Sam, who has taken refuge in a silence that he obviously enjoys, finds it difficult to break the habit. As is typical in these types of novels, Sue blames business for dehumanizing her husband, and their relationship deteriorates through a lack of communication.

Compensating for the voids in her life, Sue commits herself to a life of social service that includes embracing new ideas and "liberal" friends. These young socialists provide some satisfaction in a period when the urban settlement house had become so popular, with its particular psychology designed to increase donations from the guilt ridden. Sam views such philanthropy with many misgivings. Sue, however, is elected "to the presidency of a society for the rescue of fallen women, and [Sam] began seeing her name in the newspapers in connection with various charity and civic movements." In the meantime, "at the house a new sort of men and women began appearing at the dinner table; a strangely earnest, feverish, half fanatical people . . . with an inclination toward corsetless dresses and uncut hair, who talked far into the night and worked themselves into a sort of religious zeal over what they called their movement."

Sam is not impressed. He "found them likely to run to startling statements, noticed they sat on the edges of their chairs when they talked, and was puzzled by their tendency toward making the most revolutionary statements without pausing to back them up." Although he attempts to understand, Sam is a man of action who finds these men and women, with their chatter, to be weak and inconsequential. But, in order to get along with his wife, he tries to show some enthusiasm for various plans designed to uplift the downtrodden. He even agrees to teach "a class of young men at a settlement house in the factory district of the west side." That the project fails is due not only to Sam's attitude but also to the listlessness of the tired workers. Sam realizes "these heavy featured young men are part of the world as men have made it. Why this protest against their fate when we are all of us making more and more of them with every turn of the clock?" (pp. 225–27 passim).

Sam begins to believe, in view of his wife's disorientation by her inability to bear children and provide "service to mankind" through her offsprings, that Sue's strength in many ways had been a false front; and he turns to money-making as a substitute for a failing marriage. He is extremely successful in his new life, but clearly something is missing. Anderson suggests that Sam's display of power is now sheer compensation for his personal unhappiness. Implicit in this observation is a questioning of the motives that eventually led to the creation of "modern" America.

The final break between Sam and Sue comes after he fails to keep his promise that a proposed take-over of the Rainey Arms Company, which he has engineered, will not occur. His decision to effect the coup is predicated upon his belief that *truth* must prevail. His betrayal of Colonel Tom seems necessary even though he knows Sue will not remain with him after such a display of faithlessness toward her father. The old man's subsequent suicide as well as Sam's later suspicion that his actions may not have been as necessary as he had believed leads the dehumanized man away from the city in order to search for Truth unhampered by the demands of life in "the towering city."

Through his years in Chicago, Sam displays a rare ability to understand himself and develops a business creed based upon truth as he understands it. In a moment of self-revelation, Sam writes: "I cannot see myself believing in the rot most business men talk. . . . They are full of sentiment and ideals which are not true. Having a thing to sell they always say it is the best, although it may be third rate. I do not object to that. What I do object to is the way they have of nursing a hope within themselves that the third rate thing is first rate until the hope becomes a belief." Accepting one of the cardinal principles of advertising, Sam continues: "I would lie about goods to sell them, but I would not lie to myself. I will not stultify my own mind. If a man crosses swords with me in a business deal and I come out of the affair with the money, it is no sign that I am the greater rascal, rather it is a sign that I am the keener man" (pp. 177–78). Sam's self-knowledge and his willingness to recognize his narcissism differentiates him from many of the businessmen who do indeed lie to themselves. Thus, the reader is prepared for Sam's flight from the world of commerce.

In one of his many interpolations, Anderson tries to explain Sam, but he cautions the reader to remember how the evolution of the captains of finance took place in the nation.

> There is a widespread misunderstanding abroad regarding the motives of many of the American millionaires who sprang into prominence and affluence in the days of change and sudden bewildering growth that followed the close of the Spanish War. They were, many of them, not of the brute trader type, but were, instead, men who thought and acted quickly and with a daring and audacity impossible to the average mind. They wanted power and were, many of them, entirely unscrupulous, but for the most part they were men with a fire burning within them, men who became what they were because the world offered them no better outlet for their vast energies.

Despite Sam's initial commitment to the Chicago business world, in all probability his later financial wizardry is as much due to his failing marriage as to any other single factor.

Sam McPherson had been untiring and without scruples in the first hard, quick struggle to get his head above the great unknown body of men there in the city. He had turned aside from money getting when he heard what he took to be a call to a better way of life. Now with the fires of youth still in him and with the training and discipline that had come from two years of reading, comparative leisure and of thought, he was prepared to give the Chicago business world a display of that tremendous energy that was to write his name in the industrial history of the city as one of the first of the western giants of finance. (pp. 232–33)

With the final betrayal of Colonel Tom Rainey, who had maintained his relationships with his workers through a sense of their loyalty rather than any particularly creative leadership, "the story of Sam's life there in Chicago for the next several years ceases to be the story of a man and becomes the story of a type, a crowd, a gang" (p. 248). The importance of money-making to this crowd cannot be ignored of course, just as its need to control all facets of human life created a new class of masters and slaves. Addressing the reader on several occasions, Anderson repeatedly asserts that success is not without its price. But whatever regret Sam may feel or whatever degeneration takes place in both his spiritual and physical well-being is not necessarily true of his group. In fact, "all of his companions did not suffer equally" (p. 252).

Sam has proved the reality of the American myth of success. In a moment of reflection, he thinks of his rise in the world. "Like the novelist, it seemed to him that he should admire and bow his head before the romance of destiny." And when he considers his life and his accomplishments, "it seemed that he was in some way the master and the maker of it all" (p. 203). Yet, ultimately, "the little money grubber" understands the futility as well as the uselessness of much of his life. He knows that success has exacted a tremendous toll even though he has merely responded to the ideas and movements around him. But his introspective nature does not go unnoticed by the novelist. When he revised *Windy McPherson's Son*, Sherwood Anderson added many explanatory notes designed to reinforce Sam's tendency toward self-analysis. Clearly understanding "right" from "wrong," Sam's perversion of the good usually results from his desire to do the expedient. Without condemning Sam, Anderson tells the reader: Sam "was an American and down deep within himself was the moral fervor that is

American and that had become so strangely perverted in himself and others. As so often happened with him, when he was deeply stirred, an army of vagrant thoughts ran through his head" (p. 318).

While the ambiguity of success is obviously Anderson's concern, the possibility of failure is an explored corollary. In his revision, Anderson added, toward the end of the novel, another important intrusive statement that attempted to evaluate Sam not only within the urban setting but also as a representative of our national culture. Pointing out significant differences between the evolutionary process of European culture and the American doctrine of immediacy, Anderson notes: "For so long we have had to push forward blindly. Roads had to be cut through our forests, great towns must be built. What in Europe has been slowly building itself out of the fibre of the generations we must build now, in a lifetime." And the commentary ends cryptically: "In our father's day, at night in the forests of Michigan, Ohio, Kentucky, and on the wide prairies, wolves howled. There was fear in our fathers and mothers, pushing their way forward, making new land. When the land was conquered, fear remained, the fear of failure. Deep in our American souls the wolves still howl" (p. 325).

IV

Despite the frequency of the intrusive author passages, in many ways *Windy McPherson's Son* is typical of the novel of its genre. Certainly, the long narrative seems to follow the "from-rags-to-riches" formula placed within the Chicago setting. One might even be inclined to accept Anderson's later dismissal of the work as being essentially derivative.[26] However, the portrait of Sam McPherson in the city is augmented by Anderson's interpretation and use of other facets of urban life seldom used in the Chicago novel. Focusing upon both advertising's association with the press and its unique use of language, utilizing a free-will escape from the city, making use of the oases of nature within the city, and dealing with some religious issues are distinctive thematic alterations of the pattern of the urban novel. At the same time, these elements modify the conventional story of the rise of a businessman.

Although Chicago's novelists often have used the world of journalism as a traditional means to make public the activities of the city's reigning elites, the crusading newspaper did not play an integral role in the Chicago novel until there was a more widespread acceptance of protest fiction. When the business structure "owns" the press, the resulting publicity generally is positive and supportive. When it is an independent instrument of the people, the press becomes a device by which unsavory practices are exposed. But whether the mouthpiece of some mogul or an editor, newspapers are seldom portrayed in terms of their complex organizations.

When preparing their take-over of the Rainey Arms Company, Sam and his group make certain that the story, cast in a light favorable for them, appears in the newspapers. The exaggerated picture of Colonel Tom is printed because Sam's supporters go "from newspaper office to newspaper office . . . using their influence as big buyers of advertising space and even insisting upon reading proof on their own masterpieces" (pp. 238–39). Not only does Anderson use the press as a tool that can be manipulated by the business establishment, he is the first novelist to associate it specifically with advertising. When considered as a form of public relations, advertising can really result—as every modern American knows—in created desires and a rejection of life as it is. Although one would like to believe otherwise, the enormous advertising budgets distributed to the media might lead to a management of the news. Sam's work "put his name on the front pages of the newspapers and got him the title of a Captain of Finance" (p. 232).

Anderson is convinced that those who write advertising copy also are heroes of American Business. After noting that "the annual advertising expenditure of the firearms trust ran into millions and Sam's hold upon the press of the country was almost unbelievably strong," the novelist explains that the man in charge of this campaign "rapidly developed unusual daring and audacity in using this instrument and making it serve Sam's ends." Making facts and illusions interchangeable, he "used the newspapers as a whip to crack at the heels of congressmen, senators, and legislators, of the various states, when such matters as appropriation for firearms came before them" (p. 249).

Sam's earliest friends in Chicago are in advertising. Jack Prince introduces him to Tom Morris "the best advertising and publicity man in America." Speaking of Tom, Jack says, "he can take another man's ideas and express them so simply and forcibly that they tell the man's story better than he knew it himself. And that's all there is to advertising" (p. 129). It is Jack Prince who launches the successful campaign for Colonel Tom and Sam, which "made the name and the merits of the Rainey Arms Company's wares known to all reading Americans." As a result,

> the muzzles of Rainey-Whittaker rifles, revolvers, and shotguns looked threateningly out at one from the pages of the great popular magazines, brown fur-clad hunters did brave deeds before one's eyes, kneeling upon snow-topped crags preparing to speed winged death to waiting mountain sheep; huge open-mouthed bears rushed down from among the type at the top of the pages and seemed about to devour cool deliberate sportsmen who stood undaunted, swinging their trusty Rainey-Whittakers into place, and presidents, explorers, and Texas gun fighters loudly proclaimed the merits of Rainey-Whittakers to a gun-buying world.

Thus, it is that "big dividends, mechanical progress, and contentment" come to Colonel Tom and Sam after the well-staged advertising campaign (p. 199). As language becomes increasingly meaningless, Anderson incorporates in his consideration of advertising the selling of goods as well as the selling of personalities. Implicit is the assumptive question that if to purchase a person is a form of slavery, then might it not be possible that advertising creates a new form of slavery associated with modern America?

The abilities of these men to manipulate language is revealed most tellingly in what appears to be an inconsequential incident. As a dinner guest at the McPherson's, Maurice Morrison, another advertising man who is part of Sam's life in Chicago, usurps the conversation and overwhelms the guests with talk "of the coming revolution." Instead of being angry, Sue thinks highly of him only to have Sam later reveal to her: "Morrison was joking. I know the man. He is a friend of men like me because he wants to be and because it pays him to be. He is a talker, a writer, a talented, unscrupulous word-monger." Sue, hurt and astonished, questions her husband's invitation to such a person. Sam arrogantly explains: "First because I like him and second, because I wanted to see if I couldn't produce a man who could out-sentimentalise your socialist friends" (pp. 230–31).

Sam's departure from the city to search for the meaning of human existence marks not only the beginning of his great escape but also signals another major deviation from the traditional patterns of the Chicago novel. Although he has been able to justify his actions, Sam is shaken by his betrayal of Colonel Tom and the old man's subsequent suicide. Thus, at the height of his materially prosperous life, Sam McPherson turns his back on it in order to find Truth. Throughout *Windy McPherson's Son*, there are indications that the novelist is not altogether comfortable with the stereotypes and formulas used by his predecessors. To suggest, however, that Anderson's tale of Sam's quest is a deliberate alteration of the businessman in fiction is to lend too much weight to this first published novel as a consciously premeditated effort. Rather, it seems that the story is simply a result of another view of the city and of Anderson's instinctive belief that urban life did not have to be as powerful as had been believed. Like Sherwood Anderson, Sam is convinced that life provides solutions if a person is willing to seek them.

Furthermore, the novel seems indicative of the storyteller's rethinking of the American gospel of visible accomplishments and demonstrates his awareness that other elements should figure in the stories of those who seek success in the city. This becomes even more significant when it is remembered that Anderson had had the advantage of understanding the business world and the importance of advertising to it. He had risen through the ranks to achieve the material goals of the American Dream. On the other hand, Henry Blake Fuller had come from money but had had no interest in it and little ability to hold on to the family fortune. Hobart Chatfield-Taylor, who also had come into money, did little with the business life of the city other than to live as elegantly as possible. Roe, Payne, Dreiser, Herrick, and the others who had written novels about this phase of the city's life did so as outsiders and had mistaken notions about the lives of their heroes and heroines. Not only did they often accept money as "evil" while recognizing the power of having it, they also relied heavily upon naturalistic elements to convince their readers of the inevitability of it all. But Anderson, the businessman, gave a sense of immediacy to the work of Anderson, the novelist.

Important though Anderson's use of the worlds of journalism and advertising are in shifting the fictional use of the city, it is Sam's actual and symbolic search for Truth that separates *Windy McPherson's Son* from others in its genre. As he sets out on his quest, Sam does not realize that the first stages of his search had actually begun in Caxton. After the death of his mother, Sam sees the "thin-lipped, brown-bearded" minister who sanctimoniously tells him, "Join the work of Christ. Find truth." Since the minister's notion implies church membership and church participation, Sam dismisses the preacher and his admonition as "a meaningless jumble of words out of which he got but one thought. 'Find truth,' . . . and [he] let his mind play with the idea." He convinces himself "the best men are all trying to do that. They spend their lives at the task. They are all trying to find truth" (p. 107).

Once in Chicago, he recalls the words of the Caxton clergyman; and when he betrays Colonel Tom, Sam writes himself a note saying, "The best men spend their lives seeking truth." Again he recalls the same words after the suicide of the old businessman. Even during a drunken bout with his crowd and during a fun-filled spree, Sam calls upon his associates "of rich money spenders to think and to work and to seek Truth." As he rejects his business career, "he knew only that he would follow the message his hand had written. He would try to spend his life seeking truth" (pp. 254–55). Although he has to admit that such a search is contrary to the American Dream, he repudiates the urban version of it along with his own personal business success. Anderson describes Sam at this moment in his life as "an American multi-millionaire, a man in the midst of his money-making, one who had realized the American Dream, to have sickened at the feast and to have wandered out of a fashionable club with a bag in his hand and a roll of bills in his pocket and to have come on this strange quest—to seek Truth, to seek God" (p. 258). So begins an affirmation rather than a denial of life. What he is to learn on his quest, however, tells him just how pervasive the urban influence has really been.

Sam has to admit, after only a short time on the road, that the laborers and ordinary people with whom he is trying to identify are no better than their urban brothers and sisters. He discovers that in the small towns and villages of America people are not searching for Truth nor do they have ideals to motivate them. Rather, they want the power of the city. Sam concludes that the tales of urban success are the stories most believed by villagers for whom the city has become the only reality toward which they strive. Even the vagabonds on the road speak "of the big cities, of 'Chi' and 'Cinci' and 'Frisco' [and are] bent upon getting to one of these places. They condemned the rich and begged and stole from the poor, talked swaggeringly of their personal courage and ran whimpering and begging before country constables" (pp. 281–82). He finally remembers that even as a youngster "he was more than once startled by the flashes of brutality and coarseness in the speech and actions of kindly, well-meaning men" in Caxton. He concludes "it is a quality of our lives . . . [that] American men and women have not learned to be clean and noble and natural, like their forests and their wide, clean plains" (p. 311).

Sam also observes the same sense of greed that has permeated the city also is present in the village. After a particularly unsettling episode, Sam "looked up from among the drunken workmen and his mind had seen a city built for a people, a city independent, beautiful, strong, and free" but this has been displaced by his recognition "that at bottom he did not believe the people wanted reform; they wanted a ten per cent raise in wages. The public mind was a thing too big, too complicated and inert for a vision or an ideal to get at and move deeply." Moreover, when he is working as a laborer in a small town, Sam realizes his own motives are not altruistic. It is not that he wants "the free city for a free people, but as a work to be done by his hand" (pp. 278–79). He comes to understand that coupled with an over-powering sense of greed is the failure of people to want reform. There is an acceptance of vice as an incontrovertible way of life. "In the small towns through which [he] walked . . . vice was openly crude and mas-culine." In fact, "dissipation and vice get into the life of youth . . . [i]t gets into all modern life. The farmer boy coming up to the city to work hears lewd stories in the smoking cars of the train, and the travelling men from the cities tell tales of the city streets to the group about the stove in village stores" (p. 313).

One distinct manifestation of Sam's search is his interest in com-municating with others. Instead of *hearing* people he begins to *listen* to them. "Everywhere Sam sought people who would talk to him of themselves. He had a kind of faith that a message would come to him out of the mouth of some simple, homely dweller of the villages and farms" (p. 282). The woman at the Fort Wayne railroad station, with a realism not generally associated with tales of western expansion, admits that going West was a difficult decision because the work in pioneer settlements is both hard and uncertain. Nevertheless she is going to insist that her machinist husband leave "a bicycle factory in Buffalo" and that her two grown daughters go "to the new country" with them. "Having a sense of her hearer's interest in her story, she talked of the bigness of the west and the loneliness of the vast, silent plains, saying that they sometimes made her heart ache. Sam thought she had in some way achieved success, although he did not see how her experience could serve as a guide to him" (p. 283). Yet, the pessi-mism of much of Sam's reeducation seems somewhat balanced by the "go west" theory and its success in the story of the woman with the three sons. She has achieved her "truth."

Throughout his wanderings, Sam attempts to share his knowl-edge with others, but his new life makes him examine more honestly his own motives. One such telling episode occurs during a particu-larly bitter strike at a "Jewish shirtwaist factory." The girls are pitiful, and Sam offers to help them. When their leader questions him, Sam replies: "It is a long story. I am a rich man wandering about the world seeking Truth. I will not want that known. Take me for granted. You won't be sorry" (p. 297). But Sam is sorry. His type of leadership is neither wanted nor protected. In fact, instead of welcoming "his help," most people are openly hostile. The constant rejection of him often is based upon a lack of trust that results because people really do not want volunteered assistance and are frequently suspicious of anyone who has it to give. While this tendency "to play it close to the chest" is expected in urban life, Sam is surprised to discover how much of the covert urban behavior exists in rural communities. The message of the novel, operating on several different levels, seems to suggest that Sam's abstract search for Truth is not as abstract as might be imagined and is severely hampered by the fact that life is controlled essentially by the false.

Furthermore, while Sam is realizing that he lacks the leadership qualities to change existing conditions, Anderson suggests this is the same problem that so many urban reformers face. Sam's new insights are a direct repudiation of the more idealistic concepts of social welfare as accepted by the wealthy of the city who listened, as did Sue, to the young activists who spoke frequently of the "coming social revolution." Finding solace in philanthropy and working for the downtrodden, Sue's group believed they could effect certain changes. But Sam is convinced change can come only through the motivated individuals and not by some outsiders who might be trying to assuage feelings of unspecified guilt.

Remembering the vagabonds he met on the road, Sam is struck by their lack of direction. "They had no end in life, sought no ideal of usefulness. Walking and talking with them, the romance went out of their wandering life. They were utterly dull and stupid, they were, almost without exception, strikingly unclean, they wanted passionately to get drunk, and they seemed to be forever avoiding life with its problems and responsibilities" (p. 281). As he travels aimlessly up and down the roads of America's countryside, Sam increasingly becomes aware that life is indeed a futile struggle for everybody. This helplessness is illustrated graphically as he watches a barnyard fight between some chickens.

> Again and again they sprang into the fray, striking out with bills and spurs. Becoming exhausted, they fell to picking and scratching among the rubbish in the yard, and when they had a little recovered

renewed the struggle. For an hour Sam had looked at the scene, letting his eyes wander from the river to the grey sky and to the factory belching forth its black smoke. He had thought that the two feebly struggling fowls, immersed in their pointless struggle in the midst of such mighty force, epitomised much of man's struggle in the world, and, turning, had gone along . . . feeling old and tired. . . . (pp. 291–92)

This scene has a lasting impression on him.

Sam finally realizes the city cannot be abandoned. After years of wandering in search of the elusive truth, Sam understands "that he was not by nature a vagabond, and that the call of the wind and the sun and the brown road was not insistent in his blood. . . . [H]e was, after all, a man of the towns and the crowds. Caxton and South Water Street and LaSalle Street had all left their marks on him" (p. 324). Thus it is that Anderson gives Sam the following concluding speech in the revised edition of the novel: "I cannot run away . . . I must face it. I must begin to try to understand these other lives, to love" (p. 330). Within a larger context, Sam's resolution belongs to Anderson and is one answer not only for Chicago but also for American civilization.

Any account of Sherwood Anderson's urban vision must take into account his use of open spaces within the city, another deviation from the usual pattern of the Chicago novel. In *Windy McPherson's Son*, the artificial city is balanced by its own natural spaces that are unaffected by the man-made. Romanticists often have subscribed to an idea that claims when an individual returns to nature, the person is likely to derive additional strength from the encounter. Urban realists, on the other hand, generally have refrained from the use of this theme unless they intend to set up a contrast between the city as a concrete jungle and the surrounding countryside as being symbolic of the freeing influence of nature. Anderson's urban landscape includes specific references to the part of physical nature that exists within the city's corporate limits. Many of the crowded downtown streets lead into Michigan Avenue which is "faced by a long narrow park . . . where the city was trying to regain its lake front" (p. 152). Sam often goes to Grant Park to stand "by the lake, looking at the silent moving water" or he "push[es] his bed to the window overlooking the lake . . . [where he] would spend half the night watching the lights of boats far away" (pp. 182–83). Sam discovers that nature provides the antithesis for the city. He is fascinated by Lake Michigan "on stormy nights" when it is being "lashed by the wind." At these times, he also discovers "[g]reat masses of water moving swiftly and silently [which break] with a roar against wooden piles, backed by hills of stone and earth, and the spray from the broken waves [falls] upon [his] face and upon winter nights [freezes] on his coat." In fact, he "would stand for hours . . . looking at the moving water, filled with awe and admiration of the silent power of it" (pp. 126–27). Always it is the same. From the water he gains additional strength. Whenever he wants to think, he walks in one of the city's parks, and his courtship of Sue Rainey takes place in Jackson Park.

As soon as it is apparent that he has to make a decision that will affect his relationship with his wife even though it will give him greater control of the Rainey Arms Company, he takes a walk. "Down by the lake he went to where the railroad with the lake beyond stopped him. Upon the old wooden bridge looking over the track and down to the water he stood as he had stood at other crises in his life and thought over the struggle of the night before. In the clear morning air with the roar of the city behind him and the still waters of the lake in front," he reasons that to do other than go forward with his business takeover would be a sign of weakness and would be less than truthful. And he turns toward "the towering city before him" realizing his wife is no longer important. He convinces himself, while "still looking toward the city," that love "is a matter of truth, not lies and pretence" (pp. 245–46).

Earlier in the novel when he fears that Sue has died in childbirth, Sam runs away. On the outskirts of town he stops where "the long rank marsh grasses [are] rolling and tossing in the moonlight . . . he [sits] under a tree. Peace came over him" (pp. 217–18). The following morning he is able to return to the center of the city. Through Sam's communion with nature, the reader is told of the healing qualities of the water and prairie lands. On one level, this seems to be a repetition of a romantic escape from reality; on another, it helps to reinforce the inevitable power of the city. Yet, Sam's trips away from the city reveal the studied indifference of nature to human beings, whether he is on his honeymoon in the northern woods or wandering through America and Europe. But, instead of repeating the antagonistic approach of nature to man (much favored by the naturalists), Anderson tries to reaffirm the part of life that is unchanged by greedy, grasping human beings.

Closely related to his use of nature and unlike the usual urban novel that avoids an in-depth analysis of religious issues, Anderson's work explores several of them. Clearly, Sam has needs that cannot be satisfied by the fulfillment of material wants nor by listening to John Telfer. Neither can the men of Caxton who serve as father substitutes answer all of his questions. In an especially poignant moment Sam's future conflicts are foreshadowed as he secretly reads the Bible. "When his mother came up the stairway, he slipped [it] under the cover of the bed" because he thinks it is "not quite in keeping with his aims as a business man and a money getter to be concerned about his soul. He wanted to conceal his concern but with all his heart [he] wanted to get hold of the message of the strange book" (p. 39). In spite of his success in the city, a growing inner conflict becomes more apparent; therefore, as he optimistically justifies his life according to the new rules, the old desire for "truth" never leaves him. No longer symbolized by his passive attempt to unlock the secret of the Bible, it is a desire just as real as those furtive sessions from childhood when he examined the Scriptures.

In terms of the later developments in the novel, it is important to distinguish between a general sense of spirituality that may be the result of an intense religious belief and organized religion. Anderson was aware that the latter often utilized the more worldly characteristics of the commercial milieu. For example, there is the traveling evangelist who is "a short, athletic-looking man in a gray business suit [and who] seemed . . . out of place in the church." The preacher

> had the assured business-like air of the traveling men who came to the New Leland House, and Sam thought he looked like a man who had goods to be sold. He did not stand quietly back of the pulpit giving out the text as did the brown-bearded minister, nor did he sit with closed eyes and clasped hands waiting for the choir to finish singing. While the choir sang he ran up and down the platform waving his arms and shouting excitedly to the people on the church benches, "Sing! Sing! Sing! For the glory of God, sing!" (p. 36)

Here is the salesman par excellence badgering a public to buy his wares. Ten years before Elmer Gantry and many years before the current purveyors of a particular approach to public religious worship, Anderson had clearly indicated the extent to which salesmanship had entered into the spiritual realm.

Sam also is struck by the apparent hypocrisy displayed among church people, and his experience at the Caxton revival makes him declare he will not attend church again. But his resolve to forsake the human interpretation of God does not eliminate his need for the spiritual nor his concern about matters of immortality. In fact, Anderson makes it clear that Sam is "not without a hunger for religion." His ear-liest needs are connected to the superstitious fears of the unenlight-ened. "Once when he was taken with a fever, he fell asleep and dreamed that he had died and was walking on the trunk of a fallen tree over a ravine filled with lost souls that shrieked with terror. When he awoke he prayed. Had some one come into his room and heard his prayer he would have been ashamed." At the same time, "on winter evenings as he walked through the dark streets with the papers under his arm he thought of his soul. As he thought, a tender-ness came over him; a lump came into his throat and he pitied him-self; he felt that there was something missing from his life, something he wanted very badly" (p. 37).

Yet preachers and other emissaries of the church do little to trans-late the true message of religion to Sam who is quite aware of the in-adequacies of the many interpreters. He discovers

> on all sides of him . . . the voices of the men—the men at Wildman's who owned to no faith and yet were filled with dogmaticisms as they talked behind the stove in the grocery; the brown-bearded, thin-lipped minister in the brick church; the shouting, pleading evangelists who came to visit the town in the winter; the gentle old grocer who talked vaguely of the spirit world,—all these voices were at the mind of the boy pleading, insisting, demanding, not that Christ's simple message that men love one another to the end, that they work together for the common good, be accepted, but that their own complex interpretation of his work be taken to the end that souls be saved. (p. 40)

Among the many people whom Sam meets while on his quest for Truth is a young minister. "They talked of God and of what the thought of God meant to men." Anderson, however, notes: "The young minister did not try to give Sam an answer to his problem; on the contrary, Sam found him strikingly dissatisfied and unhappy in his way of life." The minister tells Sam:

> There is no spirit of God here. . . . The people here do not want me to talk to them of God. They have no curiosity about what He wants of them nor of why He has put them here. They want me to tell them of a city in the sky, a kind of glorified Dayton, Ohio, to which they can go when they have finished this life of work and of putting money in the savings bank. (p. 284)

Obviously, such an urbanized heaven is not desirable.

In time, during Sam's concern about the spiritual side of life, the word *soul* comes to have a negative effect. It seems to be a "shadowy something [that stands for] an act of cowardice" (p. 40). In Chicago, church membership and organized religion are coupled with the unscrupulous in business. The "oily, silent, tireless" older brother in the partnership for which Sam works is also "a great worker in a suburban church" who bears "a striking resemblance to the brownbearded minister of the church in Caxton" (p. 134). And Webster, the lawyer who advises Sam and helps work out several questionable deals, also is a member of a "suburban church" (p. 252).

How many human problems are due to the absence of a viable religion is not made clear although the reader is aware of the dichotomy between what is professed and what is desired. Perhaps Mike McCarthy in his jail-house prayer is not as crazy as some believe. When Mike calls for "a new Christ," Telfer observes: "The world will some day grope its way into some kind of an understanding of its extraordinary men. Now they suffer terribly. In success or in such failures as has come to this imaginative, strangely perverted Irishman their lot is pitiful. It is only the common, the plain, unthinking man who slides peacefully through this troubled world." At the same time, Sam begins to understand something of the nature of life.

> From the wild ravings of the man in the jail he had got hold of something. In the midst of the blasphemy of Mike McCarthy he had sensed a deep and abiding love of life. Where the church had failed the bold sensualist succeeded. Sam felt that he could have prayed in the presence of the entire town. "Oh, Father! . . . make me stick to the thought that the right living of this, my life, is my duty to you."

Telfer concludes that the McCarthy experience is good for Sam because, as he indicates to Sam's mother, "I wanted Sam to hear . . . [h]e needs a religion. All young men need a religion. I wanted him to hear how even a man like Mike McCarthy keeps instinctively trying to justify himself before God" (p. 55).

As Sam proceeds upon his search, the image of Christ does not escape him. "He thought of Christ going about seeing the world and talking to men, and thought that he too would go and talk to them, not as a teacher, but as one seeking eagerly to be taught" (p. 278). But God's purpose eludes him even though he cries out on one occasion, "Are you there, O God? Have you left your children here on earth hurting each other? Do you put the seed of a million children in a man, and the planting of a forest in one tree, and permit men to

wreck and hurt and destroy?" (p. 323). Anderson reasons that organized religion has failed to provide answers for human existence not
only because of human intervention but also because few understand
the true nature of Christianity. Toward the end of the revised edition
of the novel, he offers the following commentary: "We have called
ourselves Christians, but the sweet Christian philosophy of failure
has been unknown among us. To say of one of us that he has failed is
to take life and courage away" (pp. 324–25). When one considers his
early ambiguous feelings concerning the role of religion in human life
and his commitment to the mandate "find truth," Sam's rejection of a
"successful" life, his futile but inconclusive search, and his final acceptance of the world as it exists are not as unusual as they appear.

V

Despite the obvious weaknesses of the closing scenes of the novel,
both the original and revised versions imply that Sam once again will
become a man of affairs who is in control of his destiny. The im-
probability of his actions, however, is mitigated by a greater sense of
his introspective nature in the later edition. As he meditates upon his
return to Sue and the fates of the three children who have returned
with him, the night is still. "In the trees beneath which he stood a
bird moved on some slender branch and there was a faint rustling of
leaves. The darkness before and behind was a wall through which he
must in some way manage to thrust himself into the light" (p. 330).
Perhaps, this suggests an unwarranted optimism. From darkness to
light, from isolated nature to human society, from a nomadic life to an
ordered life, Windy McPherson's son symbolically resumes his life in
the East. How much he has learned is not stated specifically, but the
futility of looking outside of himself for truth perhaps has become as
apparent to him as to the reader. Although his return with the children of a St. Louis woman who would rather run a saloon than keep
her children raises more questions than it answers about the efficacy
of Sue's initial dreams and the ultimate meaning of marriage for them,
the suggested reconciliation is less than convincing. But of significance is the fact that Sam's quest has ended with the probable re-
sumption of his life as a city man.

   Whatever the novel may lack in credibility, the revised edition
ends with a positive statement leading to the unmistakable conclusion that Sam now is ready to face life once again. And so "with his

hand before him, as though trying to push aside some dark blinding mass, he moved out of the grove and thus moving stumbled up the steps into the house" (p. 330). The search of Windy McPherson's son, which had started in Caxton and which had been conditioned by life in Chicago, is now over; he cannot run away from himself.

With little difficulty, of course, a reader can catalogue the weaknesses of the novel, and no one of them is more glaring than the conclusion that includes Sam's "purchase" of three children and his return to Sue bringing them. So bizarre is the incident that it undoubtedly negates the validity of Sam's story for many. Even Anderson realized the episode of the three children was not really the answer for Sam's story. The revised edition of *Windy McPherson's Son* both tries to smooth out the unbelievable ending and introduces a clearer statement of the symbolic nature of the city. Inasmuch as other writers had executed the urban theme more consistently and with less authorial commentary by the time of Anderson's first published novel, it is important to examine what the work does accomplish.

That it suggests his future perceptive analyses of the small town has been noted by most critics, but its examination of the city should not be ignored. By 1916, the realistic doctrine had been codified. Fidelity to events, an emphasis upon the ordinary, the absence of the intrusive author, attempts to render specific linguistic peculiarities, and a clinical objectivity had become some of the trademarks of the urban novel before Anderson and were considered part of the credo of the major realists. The methods of Howells, James, and Mark Twain had already formed an inviolate philosophy among many of the nation's writers and critics. *Windy McPherson's Son* presents Anderson's revision, tentative at times to be sure, of the prevailing realistic doctrine.

While not denying the businessman's status as the nation's cultural hero, Anderson looked at the complexities of the character. He also questioned the inevitability of a city's power to control and order life. Although the novel, like its forerunners, attacks the single-minded commitment of business to the material aspects of life, Anderson goes further and attempts, perhaps unsuccessfully at times, to analyze the strange dichotomy between the search for one's self and Success. In both *A Life for a Life* and *The Master of the Inn*, Robert Herrick tried a similar approach; however, both works are so dependent upon the surreal and the allegorical that they seem less applicable to ordinary people. Even the use of the city is merely a tool for the execution of the tales rather than an integral part of the action. Anderson uses Chicago as the concrete example of a particular way of life. At the same time, it provides a setting for a philosophical exploration into the meaning of urbanism.

Anderson essentially agreed with many of the earlier novelists in his portrayal of the driving forces behind the urban businessman. The manipulative nature of Sam seems compatible in a city where men of affairs are expected to control enterprises as well as the destinies of others. As commonly presented, these men are unaware of the numbers of people hurt or destroyed by their machinations. Yet, it seldom matters, because such people are expendable and can be sacrificed if necessary. The treachery of Sam toward his wife, his father-in-law, and others close to him is inconsequential at the moment of his greatest success. His humanness is submerged beneath the harshness of American business, as that institution itself becomes less personal and increasingly more speculative. But the story goes beyond this. A feeling of the nightmarish quality of his life grips Sam, and his repeated successes do not give complete satisfaction.

To say of Sam that he is "the man who made good, the man who achieved, the kind of man of whom America boasts before the world" (p. 246) is not to absolve him. Not only does he understand the nature of business, he is aware of the restraints demanded by the course that he has chosen for himself. Even though he can say with expected self-justification, "I do not blame myself for anything. I am a result, not a cause" (p. 255), it is clear that he has not totally convinced himself— and the novelist introduces a new dimension to the character who had become a popular stereotype in American fiction. Instead of the usual man of commerce, who may be unhappy in Chicago but who holds on until he conquers the city or is decisively beaten by it, Anderson chronicles his hero's inner conflicts and sense of free will. The novelist also seems to subscribe initially to the notion that spiritual fulfillment and world achievement are diametrically opposed, but in the end he seems to sympathize with those men who also are victims of their times, as he presents the efforts of a particular businessman to reconcile the material world with his search for Truth.

Sam's desire to replace the expedient with the more enduring values of life is a conscious decision to reject part of himself in order to embark on an ambitious, albeit symbolic, quest for another way of life. "I will begin all over and come up to Truth through work . . . I will leave the money hunger behind me." If, however, the quest fails and he cannot lose his "hunger," he tells himself: "If it returns I will come back here to Chicago and see my fortune piled up and the men rushing about the banks and stock exchange." He feels that once he again sees "the court they pay to such fools and brutes as I have been . . . that will cure me" (p. 257). Ultimately, then, Chicago does not hold Sam captive. Whether it is the departure of a Curtis Jadwin who failed after trying to corner the market or that of a Frank Cowperwood whose bid to buy enough votes to make his traction deals worthwhile, the businessman is shown leaving Chicago only when conditions make it absolutely necessary for him to do so and never out of a free-will attempt to find a better life. If the novel is a requiem for anything, it is the final salvo of the dreamer. In Sam's search for Truth and in his momentary rejection of his life as a successful businessman, Anderson portrays the limitations of the dreamer in American society.

The desire for success leads Sam to a need to understand himself. If one accepts Anderson's many autobiographical statements, the novel is an introspective analysis of the author's own goals and life. Sam's search is an examination of Anderson's. The obvious similarities between Sam McPherson and Sherwood Anderson are many. Both came from small midwestern towns and wished to go to Chicago in order to make a mark in life. The opening pages of the novel are simply restatements of Anderson's own *A Story Teller's Story* and *Memoirs*. While Sam and Sherwood begin as hustlers who long for material success, they early display a need to understand themselves. Both do a great deal to attract notice in their towns. Once in the city, they achieve varying degrees of success; but they share similar reactions to the world of business as they both reject it when they appear to be doing well.

At one time, Anderson partially explained his novel as a fragment of his own story: "Consider the circumstances. There was I, a manufacturer in an industrial city in Ohio. I had reached near to the middle station in life and was unfitted for my place in i[t]. My own nature was in revolt against money-making as an end in life, and the history of Sam McPherson is the history of such a revolt."[27] Just as Sam, the businessman, makes certain discoveries by the end of the novel so Anderson, the businessman, made the first step toward his transformation into Anderson the artist. On this level, then, *Windy McPherson's Son* can be read as a form of testimony since it presents the author's personal attitude toward the nation's business structure. But beyond that, the novel demonstrates Anderson's early technique of storytelling.

If *Windy McPherson's Son* seems familiar, it is due to the not-so-subtle inclusion of three well-known legends. There is the restatement of the formula of the American Dream, which centers upon the success of an ambitious country boy. But instead of the fairy-tale ending that claims "and they lived happily ever after," at the height of his power, the young man begins to question his success and embarks upon a search. When he shifts to the legend of the Holy Grail, Anderson introduces into Chicago fiction one of the famous tales of world literature. In so doing, he moved the Chicago novel from a mere recital of the expected and utilized the city as a means of launching Sam's quest. As he travels throughout the land in search of that elusive *cup* of truth (a task foreshadowed in the early pages of the novel when he secretly reads the Bible), Sam McPherson assumes mythic proportions. Finally, there is the repetition of the urban tale that claims for the city the naturalistic power to corrupt. While a sense of doom generally permeates this fatalistic view, Anderson's description of the rise of Sam's crowd is a metaphor for the growth of the United States during this period. No one can deny the reality of the great financial leaders who, like Sam, could justify their lives with various explanations; neither can one deny Anderson's insistence that these men are representatives of the direction of the nation. As the city dictates his behavior at crucial moments in his life, Sam eventually recognizes that he must try "to force himself back into the ranks of life" (p. 347). Throughout the novel, Chicago is stern and unyielding, but its force has a strange attraction. Men are made or broken in the city. The urban environment itself remains uncaring, unfeeling, and unaltered; but even its force has some limitations when matched by human determination and will.

Waldo Frank suggested shortly after the appearance of the novel that it contained "a radiant glow of truth" and observed that Anderson's hero—"bewildered with his affluence and power, seeking the truth in the fair plains and the cancerous cities, ignorant and awkward and eager—is America today. And Sam McPherson, the boy, arrogant and keen and certain, hiding from himself his emptiness with the extent and occupation of the materials that his land floods upon him, is the America of our fathers."[28] Perhaps, it is this quality that ennobles Sam's story.

Like earlier urban novelists, Anderson seems to understand the pervasive influence of the city; yet, his integration of the inner city with its outward manifestations anticipates the work of later urban novelists. Unfortunately his story's disparate elements are often submerged beneath an implicit didacticism that ultimately weakens his effort to examine the myth of self-made men and women within the context of the American success story. Moreover, Sam's rediscovery of self is hampered by some naturalistic details that are not pursued. The episodic nature of the stories dealing with such women as Mary Underwood and Janet Eberly as well as the interludes on the roles of women in America needed greater development if those characters and their related incidents were intended to have meaningful connections to the narrative of Sam McPherson.

As he attempted to find a solution for the chaos and isolation of modern life, Anderson began an analysis of the role of the American city. He set forth the possibility that individuals, by their own wills, could alter a deterministic philosophy. While John Telfer's probing into the meaning of freedom as well as the novel's emphasis upon selfhood combine with Anderson's "new note" to reflect significant aspects of the renaissance occurring in Chicago at the time, of even greater importance is the sense of immediacy in the chronicle of a Chicago businessman told by a businessman who had reflected upon the meaning of Success. In a measure, then, *Windy McPherson's Son* is a confessional produced by a man who could personally testify to the disillusionment of city life.

A people calling itself great and living
in a city also called great, go to their
houses a mere disorderly mass of
humans cheaply equipped . . .

*   *   *

Chicago is one vast gulf of disorder.
Here is the passion for gain, the very
spirit of the bourgeoise [sic] gone
drunk with desire. The result is something terrible. Chicago is leaderless,
purposeless, slovenly, down at the
heels.

And back of Chicago lie the long
corn fields that are not disorderly . . .

—*Marching Men*

4

Beaut McGregor
Angry Activist
in a Disorderly City

MARCHING MEN, Anderson's second published novel, presents another dimension of his urban landscape. Beaut McGregor, the central figure, is similar to Sam McPherson in many ways. He, too, has been conditioned by village life to believe that untold opportunities exist in Chicago, and he escapes to the city in search of success. He is as self-determined and committed to a quest for Truth as Sam. That he, too, is destined to be among the strong in Darwinian terms becomes apparent as the novel develops; but he suffers from a sense of estrangement and isolation that urban life does little to alleviate. Chicago remains a mighty force, controlled by a business ethos and a political paradigm, that does not care for the weak.

Although it lacks the form of the typical "from-rags-to-riches" tale, the novel presents the success story that highlights a particular type of professional man in the city. Writers of urban fiction generally have assumed that, if characters wish to be successful, they must cooperate with the dominant structure, in spite of the assumption that this acquiescence often leads to a prostitution of professional and ethical standards. To refuse such accommodations by holding to the ideals of a chosen vocation is to be assured of financial failure. In either instance, however, the place is a negative force with its smug business community and corrupt political machines. Throughout urban literature, then, such figures as physicians, lawyers, teachers, architects, and artists have been called upon to make some hard choices and usually have been victimized by the city.

The novel also represents another confrontation between Anderson and Chicago. Written in Ohio before the author's return to the city, *Marching Men* is a product of a period characterized by Anderson's search for a means by which he could come to terms with his own life in the world of commerce. But of greater significance, the story examines the effects of urban life upon the city's laborers, who have been lured by promises of the good life. Suggesting that the dehumanizing elements of the business and industrial worlds lead to a sense of disorder that, in turn, can produce automatons who simply respond to external conditions, Anderson creates a protagonist who actively seeks to bring order to the chaos of urban living. In stressing the importance of human unity as a means of rebelling against the restrictions imposed upon laborers by industrialism, Beaut proposes that the city's leaderless workingmen actually march together in order to develop an independence from the system that binds them.

Yet, despite its specific answers to questions of urbanism, *Marching Men* has not been examined within the genre of the urban novel, perhaps for several reasons that have little to do with its weaknesses as a long narrative. First of all, the work generally seems to offer an implausible solution for issues of city life. Furthermore, most critics have summarily dismissed the "Chicago" sections (more than three-fourths of the novel) in support of their tacit belief that Anderson was the spokesman for the small town. They have neglected to realize that knowledge of the nation's villages does not mean an inability to understand the American city. In effect, they have followed the lead of H. L. Mencken who, while one of the most vocal supporters of the literary efforts coming out of Chicago, found the chapters devoted to the city to be the most ineffectual part of Anderson's novel and claimed that only the portrayal of the small town at the beginning of the work had any merit.[1] (Writing about *Windy McPherson's Son* many years later, Brom Weber ironically made a similar judgment.) It is perhaps unusual that so astute a critic as Mencken would have failed to see that Anderson's use of Chicago in *Marching Men* was one of the most penetrating in fiction up to that time.

Receptions of the novel were hampered for other reasons. Since it had the misfortune to appear so closely after the publication of *The Titan*, comparisons were inevitable. Anderson's novel seemed to suffer because it lacked the narrative force of Dreiser's work even though one could build a strong case for Beaut as an example of an equally powerful urban titan. Finally, still another problem results because time and world conditions eventually made Anderson question the idea upon which he based *Marching Men*. In "Waiting for Ben Huebsch," Anderson explains the motivation for *Marching Men*, a "piece put in the form of a novel that should have been put into the form of an epic poem," as a product not only of his brief stint in the army but also of his life in Chicago.[2]

> I was in Chicago and stood on the station of the elevated railroad. It was evening and people were pouring out of offices and stores. They came by the thousands out of side streets and into the broad city street of faces. They were a broken mob. They did not keep step. There were thousands of individuals, lost like myself. As individuals they had no strength, no courage.
> By that time I had become a writer . . . I conceived of a figure, a man, a kind of combination of Abraham Lincoln and that later American figure, John Lewis.
> I conceived of such a man really inspired, a poet.
> He would be a poet of the movement.

Speaking of his attempt "to create such a figure" in *Marching Men*, Anderson continues his retrospective analysis by admitting that he wanted "to create a great epic poem of movement in masses." Instead, he says: "When the fascist movement swept over Europe I began to see, more clearly, how such a movement, once started, may thus become identified with the state. When I saw the dream I had put into action I grew afraid of my dream."[3] But Anderson's later thoughts on his novel do not alter the urban portrait presented in *Marching Men*.

I

At the time of its appearance, Anderson's second published novel was discussed sporadically and, in later years, has received occasional recognition. The earliest reviewers were not in agreement on the work's impact, meaning, or significance. Many noted that the author demonstrated a sympathy for the nation's laboring forces but were disappointed when he seemed incapable of sustaining the hero's story, buried beneath vague and impractical incidents.[4] In trying to unite the materialism of the city with the search of Sam McPherson, Anderson had run into some structural and philosophical questions in his earlier novel. These remained unresolved even after his revision. Thus, that work ends on a puzzling note. If *Windy McPherson's Son* seemed faulty and led to its critical dismissal as an important Chicago novel, *Marching Men* also proved to be an enigma to many readers. Clearly the promise of the first novel had not been fulfilled in the second.

Among the politically liberal critics, there were those who attempted to find merit in what appeared to be the socialistic overtones of the tale. Francis Hackett praised Anderson's efforts toward making the American worker a viable figure in American fiction but found the idea of the marching men too far removed from reality. He thought Anderson had presented only "the rawest American people . . . brutal in their callous acceptance of their own ugly and shoddy material conditions." Furthermore, they were "flaccid in their personal tastes and futile in their sprints to escape banality."[5] Doris Webb also was impressed with Anderson's apparent concern for the oppressed workers but questioned the effectiveness of the dialogue that detracted from the novel's reality.[6] Oscar Cargill, on the other hand, dismissed the novel as "sentimental naturalism" and implied it presented such a set of improbable events that it had little value as either philosophy or as fiction.[7] George B. Donlin asserted that the purpose of the work was to show the importance of order in an otherwise chaotic world but decreed Anderson's "paean to order" resulted in "a naked and somewhat febrile celebration of force," which demonstrated the author's pathological fascination.[8]

Implicit in many analyses has been the suggestion that Anderson was prophetically anticipating modern fascism. In later years, Irving Howe rejected the apparent presentation of the novel's hero as an unwilling dictator and mover of men. Instead, he suggested that the central issue was a working out of Anderson's personal sense of order and disorder in his own life.[9] David D. Anderson has also noted the autobiographical nature of the work by claiming it "portrays Anderson the reformer as he saw himself after his world of commerce became meaningless in Elyria."[10] Although a certain personal level cannot be ignored, H. W. Boynton's explanation that the novel's hero was "a prophet of the masses, of mankind, the toiler finding his place in the sun" found some advocates. Boynton saw the work as a type "of parable or prophecy" in which the hero's actions emanated from a deep commitment to mysticism.[11] *The Nation*, however, declared the entire novel was flawed by the mystical,[12] and the New York *Tribune's* reviewer found merit in the novel but asserted the conclusion was dishonest.[13] John Nicholas Beffel saw little to redeem what he called "a disaster,"[14] and the *New York Times Book Review* shared the opinion that the hero as well as his story were too static to produce a narrative worth reading.[15]

Among the more recent critics, Ray Lewis White has observed the novel "was more the product of a scribbling manufacturer than of a liberated soul of the Chicago Renaissance" and found its appeal generally to have been a result of the fact that *Marching Men* "is a pro-labor work that champions the martial, disciplined force of massed men."[16] In the final analysis, however, he saw it as the "second apprentice novel, interesting only for its strange philosophy."[17] Brom Weber clearly is ambivalent about the merit of the work, which he classifies as a "social novel" that seems to be in the tradition of "Thorstein Veblen, Frank Lloyd Wright, and William James." Although it is "structurally flawed," it is "noteworthy for its stylistic fluency and its fusion of ideas and dramatic action." He asserts further "the novel struggles unsuccessfully to maintain an equilibrium between Anderson's constructive critical temper and his unabashed impulse for collective physical violence and social destruction." While "idea and form . . . were confused, . . . Anderson's style had progressed beyond the clumsy rawness of most of his earlier novels [and] had moved closer to the prose poetry of *Winesburg, Ohio*." Thus Weber could conclude the novel demonstrated a "growing mastery of imaginative details."[18]

Despite the variations in the reviews of the novel, on one level there was an underlying agreement that the work anticipates aspects of the nazi regime. Later readers might see it as evidence of Anderson's interest in communism and his assumption that such a system might serve as a salutary answer to the problems of capitalism. (This is hardly a particularly unique solution. The roster of twentieth-century American writers who embraced alternate political ideologies as possible responses to the frustrations of American life consists of some of the distinguished men and women of American letters, whose disenchantment with the nation was clearly expressed in terms that were not adverse to viewing Russia as a potential home.) Usually overlooked in considerations of the novel, however, is the work's proposal that the problems of labor and the disorder of urban life might be solved through a version of "non-violent civil disobedience."

In many ways, *Marching Men* is an urbanized twentieth-century companion to Henry David Thoreau's "Civil Disobedience" and John Jay Chapman's "The Doctrine of Non-Resistance." These Transcendentalists had cogently presented the principles by which the individual, through noncompliance, might proceed to attempt a reform of society. Setting forth the doctrine in fictional terms after nineteenth-century idealism had been replaced by a more pessimistic view of life, Anderson proposed an alternative to the dominant business structure. The solution, however, is distinguished by its ambiguity. The novel, dedicated to "American Workingmen," utilizes the techniques of nonviolent demonstration in order to portray the extent to which the workers can capture the attention of businessmen and the ruling elite through unified, dedicated, and dramatic action. Anderson shows that the use of collective marching can give the participants a sense of power and superimpose upon them an air of dignity as well as a degree of self-respect. But, in the end, people remain essentially powerless as they merely substitute one binding force for another.

Although the novel presents Anderson's restatement of the doctrine of self-reliance as popularized by the high priest of American romanticism and practiced by his apt protégé at Walden, Emersonian optimism is tempered by the novel's grim urban vision. This becomes all the more telling when one remembers the novel was published during a war that seemed full of hope and promise, as America set about "to make the world safe for democracy." Just as it celebrates collective action by asserting the strength of mankind is exhibited through a commitment to a central purpose, the work also shows that this can lead not only to the denial of the individual but also to the possibility of violence. Finally, the novel also calls into question a doctrine that, when pushed to its outermost limits, might possibly produce a Beaut McGregor.

One can speculate about Anderson's sympathies or the expressed anticapitalistic views or the novel's structure, the fact remains that the work seems to negate the very philosophy it ostensibly supports. Whether "parable or prophecy," *Marching Men* unconsciously points out the serious limitations of nonviolent civil disobedience as a technique for urban change. In spite of Beaut's commitment to order, marching "shoulder to shoulder" is difficult to sustain indefinitely as an end in itself. During the past years, there have been diverse examples of "marching men" from the SS troops in Germany to the nonviolent marches spawned by varying interpretations of civil disobedience in the United States to the activities of the IRA in Ireland. Each has revealed some of the weaknesses foreshadowed by Anderson. As men and women, led by a godlike figure, march to dramatize their commitment to a specific idea, they momentarily may achieve a sense of dignity and self-importance. But, if McGregor's movement is an example, Anderson has revealed that this particular promise of the future can reduce humans to automatons for whom collective action becomes the substitute for creativity, beauty, and truth. Whether caught in the chaotic disorder of modern life or in the cadenced order of marching, mankind remains the victim. And perhaps this is a greater tragedy than the imminent failure of mass movements.

Beyond its philosophical level, *Marching Men* is the story of a man and a city. As in his earlier work, Anderson brings several narratives together. There is the story of Beaut, a young man from a village, who becomes a lawyer in the city. Then, there is the story of Beaut, an angry activist, who becomes a leader of men. Forming a subplot in the tale are his relationships with and eventual choice between two women: one an independent milliner, the other the daughter of a wealthy magnate. As it presents the chronicle of Beaut McGregor from his youth in a Pennsylvania coal-mining town to his adulthood as a successful lawyer in Chicago, where he champions the underdog and becomes a folk hero idolized by thousands, *Marching Men* examines the chaotic nature of urban life. Although Beaut firmly believes in the power of the masses when working in unison, the theory of the nonviolent marching men grows out of his misanthropic attitudes; and his movement evolves from hatred rather than from an encompassing love.

II

As presented in the novel, Chicago is a place of brute force and great ugliness. (This is particularly ironic since the city's official motto is *Urbs in Horto,* and during the latter part of the nineteenth century it was called "the City Beautiful.") In spite of assertions that emphasize the degree of control that the urban force exercises over the minds and lives of people, Chicago novelists often write eloquently of a strange and haunting beauty in the city's power when they describe the physical city in terms of its majesty. Anderson followed this convention in *Windy McPherson's Son* by giving readers fleeting glimpses of the city's beauty from Jackson Park to the Loop and on to the North Side mansion of the McPhersons. Occasionally he transmits the sense of the buildings as he celebrates their size. Thus, the dominant tone captures the electric atmosphere of a very alive, power-filled city. But

Marching Men rejects the more acceptable and traditional literary descriptions that focus on the lives of powerful men and women in an equally powerful city, which is displayed in mythic splendor. Instead, it examines the oppressive lives of ordinary people in the midst of total urban disorder.

Such novels as Darrow's *An Eye for an Eye*, Sinclair's *The Jungle*, and other protest novels had attempted the same approach, but they relied so heavily upon their attacks of specific urban systems (the judiciary in the first instance and the packing plants in the second) that the totality of the city failed to emerge. Furthermore, these two earlier novels are closer to tracts than to fiction, but Anderson's ugly city in *Marching Men* is a forerunner of the urban center later celebrated and immortalized by the Farrell-Algren-Wright triumvirate.

To make certain that the reader understands the locale, Anderson chooses to have Beaut arrive in Chicago "late in the summer of 1893," a time usually associated with the city's most splendid and spectacular period, but it is not the ethereal effect of the World's Columbian Exposition that occupies the novelist's attention. In fact, he even errs by dating the fair in 1892 rather than in 1893. Thus, had Beaut arrived in 1893, as Anderson claims, it would have been in the midst of the Exposition rather than during the grimness of the economic depression of 1894. He is correct, however, in noting that ultimately the noble fair created chaos in the city. Consequently, the strength and phenomenal development, qualities frequently cited by histories as "the story of Chicago," are dismissed summarily by Anderson, who does not describe the city up to the time of the Exposition in terms of its greatness and promise. Rather he says "in 1893 . . . the city lay sprawling and ineffective . . . a tawdry disorderly dwelling for millions of men, built not for the making of men but for the making of millions by a few odd meat packers and drygoods merchants."[19]

Accordingly, Anderson remarks that Beaut's arrival coincides with "an ill time for boy or man in that city" because the World's Columbian Exposition "had brought multiplied thousands of restless laborers into the city and its leading citizens, who had clamored for the exposition and had loudly talked of the great growth that was to come did not know what to do with the growth now that it had come." Anderson accurately observes: "The depression that followed on the heels of that great show and the financial panic that ran over the country had set thousands of hungry men to wait dumbly on park benches, poring over want advertisements in the daily papers and looking vacantly at the lake or had driven them to tramp aimlessly through the

streets, filled with forebodings." The novelist understands the quality
of life spawned in an urban environment caught in the throes of an
unfortunate economy; and, in one of the many authorial comments,
concludes: "In time of plenty a great American city like Chicago goes
on showing a more or less cheerful face to the world while in nooks
and crannies down side streets and alleys poverty and misery sit
haunched up in little ill-smelling rooms breeding vice" (p. 61).

During an era of depression even an imagined successful city will
be victimized by unemployment, hunger, prostitution, and crime.
When such "creatures" as poverty and misery "crawl forth and joined
by thousands of the unemployed tramp the streets through the long
nights or sleep upon benches in the park," the city is doomed. Then
in a panoramic sweep of Chicago, Anderson shows some of the specific effects of the period:

> In the alleyways off Madison Street on the West Side and off State
> Street, on the South Side, eager women driven by want sold their
> bodies to passersby for twenty-five cents. An advertisement in the
> newspapers of one unfilled job brought a thousand men to block the
> streets at daylight before a factory door. In the crowds men swore
> and knocked each other about. Working-men driven to desperation
> went forth into quiet streets and knocking over citizens took their
> money and watches and ran trembling into the darkness. A girl of
> Twenty-Fourth Street was kicked and knocked into the gutter be-
> cause when attacked by thieves she had but thirty five cents in her
> purse. A professor of the University of Chicago addressing his class
> said that, having looked into the hungry distorted faces of five hun-
> dred men clamouring for a position as dishwasher in a cheap restau-
> rant, he was ready to pronounce all claims to social advancement in
> America a figment in the brains of optimistic fools. A tall, awkward
> man walking up State Street threw a stone through the window of a
> store. A policeman hustled him through the crowds. "You'll get a
> workhouse sentence for this," he said. "You fool, that's what I want.
> I want to make property, that won't employ me feed me," said the
> tall gaunt man who, trained in the cleaner and more wholesome
> poverty of the frontier, might have been a Lincoln suffering for
> mankind.

It is "into this maelstrom of misery and grim, desperate want" that
Beaut McGregor comes (pp. 62–63).

As in *Windy McPherson's Son*, *Marching Men* makes use of identifiable locations within the city. By focusing upon the names of streets,

for example, Anderson is able to give a sense of specificity to an action that is not highly dependent upon the particularized city because Beaut's dream of the marching men does not need Chicago for fulfillment. Neither is Beaut an actual product of the city, although he is affected tremendously by what he sees there. The place, however, does provide the arena for his plan, while ultimately serving as a symbol for the American urbanized industrial community that has grown in response to the false hopes used to tantalize its victims.

Following a pattern already established by earlier Chicago novelists (notably Fuller, Herrick, and Dreiser), Anderson sees the city not only as a "defiance against nature" but also as a place that supports numerous versions of the American Dream. In one of his most perceptive descriptions in the novel, he presents the "vast city [where] millions of people live within the limits of its influence" and suggests the idea of Chicago extends far beyond its corporate limits. "It stands at the heart of America almost within sound of the creaking green leaves of the corn in the vast corn fields of the Mississippi Valley. It is inhabited by hordes of men of all nations who have come across the seas or out of western corn shipping towns to make their fortunes. On all sides men are busy making fortunes." Anderson tersely presents both the myth and the reality of the city by noting: "In little Polish villages the word has been whispered about, 'In America one gets much money,' and adventurous souls have set forth only to land at last, a little perplexed and disconcerted, in narrow ill-smelling rooms in Halstead [sic] Street in Chicago." Nor is the legend limited to foreign immigrants.

> In American villages the same tale has been told. Here it has not been whispered but shouted. Magazines and newspapers have done the job. The word regarding the making of money runs over the land like a wind among the corn. The young men listen and run away to Chicago. They have vigour and youth but in them has been builded no dream, no tradition of devotion to anything but gain. (pp. 155–56)

Beaut's going to the city is the logical result of his belief in the opportunities that the metropolis will provide. He soon discovers, however, that Chicago and his home town are more similar than he realized. Commercial cities magnify the chaotic nature of life as much as industrial towns. Although Anderson does not dwell upon the evolution of the modern city, he posits the theory that large urban areas can exist because when men [lose] "step with one another,

[they] also lose a sense of their own individuality so that a thousand of them may be driven in a disorderly mass in at the door of a Chicago factory morning after morning and year after year with never an epigram from the lips of one of them" (p. 12). Beaut reflects constantly upon "the workers in the Chicago warehouse and of the millions of other workers who in that great city, in all cities, everywhere, went at the end of the day shuffling off along the streets to their houses carrying with them no song, no hope, nothing but a few paltry dollars with which to buy food and keep the endless hurtful scheme of things alive" (p. 149). This can occur because the city provides false illusions, and Anderson observes "the modern man is satisfied with what is cheap and unlovely because he expects to rise in the world. He has given his life to that dreary dream and is teaching his children to follow the same dream" (p. 101).

In the meantime, the city has little to offer to dreamers whether from the United States or Europe because "Chicago is one vast gulf of disorder. Here is the passion for gain, the very spirit of the bourgeoise [sic] gone drunk with desire." The terror of the place is increased because "Chicago is leaderless, purposeless, slovenly, down at the heels." If, however, one assumes that life itself is conditioned by a force larger than the city; it is with a degree of hope that Anderson reminds his readers "back of Chicago lie the long corn fields that are not disorderly. There is hope in the corn. Spring comes and the corn is green. It shoots up out of the black land and stands up in orderly rows. The corn grows and thinks of nothing but growth." Yet, sadly he notes: "Chicago has forgotten the lesson of the corn. All men have forgotten. It has never been told to the young men who come out of the corn fields to live in the city" (p. 156). Obviously, one of the lessons of the cornfield is to provide an example of natural order.

On the other hand, the unnatural disorders of the city, while a violation of nature, are like a magnet attracting the people from the countrysides. Although his definition of order is not absolutely clear, Anderson is convinced that "down deep in the hearts of men lay sleeping a love of order" (p. 130). It is this knowledge that leads Beaut McGregor toward a pursuit of truth, but the people of Chicago have no such compelling motivation as they endure days of unrewarding toil. They are a sad and hapless lot. "Drifting they go, in droves, hurrying along. It is a startling thing to look closely at them." Then in a penetrating description of the people of Chicago, Anderson selects their mouths as a distinguishing characteristic. "The people have bad mouths. Their mouths are slack and the jaws do not hang right. The mouths are like the shoes they wear. The shoes have become run down at the corners from too much pounding on the hard pavements and the mouths have become crooked from too much weariness of soul." Anderson continues: "Something is wrong with modern American life and we Americans do not want to look at it. We much prefer to call ourselves a great people and let it go at that."

Urban activity or that sense of electricity, which had fascinated him in *Windy McPherson's Son,* is examined more closely. Anderson now sees it as part of urban discord. With clinical dispassion, he observes:

> It is evening and the people of Chicago go home from work. Clatter, clatter, clatter, go the heels on the hard pavements, jaws wag, the wind blows and dirt drifts and sifts through the masses of the people. Every one has dirty ears. The stench in the street cars is horrible. The antiquated bridges over the rivers are packed with people. The suburban trains going away south and west are cheaply constructed and dangerous.

And he concludes by offering the following judgment:

> A people, calling itself great and living in a city also called great go to their houses a mere disorderly mass of humans cheaply equipped. Everything is cheap. When people get home to their houses they sit on cheap chairs before cheap tables and eat cheap food. They have given their lives for cheap things.

Employing a romanticized version of life in the Old World, Anderson concludes in contrast "the poorest peasant of one of the old countries is surrounded by more beauty. His very equipment for living has more solidity" (pp. 100–101).

What does all of this ultimately mean? Is the American Dream really the American Nightmare? Whatever else it might be, the Dream is responsible for the conditions that Anderson, rejecting the commonly held notion that the city had achieved an urban integrity of its own during this era, finds in Chicago. Instead he describes the world's fair city as being "big" and "disorderly." He contends throughout the novel that the "restless moving people" in Chicago are too complacent about the "vast disorder of life." To Beaut, much of what he sees reinforces "the disorder and ugliness of the city." It is not Chicago's praiseworthy architecture, with its skeleton frame construction, that captures Anderson's attention. Rather he notes the "rows of tall smoke-begrimed brick buildings hanging black and ominous against the sky" (p. 158).

The various descriptions of the city give a graphic sense of the disorder, filth, and broken hopes to be found within its crowded confines. Instead of focusing on the great financial institutions and magnificent commercial structures of the downtown area, as was customary in the early novels about the city, Anderson turns his attention to the corruption of the First Ward, the vice of the red-light district, and the world of South State Street—the ignored sections of the business district. This is not the universe of the commercial titans nor of the socially elite. In fact, given Anderson's tendency to pinpoint such fixed landmarks in the area as the Harrison Street Police Station or the elevated station platform at Van Buren Street or the Illinois Central terminal at Twelfth Street in order to give the reader a sense of location, one might find it interesting that he avoids mentioning the Rookery or the Monadnock, which are buildings in the same general area. In his frequent use of city street names, he does not include LaSalle Street. After Beaut has become an attorney, Anderson correctly notes that there are "thousands of young lawyers scattered over the Chicago loop district" (p. 172), but Beaut's office is not in a popular firm. His is "upstairs over a second-hand clothing store in Van Buren Street" (p. 176). As a result, the most vivid picture of the Loop revolves around South State where "the people . . . [wander] here and there going without purpose like cattle confined in a corral" (p. 173), hardly the portrait generally associated with the financial center of the Midwest.

Once again, demonstrating his awareness of the three "sides" of Chicago, Anderson recognizes one must cross a bridge in order to go from one section to another. Details of the North Side are not as numerous as those dealing with the Loop. Beaut's first job (like Anderson's) is in an apple warehouse. Many years later, after he has become a lawyer, he meets a client "in the old Cook County jail on Chicago's Northside." Leaving the prison, Beaut "walked along the street and came to the bridge that led over the river into the loop district." Then, his first major legal victory results in a celebration walk. "His way led over a bridge into the North Side, and in his wanderings he passed the apple warehouse where he had made his start in the city. . . . When night came he walked in North Clark Street and heard the newsboys shouting of his victory." Thrilled with himself and his accomplishment, he has "a new vision . . . of himself as a big figure in the city . . . he felt the power to stand forth among men, to outwit them and outfight them, to get for himself power and place in the world." With the assurance of a winner, he begins to have a different sense of the city which, the reader is to learn, does not last. "Out of Clark Street he walked east along a residence street to the lake." In a momentary glance at the localized beauty of the city, Anderson notes: "By the lake he saw a street of great houses surrounded by gardens and the thought came that at some time he might have such a house of his own. The disorderly clatter of modern life seemed very far away" (p. 197).

The North Side appears again briefly near the end of the novel. Beaut attends "a big outdoor meeting" there. In an unnecessary revision of Chicago history, Anderson claims that a Dr. Cowell "the big English statesman and writer who later was drowned on the Titanic . . . was in Chicago to see McGregor and try to understand what he was doing" (p. 284). (This is an obvious reference to the Reverend Mr. William T. Stead, who visited Chicago to see the World's Columbian Exposition and stayed long enough to write of the city's vice districts in the famed *If Christ Came to Chicago*. He indeed later was a passenger on the ill-fated *Titanic*.)

The novel also includes allusions to the city's South Side; but, with few exceptions, they are used, like their North Side counterparts, to give simply a sense of the scope of the urban landscape. On one of his many walks through the city streets, he visits a neighborhood bar "in Wabash Avenue near Twenty-third Street." Later "at Thirty-ninth Street a crowd of youths scuffling on the sidewalk pushed against" him. And in the midst of his thoughts, Beaut is impressed with the obvious "pitiful insignificance of the individual." Finally, "in his wanderings [he] came to an out-of-door restaurant and garden far out on the south side. The garden had been built for the amusement of the rich and successful. Upon a little platform a band played. Although the garden was walled about it was open to the sky and above the laughing people seated at the tables shone the stars" (pp. 215–17 *passim*). His attention is given to the successful men seated about the tables on the terrace. The long walk, which in effect covers the length of the South Side of Anderson's day, extends from Beaut's office at the outskirts of the Loop to the Midway Gardens at Sixty-Third Street. While it serves as a means to recount Beaut's thoughts, the walk gives a sense of the city's neighborhoods.

In the midst of the usual urban confusion, there are some South Side spots that seem strangely untouched—one of which is the University of Chicago. Beaut is aware of "the massive buildings, erected for the most part through the bounty of one of [America's] leading business men." He thinks that "the great centre of learning seemed so little a part of the city. To him the University seemed something entirely apart, not in tune with its surroundings. It was like an expensive ornament worn on the soiled hand of a street urchin" (p. 165). Then there is the description of the mansion of the David Ormsby family on Drexel Boulevard, which, like the university, is a foreign oasis in the midst of the actuality of the city.

Much of the action of *Marching Men* takes place on the West Side. Instead of focusing upon the single-family homes of the area as well as its palatial mansions, as was common in the early stages of the Chicago novel, Anderson was one of the first novelists to give a sense of the decadence and prevailing disorder in a section that combines houses and factories with little regard for the aesthetics of urban planning. "The street in which McGregor lived . . . was complete in its hideousness. Nothing more unlovely could be imagined. Given a free hand an indiscriminate lot of badly trained carpenters and bricklayers had builded houses beside the cobblestone road that touched the fantastic in their unsightliness and inconvenience." And Anderson correctly observes: "The great west side of Chicago has hundreds of such streets." He continues:

> Foul dust filled the air. All day the street rumbled and roared under the wheels of trucks and light hurrying delivery wagons. Soot from factory chimneys was caught up by the wind and having been mixed with powdered horse manure from the roadway flew into the eyes and the nostrils of pedestrians. Always a babble of voices went on. At a corner saloon teamsters stopped to have their drinking cans filled with beer and stood about swearing and shouting. In the evening women and children went back and forth from their houses carrying beer in pitchers from the same saloon. Dogs howled and fought, drunken men reeled along the sidewalk and the women of the town appeared in their cheap finery and paraded before the idlers about the saloon door. (pp. 75–76)

III

Anderson's vision of Chicago is highly dependent upon Beaut McGregor, who like the city is a mass of contradictions. Hence, the ultimate success of the novel is partially based upon how well a reader accepts Beaut as a believable character. For this reason, it is important that the novel should open in Coal Creek, a small mining town in Pennsylvania. A feeling of desolation is pervasive and is reinforced through the young Beaut, who is quite aware of the effects of the town upon his parents. His father is a sensitive soul, and his mother is a woman struggling to keep her family intact. Because he is embittered by the shabby treatment accorded to his father by the townspeople, Beaut lashes out at everybody and everything. In the meantime, the young boy suspects that there are some discrepancies in the American Dream. But unlike Sam McPherson, he appears to be a sullen, unmotivated, rebellious youngster. Thus, as his story unfolds, there initially seems to be nothing in his early life that could have foreshadowed his later fame.

After his father's heroic death trying to save some trapped miners, Beaut sees his mother attempt to eke out an existence as the proprietor of a small bakery. But her fortunes are tied directly to those of the people around her. When the miners are out of work, her central concern is whether to provide bread for them. To feed the hungry means that she will face certain poverty and will be unable to maintain herself and her son. But to deny the miners when they need her help during a labor crisis seems inhumane to her. On the other hand, the mine operators do not want her to aid the workers; and they give her a job as a charwoman in their offices when the bakery fails. Beaut understands his mother's dilemma at first, but he finally blames the townspeople for ruining her. Although he wants to alleviate the hard work imposed upon her, he selfishly determines that he will not go into the mines to work.

As he realizes his own impotence in Coal Creek, he becomes more bitter. He cannot understand why the men and boys shuffle into the darkness of the mines every day nor why the women and children suffer so silently. He sees them as willing pawns, who are at the mercy not only of the mine operators but also of their own lack of direction and ineptitude. While it is made clear that the growing spirit of industrialism is responsible for the inability of the residents of Coal Creek to be free souls, it is equally apparent that many of them have accepted without question their roles as determined by the mine operators, who represent the mercilessness of the system. The workers have traded their free will for a security that is subject to the whim of the mine operators. It is not surprising that they go about the business of living in a haphazard way, often feuding with each other as a substitute for their helplessness.

Anderson suggests that the growing entrapment of industrialism is victimizing the characters; yet, the portrayal of the angry Beaut is more convincing at this point than the notions of a predestined universe. Early in the novel, Anderson shows that Beaut's tendency toward violence is a result of his frustrations, but those against whom he turns his wrath view him merely as a strong man who must be feared, the son of Cracked McGregor, who is not to be trusted. That much of his anger is directed toward the leaderless people who act stupidly even though they are caught in the circumstances that govern coal mining operations is inconsequential.

Throughout his life, Anderson repeatedly emphasized the importance of single moments in human life. He was convinced that insignificant scenes assumed meanings that often defy explanation. Using this notion in his novel, Anderson has Beaut's commitment to the idea of organized behavior's power come from the young man's reflection upon the meaning of a single incident. During a bitter strike at the mines, soldiers arrive at the request of the owners, who wish to frighten the laborers back to work. Fascinated by the effects of this show of force and by the sense of dedication demonstrated by the marching soldiers, Beaut is "thrilled by the sight of trained orderly men moving along shoulder to shoulder. In the presence of these men the disorganized miners seemed pitifully weak and insignificant" (p. 49). When Barney Butterlips, the town's socialist, had earlier suggested the need for the miners to unite, Beaut rejected the idealistic talk "of a day coming when men would march shoulder to shoulder and life in Coal Creek, life everywhere, should cease being aimless and become definite and full of meaning" (p. 13). Because he cannot tolerate idle chatter and finds language to be deficient as a means of communication, Beaut initially feels that the spoken dreams of Butterlips are intolerable; now he thinks the actions of the soldiers are admirable. With the scene of the marching soldiers before him, he begins to think that the working people of the nation should be organized into a large marching army.

During this period, when his vague purpose is taking shape in his mind, Beaut also is influenced by another force. Like other young people in the small towns of America, he often thinks "of life in the city and of the part he should play there" (p. 26). Lured to the city by the promise of success, Beaut selects Chicago, where opportunities for advancement are imagined to be immediate for those willing to gamble in the impersonal urban world. Yet, if Coal Creek suggests a deterministic life, the sense of destiny becomes even more apparent, rather than less so, once he arrives in the city.

While city dwellers might have a difficult time coping with the cataclysmic changes of life, it is equally true that the people from the small towns, whose ideals of the city frequently are destroyed by the reality of it, are victimized by their illusions and disappointments. The elements of naturalism, so common in the Chicago novel, are not particularly subtle in *Marching Men*, as Anderson repeats the oft-used observation that the urban force envelops the individual. The "big, disorderly city" casts a spell and the "air of disorderly ineffectiveness" surrounds everybody. Yet, Beaut McGregor is convinced that he can exercise his free will in the midst of so much obvious determinism, despite his twin discoveries that the disease of mechanization has curtailed life in the city and the emphasis upon worldly gain has created its own group of isolatoes. He believes that he can stem the tide of the inevitable urban force. He realizes that his rise in the city is not going to be as effortless as he had imagined, and he comes to understand that success is not waiting for everybody.

Looking at the grim view from the window of his West Side boardinghouse, he can watch "the discarded newspapers, worried by the whirlpools of wind in the court, run here and there, dashing against the warehouse walls and vainly trying to escape over the roof." Contemplating the scene, he comes to the conclusion that "the lives of most people about him were much like the dirty newspaper harried by adverse winds and surrounded by ugly walls of facts" (p. 79). Although he believes that men and women are inextricably caught by forces over which they have no control, he is convinced that he will be a "master player" despite his understanding that possibilities for advancement must be tempered by a recognition of human frailty. But the more evidence he sees of the city's power the more convinced he becomes that he can find a solution for the apparent disorder of life. That he chooses the legal profession suggests his plan for remedying urban ills by championing causes through legal means. Despite his hero's certainty and his own latent optimism, Anderson seemed convinced at this point in his creative life that a quality existed in Chicago that constantly asserted itself over people and rendered them helpless.

Even Beaut at times succumbs to a fatalistic viewpoint as he thinks "of all men as counters in some vast games at which he was presently to be a master player" (p. 84). Underlying his belief in his ability to rise in the city are contradictory signs. As he walks about Chicago, he is struck by the sense of disorder and by the complacency of people who exist in this "vast disorder of life" (pp. 107–108). Anderson accepts the mythic Chicago and repeats the patterns common to the urban novel, which focus on the attitudes of characters who are generally impressed by the obvious power of the huge metropolis as they face the city for the first time.

Eventually, the anger that had overwhelmed the younger Beaut finds an outlet when he moves to Chicago and is displayed in varying ways. While his hatred of things as they appear to be seems to inform much of his action, the chaos and hopelessness of the city are reinforced by a fascinating character momentarily inserted in the novel. "The man is from Ohio . . . [and] owns a factory in one of the large industrial towns there and has come to the city to sell his product." One evening this unnamed character (a not-so-subtle Anderson self-portrait) takes a walk. What he sees is largely conditioned by his background, for he is a man of the better sort, quiet, efficient, kindly." One of his first reactions to the city is to conclude "life is good" as he passes familiar family scenes. When he sees a drunkard, the man from Ohio, so Anderson notes, is not unduly disturbed. (In retrospect a reader can conclude that here is another presentation of the novelist's alter ego drawn from the days when he was too blind to the reality of the city and saw it, as did other salesmen and travelers, as simply one more market.) The visitor "knows that drunken men are often but gay-spending dogs who tomorrow morning will settle down to their work feeling secretly better for the night of wine and song." In rapid succession "the man from Ohio" sees a fight, great dirty buildings, a ship being loaded at the river's edge, and "a street filled with pawn shops, clothing stores, and the clamor of voices." He also, in a flash, sees Beaut who seems to be hurling curses to heaven. The city's people, then, include newsboys, policemen on call in a patrol wagon, prostitutes, and Beaut whose threatening, ugly face intrudes upon the visitor. What had started out as a pleasant walk after an equally pleasant dinner ends on a discordant note as "the man from Ohio" senses his "pleasant evening has been in some way spoiled."

At the very instant that the traveler has passed him, Beaut is also lost in his own thoughts as he is trying to decide what should be his role in the brutal city. In a moment of commitment Beaut has indeed "thrust his fist up in the air" vowing: "I'll get ready to use that intelligently . . . a man wants trained brains backed up by a big fist in the struggle I am going into." The stranger in the city and Beaut momentarily meet at that second. The visitor simply sees a "man raise his fist to the sky and notes with a shock the movement of the lips and the hugeness and ugliness of the face in the lamplight." On the other hand, the incidental meeting has a profound effect on Beaut. "To McGregor's nostrils came the odour of rich fragrant tobacco. He turned and stood, staring at the intruder on his thoughts" (pp. 157–64 *passim*). The chance meeting between "the man from Ohio" and Beaut exemplifies not only the lack of meaningful communication as a significant urban characteristic but also the random nature of it. The two people merely respond to the external reality and actions of each other. By capturing this isolated moment Anderson reveals that the effects of such unplanned meetings are predicated upon the vantage points of the responding observers.

In another particularly telling incident Anderson relates the episode of Beaut and a Lake Street prostitute, who lures him into her house. When her companion attempts to rob him, Beaut rages at both of them and is convinced more than ever that the city is chaotic and ugly. "Again a great hatred of the disorder of life took hold of him and as though all of the disorderly people of the world were personified in her he swore and shook the woman as a dog might have shaken a foul rag" (p. 104).

Beaut's experiences in the city do little to alter his negative view of life. And always on the streets of Chicago are "the restless moving people" who have become victims of the city.

> On the sidewalks along Canal Street he saw strong-bodied men loitering before cheap lodging houses. Their clothing was filthy with long wear and there was no light of determination in their faces. In the little fine interstices of the cloth of which their clothes were made was gathered the filth of the city in which they lived and in the stuff of their natures the filth and disorder of modern civilization had also found lodging. (p. 107)

The filth and disorder are accompanied by aimlessness and loneliness which are just as pervasive. Can the human element ever gain control in the midst of such chaos? Is the survival of the fittest the only operating principle? *Marching Men* is an attempt to answer both queries.

Novelists have assumed that certain types of people are partially responsible for the conditions of places like Chicago. Among them, according to Anderson, are the political bosses who gain power through a repression of the electorate and successful businessmen who assuage their guilt in many ways. David Ormsby, a great financier, continually justifies his life as being necessary for progress. His daughter, Margaret, tries to give her useless life meaning and follows a pattern established by many wives and daughters of the elite. She becomes involved in great philanthropic endeavors and moves into a settlement house in the notorious First Ward in order to help the very downtrodden who have been created by her father and the insensitive political bosses. While one would not wish to question her dedication or her sincerity, it is interesting that her life in the slums is mitigated by daily luncheons with her father in one of the city's fashionable restaurants.

Political corruption has been a common device by which the city's novelists have defined Chicago, but the crime or syndicate story did not really become popular until the Prohibition era. Although nineteenth-century dime novels were content to dwell upon "the lower elements" of the city, the so-called mainstream novels generally alluded to the relationship between some businessman's use of the law to exercise his will without going into specific details. Anderson, however, examines the First Ward as further proof of the city's shortcomings. Henry Hunt, who shares a desk in Beaut's office and who has become trapped by a system that goes against his better self, exemplifies another victim of the city's life. He is "lieutenant to the 'boss' of the First Ward" and is nominally a real estate broker. He actually is "a collector of tithes for the political bosses. . . . All day he went from place to place through the ward interviewing women, checking their names off a little red book he carried in his pocket, promising, demanding, making veiled threats" (pp. 179–80).

Another helpless character caught in the evil maelstrom of the city's First Ward is a young man, "son of one of the city's plunging millionaire wheat speculators [who] was found dead [one night] in a little blind alley back of a resort known as Polk Street Mary's place." Expectedly, the policeman on duty nearby in the alley hears nothing. As a result of the cry for change that fills the city's newspapers, "the powers that ruled the First [Ward]—quiet shrewd men who knew how to make and to take profits, the very flower of commercialism— were frightened." To satisfy the cry for reform and to silence the newspapers, the political bosses decide there must be a sacrificial lamb. They realize that the newspapers, which rely heavily upon oversimplification and repetition, play an obvious role not only in the distribution of information but also in the creation of an awareness of urban problems. Highly dependent upon the sensational, journalists have a self-serving interest in exposés and are not always motivated by a sense of altruism. At the same time, many politicians and businessmen know that the public servants of the press can be bought like any other commodity. In a case reminiscent of the rumor regarding the death of Marshall Field's son, Anderson presents the dilemma of the politicians who recognize "in the prominence of the dead man a real opportunity for their momentary enemies—the press."

At all costs, the First Ward must be protected. "For weeks they had been sitting quietly, weathering the storm of public disapproval. In their minds they thought of the ward as a kingdom in itself, something foreign and apart from the city. Among their followers were men who had not been across the Van Buren Street line into foreign territory for years" (pp. 180–82 *passim*). After a consultation with Henry Hunt and "a police official," the presiding boss of the First Ward selects a scapegoat who is accused in order to quiet the public. When they have a victim, as the big and little city bosses know, "the newspapers dropped the clamorous cry for reform and began demanding instead the life of Andrew Brown" (p. 183) and would no longer seek the truth.

The murder trial is "both an opportunity and a test for McGregor." Momentarily, the unlikely criminal and the reluctant lawyer come together to affect each other. Up to this time Beaut had "for a number of years . . . lived a lonely life in Chicago . . . a solitary figure aloof from life." This case draws him "into the maelstrom" of life (p. 186). In defending Andy Brown, McGregor takes on an entire system. If it seems out of place and contrived in the novel, the episode permits Anderson to point out the whimsical nature of calls for reform as well as the weaknesses of a legal process responsive to political and commercial interests. But of even greater importance, it gives him an opportunity to establish the credibility of Beaut McGregor as a folk hero in the city. Demonstrating the growing appeal of his protagonist, an appeal that is reinforced by the news media, Anderson makes the reader realize the force of both publicity and emotional oratory in mass movements.

Beaut's success is predicated upon his manipulation of words. Recounting the famous Andy Brown trial, Anderson comments:

> The city caught fire . . . at the time of that terrible speech of his in the court room when Polk Street Mary grew afraid and told the truth. There he stood, the raw untried red-haired miner from the mines and the Tenderloin, facing an angry court and a swarm of protesting lawyers and uttering that city-shaking philippic against the old rotten first ward, and the creeping cowardice in men that lets vice and disease go on and pervade all modern life. (pp. 278–79)

The novelist continues by calling the speech another example of "J'Accuse!" and maintains that "when he had finished in the whole court no man spoke and no man dared feel guiltless. For the moment something—a section, a cell, a figment, of men's brains opened—and in that terrible illuminating instant they saw themselves as they were and what they had let life become" (p. 279). While law firms and popular lawyers vie for his attention, Beaut the silent one, has come to understand the indispensable nature of language.

When he recognizes the need to articulate his dream to others, Beaut realizes the importance of study, but finds that education alone will not solve the problem of communication. His immediate need for language is ironic inasmuch as he has always railed at its ineffectiveness. In a particularly revealing scene, Anderson notes that during a lecture at the university given by a professor who is concerned with world conditions, Beaut interrupts and in a tirade charges: "We go from room to room hearing talk . . . [on] the street corners downtown in the evenings and in towns and villages men talk and talk. Books are written, jaws wag. The jaws of men are loose. They wabble about—saying nothing." Then in a pointed reference to the professor, he raises the question: "If there is all this unrest . . . [why] do not you who have trained brains strive to find the secret of order in the midst of this disorder? Why is something not done?" The professor, misunderstanding Beaut's concern and assuming the query is a call for violence, dismisses the class with the observation: "I understand your kind" (pp. 167–68). Inherent in the professor's reaction is a response to the efforts of active reformers.

In the meantime, the professor's wordiness has affected Beaut as had that of Coal Creek's socialist many years before. Throughout his life, Anderson was to be concerned about the shortcomings of language as a means of communication. In *Marching Men*, while examining this deficiency, he intrudes to note:

> It is a terrible thing to speculate on how man has been defeated by his ability to say words. The brown bear in the forest has no such power and the lack of it has enabled him to retain a kind of nobility of bearing sadly lacking in us. On and on through life we go, social ists, dreamers, makers of laws, sellers of goods and believers in suffrage for women and we continuously say words, worn-out words, crooked words, words without power or pregnancy in them. (p. 123)

Eventually, Anderson's hero knows that he must control language in order to convince others of the efficacy of his plan, and he learns to stir people with his oratory. His display as a defense attorney is simply one example of his ability.

Successful though Beaut is as a lawyer, his dream of a day when there might appear an organized mass movement of workingmen never leaves him. He knows it could represent "a vast order coming out of disorder." Yet, as he meditates upon his life in the city, he thinks it is "like . . . standing in the presence of some gigantic machine with many intricate parts that had begun to run crazily, each part without regard to the purpose of the whole" (p. 129). It is not until he returns to Coal Creek for the funeral services of his mother that he begins to understand, once again through an isolated incident, the possibility that his dream for the marching men might be realized and that his life might gain a greater sense of purpose.

On his way to the cemetery, his carriage is followed at a short distance by several groups of miners who, though they still fear Beaut, are genuinely saddened by the death of Nance McGregor. As these men shuffle behind the carriage, as it moves from the heart of the mining town, Anderson asserts: "An instantaneous impulse seemed to run through the ranks of stooped toiling figures. . . . With a swing the marching men fell into step." In that moment when the shufflers become marchers, McGregor realizes the significance of his dream. "With Napoleonic insight he read a lesson into the accident of the men's falling into step . . . ," and Beaut muses: "Some day a man will come who will swing all of the workers of the world into step like that. . . . He will make them conquer, not one another but the terrifying disorder of life. If their lives have been wrecked by disorder it is not their fault. They have been betrayed by the ambitions of their leaders, all men have betrayed them" (pp. 148–49).

It is at this emotional time in his life that he rededicates himself to the consummation of his once formless idea. He dreams now of "the great disorderly city on the western plains rocked by the swing and the rhythm of men, aroused and awakened with their bodies a song of new life" (p. 154). Beginning in Chicago, his movement would in time, Beaut thinks, sweep the nation and eventually the world. It is to be a mass demonstration of labor's force and will counteract a political system designed through corruption and human sacrifices to keep the oppressed from understanding that they are little more than victims of the ambitious greed of a select few. Moreover, his plan is designed to eliminate the disorder of life while "driving the great song of order[,] purpose[,] and discipline into the souls of Americans" (p. 178).

Given the nature of Chicago, it is not surprising that the concept of the marching men finds a congenial atmosphere. At first, however, Beaut gets few converts. The inability to communicate clearly the specifics of the movement is foreshadowed throughout the novel by a general lack of understanding between the characters. When the plan, with its hypnotic powers, does become somewhat successful, publicity of Beaut becomes the substitute for an adequate explanation of what really is occurring, primarily because newspapermen who are committed to the use of words find they can neither report the force nor the effect of McGregor's words. As they turn their collective attention to the central figure of the movement, journalists do not distinguish between the ideals of the marching men and the adoration of its leader. The press follows the little bands of marching men, but it is Beaut who becomes the subject of interest for most editors. "Every train brought writers tumbling into Chicago" (p. 282). Although the nation's newspapers promote the marching men through exposure, Anderson casts doubt upon the extent to which they really understand what is occurring.

The simplicity of Beaut's plan heightens the probability that it will be distorted. Based upon the notion that order can be created out of disorder, the movement requires that the marchers be disciplined. In its early days, the participants are commanded to remain silent as they march "shoulder to shoulder." The silence adds mystery and gives Beaut a psychological advantage, whereas the marching itself strikes a sense of terror among those who are suspicious of this new phenomenon sweeping the city. The dread, in part, is a result of the inability of "the men of affairs" to understand the underlying motives of labor. Had there been strikes or other overt actions, they would have had no such difficulty. But what defense do they have against a group of workers who simply march "shoulder to shoulder"? As fears in the city grow, the spirit of the workers' revenge is revealed as they are "made glad" by the effects of their marching. Anderson comments that there is a "grim satisfaction" about the turn of events. The laborers recognize that they are "part of something vast" and gain a sense of dignity from that knowledge. "When in the past they had been told that power dwelt in them they had not believed" (p. 266). But with the increased publicity, even greater fears are generated as the marchers assume a power they really do not have, but "the comfortable, well-fed middle class people were afraid! It swept over the country like a religious revival, the creeping dread" (p. 283).

In time the silent marchers begin to chant a haunting melody that is described as "the most persistently penetrating thing Americans had ever heard." The description of the song emphasizes the religious nature of the melody that was written by a man who "bore the marks of the shackles on his legs" and that, Anderson says, has *soul*. What he observes about the song might, with a few changes, be applicable to all such airs. "Who could forget it? Its high pitched harsh feminine strain rang in the brain. How it went pitching and tumbling along in that wailing calling endless note. It had strange breaks and intervals in the rendering." This essentially harmless song tends to inspire a very negative reaction. Law enforcement agents are especially annoyed by the singing, marching men, but "the police could not arrest a hundred thousand men because they marched shoulder to shoulder along the streets and chanted a weird march song as they went." How much greater would have been the displeasure if all of its hearers had realized that the song had been written by a Russian! "There was in it just the weird haunting something the Russians know how to put into their songs and into the books they write. It isn't the quality of the soil. Some of our own music has that. But in this Russian song there was something else, something world-wide and religious—a soul, a spirit. Perhaps it is just the spirit that broods over that strange land and people." Anderson concludes with the observation that "there was something of Russia in McGregor himself" (pp. 280–82 *passim*).

It is not long before all of Chicago is swept up in the movement either out of respect or fear. No one doubts that Beaut is successful and powerful. He seems destined for greatness. He has given the working classes a mission. However, unlike his wealthy comrades, David Ormsby is not disturbed. He knows "in the end . . . the silent patient power of money [will] bring his people the victory" (p. 299). Furthermore, in the practical application of Beaut's attempt to create an ordered universe, there are external and internal forces that operate against him. Therefore, at the height of the movement's vitality, the probability of its failure is inherent in its success, because its nobility of purpose will be hampered by the nature of human beings.

By implication, then, the "marching men" do not offer a viable answer to the problems of the city. First of all, the popularity of the cause creates some immoral leaders who, through their greed, sabotage the integrity of Beaut's program. David Ormsby has an encounter with such a labor leader, who is described as "a miniature McGregor with a crooked twist to him." The businessman knows that the man is "a rascal." Ormsby admits "the things he said to my men were all true enough. I was making money for my investors, a lot of it. They might have won in a fight with me." Then he adds: "I bought the man off . . . I used the cruel weapon men like me have to use. I gave him money and told him to get out, to let me alone. I did it because I had to win. My kind of men always have to win" (p. 309).

In addition to the rich, who have the ability to buy people as they might purchase any commodity, are those who imitate the movement without understanding its meaning or significance. As David Ormsby travels through the city with his daughter, attempting to get her to regain her confidence after an infatuation with Beaut, they see "before a saloon a troop of street urchins, led by a drunken man without a hat [who] gave a grotesque imitation of McGregor's Marchers before a crowd of laughing idlers. With a sinking heart Margaret realised that even at the height of his power the forces that would eventually destroy the impulses back of McGregor's Marchers were at work" (p. 312).

Interestingly enough, Beaut's idea does not encompass all segments of life. During the final triumphant moment, as the men assemble for the big rally, the women and children remain behind in the old neighborhoods. "Everywhere was dirt and disorder, the terrible evidence of men's failure in the difficult and delicate art of living" (p. 303). Occasionally, David and Margaret see some pathetic attempt to create beauty, but substantially the area is barren and desolate. Anderson, in spite of his sympathies, seems convinced that power without a concern for beauty is just as deadly as the oppressions of the world of commerce. In the end, it is clear that the new-found independence of the marchers will not survive in a materialistic society that tends to celebrate the producer rather than the consumer. Marching might lead to solidarity, but this does not alter the fact that the participants still are at the mercy of the economic system.

Central to the predictable disintegration of the movement is Beaut himself. Although he does not succumb to the standards or the morality of the city as he attempts to pursue his goal of unifying all laboring forces, his passionate desire to create the movement of the marching men is an end in itself rather than a means to better society. A vision of marching men as an answer to the disorder of life does not seem to be a feasible response. His single-minded devotion to his idea makes him one of Anderson's early grotesques; however, the contradictions in him remain unresolved. Exhibiting little compassion, Beaut appears as a demigod whose contempt for mankind is one of his strongest motivating forces. His hatred develops from his personal reactions to Coal Creek where the miners were "weak and disorganised like cattle" (p. 53).

In addition to a misanthropic trait, Beaut's repressed violent streak surfaces whenever he feels the futility of his life. Early, the reader learns that when McGregor is on his way to Chicago for the first time, he "look[s] back at Coal Creek, full of hate. Like Nero he might have wished that all of the people of the town had but one head so that he might have cut it off with a sweep of a sword or knocked it into the gutter with one swinging blow" (p. 59). As he walks the streets of Chicago, his dream of city life is changed considerably by the "filth and disorder" he sees, and "the flame of anger within burned stronger and stronger" as his contempt continues to grow. Anderson explains: Beaut "saw the drifting clouds of people of all nations that wander at night in Halstead [sic] Street and turning into a side street saw also the Italians, Poles, and Russians that at evening gather on the sidewalks before tenements in that district." The novelist continues: "The desire in McGregor for some kind of activity became a madness. His body shook with the strength of his desire to end the vast disorder of life. With all the ardour of youth he wanted to see if with the strength of his arm he could shake mankind out of its sloth." Instead, he strikes out at a passerby who is "like a child without muscles and hardness, clinging to the skirts of life" (pp. 107–108). As he rolls in the gutter, Beaut's victim is so surprised by the unwarranted attack that he crawls around like a child begging for help. The incident reinforces Beaut's contempt for humanity, a contempt that he justifies by his perception of a people without purpose and a disorganized environment.

On one occasion, as he watches a spider, it seems that Beaut is beginning to understand the nature of life, but even this moment of recognition ends in violence.

> In the hideous body of the insect there was something that suggested to the mind of the struggling thinker the sloth of the world. Vaguely his mind groped about trying to get hold of words and ideas to express what was in his brain. "Ugly crawling things that look at the floor," he muttered. "If they have children it is without order or orderly purpose. It is an accident like the accident of the fly that falls into the net built by the insect here. The coming of the children is like the coming of the flies, it feeds a kind of cowardice in men. In the children men hope vainly to see done what they have not the courage to try to do."

Beaut's speculations end "with an oath," and he crushes "with his heavy leather glove the fat thing wandering aimlessly across the light" (p. 127).

From an innocent passerby to a spider, McGregor sees in them a

personification of the disorder of life. Recalling his fascination with
the order displayed by those in the military, it dawns on him that "the
soldiers who had led thousands of men into battle had appealed to
him because in the working out of their purposes they had used human lives with the recklessness of gods. They had found the courage
to do that." And Beaut decides "away down deep in the hearts of men
lay sleeping a love of order and they had taken hold of that love. If
they had used it badly, did that matter? Had not they pointed out the
way?" Anderson gradually reveals that Beaut, a potential leader of
men, adopts the dangerous notion that the end always justifies the
means. He recognizes that the power of the marching men is predicated upon the belief that unified action can make ordinary people
seem extraordinary. Remembering the soldiers again, he reasons
when "they went swinging along, all as one man[, s]omething in that
fact ennobled them" (p. 130).

Occasionally, in reflective moments, McGregor's contempt for
mankind is tempered slightly by his genuine desire to alter the conditions caused by the disorder and chaos of modern life. There sometimes is a vague yearning for a true brotherhood of mankind. He realizes that the army has recognized the importance of the silent power
of marching but "men have taught them that big lesson only when
they wanted to kill. This must be different. Some one must teach
them the big lesson just for their own sakes, that they may also know.
They must march fear and disorder and purposelessness away. That
must come first" (p. 150).

In any atmosphere where collective behavior is the goal, it is
necessary that the participants follow the leader without question.
A single doubter will negate the entire movement. McGregor demands loyalty. Yet, he questions the commitment of previous leaders
maintaining they have taught "the secret" of unity "only to betray"
their followers. This includes "the men of books and of brains." At-
tacking language as a poor substitute for action, Beaut muses:

> Words mean nothing but when a man marches with a thousand
> other men and is not doing it for the glory of some king, then it will
> mean something. He will know then that he is part of something real
> and he will catch the rhythm of the mass and glory in the fact that he
> is part of the mass and that the mass has meaning. He will begin to
> feel great and powerful. . . . That is what the great leaders of armies
> have known . . . [a]nd they have sold men out. They have used that
> knowledge to subdue men, to make them serve their own little ends.
> (pp. 150–51)

Although he seems to understand that many leaders often have deceived the very people they ostensibly are trying to serve, Beaut also demonstrates the same potential for betrayal when he becomes a leader. By giving to the marching men the hope that their collective behavior will be ameliorative, he does not make clear that such an act might provide temporary order without creating a climate for those lasting changes that require more than a demonstration of elementary strength or a proclivity for endurance. Nonetheless, he continues to dream "of the actual physical phenomena of the men of labour marching their way into power and of the thunder of a million feet rocking the world and driving the great song of order[,] purpose[,] and discipline into the soul of Americans" (p. 178). Beaut's dream based upon the destruction of *what is* never includes the actual creation of *what might be.*

Given the anticapitalistic nature of the novel, it is ironic that David Ormsby, the consummate businessman, often is far more pragmatic than Beaut McGregor. He not only understands the apparent weaknesses and limitations of Beaut's movement but also becomes a voice of reason. As the ever-present observer, he consistently turns either to his knowledge of history or to his awareness of human nature to indicate that the real world will not be altered permanently by moments of idealism. Consequently, as Beaut's godlike power over men seems impressive through his control of their minds and actions, Ormsby reminds him that the real leaders are not popular figures but those of wealth and business. "The really strong men of the world . . .," David tells McGregor, "have had no place in history . . . [t]hey were in Rome and in Germany in the time of Martin Luther but nothing is said of them. Although they do not mind the silence of history they would like other strong men to understand." He continues: "The march of the world is a greater thing than the dust raised by the heels of some few workers walking through the streets and these men are responsible for the march of the world. . . . If you plan to upset things you may get yourself into history but you will not really count. What you are trying to do will not work" (p. 271). Ormsby's injunction is perhaps more true than Beaut realizes. Utlimately, getting into the history books is his only major achievement; and by implication, it is usually the only reward of those who lead mass movements.

During the great meeting on the lakefront in Grant Park, Ormsby and his daughter look on the gathering from the edge of the crowd while Beaut passionately addresses his followers. This is "the day of the great demonstration when McGregor's power over the minds and the bodies of the men of labour sent hundreds of thousands marching and singing in the streets" (p. 299). At this moment when Beaut appears most triumphant, Ormsby, who also understands the short-comings of language, says: "It is too bad one has to talk. Talk kills dreams and talk will also kill all such men as McGregor. Now that he has begun to talk we will get the best of him. I do not worry about McGregor. Time and talk will bring about his destruction" (p. 309).

Despite the profoundly valid commentary about the nature of modern urban life in *Marching Men* and the plea for change, Anderson practically forces his readers to join Ormsby who, in Beaut's finest hour, is "untouched" by the leader's great success. As he translates a philosophical concept into the actuality of a realistic portrayal of his fictional world, the novelist implicitly reveals (in spite of his own views and perhaps those of his readers) the possible ineffectiveness of mass movements as a device for urban change. Furthermore, he raises several uncomfortable questions, many of which remain unanswered. Correctly observing the characteristic weaknesses of large urban areas, the novel tries to offer an alternative for the dominant business culture and the disorderly city that results from it. The solution, however, is distinguished by its ambiguity. On the one hand, it celebrates collective action by asserting the strength of mankind rests in such unity. Yet, collectivism can lead not only to the denial of the individual but also to the violence of the organized mob.

IV

Anderson makes it clear that the issues raised by Beaut McGregor certainly are valid. Yet, his hero's struggle for order and discipline, a dream shared by dictators and Christlike figures, conceivably might be an illusion after all. The world has seen many Beaut McGregors come and go. Their movements momentarily capture the imaginations of the masses, but seldom do they make lasting changes. Perhaps the psychology of marching demands more of the participants than they can possibly give. Perhaps it replaces one order with another while it continues to deny the freedom of the human spirit. Or perhaps such a movement created out of a leader's personal contempt for humanity can never rise above the hatred that created it. Even Beaut's relationship with Edith Carson and his tenuous fling with Margaret Ormsby are tainted with his own selfishness.

But would his plan for the alleviation of the disorder of urban

life have been more successful had he been motivated by love rather
than revenge and hatred? If one accepts Thoreau's concept of civil disobedience that seems to form the broad base from which many modern demonstrative acts appear to have emanated, *love* and *hate* are
inconsequential. One discovers that the theory of the sage of Walden is designed to dramatize, rather than correct, the flaws in society and does not make provisions for group behavior. When applied
to a mass movement, it results in a disregard for the rights of the
nonparticipants.

Anderson sadly notes that Beaut and his movement do not alter
appreciably the nature of the city.

> Chicago is still here—Chicago after McGregor and the Marching
> Men. The elevated trains still clatter over the frogs at the turning into
> Wabash Avenue; the surface cars clang their bells; the crowds pour
> up in the morning from the runway leading to the Illinois Central
> trains; life goes on. And men in their offices sit in their chairs and say
> that the thing that happened was abortive, a brain storm, a wild out-
> break of the rebellious[,] the disorderly[,] and the hunger in the
> minds of men.

Yet Anderson justifies the movement by asserting: "The very soul of
the Marching Men was a sense of order. That was the message of it . . .
[m]en have not learned that we must come to understand the impulse
toward order, have that burned into our consciousness, before we
move on to other things." So much is made of the importance of the
individual in American culture that there is a tendency to overlook a
good that can arise out of the activities that may be mutually bene-
ficial. Hence, the novelist reminds his readers: "There is in us this
madness for individual expression. For each of us the little moment of
running forward and lifting our thin childish voices in the midst of the
great silence." In the end, according to Anderson, Beaut could not
teach the great lesson. "We have not learned that out of us all, walking shoulder to shoulder, there might arise a greater voice, something
to make the waters of the very seas to tremble" (pp. 277–78).

The notion that strength comes out of unity obviously is not
unique to Sherwood Anderson. Neither is the doctrine of self-reliance
that has had periodic appeals. The wisdom of collective action has
been discussed throughout history, and individuals who have with-
stood external pressures by publicly rebelling against them in time
have become heroes and heroines of the doctrine of self-reliance.
Consequently, the message of *Marching Men* is as old as the desire to
stem the tide of the inevitable through individual commitment and

unified action. Repeatedly, however, the efficacy of the idea has been challenged seriously by the impossibility of its achievement. In fact, recent developments perhaps have made the modern world more aware of the effects of such collectivism while emphasizing the differences between the theoretical and the actual. Philosophically the goal of Thoreau's "civil disobedience" and Chapman's "practical agitation" was to alter public opinion or create a public awareness. Although each gave evidence of how the objective was to be reached, both men relied heavily upon the individual to make certain choices.

As Anderson reinterprets the concept of civil disobedience, the process is expressed in mass activity rather than in individual terms. Furthermore, it is rooted in the personality of Beaut McGregor; and his flaws become those of the movement. At the same time, his success carried with it the seeds for his eventual failure. Whether Anderson understood the ultimate tragedy that could result when individuals pitted themselves against stronger and superior forces is not clear. Beaut McGregor certainly is not Antigone rejecting the law of Creon in order to obey a higher law; yet, he joins those who, through the years, have advocated the need of the individual to rebel against existing conditions by placing the moral law above the rules of society. Often they have employed the techniques of "civil disobedience" or "practical agitation" to withstand the injustices of their eras, and frequently their confrontations were tragic.

The essence of tragedy, however, is missing in *Marching Men*. Instead, there is a disordered universe, where communication is difficult among some inarticulate individuals and isolated groups, where unreasoned fear replaces attempts to understand prevailing conditions, where the participants in the movement never seem to rise to the greatness of the idea that motivates them, and where the fanaticism of Beaut McGregor robs him of human warmth and compassion. That Anderson was willing to explore the "marching men" as a possible answer for urban chaos indicates more about his idealism than his understanding of either the city or human nature. Ultimately, the value of *Marching Men* goes beyond the tale, which does often tax credulity. The narrative reveals the extent to which Anderson, at least at one moment in his life, was willing to offer an emphasis upon order as the response to the chaos of urban life. The novel also reveals his vision of the artist's role. He saw it as an ability to bring life to one's imagination without negating one's obligation to be an observant human being. Such an attempt might be met with failure, but like Beaut McGregor an artist should have the courage to fail.

The life of reality is confused, disorderly, almost without apparent purpose, whereas in the artist's imaginative life there is purpose.

—*Sherwood Anderson's Notebook*

5

"Disorderly" Realism

WHATEVER SOCIAL or political message one may read into *Marching Men*, the conclusion of the novel holds little promise for the betterment of the city. In an examination of rising concerns (capital versus labor, political corruption, failure of reform and reformers, as well as the general status of the urban population), Anderson highlights the issues that still plague the American city. One might insist that the American Dream can be realized (and certainly both Sam and Beaut move from low positions to higher ones), but the illusion is limited to an increasingly smaller number. The reality of the disorderly city prevails. Within Anderson's created universe, even the strong are doomed to fail, and the cynical observations of a David Ormsby seem to be the operative laws of urban life. Despite his insistence that the individual often can withstand the overpowering forces of life, the novelist resignedly comments that "Chicago is still here," after Beaut McGregor's movement rocked both the city and the nation. That "life goes on" suggests the inevitability of urban disorder.

In spite of their artistic weaknesses, *Windy McPherson's Son* and *Marching Men* give excellent portraits of both Anderson's Chicago and Anderson in Chicago. The issues in and the patterns of the city, as Sherwood Anderson first knew the place, are set forth clearly in these two novels. He was drawn to the city but also repelled by it. The all-consuming sense of power that Louis Sullivan found so fascinating, Anderson often found merely depressing. Although he does not

duplicate each episode of his life, there are enough similarities between Sam McPherson, Beaut McGregor, and Sherwood Anderson to
suggest more than coincidence. Just as the early pages of both novels
seem to be restatements of portions of his autobiographies, so many
of his descriptions of Chicago are based upon his reactions to the city
as he walked its "hopeless, endless streets."

These early tales conclusively illustrate the novelist's contention
that life formed the basis for art. Because Anderson relied so heavily
upon his experiences and observations, the personal element seems
as apparent in *Marching Men* as in *Windy McPherson's Son.* Certainly,
the city provided a means of self-definition for Anderson as for his
characters. At the same time, his novels repeat the major traits of the
mythic city as perpetuated by the early historians and novelists.
When he deviated from already established fictional patterns, it was
to suggest others that were to become significant in the literature of
the city. Undeniably, then, a sense of Chicago pervades his early novels. There is a rebellion, half-hearted at times, against the dominant
business culture; but even the rebellion, as in some of the long passages of *Marching Men,* is converted into an aesthetic experience.
Thus, in spite of the apparent similarities between his life and his fiction, to read his novels as sheer autobiography is to miss a basic element in his view of the writer's role.

Even though his literary theory does not always appear well developed, by the early 1920s he was able to offer an explanation for the
autobiographical nature of art.

> The life of the imagination will always remain separated from the life
> of reality. It feeds upon the life of reality, but it is not that life—can-
> not be . . . upon the facts in nature the imagination must constantly
> feed in order that the imaginative life remain significant . . . The life
> of reality is confused, disorderly, almost without apparent purpose,
> whereas in the artist's imaginative life there is purpose. There is de-
> termination to give the tale, the song, the painting Form—to make it
> true and real to the theme, not to life. Often the better the job is done
> the greater the confusion.[1]

Anderson came to believe that there are "two kinds of realism."
One he defined as "the realism to actual life that is the challenge of
the journalist." The other is somewhat ambiguously identified as "the
realism to the book or the story life." And he concluded that the latter
"is the job of your real story teller."[2] As he moved from journalistic

realism to a faithful presentation of his imaginative universe, he never lost sight of the fact that such a cosmos was based upon both the observable world and the perceptions of the author. He also was convinced that the real stories of the United States must in some way reflect the national life. In fact, the nature of American fiction in general and of his work in particular came to concern him greatly.

As early as 1917, in his "Apology for Crudity," Anderson assumed that since crudity and ugliness were integral parts of an American culture that had made a god out of industrialism, it was only natural that a literature produced by this civilization would mirror its disturbing elements.[3] By focusing upon the more obvious elements of crudity, he ultimately overlooked his development, which grew as a result of his willingness to transcend journalistic transcriptions to get to the dominant imaginative impression that would propel his stories forward. Later he came to understand "the words used by the tale-teller were as the colors used by the painter." However, he quickly admitted: "Form was another matter. It grew out of the materials of the tale and the teller's reaction to them." Given the importance of words, he was struck by "the sudden realization of how little native American words had been used by American story-writers." In fact, "when most American writers wanted to be very American they went in for slang."[4] Increasingly, he was convinced that America's cultural heritage from England had done much to defer the development of a distinctive national literature.

Admitting that Howells and James were prose "masters," he found their "realism" to be of little value, for it was either too intellectual or subtle. He did not face the same "Howells or James" question that had perplexed Henry Blake Fuller. On the other hand, while it seems relatively clear that Anderson did not always understand James's insistence upon the importance of imagination in the presentation of reality, in some respects he was closer to James than he realized. However, by aligning himself with those writers for whom the "common" had inherent significance if not beauty, he became part of a tradition that included Whitman, Mark Twain, and Dreiser. Without becoming as committed to regionalism as Hamlin Garland, Anderson doubted that the East could make a major contribution to the articulation of the Midwest in literature. Writing to Paul Rosenfeld of his own perceptions, Anderson said: "I have in my inner consciousness conceived of what we roughly speak of as the Middle West . . . as an empire with its capital in Chicago."[5]

Eventually Anderson offered a revision of the more traditional and older philosophical doctrine of literary realism. In the beginning of his career, there is a faithfulness to external manifestations of the physical world. He recorded, sometimes in minute detail, what could be seen or heard; however, the imaginative, although it does not consciously alter the observable universe in either *Windy McPherson's Son* or in *Marching Men*, is equally important and serves as a more fundamental explanation of the actual. In the same letter to Rosenfeld, he explained that he wished to "take these little ugly factory towns [as well as] these big sprawling cities" and "pour a dream" over them in order "to write beautifully, create beautifully, not outside but in this thing in which I am born, in this place where, in the midst of ugly towns, cities, Fords, moving pictures, I have always lived, must always live." In the end, he did "not want . . . even those old monks at Chartres, building their cathedral, to be at bottom any purer than myself."

Anderson argued that the imagination is not the special province of the artist. He saw its use as a practical means of solving problems, and in "Man and His Imagination" he said that everybody could

> employ something of the writer's technique. When you are puzzled about your own life, as we all are most of the time, you can throw imagined figures of others against a background very like your own, put these imagined figures through situations in which you have been involved. It is a very comforting thing to do, a great relief at times, this occasionally losing of self, living in these imagined figures.[6]

A cynic might be inclined to dismiss Anderson's use of imagination as a problem-solving technique as nothing more than daydreaming, escapism, or a refusal to come face to face with the real world. This certainly would be true if the realm of the imagination were simply reduced to a practical device for working out inane and insignificant problems. William Sutton has explained this tendency further by exploring the "therapeutic" nature of Anderson's "basic approach to literature." Such a method was

> to give him release from consciousness of his world, to work out through the manipulation of imagined life the problems of his own, to find understanding for himself through probing lives of his imagined characters. This is a veritable refrain, as many biographical passages show. The fantasy world of the fictional Elsinore so closely

identified with his kindred sufferer, Hamlet, is the doorway to escape, to the pleasant land where the head no longer hurts.[7]

By the time of *Windy McPherson's Son*, the Chicago novel had assumed a discernibly pessimistic tone and was based upon the idea
that life indeed was conditioned by the urban environment. The literary city was designated as a "spiritual wasteland." Because Chicago
was considered as a place of power with a life of its own, the philosophy of naturalism seemed compatible with such a life. At a significant
moment in Anderson's artistic development, Chicago and his perceptions of it intruded upon his consciousness. Although he accepted
the basic premises that governed the development of the urban novel,
even his early work moved beyond a mere repetition of it; and he became a pivotal figure who emerged at the end of one era of urban fiction and initiated another. Despite the tendency of the city's novelists
to emphasize the role of place and Anderson's own admission that
Chicago had "scarred his soul," increasingly his city was transmitted
through impressions, moods, and ideas rather than through descriptions of specific sites within the corporate and municipal boundaries.
The evolution of his urban vision may not "explain" the writer to the
total satisfaction of everybody; however, a recognition of it not only
provides further insight into the relationship between a writer's imagination and reality but also serves as an important forerunner to *Mid-
American Chants* and *Winesburg, Ohio*. In time, his perceived city became more important than the actual one.

"The artist is, after all, partly a product of his environment. . . .
He does not escape the general tone and mood of the world in any
event," so Anderson wrote to a friend in 1930.[8] Before his metaphoric
shift from the specificity of his own life to the universality of his observations as a condition of art, he was concerned with an examination of the validity of the American Dream as promulgated at the turn
of the century. Instead of happiness, fulfillment, and material success, generations have discovered in such large urban areas as Chicago that the actual city is ugly, chaotic, filled with strange buildings
and dirty streets which are crowded with isolated, gloomy people. In
such a setting, people seemed doomed not only by locale but also by
themselves, since they cannot cope effectively with the disorder. In
the midst of all of this, the city emerges as an artifical unit designed
more as a battleground than as a background for meaningful relationships. Generally, characters are caught by the cataclysmic circumstances of urban life and have no means of freeing themselves.

Although they are stronger than most, Sam McPherson and Beaut McGregor also are victims of what they see as the demands of the city. But whether one becomes materially successful, as in the case of Sam, or a spiritual superman, like Beaut, there looms as a constant the conditions of a materialistic culture with its disorder and corrupting influence of money. There also is the urban isolato whose pathetic human will is no match for the overpowering force of the city.

The very nature of the city as an artificial entity created for the fulfillment of human wants and desires, with its crowds and unnamed masses, reinforces the notion of the lack of personal identification. One may argue convincingly that a sense of stability is possible in a small town that relies heavily upon the idea of like-minded people coming together for similar reasons. Because such relationships are increasingly fluid and tenuous in the city, the basic human isolation of those suspended in time and place becomes further evidence of the reality of modern life and is more apparent in cities, which are not governed by the surface connections of a small town. But the issue is not a simple either/or situation. Traditionally, social scientists have stressed family units, the acceptance of a recognizable social class, and an identifiable community as significant stabilizing forces. However, Anderson's heroes do not have these. Even the strongest figures in his novels substantially lose their identities. Sam becomes part of what is called the McPherson crowd, and Beaut functions as an urban antagonist rather than as an individual.

While the city-as-brute-force exists in Anderson, he tempers this concept with an insistence that people, properly motivated, have the power to move and determine their destinies. In fact, the shortcomings of the city are largely the result of human action and inaction. The physical ugliness, often a result of greedy real estate operators and uncaring politicians, does not have to exist. The confusion and lack of motivation that grip people often result from their inability to cope with conditions, even though most of them have been called to the city by the "dream of success." Reform movements do not succeed because too frequently they are replaced by the scapegoat theory, which gives short-term solutions for more complicated long-range problems. And so one could continue to list all of the urban ills singled out by Anderson and realize that the naturalistic control does not have to be as powerful if the human element maintains its strength and integrity.

Evoking the image of a large, impersonal, chaotic disorderly place, Anderson was interested in the totality of the city rather than in the neighborhoods of a Farrell or an Algren or a Wright; but it is a particular kind of place, whose possible symbolic interpretations go beyond an analysis of the shortcomings of the American Dream. City life, to many observers, is characterized by the hustle and bustle associated with the diversity and movements of teeming thousands, who go about their lives in active pursuit of what the city offers; but Anderson's city, chaotic though it is, is marked by a strange silence. Furthermore, Anderson noted "we Americans are, in spite of our great achievements, an essentially lonely people, and this may be true because we were, in the beginning, a transplanted people."[9]

Anderson's city is more inclusive than the name of a single city would suggest. In a balance between the earthly and the spiritual, the search for Truth becomes a search for a workable reality, whether it leads a figure on a picaresque journey or to an insistence that individuals are imbued with the power to make a difference in their daily lives. Within Anderson's created universe is a place for a revitalized religion, even though he saw the clergy and churches as being ill-prepared to deal with the conditions of modern life. Chaos and isolation were not to be dispelled through religious insurance policies nor by any of the current church-related activities. In the meantime, the possibility of failure is ultimately not the final tragedy. As the magnate David Ormsby observes at the end of *Marching Men*, Beaut McGregor perhaps "knew he would fail and . . . had the courage of failure" (p. 314).

With the exception of the West Side, the city's neighborhoods seldom are his final concern although Anderson does offer general descriptions of the "sides" of Chicago. Even as Sam McPherson and Beaut McGregor walk through the streets, the city does not have the same sense of immediacy for them as it does for Dreiser's Carrie as she trudges through many of the same streets. But Anderson's West Side offers an example of the novelist's use of national folklore. It is a fact of Chicago history that many young men and women who moved into the city first found lodging in the western section of the city. Once they became successful, they moved elsewhere. In a subtle revision of the American metaphor, "go-West-young-man-go-West," Anderson has his characters discover that the directive is fallacious. Success is not to be found on the city's West Side, which is a place of deadly impasse for the nonadventurous. But only the persevering urban pioneers can discover this. Those who follow their own sense of what is needed rather than accepting blindly what others have said have a greater chance for survival.

In many ways, Anderson utilizes the death-and-resurrection formula. His heroes, through rites of passage, go from their small towns to be reborn in the city. But instead of finding the city of their dreams, they discover ordinary people moving in massed crowds, incapable of achieving the expected rewards of urban life. Anderson's characters assume that since success is possible for some, failure is in some way a judgment on the individual rather than on the American Dream. Once they recognize their predicaments, they frequently are incapable of communicating their discoveries because they are inarticulate. If they have the gift of speech, they often are intent merely upon imparting that which is false.

To examine Anderson's urban heroes and heroines is to survey a host of men and women who for one reason or another are incapable of breaking through existing barriers. Part of their inability to relate to others is their denial of the importance of either the need for dialogue or the acceptance of true love as a humanizing force. Thus, in many ways Anderson became the spokesman for these inarticulate ones with their frustrated and thwarted lives. Moreover, Anderson's early work introduced the grotesque figure, who eventually is defined in *Winesburg, Ohio*. Both Sam and Beaut are grotesques, who not only embrace a specific truth but also seem to float in and out of reality. Then, at significant moments, they lose the power of speech; hence, they lose the power to communicate. The later role assumed by George Willard is taken by Anderson himself in his first novels. This results in a series of intrusive author comments that attempt to interpret the stories of his city people.

During his first period in Chicago, he frequently referred to the loneliness of life in the small rooms of a boarding house. His artistic rendering of this idea occurs in both *Windy McPherson's Son* and *Marching Men*. The tremendous effects of loneliness perhaps are more important in the understanding of Beaut McGregor, whose isolated spirit might have led to his sense of self-reliance, but as a leader of men his loneliness did not prepare him for the sense of communication necessary for leadership. That he could inspire workers to action is apparent, but his distance from them and his coldness are to signal his own defeat. Such an isolato concerns Anderson greatly, and this theme was expanded beyond those small rooms, which both he and McGregor shared on a cheerless street in a large city.

In any review of the urban elements in American literature, there is an underlying premise that suggests that city life has had a significant influence upon those who, by choice or force, remained in such an environment. Attempts to explain this phenomenon have been varied. Joseph Hudnut in his *Architecture and the Spirit of Man* presents a view of urban life that takes into account both the spoken and unspoken appeals of the city. He has noted that modern life is city-related not essentially from economic necessity (although one cannot deny the importance of the economic) nor for the pleasures that come from the metropolis "but by a hunger which transcends both practical and sensuous experience, a hunger seldom revealed by appearances, seldom acknowledged in our consciousness." Furthermore,

> We are held in the city by our need of a collective life; by our need of belonging and sharing; by our need of that direction and frame which our individual lives gain from a larger life lived together.
>
> There are city habits and city thoughts, city moralities and loyalties, city harmonies . . . which surround us in cities. . . . Beneath the visible city . . . there lies an invisible city laid out in patterns of idea and behavior, which channels the citizen with silent persistent pressures and, beneath the confusion, noise, and struggle of the material and visible city, makes itself known and reconciles us to all of these.[10]

Windy McPherson's Son and *Marching Men* gave Anderson the opportunity to work out in his own mind not only the relationship between the human and the urban but also the interconnections between the "visible city" and the "invisible" one. However, the tale of Beaut McGregor was a more ambitious project for a writer who had obvious difficulty in sustaining the necessary dramatic action demanded by the structure of the novel form as he understood it. Anderson's tendency to intrude often hinders the development of his narrative and leads to the introduction of "mini-sermons" more distinguished by their observations than by their gospel messages. Seemingly violating some of the major principles espoused by the Mark Twain-Howells-James school of realism commonly used in the Chicago novel, Sherwood Anderson evidently was groping for a narrative method that would best explore the disorder of urban life. As the novelist confronted the city, utilizing its physical geography as well as the facts of its existence, certain stylistic devices and methods became apparent. The matter-of-factness, the cajoling, even the misstatements—so much a necessary part of advertising—were altered to fit his needs. And, always, there was the storyteller intruding upon the action to furnish commentary upon the scene, the situation, the characters, and the action. For those accustomed to the fast-paced modern novel, Anderson's long fiction seems to stall at the very moment when the reader expects "to see" life rather than "to be told" about it. Yet, many of these interpolations contain some of the most perceptive views of American city life.

While Anderson includes suggestions of a determinism in both *Windy McPherson's Son* and *Marching Men,* the result is not always naturalistic, although the novelist often seems thoroughly convinced that human beings are inextricably caught in a web of overpowering forces and are victims of either their environments or their darker selves. There is an element in his urban work that refuses to accept the idea that all characters must fall victim to the city,. Without claiming undeserved merit for these early works, readers must remember, in a society inclined to categorize writers as being *romantic, realistic,* or *naturalistic,* Anderson is difficult to identify. One can build a solid case for him as a romanticist, who looks either to the "corn-fields back of Chicago" or backward to an idyllic age that perhaps never existed except in his own mind. There also is the realistic Anderson, who deals faithfully and truthfully with the setting as well as the human condition, who describes the minutiae of life but whose characters often are imbued with the ability to chart their own destinies. Free will is infinitely more powerful than some abstract power causing human action. This, then, is a partial explanation for Sam McPherson's search and for the isolation of Beaut McGregor, whose strength alone would have made him a success in a city that worshipped strong men. Because Anderson's first two published novels, which clearly indicate his later development as a storyteller, are cast in the mold of a type of long narrative that had gained popularity, one is apt to take their deviations as weaknesses. To focus on one Anderson is to deny the total scope of his work.

By the time of his writing *Winesburg, Ohio,* Anderson had perfected his approach to prose diction; but his groping for a distinctive style can be seen in his earliest novels in spite of the anger and so-called social messages in these works. If he merely had been concerned with a critique of society, one might legitimately conclude that *Marching Men* could have been thoroughly treated by either a sociologist or psychologist. However, the novel is an exploration into an experimental use of language. For example, the words *chaos, disorder,* and *disorderly* are invoked so much that they practically become part of an incantation designed to hypnotize the reader. At the same time,

Anderson was obviously beginning to understand the nature and the importance of prose rhythm; hence, the descriptive passages dealing with the city repeat the disordered rhythm of the urban structure in short staccato sentences that undoubtedly serve to reinforce the lack of form in the city. However, when he looks at the force of the marching men, his sentences assume the sonorous roll approximating the rhythm of such a unified force. On the other hand, when he describes the urban alternative, the language graphically seems to reproduce the langorous rhythms of the cornfields. The sentences now assume a soothing quality almost lullabylike in their appeal. Anderson understood the need of language to communicate feelings and moods as much as ideas. There have been those critics, such as Brom Weber, who have suggested that Anderson's experimentation with langauge is direct evidence of the influence of Gertrude Stein's *Tender Buttons* on him. But his broadening of its effects are his contribution to the American urban novel.

Windy McPherson's Son and *Marching Men* have been called works of his apprenticeship. This is a correct assessment if one insists that *Winesburg, Ohio* indeed is his masterpiece or if one is committed to the belief that Sherwood Anderson simply is the voice of the small midwestern town. On the other hand, his merger of town and city, his analysis of the prevailing business structure, and his determination about the nature of urban life with its disorder and corruption place his first two published works within the orbit of the urban novel, which had been and still was being produced in Chicago in the opening decades of the twentieth century.

Had his life's work ended with *Windy McPherson's Son* and *Marching Men*, Anderson would have made a lasting contribution to the American city novel. Up to this point in his career, as he confronted the urban, he had examined the extent to which the disorderly nature of the city could influence human beings. After a less-than-rewarding escape, Sam McPherson rejects a life of wandering convinced that he has a greater understanding of himself. The optimism or naivete of a Sam McPherson, who eventually decides after he has succumbed to the mirage of the American Dream that the individual can cope with urban forces without capitulation, is replaced by the puzzling and angry Beaut, who rails against the city's chaotic nature. Beaut McGregor does not accept quietly the mandates of the city. Although neither character has an answer that proves to be completely feasible and the reader understands the impotence of the individual, Anderson seemed committed to making the human rather than some powerful urban force the center of his universe. At the same time, in his revision of the currently accepted notion of the realistic theory, he forged a distinctive literary style that he would perfect later in his writing career.

Sherwood Anderson, 1876–1941
(The Newberry Library)

BusinessTypes
SHERWOOD ANDERSON

The Undeveloped Man.

THE advertising man sat upon his upturned grip at a railroad junction. It was midnight, a drizzle of rain was in the air and close about him lay the unbroken blackness of a cloudy night.

Down the tracks in the railroad yards a freight engine was making up a train. The banging of the cars, the rumbling of the wheels, the swinging lanterns and the voices of the trainmen lent interest to a long, dull wait. Suddenly up the track there came a rippling string of oaths, and for the next ten minutes the air was filled with them. In the words of Mark Twain, there was "swearing in that railroad yard, swearing that just laid over any swearing ever heard before."

The engineer swore and he wasn't half bad; the conductor deftly caught up the refrain and embellished it, and then from far down in the yards the voice of a brakeman cut into the game.

It was all about a box car and a coupling pin that wouldn't catch, and it was nothing less than genius the way that brakeman handled his subject. He swore scientifically. He worked over the ground already covered by the engineer and conductor and from it harvested another crop, and then he caught his breath, waved his lantern and started into the dense forest of untried oaths. The best part of it all was the way he clung to that box car, he went far enough afield for words but when he used them they were pat, they were all descriptive of the car and its peculiar and general uselessness.

"He is a sort of genius in his way, ain't he?" said a weak, piping little voice at the advertising man's elbow.

SHERWOOD ANDERSON.

By May of 1904 when this vignette appeared in *Agricultural Advertising*, Anderson, at twenty-eight, was a copywriter in Chicago.
(The Newberry Library)

"A New Celebrity" from the *Chicago Daily News*. The spoof appeared after the publication of *Marching Men*.
(The Newberry Library)

Tennessee Mitchell Anderson, 1874–1929, was a sculptor and Anderson's second wife. They were married in Chicago 31 July 1916. He divorced her in April of 1924 after a fourteen-month stay in Reno, Nevada.
(The Newberry Library)

"Marching Men." The high unemployment rate between 1880 and 1930 made city living less than ideal for many. This photograph was taken during the 1914 march by the unemployed on City Hall for the purpose of seeking jobs and relief.

(Chicago Historical Society, DN# 62,263)

South Water Street Market.
(Chicago Historical Society, ICHi 19429)

South Water and Clark Streets, 1908.
(Chicago Historical Society, DN# 5902)

PART TWO
Reconciliation

A city to be a real one has to have
something back of it. Land, a lot of it.
Rich land—corn, wheat, iron, rivers,
mountains, hogs, cattle. Chicago back
of it has the Middle West—the empire
called Mid-America. Corn, hogs,
wheat, iron, coal, industrialism—a
new age moving across a continent
by railroads, moving unbelievable
quantities of goods across a vast
place, in the center of which Chicago
stands.

—Memoirs

[The Renaissance] was the time in which something blossomed in Chicago and the Middle West. . . . Something which had been very hard in American life was beginning to crack, and in our group we often spoke of it hopefully. And how exciting it was. Something seemingly new and fresh was in the very air we breathed. . . . What ho! for the new world.

—*Memoirs*

6

"Something Blossomed in Chicago"
Renaissance Days

S HERWOOD ANDERSON returned to Chicago at a time when a cultural revolution was taking place in the city, and it provided a congenial climate for the growth and development of a man who no longer was convinced that the methods of business were the most rewarding goals of life. Success and money, he concluded, would not guarantee happiness. Much like his Sam McPherson, Sherwood Anderson embarked upon a search without exactly knowing what he wanted. Having been tempted to become a city man, he realized that urban life offered no panacea for the problems of human relationships; yet, fortunately for him, he met a group of people who understood his creative urges and sympathized with his desire to become a writer. By this time, novels set in Chicago were receiving national attention; consequently, Anderson not only found an audience for *Windy McPherson's Son* and *Marching Men* but also was encouraged to pursue a literary career. The so-called Chicago Renaissance of the twentieth century, however, was not as monolithic as some critics have assumed. Few realized in 1913 that the cultural ferment of the era, described by Anderson as a time in which "something blossomed in Chicago and [in] the Middle West"[1] was just as applicable to the nineteenth century.

The early settlers, like the later ones, rejected those principles that would have made them part of some great system. Instead, they constantly supported the notion of the self-sufficiency of the individual. It was a sense of liberty devoid of philosophical overtones, one that often bordered on license. From the beginning of Chicago's civic life, *freedom* was the city's watchword; and very few failed to answer its call. Among businessmen, this led to the unbridled search for money and new ways to make it; among artists, it was the repudiation of traditional forms, patterns, and structures. The development of the Chicago School of Architecture is a most telling example of this artistic freedom. In conjunction with the needs of businessmen and in response to the limitations of the commercial districts as well as of the land, the architect, in seeking new ways to accommodate both the human and the region, discovered the beauty of skeleton frame construction. At the same time, conditions in the city eventually paved the way for a more vibrant literature that reinterpreted the Midwest and used the region as a symbol for modern America. Thus, the notion of a cultural rebirth, in effect, was an on-going process and was part of an urban community's attempt to define itself.

I

In the late 1830s and into the 1840s, there was an apparent concern in Chicago, at least among some of its citizens, about the image of the city. Unwilling to be considered products of the vulgar pioneer life of the western frontier, many wished to prove their close kinship with older sections of the nation. Embarking upon what Bessie Pierce has called "the quest for the refinements of life,"[2] early Chicagoans were often intent upon demonstrating that cultural activities were not out of place in the Midwest. The resulting "renaissance spirit" took many forms, not the least of which was an interest in literary productions.[3]

Several nineteenth-century groups contributed to Chicago's literary life, including the city's business and social leaders, who had pretensions of culture. Initially, this found expression in organizations patterned after the Young Men's Club of the 1840s. In the days following the Civil War, advocates of the genteel tradition tried to establish "the East" as the role model for the city's cultural life. And, because many of the supporters of the idea were part of the elite, it is often mistakenly thought that this tradition had more influence than it ultimately did. Then came such clubs as the all-male Chicago Literary Club of 1874 or the Fortnightly, its female counterpart, established a few years later. By the end of the century, the elite often came together in various loosely formed groups, of which the Little Room was probably the best known. Although the purposes and rosters of these "literary" organizations reveal that money rather than culture held them together, in their informal meetings and conversations, in their devotion in "the arts," they did not differ greatly from the twentieth-century "renaissance groups" in the city.

Even if one discounts the papers issued by some of these nineteenth-century clubs and assumes that they did not make great literary contributions, one must acknowledge that at least they provided an atmosphere of interest in creativity and authorship. The first tangible evidence of the "new" literature or a "renaissance spirit" appeared in the multitude of nineteenth-century newspapers and magazines devoted to a realistic portrayal of life in the city. Long before Howells became the spokesman for the realistic movement, Chicago editors were enjoining their writers to present the ordinary life of the city faithfully in a language that would appeal to their readers. While a number of sentimental tales were written in keeping with the tastes of the period for the sensational and melodramatic, there were strong manifestations in Wilbur Storey's *The Times*, Horace White's *Tribune*, and later Melville Stone's *Daily News* demonstrating the literary innovations of journalists. (In fact, between the 1860s and the end of the 1920s, the city's press corps was extremely active and made outstanding contributions to the development of modern American literature. In time, it included such writers as George P. Upton, Franc B. Wilkie, Charles Harris, Eugene Field, Finley Peter Dunne, George Ade, Ring Lardner, Ben Hecht, Charles MacArthur, Theodore Dreiser, Carl Sandburg, Floyd Dell, and Sherwood Anderson. A flourishing school of literary criticism was also supported by the "literary pages" associated with the daily newspapers.) In the meantime, the growth of the ethnic press was accompanied by attempts to integrate some Old-World customs into the city's cultural life, despite the hysteria of the native press culminating with the diatribes of *America*. Far more significant were the informal gatherings that centered in the city's bookstores. Perhaps, the best remembered today is the Saints and Sinners Corner (over which Eugene Field presided) at McClurg's Bookstore.

During the last decade of the nineteenth century, there were several attempts to present the city's artistic and cultural life to the rest of the nation. Even the staid *Dial* and the conservative Henry B. Fuller contributed to the uniqueness of literary developments in Chicago. The explanations that followed the World's Columbian Exposition were not as apologetic as those preceding the fair. While William Payne, the city's resident literary critic, had written some long articles that were noticeably dull recitations of what had been published in the city, the exciting "Chicago letters" by Lucy Monroe appeared in the New York-based *The Critic* and ran intermittently from March 18, 1893, to June 27, 1896.[4] Harriet Monroe's sister proved to be an astute observer of the midwestern urban scene. Although Hamlin Garland often was given to excesses, his *Crumbling Idols* (1894) was one of the first theoretical works to recognize the unlimited possibilities of the city in American literature and came in the aftermath of his assertion that the World's Columbian Exposition had ushered in a new age of literary study that would emphasize both realism and regionalism. In fact, enough had transpired in Chicago to make him conclude that the city was destined to become the literary capital of the United States. He became a staunch defender of his idea. Eugene Field and others simply laughed and dismissed such enthusiasm.

But by the time of the World's Columbian Exposition, Chicago had become an artistic and cultural center of some note, one marked by diversity as well as great activity. For example, there was tremendous support within the city for the architectural innovations of men such as Louis Sullivan. The Chicago skyscraper was deemed an objet d'art worthy of consideration. Certainly the architects had proved that a business culture, in response to its needs, could produce its own art despite those, including Fuller, who found the new buildings to be horrendous displays lacking a sense of aesthetics. Many applauded Mrs. Potter Palmer's foresight, as she collected the paintings of French Impressionists long before their importance was established by the so-called knowledgeable, even though some detractors claimed that she was simply gathering "pretty pictures" and had no idea of what she was doing. The worldwide meeting of authors in 1893 provided an adequate forum for the discussion of new directions in literature and showcased literary activities in the city.

In the midst of several debates on such questions that might further define matters of refinement and taste, the city at least emerged as a place congenial to the new and untried. It had made its mark in the evolution of American literature. Journalistic wits, led by Eugene Field and Charles Harris, had become part of the nation's comic tradition. *The Daily News* had proved that newspapers could fulfill their roles as disseminators of news and at the same time make literary contributions. The American novel had been given a different direction in Chicago by the genteel Fuller, the academic Herrick, and the journalistic Dreiser. Floyd Dell, writing in *The Bookman* in 1913, presented several of the earlier novelists in a series entitled "Chicago in Fiction." In his judgment, Fuller, Dreiser, Herrick, and Norris had produced important American novels with the city as the background. Although Fuller was a native Chicagoan, the urban sense was as great, if not greater, in the work of the other writers. Furthermore, William Vaughn Moody had proved that poetry was not to suffer in the city, and Francis Fisher Browne's *Dial* was a journal devoted to literary standards. That it was published in Chicago was not as unusual as some easterners thought. Thus, the literary movement that made Chicago, at least for a moment in the nation's history, a significant locale was as firmly rooted in the nineteenth century as was the myth of the city.

II

For a brief period in the twentieth century, some men and women from small, isolated midwestern towns accidentally came together in Chicago. From Davenport, Iowa, had come Floyd Dell and George Cram Cooke. Ben Hecht was from Racine, Wisconsin, and Edgar Lee Masters hailed from Garnet, Kansas, by way of what Chicagoans call "downstate Illinois." Carl Sandburg was from Galesburg, Illinois, and Sherwood Anderson had arrived once from Clyde and later from Elyria, small Ohio towns. Earlier, Theodore Dreiser had come from Terre Haute, Indiana, and later Margaret Anderson was to arrive from Columbia, Indiana. In another age and in another place, many of these people probably would not have met, but in the early years of the twentieth century they derived strength and inspiration from their associations with each other, which were made more frequent by their sense of community, by their kinship with the city's journalists, and later by the presence of *Poetry: A Magazine of Verse* and the *Little Review*.

They also were held together by their antipathy for their home towns, by their fascination with the possibilities to be found in Chicago, and by the power of their search for elusive truth, which often translated into a selfish commitment to themselves. They refused to accept placidly the nature of Chicago and agreed that the place might be devoted to money-making (certainly its phenomenal growth had been predicated upon this); but, in their desire to live in the city, they were convinced that the place would provide opportunities unavailable "back home." They had been nurtured on the tales of urban success. While they denied money-making as the only goal of life, each pursuing individual goals was motivated by the American Dream unencumbered and unfettered by the limitations of a small town. At the same time, believing fervently in visions of personal triumph, they attempted to rediscover some of the basic verities of human existence. In so doing, they joined those Americans and Europeans, moderns and ancients who have created codes of art based upon the freedom of the individual. They were destined, however, to capture the attention of critics and urban observers from that day to the present. United under the banner of the Chicago Renaissance, the definition of which commonly has been localized in terms of time and place, they have been singled out as forming an identifiable movement in American literature.[5]

Indifferent to traditions and unaware of history, these recently arrived urban dwellers did not realize at the time that their ideas were not as new as some of them thought. They implicitly adopted the Emersonian principle of self-reliance and made "trust thyself" the cornerstone of much of what they said and did. Emerson's further directive, "never imitate," gave them justification for their work. It may be, in retrospect, they misunderstood the nature of the city that with a characteristic lack of concern and enthusiasm for them unconsciously provided the arena for their explorations by offering a challenge for growth as it provided the tensions necessary to make such development possible. They also overestimated their own importance. Even the shock value of free love as a means to signify independence of expression faded quickly in a city willing to accept many variations of standard behavior. Ultimately, they did not in any way alter the pattern of urban life, but they did prove that artists could survive and create in a commercial marketplace. Despite their small-town backgrounds, they helped to promote an urban art that placed Chicago in the center of the nation's cultural universe. Certainly, some of the livelier and more picturesque aspects of the movement were centered in those dilapidated remnants of shops on Fifty-seventh Street left over from the World's Columbian Exposition near the Midway in the shadow of the University of Chicago. Perhaps, it is ironic that here the city's Bohemian life reached a peak before that of New York's Greenwich Village. The various relationships of the group that congregated in this area have been the subject of much speculation, gossip, and interest. Into the separate studios of Margery Currey and her estranged husband, Floyd Dell, came both the major and minor figures of the era.

Initially, Sherwood Anderson was a shy visitor. Older and more experienced in some ways than the Dell circle, he believed himself to be an outsider. Alone among the group, he was not quite as optimistic about Chicago. He had lived in the city on two previous occasions and now realized that he had expected too much from urban life. Yet, as he began to rebuild his life after a series of disillusionments, he discovered that the dreary routine of the advertising business to which he had returned was balanced by his exciting contacts with some of the so-called "renaissance makers." He soon became an active member of the informal group from Fifty-seventh Street, reading his works and listening to the stories and poems of others. His separation from his first wife led to a divorce late in 1915. His marriage the following year to Tennessee Mitchell, a sculptor who also was the high-spirited companion of Edgar Lee Masters, promised a freedom that he had not had. She was a "liberated" woman who would not make demands upon his time and life, or so he thought.

It frequently is difficult to realize that the more well-known "renaissance makers," given the nature of their influence, did not remain in Chicago very long. In fact, by the late 1920s, this most transient immigrant group had departed. Francis Hackett went to New York City in 1911. Dell followed in 1913. The mercurial Margaret Anderson fled briefly to San Francisco in 1916, then escaped cross-country to New York, and finally settled in Paris. Although he remained in Chicago until the early 1920s, even Sherwood Anderson did a great deal of wandering during this period. His daily grind at his advertising job was mitigated by his travels and by his friends, who seemed to understand his disquietude. In 1918, he spent several months in New York, where he joined that city's Bohemian crowd. Even though he was not part of the inner circle of the *Poetry* group in Chicago, in the East he was associated with the advocates of the new poetry and was apparently inspired to write verse. January 1920 found him taking another long trip, this time to Mobile and Fairhope, Alabama, ostensibly in order to recover from influenza; however, his second marriage was irritating, despite its promises of "freedom" and "openness." His job was restrictive and unrewarding. Thus, he took another leave of absence from advertising, as well as a vacation from his wife.

Meeting Gertrude Stein was one of the highlights of his 1921 trip to Europe, an experience that was to have a profound effect upon him. After winning the *Dial* prize of $2000 for fiction, Anderson again took a leave from his advertising job in 1922. This time he went to New Orleans but was forced to return to his Chicago job after a few months of "freedom." Soon, however, he closed his last advertising account and, except for occasional visits, left the city. The same sense of restlessness that had bothered him in Ohio became more evident.

Increasingly, he found Chicago, in spite of the prevailing "renaissance spirit," to be disappointing; and the city served as his base rather than as his home, if the latter term is defined primarily as a place of legal residence.

In many ways, however, Anderson was a "product" of Chicago; and, as he perfected his writing style and began his writing career, his stories, poems, and novels were either conceived or written in Chicago. Even his later journalistic work and last novels often returned to ideas and issues first explored during his Chicago days. One might argue convincingly that the city was his psychological "home" years after his departure. In his *Memoirs*, Anderson admitted:

> [Chicago] remained my city after I had begun to comprehend the distinctiveness of the great city, almost as great as that of individuals, nations, trees, people, hills.
>
> There I saw the first woman who rejected me—felt what men feel when they are so rejected. There I first made ink flow, sang my first song. There after many efforts I wrote a sentence I could bear reading the next day.
>
> There I first heard the sound of men's voices—related to streets, houses, cities—saw my first real actor walk upon a stage, heard music first, saw painting.
>
> When I visit any other great city of the world I am a guest. When I am in Chicago I am at home. It is a little what I am. I am more than a little what Chicago is. No man can escape this city.
>
> I am not proud of it. Chicago will not be proud. But it is a real city—my city. (p. 109)

Without diminishing its significance or minimizing Sherwood Anderson's activities in it, *the* Chicago Renaissance was not an integrated era with a spectacular beginning that is easily dated; neither did it end when a few writers left the city. While they were insisting upon the right to explore life without restraint, seldom did the midwestern villagers who had gathered in the city recognize that the artistic ferment of the age extended beyond their restricted Fifty-seventh Street group. In reality, there were several movements and "cultural centers" that involved the entire city. It is customary to locate the so-called Chicago Renaissance in the early years of the twentieth century, with the assumption that it had ended by the 1920s, after many of its participants and the *Dial* had moved to New York. Furthermore, it generally is interpreted in terms of the Fifty-seventh Street group, perhaps because they were more dazzling in their personal

lives and have repeatedly received more publicity and critical attention as "the renaissance makers." However, it is important to remember that the movement of which they had been a part continued in the
city. Clearly, the Chicago Renaissance was far more fragmented than
most of its twentieth-century participants knew. Fanny Butcher, who
was quite active in several literary circles first as a reviewer for Dell's
Friday Literary Review and ending her career with the *Tribune*, reminded later generations that the "so-called . . . Renaissance" did not
have the "mass psychology of being part of a movement."[6]

After the early 1920s, there remained an active literary group.
Henry Blake Fuller and Harriet Monroe, both of whom began their
work in nineteenth-century Chicago, were, until their deaths, the un-
official leaders about whom gathered many of the city's writers. The
newspapers still attracted outstanding journalists. It may well have
been that the emerging critical establishment was not as colorful as
the men and women who had congregated around Floyd Dell and
Ben Hecht, but they were producing some solid work. *Poetry* and
other journals maintained their importance in the "little magazine"
movement. Moreover, in spite of the death of William Vaughn Moody
and the departure of Robert Herrick, the University of Chicago remained an active literary center.

The twentieth-century cultural ferment in Chicago was citywide,
and the scope of the Renaissance can be expressed, at least in part,
through the sectional landmarks related to it. Located a few blocks
from the Dell-Currey households, the University of Chicago has always been associated with the city's South Side. (Unlike cities that
nominally have a four-part structure, Chicago is divided into three
parts originally designated as the South, West, and North divisions.
These are basically separated by the South and North branches of the
Chicago River. Even the symbol of Chicago, the Y-shaped insignia, is
designed to specify the three divisions or "sides" as are the white bars
of the Chicago flag.) The forerunner of the university had existed near
the lakefront at Thirty-fifth Street on the old Stephen Douglas estate;
and part of the present university had been founded on the outermost limits in Morgan Park at 2204 West 111th Street, in the living
room of the Reverend Justin Smith whose son, Henry Justin, was an
active participant in one phase of the renaissance era.

In the university's formative period, William Rainey Harper, the
great Old Testament scholar, gathered some of the most outstanding,
progressive, and productive thinkers of the nation to be part of the
new institution. The growth and development of the University of

Chicago is one of the city's success stories translated into educational rather than mercantile terms. Businessmen were not far removed from its early life, much to the chagrin of Robert Herrick. John D. Rockefeller, an outstanding Baptist layman, willingly gave money to help bring the dreams of William Rainey Harper to fulfillment and Marshall Field donated some of his valuable South Side land. These three—Harper, Field, and Rockefeller—made the University of Chicago a phenomenon in its early days. Legend has it that eastern scholars considered it the highest honor to have Harper bestow upon them the C.T.C., meaning "Called to Chicago." Thus, when the institution opened on October 1, 1892, a distinguished faculty (rumored to include eight former college presidents as well as practically the entire faculty of Clark University) and a distinguished program combined to suggest that an academic renaissance had indeed taken place in the commercial marketplace of the Middle West. Hence, from the 1890s, the university has played a significant role in the literary life of the city.

In addition to Robert Herrick, Robert Morss Lovett (with whom Sherwood Anderson had a rewarding relationship), William Vaughn Moody, and Percy Boynton in the Department of English, other writers (many of whom had been called to Chicago from Harvard) were associated with the development of a literary awareness in the city. For several years, James Weber Linn was in the English Department. His novel about the university may not rival Herrick's *Chimes* (1926), but *Winds Over the Campus* (1936) certainly captures the spirit of the South Side's intellectual island. And James T. Farrell first began to explore his neighborhood in fiction while a student. When he arrived at the university, Thornton Wilder, in addition to his scheduled work, established a small writing class that included Dorothy Aldis, Marion Strobel (both of whom produced some popular Chicago-based novels), Arthur Meeker, Jr. (whose *Prairie Avenue* and *Chicago, With Love* give first-hand insight into the lives of the city's upper class not frequently on display), Kate Brewer, Fanny Butcher, and David Hamilton. It is probably an interesting footnote to history to recognize that while a select few were seriously studying in "Thornton Wilder's Writing Class," Nelson Algren and, somewhat later, Richard Wright, primarily educated in the streets, also were beginning to explore new approaches to the Chicago novel.

Other South Side locations were important in the development of the city's literary vitality. By this time, there was a strong Negro community in the area with financiers, artists, and the celebrated Olivet

Baptist Church which had been founded in 1850. Eventually, the section was to become important in the literature of Chicago. Ironically, Groveland Park (still standing approximately midway between the University of Chicago and the downtown business district) is very close to the former Stephen Douglas property. Now located near the famed Douglas monument, Groveland Park is a reminder of a day that used to be. Mrs. William Vaughn Moody lived on Ellis Avenue, and her home was as close to an actual literary salon as any that the city has even seen although, to be sure, many women have played hostess to the literati.

Traveling toward the center of the city, as Anderson did almost daily before moving to what is euphemistically called "the near northside," one discovers several public buildings that served as meeting places for the city's artistic community. The Studebaker Block, renamed the Fine Arts Building in 1898, was a creative center. Designed by Solon S. Beman and constructed in 1886 for early entrepreneurs, it achieved a reputation in its own right as the first "art colony" and has served as such since that time. For a number of years, it was the hub of speculative activities in the arts because it was the site of Franklin J. Meine's Chicago Book and Art Auction, which attracted buyers from all over the country. Frank Lloyd Wright, John T. McCutcheon (the *Tribune* cartoonist), and Frank Denslow, whose major claim to popular attention was his illustrations for Frank Baum's *The Wizard of Oz,* had studios on the tenth floor, which had been redesigned with high ceilings and skylights for the convenience of artists.

Other tenants of the Fine Arts Building at various times during this cultural ferment included Anna Morgan and Maurice Browne. The former had a famous studio there. Part of the literary group known as the Little Room, Morgan also produced the first American performances of several works by George Bernard Shaw and Henrik Ibsen. Thus, by the time it became the home of Maurice Browne's Little Theatre, where men and women of the arts were joined by the city's elite for weekly discussions and for previews of the avant garde, drama was no stranger in the Fine Arts Building. From the work of August Strindberg to local playwrights, Browne (aided by Ellen von Volkenburg) showcased them all. Interest in Browne's Little Theatre eventually led to the national movement and gave rise to the more famous Provincetown Players, with Eugene O'Neill practically becoming the resident playwright for that group and the Washington Square Players of New York.

The building housed the editorial offices of a number of journals.

For a brief period *The Saturday Evening Post* was issued from the Fine Arts Building, which also provided space for two other, more influential periodicals. The *Dial* had been founded in 1880 by Francis Fisher Browne, whose beautiful bookstore remained in the building from 1910 to 1913. Frank Lloyd Wright had designed the interior for this famous meeting place that, although a commercial disaster for Browne, undoubtedly was the place where Margaret Anderson, newly arrived in Chicago, heard many literary debates as she worked as one of the store's clerks.

Until his death in 1913, Browne meticulously guided the *Dial*. It avoided any chauvinistic regionalism, until the agitation for the World's Columbian Exposition. When eastern journals began to decry the cultural sterility of the area, the *Dial* became the locale's leading apologist; however, it remained committed to literary standards. This fortnightly, by its very existence, was more persuasive in its contention that "good" literature could emerge out of Chicago than any newspaper diatribe. Because its editors announced on June 20, 1918, that the journal was going to move to New York, the *Dial* is associated with the great cultural exodus from Chicago; however, for a number of years it was an integral part of the city. Writing about the magazine in later years, Nicholas Joost remembered "The *Dial* was not a glittering, and occasionally silly, hodge-podge like the *Little Review* but was a disciplined and ordered artifact." In addition to "self-expression," it was committed "to an articulated consistent point of view about art." In the end "what interested the *Dial* was 'aesthetic perfection,' keeping the eye on the object and letting 'economics and interpretation and analysis go hang.'"[7]

Although the *Little Review* did not remain in the Fine Arts Building for long, it perhaps is of some interest that the journal was based briefly in a structure whose entrance arch declares: "All passes—Art endures." The "occasionally silly, hodge-podge," however, made certain significant contributions not only to the literary life of Chicago but also to American literature. As eccentric as Margaret Anderson might appear to later generations, the *Little Review* took some notable steps toward the development of modernism in world literature by providing an outlet and an audience, limited though it was at times, for the new and untried committed to unadorned honesty. The presentation of sex in literature is no longer shocking, and the publication of a latter-day *Ulysses* would not be a criminal offense. If the Chicago movement did nothing else, it proved that truthful writing and modern life could coexist. To read now the list of contributors is to become aware that many of those credited with innovative approaches to the art of writing were major contributors to and supporters of the *Little Review*. For example, works by the following writers appeared in the magazine between 1914 and 1929: T. S. Eliot, Ezra Pound, William Butler Yeats, James Joyce, Sherwood Anderson, Hart Crane, Ernest Hemingway, William Carlos Williams, Ford Madox Ford, Wyndham Lewis, Marianne Moore, Gertrude Stein, Amy Lowell, Wallace Stevens, Baroness Else von Freitag-Loringhaven, and Maxwell Bodenheim.

Like other editors of little magazines that flourished during the first three decades of the century, Margaret Anderson and Jane Heap talked glibly of *truth in art, aesthetic principles, freedom of expression,* and used such code terms as *new search* and *artistic integrity* without translating abstract concepts into concrete principles. In the final analysis, what was published often was simply a matter of what appealed to them or what seemed to have the greatest shock value. Yet, out of the work of people like Margaret Anderson, there evolved the present-day literary attitudes that do not seem unusual but certainly were hastened by those who dared to defy conventions and rebel against former taboos. Modern literature has become so respectable that even nonreaders can expect to see at least one writer on every television talk show. This appeal to the masses may have obvious negative overtones to some, but in essence this was one of the aims of editors such as Francis Fisher Browne, Harriet Monroe, and Margaret Anderson. Different though many of their activities were, they achieved a unity through their proximity in the Fine Arts Building.

North of this cultural citadel stands Orchestra Hall at 220 South Michigan Avenue. Built in 1905 by the D. H. Burnham Company for Theodore Thomas's musical aggregation and now the home of the Chicago Symphony Orchestra, the structure became part of the literary world by the presence of the Cliff Dwellers Club on its top floor. Founded by Hamlin Garland as a social outlet for those in and sympathetic to the arts, in the rooms of this club, the broken, destitute, and despondent Louis Sullivan, in the weeks before his death, completed his monumental *The Autobiography of an Idea*.

When the Monadnock was erected in 1891 by the firm of Burnham and Root, it was destined to become a significant part of the city's architectural history. Known today as the tallest commercial building with load-bearing walls, the thickness of those walls at the base of the structure has become just as legendary as its dark and foreboding exterior. While it has always been considered primarily as an office complex, it, too, contributed to the literary world of the Midwest. Shortly after its completion, there is evidence to suggest that Fuller had it in mind as "The Clifton" of his *The Cliff-Dwellers;* however, there were enough commercial buildings (called business blocks) in Chicago at this time to suggest that Fuller's structure was a type rather than a specific one. In fact, in Maitland's *Dictionary of American Slang,* issued during the 1890s, a skyscraper is defined as "a very tall building such as now being built in Chicago." In spite of the fame of the city's buildings, many novelists shared Sherwood Anderson's attitude about the "tall, begrimed" structures. Nonetheless, in the 1920s, John Y. Frederick maintained his office in the Monadnock while he edited *The Midland,* which was somewhat more inclusive than many of the city-based journals, because it attempted to publish stories, poems, and essays by midwesterners regardless of their places of residence. In so doing, he made important strides toward nationalizing the provincial nature of some local writers and work. Eventually, he edited *Out of the Midwest.*

Although much of the literary work of the period was centered in the city, Frederick, in the cause of regionalism, attempted to clarify the significance of locale in American writing. Beginning with the obvious premise that "a good regional writer is a good writer who uses regional materials," he defined regionalism as "an incident and condition, not a purpose or motive." He suggested that writers use "the literary substance" of their areas, but he cautioned that the merit of such work should be dependent upon its meeting "the standards of good writing at all times and in all places." He then articulated a major philosophical concept of the use of localisms: "In a country so vast and varied as ours the regional writer gives special service to the nation as a whole by revealing and interpreting the people of his own region to those of other regions. He serves most significantly if he can reveal and interpret the people of his region to themselves."[8] For those who would accuse advocates of Chicago literature of a particular kind of chauvinism, critics such as John Frederick made it clear that regionalism and literary standards were not antithetical.

Several bookstores in the city's downtown area continued to be small independent literary centers, frequented by Sherwood Anderson and others. In addition to McClurg's, at one time considered to have been the largest bookstore in the country, there was the Covici-McGee Bookshop. Like Eugene Field at McClurg's, Ben Hecht presided over the activities of the group that met regularly at the store. Maxwell Bodenheim who, according to Fanny Butcher, was "the original hippie in our town [because] he never bathed and had long unwashed blonde hair"[9] spent much time with Hecht and Pascal Covici. For a while the latter published Hecht's ill-fated *Chicago Literary Times*. Hecht also was a key figure in the group that met in Schlogl's Restaurant, which was west of the downtown area near the Chicago River and the Daily News Building. Others who met there consisted of Henry Sell, the first literary editor of the *News*; Harry Hansen, who succeeded him; the humorist Keith Preston; sports writer Lloyd Lewis; Henry Justin Smith; and Vincent Starrett. Not infrequently they were joined by Carl Sandburg, John Gunther, Burton Rascoe, Lewis Galantière, and Sherwood Anderson.

The cultural life of the North Side of the city was not nearly as localized as that in other sections; however, it also had some important landmarks. For example, between Ontario and Ohio Streets there are still the inconspicuous doorways leading to the Tree Studios. Designed very much like an English courtyard with a fountain and winding walkways in a parklike setting, these buildings were the center for the more avant garde painters and sculptors during the 1920s. While the traditional artists, led by Lorado Taft, met in the Fine Arts Building, the Tree Studios became the headquarters for those who espoused the elimination of juried shows and offered support for cubism and abstractionism in a post-impressionistic age.

Poetry finally established its offices at 232 East Erie Street where, according to Harriet Monroe, the staff played host to local and visiting poets, who used the office as a gathering place. Within a three-year period of its establishment, *Poetry* rocked the traditional poetic world with the publication in 1913 of Vachel Lindsay's "General William Booth Enters into Heaven." During the next year it issued Lindsay's "The Congo" and Carl Sandburg's "Chicago." Then, in 1915, T. S. Eliot's "Love Song of J. Alfred Prufrock" appeared in the magazine. Harriet Monroe lived in the area, at 1310 Astor, in a house designed by John Root, her brother-in-law, whose partnership before his death in 1891 with Daniel Burnham formed one of the important components of the Chicago School of Architecture. In the meantime, close by at 735 Cass Street (but social worlds away) was the boarding house where Sherwood Anderson read *Spoon River Anthology* and completed *Winesburg, Ohio*.

Informal groups gathered in private homes, although few of them reached the status of "salons." With a degree of regularity Ben Hecht (accompanied by his first wife), Lloyd Lewis, Charles MacArthur, and Carl Sandburg met at Fanny Butcher's home. Hecht and

MacArthur were to collaborate on *Front Page*, which seems so representative of an exciting period of journalism. Lloyd Lewis eventually was to become one of the more popular historians of Chicago, Sandburg the poet laureate of Illinois, and Butcher the editor of the *Tribune's* "Book World." Recalling those days, Fanny Butcher later said: "I assure you the talk was never about any potential Chicago Renaissance. . . . We were certainly not crusaders bent on going down in history as members of a movement."[10]

In addition to specific locations in the city that played a role in the literary activities of the day, more organizations devoted to a recognition of the city's writers appeared. In 1915, the Society of Midland Authors was established in Chicago. Its purpose was to bring together midwestern writers in a mutually supportive body. Among the fifty-two charter members (some of whom were closely associated with Sherwood Anderson) were George Ade, Hobart C. Chatfield-Taylor, Clarence Darrow, Edna Ferber, Arthur Davison Ficke, Zona Gale, Hamlin Garland, Vachel Lindsay, John T. McCutcheon, Douglas Malloch (whose didactic poetry inspired a generation of midwesterners), Harriet Monroe, James Whitcomb Riley, and William Allen White. Later Jane Addams, Louis Bromfield, George Barr McCutcheon, Gene Stratton Porter, and Carl Sandburg were associated with the society. The major work was carried, as it is now, by the Chicago members, and the organization made no attempt to screen its members as the great and the not-so-great came together under its loose structure.

Far more discriminating than the Society of Midland Authors in its membership was the Chicago chapter of P.E.N., founded in 1932, which required that each applicant present evidence that at least one "distinguished" work already had been published. Mrs. Butcher credited this club with "the resurgence of interest in reading and writing in our town."[11] Although the group had less than forty members in the 1930s, among them were three Pulitzer Prize winners (Dr. Bernadotte Schmitt, the poet George Dillon, and the novelist Margaret Ayer Barnes), a Pulitzer Prize runner-up (Janet Ayer Fairbanks), and a Nobel Prize winner (Arthur Compton). Others eligible for membership were novelists Mary Hastings Bradley, Edith Franklin Wyatt (who was, according to Howells, "Chicago's Jane Austen"), Marion Strobel, Dorothy Aldis, and Mignon G. Eberhart (who did a great deal to perfect the "Chicago mystery novel"). From the academic world came the famous Dr. Edgar J. Goodspeed, whose translation of the New Testament impressed both biblical scholars and the literati,

Robert Morss Lovett, Percy Boynton, and G. A. Borghese, whose father-in-law was Thomas Mann. Elia Peattie's son, Donald Culross, whose nature studies of the prairie achieved much fame, was active, as were Clara Laughlin (well known writer of travel guides), and journalists Tiffany Blake of the *Tribune* and Paul Scott Mowrer of the *Daily News*.

The later disillusionment of Hamlin Garland and the ambivalence of Sherwood Anderson toward the city's cultural life cannot alter the continued presence of a large group of active artists and writers who remained in Chicago. Having come to terms with the urban milieu, they were able to survive and create. It was a time for versifiers. Robert Morss Lovett observed "poetry was in the air," and the Poetry Club at the University of Chicago "received much attention."[12] In its heyday it included Gladys Campbell, George Dillon who became an editor of *Poetry*, Janet Lewis, Jessica and Sterling North, Elizabeth Madox Roberts, Vincent Sheean, Glenway Wescott, and Yvor Winters, whose correspondence with Sherwood Anderson forms an interesting chapter in the lives of both men. Many of the club's members went on to make distinguished contributions to literary studies. After the death of Harriet Monroe in 1936, Morton D. Zabel (who had been the associate editor since 1929) became the editor of *Poetry*. In the meantime, the newspaper crowd gathered around the popular journalists of the *Tribune* and *Daily News* with the Press Club providing a mutual meeting place for the fourth estate.

During this period, two types of novelists were gaining recognition. In addition to the ever popular crime story set in Chicago, one group emerged from the social elite and seemed to revolve around the Ayer sisters. In 1926 Janet Ayer Fairbanks's *The Smiths* had been the runner-up for the Pulitzer Prize for fiction, and in 1930 Margaret Ayer Barnes won the prize for *Years of Grace*. Both novels focus on the development of Chicago as exhibited through family histories. It was an era of James T. Farrell, Nelson Algren, and Richard Wright. They presented a decidedly different view of the city. Focusing upon single-ethnic neighborhoods, they retold portions of the urban story, not in terms of the business structure and its accompanying social world but through the eyes of the disenchanted and downtrodden.

The Chicago novel, then, as developed by such a varied group as Farrell, Barnes, Fairbanks, Algren, and Wright was to continue as a viable genre into the 1930s and 1940s culminating several decades later in the work of Saul Bellow and Ronald Fair. Yet, during the very period when H. L. Mencken was declaring that Chicago was the literary capital of the United States, the list of writers who had lived briefly in the city and who had escaped from it read like a who's who of modern American literature: Theodore Dreiser, Hamlin Garland, Upton Sinclair, Floyd Dell, Margaret Anderson, Ben Hecht, ad infinitum. That most of them gravitated toward New York is a known fact, but their reasons for leaving the city, which according to Alson J. Smith had "stamped them [and had] brought out the best . . . in them," were complex despite Smith's further assertion that "they were never more creative than when they were working there."

It generally has been assumed that the exodus was a result of New York becoming a publishing center housing the editorial offices of the major companies and literary agents. Furthermore, because of the cluster of writers who lived and worked in it, New York was considered a cultural center. Smith, however, suggested that Chicago was somehow to blame for the departure of those artists "who were set down in the midst of the most cynical and materialistic society on the face of the earth," which he described as "a proudly idolatrous society that bowed openly before the Golden Calf." He acknowledged that "Chicago's tremendous energy, vitality and brutality attracted them and held them for a time, but the city was contemptuously indifferent to them, even to the ones who sang its praises, and that, in the long run, was unforgivable." He claimed the city's indifference forced "the writer in upon himself; his loneliness in the midst of so much bustle begat activity; he wrote and he wrote well, but the city didn't care; only money and power got recognition in Chicago." One may not agree with Smith's contention that the city "made her writers strong by resisting them" or with his assertion that the city made writers wealthy, but his conclusion seems valid: "Chicago had scarred them all, and as time went on they were proud of their scars."[13] For many artists, Chicago came to represent *the* American city; and they used it consistently to symbolize American urbanism.

Isolated though the literary community may have been from the dominant life of the city, there were many contacts between some writers and urban powerbrokers just as in the nineteenth century. Writing about the 1930s, Fanny Butcher observed "a phenomenon happened in Chicago. Literature became fashionable. Hostesses snared visiting literati as dinner table centerpieces."[14] While this had always been a custom in the city, after the World's Columbian Exposition these visitors became increasingly more frequent. Often they lectured to large crowds. Chicago may have become known as "the hog butcher of the world" and "the stacker of wheat," but it also had a large population receptive to the advancement of literary causes.

To read the autobiographies of some of the writers who lived in the city (if only briefly) is to discover the scope of such interests. In addition to Sherwood Anderson's memories of Chicago, others recalled both their involvement in the city's artistic life during this era and of the effects the city had upon them. Despite obvious differences in the poetry of Vachel Lindsay, Edgar Lee Masters, Harriet Monroe, Carl Sandburg, and Eunice Tietjens, these poets saw Chicago not only as historical reality but also insisted that the place held a strange fascination for them. Dreiser and other novelists as well as Floyd Dell, Ben Hecht, Hamlin Garland, Margaret Anderson, and Maurice Browne viewed Chicago as a metaphor that provided an explanation for the values of American civilization. Burton Rascoe, Melville Stone, and Opie Read understood that as journalism moved from the intensely personal to "Big Business," Chicago's writers were redefining the meaning of the urban experience. Even Anna Morgan, Fanny Butcher, and Arthur Meeker, Jr., long-time residents of Chicago, looked objectively, albeit lovingly, at their city and understood the importance of the tensions created by the conflict between the earthly place and the image of an ideal metropolis where pragmatism was an important god. Although the academic Robert Morss Lovett tried to put his life in Chicago within the context of the shifting mission of the nation, Sherwood Anderson could view his experience, at least on some levels, as representative of the "education" gained by an American artist in the city. Thus, it was that Chicago's loosely structured literary community contributed greatly (through individual memoirs) to the portrait of an urban literary center and of a dominant locale that "had scarred them all."

It was not until World War II that a significant phase of Chicago's cultural life ended. The literary trends rooted in the nineteenth century fundamentally came to a close in the 1940s, when the Chicago chapter of P.E.N. became moribund. Although the Press Club continued its activities, the movement in which Sherwood Anderson had participated was over. An appraisal of all facets of the Chicago Renaissance ultimately depends upon whether they are viewed as a single course of ideas and people or a series of continuing and interrelated eras. Rebellion, one of its main characteristics, always has been an important element for the development of literature in the city. Comfortable standards and ideas frequently have been questioned. Chicago's writers have been realistic enough, however, to know that they could not change the city; but, of perhaps greater importance, they have generally insisted that they would not let the city change them. Many fought against any attempts toward conformity as they asserted themselves. If some of them accomplished anything, it was to suggest strongly that even Chicago could provide the setting for imagination, for creativity, and for a new spirituality developed in response to the mechanistic nature of the urban world.

III

In many ways, the early twentieth-century participants in the so-called Chicago Renaissance were removed from the reality of the commercial city; yet, they contributed much to the understanding of the place and to a perception of the increasing urbanization of American literature, while reinforcing the image of Chicago as the center of their initial universe. What some have chosen to call "the revolt from the village" received additional attention as writers once again looked at the existing relationships between the nation's towns and urban centers. Eventually, it became clear that the differences were not nearly as great as geographical distances might have suggested. The pettiness, alienation, and loneliness of the small town also were present in the city. Moreover, urban freedom was neither as appealing nor as free as the legends had claimed, in spite of the emancipated women who seemed to play a greater role in the urban environment.

While the accomplishments of the city's writers may seem minimal to some, their work made it clear to future generations that the place which had generated the collective fortunes of Marshall Field, George M. Pullman, the Armours, and the Swifts also spawned the lonely genius of a Henry Blake Fuller or a Theodore Dreiser, later providing a forum for Carl Sandburg, Vachel Lindsay, Edgar Lee Masters, Margaret Anderson, and Sherwood Anderson. It permitted Floyd Dell and Ben Hecht to establish an audience for their avant garde journalistic endeavors and made possible the survival of Harriet Monroe's *Poetry*. It provided an outlet for James. T. Farrell, Nelson Algren, and Richard Wright as Studs Lonigan, Frankie Machine, and Bigger Thomas became representative of particularized aspects of modern life, not only in Chicago but also in the nation. At the same time, it celebrated the emerging dynasties as portrayed by Janet Fairbanks, Margaret Barnes, and the host of imitators who followed them. Eventually the optimistic vision of the city substantively was replaced by a recognition that many writers, like their characters, had come to Chicago in search of a happiness that remained elusive and unfulfilled. The work of later novelists simply reemphasized much that was already believed about the futility of modern life.

Unfortunately, Sherwood Anderson never wrote a complete history of the so-called Renaissance days, an era about which he was equivocal. Publicly, he supported the tenets of the Renaissance and could optimistically exclaim "what ho! for the new world," but privately he was unsure of its purposes and accomplishments, especially since "the new world" did not last very long. He realized "it was the time of a kind of renaissance in the arts, in literature, a Robin's Egg Renaissance." Admitting that "many of us began [in Chicago], got our early impression of life there, made friends there," he reasoned "had we stayed in the home nest, in Chicago, where it all began for so many of us, the Robin's Egg might have hatched."[15] Later, he questioned its motives as well as its results in his fiction and in his letters. He recognized that there was much cheap talk about life and art and a lack of real camaraderie among intellectuals despite avowals of kinship. All of this puzzled him, and in time he came to see the pretensions of the Renaissance as a logical outgrowth of uncommitted artists trying to survive in a mercantile culture, but, like the others, he was "marked" by the city.

As a product of a small midwestern town, as an associate of the "renaissance makers" of Fifty-seventh Street, and as a resident of Chicago, Anderson had already abandoned his youthful dreams. They had been replaced by an intense need to discover for himself the meaning of life. He realized that he had misplaced his values; that happiness, which he thought would have come from the world of business, was out of reach; and that, measured in the world's terms, success was empty. His rediscovery of himself and his commitment to writing were aided by the Dell group, who also had come to the city in search of the elusive dream of success and stayed long enough to find themselves.

Detached though he was from some of the activities of Fifty-seventh Street, what would his career have been had he not received the encouragement of the participants in the philosophical and artistic dialogue that was destined to change the course of American literature? Not only was Floyd Dell, one of the era's spokesmen, Anderson's first advocate but also the movement's sense of self-consciousness fitted the mood of Sherwood Anderson. His article, "The New Note," appeared in the first issue of the *Little Review.* Although he had nothing "new" to say, the work gave voice to his creed and now serves as a philosophical statement for the entire period.

> In the trade of writing the so-called new note is as old as the world. Simply stated, it is a cry for the reinjection of truth and honesty into the craft; it is an appeal from the standards set up by money-making magazines and book publishers in Europe and America to the older, sweeter standards of the craft itself; it is the voice of the new man, come into a new world, proclaiming his right to speak out of the body and soul of youth, rather than through the bodies and souls of the master craftsmen who are gone.[16]

Sherwood Anderson's first two published novels, although not immediate products of the so-called Renaissance, benefited from the national interest in events occurring in Chicago; however, like the stories produced by most of the city's novelists who preceded Anderson, *Windy McPherson's Son* and *Marching Men*, at least in part, result from submerged authorial anger. The feeling that Chicago controlled the lives of its citizens and made them urban statistics informed much of the work of urban artists. But, in time, writers replaced the sense of helplessness that seemed to grip urban characters with an intense interest in the magnificence of the city's power. In poetry, this was perhaps signaled by Carl Sandburg's celebration to the "hog butcher of the world," notwithstanding the tendency of later writers to return to views of the naturalistic city.

Perhaps as an immediate response to his association with the Fifty-seventh Street group or as a result of his own determination to avoid letting the city restrict his vision, Sherwood Anderson came to accept Chicago on its own terms. From the undercurrents of rebellion against what the city could do to those people not strong enough to counteract its force that mark *Windy McPherson's Son* and *Marching Men*, Sherwood Anderson seemed to adopt a different approach in his next published works. In a measure, this new attitude not only informed his productions but also resulted in a diversified use of genres. Thus, between 1918 and 1920, he would issue a collection of verse, a series of short stories, and a novel. *Mid-American Chants* (1918), *Winesburg, Ohio* (1919), and *Poor White* (1920) exhibit, in varying degrees, the extent to which he was able to use the urban milieu aesthetically despite his personal discomfort in the city. Anderson effected a form of reconciliation with the very place that had served as his antagonistic force.

While *Marching Men* displays his growing interest in language, *Mid-American Chants* illustrates his momentary fascination with poetry and the free verse movement. From a variety of poetic acceptances of the brute force and disorder of an urbanized world celebrated in his "chants" he moved to a consideration of those who might wish to escape *to* the city as well as those who had to flee *from* it. The publication of *Winesburg, Ohio,* in 1919, brought him critical recognition as an important literary voice of the postwar era. By focusing upon the grotesques in a village, the short tales mask their urban origins; yet, in the aftermath of that work he did not find the contentment he so desperately wanted.

Whatever misgivings Anderson may have had later about the directions of the artistic movement with which he is associated, and they apparently were many, he echoed its positive philosophy and the unspoken notion of optimistic Chicagoans in the words that became his epitaph: "Life, not death, is the great adventure." From the time of its founding to the time when Sherwood Anderson decided to leave it, Chicago had undergone a series of rebirths, which had resulted in the adoption of many new directions in American life and culture. The Chicago Renaissance was merely one manifestation of the cultural and creative ferment in the city. One might even conclude it was specifically *"life" in Chicago* that was "the great adventure."

I

Over my city Chicago a singer arises
    to sing,
I greet thee, hoarse and terrible
    singer . . . .

            * * *

In all your cries so little that is
    beautiful,
Only the fact that you have risen out
    of the din and roar to float and
    wait and point the way to song.

          —from "Song to New Song,"
              Mid-American Chants

7

Songs of the City
and Some Rooming
House People

MID-AMERICAN CHANTS, a collection of Anderson's free verse, appeared with little fanfare in 1918. His move toward poetry had been partially foreshadowed by the poetic prose of *Marching Men* as well as by his increasing preoccupation with the lyricism and rhythm of language. In his poetry, Anderson comes to terms with the city unencumbered by the disappointments resulting from the inability to find the "Dream." As in *Marching Men*, he reminds his readers of the juxtaposition of the natural and the superficial. He again suggests that they remember the cornfields back of Chicago. Although this can be dismissed as either sheer romanticism or a covert desire to return to the land, the cornfields also are a means of reaffirming the on-going elements of Life. Expressing the relationship between the naturalness of Nature and the artificiality of the urban, the cornfields of *Marching Men* represent a transitional statement looking toward the positivism of *Mid-American Chants*. At the same time, the poetic persona celebrates the growth, development, and the strength of the urban. Anderson was now beginning to understand, as had Louis Sullivan years before, that in the city's perceived chaos was the possibility of a form of order created by the industrial and the mechanical. "New songs" will come out of the city, the "old songs" are not the only ones that should be heard in the land. In the end, Anderson's affirmation of midwestern life, undoubtedly a partial response to his growing sense of regional loyalty, included an affirmation of Chicago.

His poems were written in New York and Chicago as a response to the freedom of expression so widely touted and practiced by the "renaissance makers" and represent his experimental use of a distinctive idiom. However, his attraction to verse ultimately must be considered within the context of the renewed national and international interest in poetry. Yet, by 1918, much of this initial attention had settled into a series of philosophical and aesthetic confrontations, many of which found a forum in *Poetry: A Magazine of Verse* established in Chicago by Harriet Monroe in 1912. Although she was associated with the genteel tradition, the journal soon became identified with the avant garde in literary circles.

Notwithstanding the appearance of Anderson's "Mid-American Songs" in the September (1917) issue of *Poetry*, Harriet Monroe was apparently unimpressed by his work. The acceptance of it was obviously a result of the enthusiasm of Monroe's confidante, Alice Corbin Henderson, a former associate editor of *Poetry*, whose early work on the journal had been invaluable. Whether one would place Anderson's verse with that of Vachel Lindsay, Edgar Lee Masters, and Carl Sandburg—as did Henderson—is now questionable; however, when *Mid-American Chants* appeared, it was with a figurative seal of approval that came from *Poetry's* publication of some sections of the work just a year earlier.

As might be expected, initial reaction to Anderson's verse was decidedly mixed, ranging from Grace Hazard Conkling's assertion that the poems were "half-utterances"[1] to Alice Corbin Henderson's belief that they represented a new midwestern voice.[2] Thus, Conkling's questioning of the form of the poems, which she called "improvisations on life," was balanced by the energetic praise of Henderson, who used her review to plead the cause of regionalism as she declared that art could be both local and "cosmopolitan." Later, she credited Anderson with being more aware of the necessary discipline needed for poetry than the simplicity of his work might reveal. And she found his desire "to sing" while he was mired in a debilitating industrial culture evidence of his commitment to be a voice not only of humanity in general but also of that humanity specifically in Chicago.

Writing in the *Dial*, Louis Untermeyer was less than optimistic about the possible career of Anderson; he found the poems self-conscious attempts rather than honest expressions of locale.[3] On the other hand, Llewellyn Jones of the *Friday Literary Review* saw in Anderson's poetic efforts the possibility that this "unterrified romanticist" in the future might produce something of merit.[4] Whatever faults were apparent in Anderson's exercises in free verse, *Mid-American Chants* was praised for its faithfulness to the Midwest and thus took its place among the regional works of the period. The obvious similarities between his work and that of better known poets also diminished the acceptance of his attempts to define the Midwest in poetic terms, but the *New York Times Book Review* noted that Anderson introduced a mystical tone into his portrait of the region.[5]

Generally, however, eastern critics were less likely to see much to commend and were more concerned with the lack of mastery of poetic techniques. Yet, William Stanley Braithwaite, who had little sympathy for the Chicago movement in poetry and who found the poems deficient, admitted there was evidence that the poet had some lyrical tendencies.[6] But, it was the absence of "singing" that Thomas Walsh found most disconcerting.[7] On the other hand, in his *Our Poets of Today*, Howard W. Cook cited "Spring Song" as "one of the most admirable poems to come from this writer of the Midwest."[8] He continued by identifying it as a poem of life and affirmation and claimed it superficially had greater structure than most of Anderson's poems.

While they are clearly a response to a particular poetic mood of the era, "the chants" also represent a significant step in the evolution of Anderson's urban vision. The truth of the former has undoubtedly obscured the validity of the latter. Among his published works issued before *Winesburg, Ohio,* his poems mark an important turning point in his career and have historic value as they signal the end of his apprenticeship and speculative period in the city. It is clear that his trip to New York and life there in 1918, at the height of both midwestern and eastern interest in poetry, convinced him that the West needed increased and fuller poetic explanations. Furthermore, by the completion of *Marching Men* his interest in language usage was as great as his proclivity for the telling of a tale. What could language do, or at least what could he do with it became a central aesthetic question for him.

Part of his answer came in *Mid-American Chants*. The businessmen who believe in the formula of success and the dreamers who reject the commercial life were no longer central to Anderson's personae. Accepting the inevitability of the power of industrialism without condoning the invidious aspects of the materialistic world, Anderson turned his attention to the power of the Midwest and to its potentialities. While the autobiographical element is as strong as in his first two published novels, he was now able to transcend the mere inclusion of specific events and begin to integrate these into moods and impressions.

The poems, many of which lack the polish of even mediocre verse, are not spectacular; indeed on one level they seem to be pitiful imitations of the combined Whitman-Sandburg approach to poetic diction and rhythm. "Song to New Song," for example, is reminiscent of Whitman's "Song of Myself" in such obvious ways that to survey them would be to belabor the apparent. Sandburg's *Chicago Poems* as well as his interest in the folk of the region already had provided evidence of the vast possibilities of a poetic rendering of the Midwest. In portions of *Marching Men* Anderson had explored and juxtaposed—albeit briefly—the chaos of the city with the order of the cornfields. In so doing, he created some memorable lines of poetic prose. As a transition and bridge to his later work, his poetry indicates that he was beginning to accept the creative force of the city in spite of its limitation. Thus, he could join in the celebration of the city as a symbolic statement of the effects of industrialization and urbanization in America. This was an important concession if not for his work at least for his life. Furthermore, the verses, which combine the excesses of his understanding of lyricism with his tendency toward the realistic tradition, represent the beginning of an increasingly important literary freedom for him.

That he could remember "west of Chicago the endless cornfields" are waiting is an acceptance of *what is* rather than a rejection of *what never was*. This was to take several directions before the end of his life. The negativism of *Windy McPherson's Son* and *Marching Men* is missing from *Mid-American Chants*, as are the more pronounced naturalistic elements that intrude into the novels written from the vantage point of the disillusioned outsider unable to make his peace with the city and what it represented. Now Anderson realizes that the city will not change, but he proudly proclaims man's capacity for good and a need to recognize the city on its own terms. Big, dirty, sprawling, and chaotic though Chicago may be, Anderson is willing to reaffirm the importance of life and to suggest that the individual can have a strength independent of the environment. In "Song of Industrial America," Anderson observes:

> You know my city—Chicago triumphant—factories and
> marts and the roar of machines—horrible, terrible, ugly
> and brutal.

It crushed things down and down. Nobody wanted to hurt.
  They didn't want to hurt me or you. They were caught
  themselves. I know the old men here—millionaires. . . .

Then he raises the question:

Can a singer arise and sing in this smoke and grime? Can
  he keep his throat clear? Can his courage survive?

After several exploratory lines, the answer is presented:

We have to sing, you see, here in the darkness. All men
  have to sing—poor broken things. We have to sing here
  in the darkness in the roaring floor. We have to find
  each other. Have you courage tonight for a song? Lift
  your voices. Come.[9]

As in "Song of the Soul of Chicago," he turned once again to the
image of the bridge (one aspect of the city's landscape that never
ceased to fascinate him) in "Song of Industrial America" and offered
another reaffirmation of his faith in the individual with his acceptance
of the inevitability of the urban.

They tell themselves so many little lies, my beloved. Now
  wait, little one—we can't sing. We are standing in a
  crowd by a bridge, in the West. Here the voices—
  turn around—let's go home—I am tired. They tell
  themselves so many little lies.

You remember in the night we arose. We were young.
  There was smoke in the passage and you laughed. Was
  it good—that black smoke? Look away to the streams
  and the lake. We're alive. See my hand—how it
  trembles on the rail.

*   *   *

You watch my hand on the rail of this bridge. I press
  down. The blood goes down—there. That steadies me—
  it makes me all right.

*   *   *

First there are the broken things—myself and the others.
  I don't mind that—I'm gone—shot to pieces. I'm part

of the scheme—I'm the broken end of a song myself.
We are all that, here in the West, here in Chicago.
Tongues clatter against teeth. There's nothing but shrill
screams and a rattle. that had to be—it's part of the
scheme. (p. 15)

Many of the poems in *Mid-American Chants* emphasize the greatness of the prairie as well as the presence of the indestructible cornfields. They employ images from love, war, and death. But central to
life is the beauty and power of the western lands. When he turned his
attention specifically to Chicago, the poems, following the thematic
pattern of "Song of Industrial America," reflect the ambiguity of the
city itself rather than the unity or harmony of the prairie. Love–hate,
strength–weakness, light–dark, greatness–insignificance are a few of
the ambivalent qualities that exist. In "Chicago," the basic tensions
caused by these dichotomies become the basis for the opening of the
poet's chant.

I am mature, a man child in America, in the West, in the great
        valley of the Mississippi. My head arises above the cornfields.
        I stand up among the new corn.
I am a child, a confused child in a confused world. There are no
        clothes made that fit me. The minds of men cannot clothe me.
        Great projects arise within me. I have a brain and it is cunning
        and shrewd.

Despite the uncertainties of life, the poem's persona is convinced
"songs shall arise in my throat and hurt me." Although it is clearly
possible to read the poem as an autobiographical statement or as a
plea for the freedom of the artist within the urban milieu, it also is
possible to view the speaker as the personified city that recognizes its
limitations. "Chicago" continues:

I am a little thing, a tiny little thing on the vast prairies.
        I know nothing. My mouth is dirty. I cannot tell what
        I want. My feet are sunk in the black swamp land, but
        I am a lover. I love life. In the end, love shall save me. (p. 13)

In "Song of the Soul of Chicago," the ambiguities of the former
poem are replaced by the boldness and pride that many have come to
associate with Chicago literature. Using the city's bridges as his cen-

tral symbol, Sherwood Anderson moves from the divided city to the dynamism of life itself.

> On the bridges, on the bridges—swooping and rising, whirl-
> ing and circling—back to the bridges, always the bridges.
> I'll talk forever—I'm damned if I'll sing. Don't you see
> that mine is not a singing people? We're just a lot of
> muddy things caught up by the stream. You can't fool
> us. Don't we know ourselves?
> Here we are, out here in Chicago. You think we're not
> humble? You're a liar. We are like the sewerage of our
> town, swept up by a kind of mechanical triumph
> —that's what we are.
> On the bridges, on the bridges—wagons and motors, horses
> and men—not flying, just tearing along and swearing.
> By God we'll love each other or die trying. We'll get to
> understanding too. In some grim way our own song shall
> work through.
> We'll stay down in the muddy depths of our stream—we
> will. There can't any poet come out here and sit on the
> shaky rail of our ugly bridges and sing us into paradise.
> We're finding out—that's what I want to say. We'll get
> at our own thing out here or die for it. We're going
> down, numberless thousands of us, into ugly oblivion.
> We know that.
> But say, bards, you keep off our bridges. Keep out of our
> dreams, dreamers. We want to give this democracy thing
> they talk so big about a whirl. We want to see if we
> are any good out here, we Americans from all hell.
> That's what we want. (pp. 62–63)

Throughout his career, first as a copywriter then as a teller of tales, Sherwood Anderson exhibited an apprehension about the inability of human beings to communicate. This concern often appeared in his preoccupation with the limitations of language and the inadequacy of words. To say that love might be a viable substitute for human interaction perhaps is too vague to be meaningful; but increasingly, he associated lack of communication with the urban environment that heightened rather than lessened the problem. One can argue convincingly that the small-town isolato is no better off in Anderson's canon; but the city with its crowds and activity traditionally seems a less likely place for such isolation. Yet, the poet is aware that part of the inability to communicate is caused by the hostility of the urban setting. It is not, therefore, unusual that *Mid-American Chants* begins with the lines:

> I am pregnant with song. My body aches but do not betray
>   me. I will sing songs and hide them away. I will tear
>   them into bits and throw them in the street. The streets
>   of my city are full of dark holes. I will hide my songs
>   in the holes of the streets.

Somewhat later he observes:

> In the cities my people had gathered. They had become
>   dizzy with words. Words had choked them. They
>   could not breathe. (p. 11)

Rather than an escape to a more congenial atmosphere, the poet remains an urban persona though "in the woven cloth that covered my body the dust of my city had lodged." Whatever fears may exist eventually are alleviated through the writing process. The second verse paragraph of "Song of Theodore" notes:

> . . . What cunning fingers I have. They
>   make intricate designs on the white paper. See, the de-
>   signs are words and sentences. I am not a priest but a
>   lover, a new kind of lover, one who is of the flesh and
>   not of the flesh. They are like me and I would make love
>   always, to all
>   people—men and women—here—in Chicago—in America
>   —everywhere—always—forever—while my life lasts.

Then Anderson says:

> There is a song in the pencil that is held in my cunning
>   fingers. Out—out—out—dear words. The words have
>   saved me. There is rhythm in the pencil. It sings and
>   swings. It sings a great song. It is singing the song of
>   my life. It is bringing life into me, into my close place.

And the poem ends with the repetition of an earlier statement that reasserts not only the shrewdness and ingenuity of the urban writer but also the sense of freedom that comes with the ability for self-expression, an idea constantly repeated through the volume.

> What cunning fingers I have. They make intricate designs
>   on white paper. My cunning fingers are of flesh.
>   They are like me and I would make love always—to all
>   people—men and women—here—in Chicago—in America
>   —everywhere—always—forever—while my life lasts.
>   (pp. 25–28 *passim*)

Whether specifically stated or merely implied, central to *Mid-American Chants* and the development of Anderson's urban vision is his conviction that "over my city Chicago a singer arises to sing." The ability to *sing* is made more significant because "you and I have risen out of the din and roar to . . . point the way to song." But of still greater importance is the observation in "Song to New Song":

> Back of your grim city, singer, the long flat fields.
> Corn that stands up in orderly rows, full of purpose.
> As you float and wait, uttering your hoarse cries
> I see new beauties in the standing corn,
> And dream of singers yet to come,
> When you and your rude kind, choked by the fury of your
>   furnaces,
> Have fallen dead upon this coal heap here. (p. 47)

Ultimately, knowledge of the city can be more inclusive if one can realize the greatness of what lies beyond. And, in "Evening Song," Anderson celebrates that place.

> Back of Chicago the open fields—were you ever there?
> Trains coming toward you out of the West—
> Streaks of light on the long grey plains—many a song—
> Aching to sing.

Recognizing the central position of the city as a transportation transfer point, the poetic persona, with "a grey and ragged brother in [his] breast," has an urge "to sing."

> Trains going from you into the West—
> Clouds of dust on the long grey plains.

Long trains go West, too—in the silence
Always the song—(p. 81)

The forty-nine poems that constitute *Mid-American Chants* show the extent to which Anderson had been influenced by the spirit of literary experimentation that prevailed during this period in Chicago. These poems are clearly explorations into the possibilities of the diction of the midwestern oral tradition for artistic purposes. Perhaps his chants are not as polished as Vachel Lindsay's nor as filled with various theatrical effects, but the drama of them is rooted in a profound sense of place. The major ideas of the collection are conveyed through impressionistic images expressed in the vernacular of the people. The long explanations in his earlier works have been replaced by short phrases designed to evoke particular moods rather than transmit specific messages.

Like the other "renaissance makers," Anderson now saw the beauty of the city's brute force, and the disorder of the city that had concerned him in *Marching Men* was recognized as a new order whose significance was related directly to an understanding and acceptance of it. As if in answer to his own question, Anderson affirmed that "a singer" could "arise and sing in this smoke and grime" although in his Foreword he said:

I do not believe that we people of mid-western America, immersed as we are in affairs, hurried and harried through life by the terrible engine—industrialism—have come to the time of song. To me it seems that song belongs with and has its birth in the memory of older things than we know. In the beaten paths of life, when many generations of men have walked the streets of a city or wandered at night in the hills of an old land, the singer arises. (p. 7)

He was voicing the same reservations that have been repeated time and time again about the very nature of American writing. Those interested in the rise of a national literature immediately after the Revolutionary War lamented the lack of a sense of historic continuity and the absence of traditions that, in the views of many, were absolutely essential to the aesthetics and production of a distinctive culture. Throughout the nineteenth century various writers made attempts to recapture a *usable past* that would lend an aura of distance to their work. But underlying much of what was produced was the unspoken question finally posited by Sydney Smith: "Who reads an American book?" His query became the raison d'être of untold defenses of our national literature. During the latter part of the nineteenth century and well into the twentieth, many midwestern writers had the same feeling of inadequacy when they thought of their literature pitted against that of the eastern seaboard and of the great traditions of Europe. Those critics who overlooked the significance of the region expected midwestern literature to reproduce the concerns and interests of the East.

As if to excuse the shortcomings of his own verse, Anderson ended his Foreword with the request that "this book of chants . . . be allowed to stand stark against the background of my own place and generation." Then he offered further explanation: "Honest Americans will not demand beauty that is not yet native to our cities and fields. In secret a million men and women are trying, as I have tried here, to express the hunger within and I have dared to put these chants forth only because I hope and believe they may find an answering and clearer call in the hearts of other Mid-Americans" (p. 8). While his later use of the small town is not to be ignored, his first collection of verse made it clear that the geography of the Midwest included not only the villages and countryside but also its cities.

In a period rich with poetic experimentation and filled with free verse offerings, *Mid-American Chants* both delights and confuses some readers. Perhaps because *Winesburg, Ohio* appeared so shortly after the collection of verse, Anderson's poetry was overlooked in the burst of enthusiasm for his short stories. It was difficult for many to see the verse as a logical outgrowth of the lyrical passages that occurred with amazing frequency in *Marching Men* or to view his poetry as a transition leading to his acclaimed work. Furthermore, by 1918, naturalists had convinced readers that, in the conflict between urban industrialism and mankind, the material or the machine would win. *Mid-American Chants* offers another answer and suggests that love does not have to disappear; indeed love is the humanizing force in an otherwise depersonalized existence. And, if *Marching Men* is a denial of the life of the soul, *Mid-American Chants* is a positive confirmation of life in the midst of the industrialized, the ugly, the urban, and the terrible. Out of the grimness of life, it is possible to capture the beauty of such enduring elements as love; hence, when he chants, "over my city Chicago a singer arises to sing," Anderson celebrates the creative factor in humanity that ultimately can and will transcend the reality of a particular moment.

From the standpoint of his later career, the affirmation of *Mid-American Chants* seems central to his philosophy, just as the lyricism of the collection became an integral part of his prose technique. Whereas it may be too much to claim that the breakdown in the naturalistic mode was his doing (especially in view of the continued work of Dreiser, Farrell, and eventually Wright), certainly he offered, perhaps unknowingly at first, another answer to modern life in Chicago. With the appearance of *Winesburg, Ohio* in 1919, the year after the collection of poems, Sherwood Anderson was praised for his ability to capture the emptiness of small-town life. Overshadowed was his role in giving renewed literary vitality to the urban mecca of the Midwest.

His return to free verse in a second volume of poetry was unfortunate. Whatever promise Anderson may have shown in *Mid-American Chants* as a practitioner of the "new techniques" is lost in *A New Testament* (1927). The work is so self-conscious that despite any merit that it might exhibit, John Farrar's assertion that it represents "fragments of [a] distilled ego"[10] is painfully true. On the other hand, Clifton Fadiman's dismissal of the work as an "absurd collection of Zarathustrian aphorisms"[11] is unduly harsh. Read within the context of biblical literature, *A New Testament* dispenses the good news of the rediscovered truths that had become important to Anderson and makes an attempt to synthesize his philosophy into a poetic manifesto. His letters during the era show how much he thought of his "testaments." Hamish Miles[12] and Herbert Seligman[13] were among those who found *A New Testament* less than impressive; yet, neither considered the work within the framework of Anderson's career. Miles simply thought that the absence of an identifiable dogma weakened the verse; but he did not recognize that this very lack reechoed the formlessness of modern life Anderson found so disconcerting.

In the midst of the discordant elements, there is a clear rejection of the urban and an embracing of the rural as a significant step not only in the rediscovery of self but also in the redefinition of the American experience.

> I am one who has walked out of a tall building into the streets of a city and over plains into a forest that fringes a river. My notion is one of escape . . .[14]

Escape alone, however, could not bring satisfaction; but his psychological acceptance of himself brought a sense of peace.

I have remade the land of my fathers,
I have come out of my house to remake the land. (p. 39)

Reexamining part of the message of *Marching Men*, Anderson now seemed more convinced than ever that organized protest was not a viable answer for the demands of the city. He agreed that sucess or failure was more dependent upon the individual who had the stamina to reject those values symbolized by the city than upon some abstract urban force that was substantially larger than life. In a measure, then, ten years after he had begun his exploration into America's urban power, he declared his personal independence from it in *A New Testament*. If *Mid-American Chants* represented an acceptance of the chaotic nature of life, his later volume of poetry refocused Anderson's attention upon the enduring values of human existence, which were so apparent to him as a country editor in Virginia.

Contrary to the beliefs of some friends, his career was not over, but it had changed. What is of paramount importance is his return to the use of a poetic diction associated with the Midwest. He had strayed from that language usage in *Many Marriages* and *Horses and Men*, his two major works of 1923, which focus upon the despair of modern life and the inability of the human to assert itself in the midst of the material. At times however, the optimistic nature of *A New Testament* is overwhelming; and Seligman admitted that the Whitmanesque quality and biblical cadence of the work was a portent of what could have been accomplished by a better artist but lamented that Anderson had simply produced some "dreamlike avowals in psalmodic."

Few read the work as a psychological declaration of independence. Although he occasionally returned to literary uses of the city after 1927, he became more detached. Chicago might be a reality of history or representative of the direction of American civilization or even symbolic of a powerful force; however, Anderson was convinced that its awesome qualities could be challenged by the human spirit. But, before *A New Testament*, Chicago was to figure in his work, tangentially at times to be sure. Eventually, his recollections of the city were not only modified by time and distance but were conditioned by

the contentment that came from life at Ripshin, a life so far removed
from the turbulence of the Middle Border's central metropolis that, by
the time of his incomplete notes for his *Memoirs*, he truly could view
the urban as if through a glass darkly. But through all of his avowals
of being "a country man," at a given moment he was indeed a man of
the city.

II

I remember with what shock I heard people say that . . . *Winesburg,
Ohio* was an exact picture of Ohio life. The book was written in a
crowded tenement district of Chicago. The hint for almost every
character was taken from my fellow-lodgers in a large rooming
house, many of whom had never lived in a village.

—*Sherwood Anderson's Notebook*

The idea I had was to take them, just as they were, as I felt them,
and transfer them from the city rooming house to an imagined
small town.

—*Memoirs*

The undistinguished rooming house at 735 Cass Street (two
blocks from the *Poetry* offices) long since has been destroyed to make
way for a parking lot (one of the traditional signs of "urban progress"). In the early years of the twentieth century, it was a rather typical building, no better or worse than most buildings in that section of
the city. Like so many others to be found on Chicago's North Side, it
was a result of the changing times. Briefly, in the post-Fire era, Cass
Street was one of the residential areas for the wealthy. When they
moved farther north and closer to the lake, the elite left their former
mansions to enterprising real estate agents who saw the advantages
of converting these dwellings into boarding houses of varying degrees
of respectability. Eventually, many of Chicago's renowned "kitchen-
ettes" were located in houses intended for the rich and famous. If, in
the annals of our literature, Americans were in the habit of venerating
literary shrines, Anderson's Cass Street address might have assumed
some momentary significance, because he wrote some of the tales
destined to change the nature of modern literature while living there.
But his greatest acclaim was to come long after his Cass Street days.

Winesburg, Ohio has generated much critical commentary. Since
its appearance in 1919, seldom has a year passed without additional

interpretations of the work or some part of it. Undoubtedly, the continued interest is a measure of the book's importance. At the time of its publication, there was a general feeling that he had done something unique with the genre that had been the forte of such diverse writers as Poe, Hawthorne, and Harte; but there also was some concern about the perceived "ugliness," "obscenity," and "gutter level" of the stories.[15] Yet, his presentation of the small town has fascinated critics from the work's publication to the present,[16] although it was initially plagued by critical associations with other regional works, primarily Edgar Lee Masters' *Spoon River Anthology* and Sinclair Lewis's *Main Street*.[17]

It is generally assumed that *Winesburg, Ohio*, following in the tradition of Edward Eggleston's *The Hoosier Schoolmaster* and Edgar W. Howe's *Story of a Country Town*, not only presents a portrait of those tortured souls condemned to life in a small midwestern village but also includes a benediction for an era of American civilization celebrated in pastoral literature. That people in Clyde, Ohio, felt a sense of embarrassment for a number of years because they thought Anderson had deliberately paraded his home town before the world may have been as much a result of civic egomania as an expression of the terrible sameness of the Midwest. In capturing the spirit of Winesburg, Anderson caught the psychological and historic towns of Mid America at the moment when the growing urban areas seemed to offer a respite and panacea for those human beings caught in the trap of village life. Certainly, his later development of Bidwell in *Poor White* is a clear testimony to his understanding of town life and characters. In fact, in some ways, Winesburg and Bidwell are similar, although Anderson moved from internalizing the effects of Winesburg to observing the external qualities of Bidwell. The latter community is essentially a civic grotesque, but the human grotesques are as prominent as in Winesburg.

Because it is so often associated with the nation's fading small towns, *Winesburg, Ohio*'s display of urban elements has been overlooked and totally neglected. Furthermore, the concern with trying to determine the effect of generalized urban factors, which reached a fulfillment in *Poor White*, actually is apparent in his earlier work. Anderson was unconvinced that the boarding-house figures, who were unrealized in the city, would have been less lonely if they had been placed in a small town. In fact, both the city and the town suffer from false illusions and faulty interpretations. Viewed as a place of freedom, in reality, the city became for too many a place of broken dreams, misplaced truths, deadly illusions, and physical as well as spiritual slavery.

The revolt-from-the-village movement had rejected towns as representative of a sense of community and togetherness, rather they were assumed to be places of as much sham and isolation as urban areas. The sense of loneliness and despair, the inability to communicate, and the absence of meaningful relationships are human and spiritual problems that have never been completely conditioned by place. If one ignores the significance of physical setting or its reality, the life of the mind or spirit ultimately can become the real world, especially when it is caught in that single moment of illumination that leads to some form of self-revelation. Perhaps, what makes the inhabitants of Winesburg particularly pathetic is the pervasiveness of their discontent, the sources of which are unidentified. Those in the village want to go to the city. Many of those in the city want to get back to Winesburg. And, happiness eludes them all.

Of the twenty-one tales in *Winesburg, Ohio,* sixteen make some reference to urban life. With the exception of New York, Anderson uses midwestern cities: Cleveland, Dayton, Cincinnati, and Chicago. Generally the city is used in traditional ways. For example, there is the expected assertion that life in the city is a means by which people might improve their lots. Elizabeth Willard, as a young girl, continually had asked traveling salesmen "to tell her of life in the cities out of which they had come."[18] And when her son suggests that he would like to get away, she raises a question with him: "You will go to the city and make money, eh? It will be better for you, you think, to be a business man, to be brisk and smart and alive?" (p. 36) Although her life holds little promise, Elizabeth Willard feels there are opportunities in the city. To rise in the world means to move to the city, where success is possible. Her son shares her optimism; and after Elizabeth's death, George Willard declares that he will "go to some city" in search of "a job on some newspaper" (p. 282). Even though he is only eighteen years old, he is beginning to feel very sophisticated as he determines to seek his fortune in the city as have many before him.

Tom Little, the train conductor from Winesburg, "had seen a thousand George Willards go out of their towns to the city." George, on the other hand, "going out of his town to meet the adventure of life, began to think but he did not think of anything very big or dramatic." His father, however, has warned him about the possible evil of the city and has offered words of advice: "Be a sharp one . . . keep your eyes on your money. Be awake. . . . Don't let anyone think you're a greenhorn" (p. 302).

If, to George Willard, the city offers the possibility of success, to others it offers much-desired anonymity. When he is leaving Winesburg in order to go to Cleveland, Ned Currie hopes "to get a place on a city newspaper and rise in the world." His sixteen-year-old girl-friend, Alice Hindman, wants to go with him, not to get married but to work so that the two of them can be together. Stressing the possibility of anonymity in the urban environment, she says: "In the city we will be unknown and people will pay no attention to us" (p. 124). Ned does not keep his promise to return "as soon as I get a good job." In fact, he does not get a "place on a Cleveland paper and [goes] west to Chicago" instead. At first he writes to Alice, "then he was caught up by the life of the city" with new friends and interests. Long after it is apparent that she will never go to the city, Alice, a pathetic victim of a broken dream, continues to save to "follow her love to the city" (p. 126). In the meantime, she believes "in the city where [Ned] is living men are perpetually young. There is so much going on that they do not have time to grow old" (p. 130).

Both Seth Richmond and Elmer Cowley, who do not "fit" in Winesburg, also view the possibility of life in the city. Cowley, looking forward to getting out of Winesburg, knows that a local freight train bound for Cleveland passes through the town at midnight. "He would steal a ride . . . and when he got to Cleveland would lose himself in the crowds there. He would get work in some shop and become friends with the other workmen and would be indistinguishable. Then he could talk and laugh. He would no longer be queer and would make friends. Life would begin to have warmth and meaning for him as it had for others" (pp. 241–42). Once again the promise of the city to provide work and companionship is balanced by the discovery that there is a lack of friendship and communication. If the last two qualities represent the reality of the city they also symbolize the reality of Winesburg.

That the city is a place of mystery and violent crime is suggested by the vague reference to the famous Dr. Cronin murder case of 1889 which often is used to illustrate the laxity of Chicago's judicial system.[19] Anderson's allusion to the case is a brief aside, but it does raise a question about Dr. Parcival who has come to Winesburg from Chicago and who refers to the murdered Dr. Cronin. Is it possible that he

was part of the unidentified mob? Although he has a great deal of
money and clearly has ability, he has few patients. Such characters as
Dr. Parcival use Winesburg as a haven from the complexity of urban
life or as a refuge from justice.

Then there is "the son of a rich merchant of Cleveland" who jour-
neys to Winesburg "on a mission . . . to cure himself of the habit of
drink and [who thinks] by escaping from his city associates and living
in a rural community he would have a better chance in the struggle
with the appetite that was destroying him" (pp. 166–67). He is not
successful because the dullness of Winesburg simply makes him
drink more. Tom Foster and his grandmother, both of whom understand the limitations of city life as well as its ugliness, move to Winesburg in order to escape from urban problems. They have led a hard
life, often without the basic necessities for survival. Even the gentle
Tom has had to resort to stealing $1.75 from the harness shop where
he worked in order to get food for his ill grandmother. "Urban opportunity" comes when she finds a purse containing $37.00. The two of
them leave the city that night, fearing if they wait until morning, the
owner of the pocketbook might appear. The move does not change
Tom appreciably. "As in the city in the houses of prostitution and
with the rowdy boys running through the streets at night, so in
Winesburg among its citizens he had always the power to be part of
and yet distinctly apart from the life about him" (p. 259).

Enoch Robinson returns to live out his days in Winesburg because his friends and associates in the city do not understand the importance of his imaginary people. He has been "a city man for fifteen
years. . . . In New York City, when he first went there to live and before he became confused and disconcerted by the facts of life, [he]
went about a good deal with young men" (p. 198). He had been
twenty-one when he first went to the city. Like others, he had a
dream that remained unfulfilled. "He studied French and went to art
school, hoping to develop a faculty he had for drawing. In his own
mind he planned to go to Paris and to finish his art education among
the masters there, but that never turned out" (p. 197). In his Washington Square area, there is a great deal of talk about art and life but little
communication, as was true during the so-called Chicago Renaissance. The silence of Enoch eventually gives way to his created internal world. His marriage and his job as a commercial artist for an advertising agency prove unrewarding. He is consumed increasingly by
loneliness. The pace of urban life does not allow for the internal world

of the spirit, and Enoch, unlike the later Bruce Dudley, realizes this too late; hence, his return to Winesburg is marked by a sense of defeat.

Jesse Bentley is "in the city" when he is forced to return to Winesburg to take care of the family farm after his father is incapacitated. But, if they expect an idyllic interlude, readers are disappointed. As a partial explanation for Bentley, Anderson theorizes: Jesse "had grown into maturity in the years after the Civil War and he, like all men of his time, had been touched by the deep influences that were at work in the country during those years when modern industrialism was being born" (p. 79). His "mind was fixed upon the things read in newspapers and magazines, on fortunes to be made almost without effort by shrewd men who bought and sold" (p. 81). While it is true that industrialism, immigration, and mass transportation as well as the news media changed irrevocably the small towns of the nation, Anderson, at this point in his career, does not seem totally committed to the notion that *what was* has to be better than *what is*. And Bentley, despite his new life in Winesburg, is well aware of the city habit of mind.

To many of Anderson's characters, the small town is a sanctuary after their unsuccessful attempts to live in the city. Whatever promise the city might have suggested to Elizabeth Willard and subsequently to her son is not substantiated by those of Winesburg who have been to various metropolitan areas. Of course, there are the thwarted lives of those who suffer perpetual disappointments in life; but one of the possible positive notes to come from these warped souls is presented in Anderson's comparative analogy between the good apples that have been "shipped to the cities where they will be eaten in apartments that are filled with books, magazines, furniture, and people" and those "gnarled apples that the pickers have rejected." Although the "round perfect fruit [is] eaten in . . . city apartments," those distorted apples that are not shipped are in reality much better. "One nibbles at them and they are delicious. Into a little round place at the side of the apple has been gathered all of its sweetness. One runs from tree to tree over the frosted ground picking the gnarled, twisted apples and filling his pocket with them. Only the few know the sweetness of the twisted apples" (pp. 19–20).

A growing sense of the standardization of life does not allow for deviation in things or people. There is a mind set that makes a Helen White feel "that the months she had spent in the city . . . had changed her profoundly" (p. 289) or influenced her visiting instructor who had "been raised in an Ohio town . . . to put on the airs of the city [because] he wanted to appear cosmopolitan" (pp. 292–93). Even Rev. Mr. Curtis Hartman, as he is being tempted by worldly thoughts, begins to think he might leave the ministry and "go to some city and get into business" (p. 180). For him, going into business is equated with giving himself to sin, although it might provide respite from the perceived demands of life in Winesburg.

Anderson explains that "in the last fifty years a vast change has taken place in the lives of our people." The "revolution" is described as

> the coming of industrialism, attended by all the roar and rattle of af-
> fairs, the shrill cries of millions of new voices that have come among
> us from overseas, the going and coming of trains, the growth of
> cities, the building of the interurban car lines that weave in and out
> of towns and past farmhouses, and now in these later days the com-
> ing of the automobiles has worked a tremendous change in the lives
> and in the habits of thought of our people of Mid-America.

Writers, Anderson continues, must share part of the responsibility for these changes. Although one cannot measure the vicarious effects of reading materials,

> books, badly imagined and written though they may be in the hurry
> of our times, are in every household, magazines circulate by the mil-
> lions of copies, newspapers are everywhere. In our day a farmer
> standing by the stove in his village has his mind filled to overflowing
> with the words of other men. The newspapers and the magazines
> have pumped him full. Much of the old brutal ignorance that had in
> it also a kind of beautiful childlike innocence is gone forever.

But it is important to remember "the farmer by the stove is brother to the men of the cities, and if you listen you will find him talking as glibly and as senselessly as the best city man of us all." The recording of this historic moment of change is not necessarily a nostalgic plea for the past. In fact, Anderson hastens to remind the reader that be-fore industrialism came into being with its labor-saving devices "men labored too hard and were too tired to read" (pp. 65–66).

Much of the critical emphasis of *Winesburg, Ohio* has focused upon the reality of the place within the parameters of the revolt-from-the-village movement or upon the isolation of those who live in small towns struggling to deal with their hopes and fears. Often they have had either disappointing urban experiences or dreams of the city predicated upon false hopes. Whatever the promises of an urban area, Anderson clearly established that the city also often was a place of loneliness, where the lack of human companionship and the absence of meaningful communication haunted its residents. Furthermore, its treadmill work promised much but offered little to the vast majority of people. Unfortunately, residents of Winesburg do not realize that modern life in their town does not differ substantially from life in the city. Only George Willard, "going out of his town to meet the adventure of life," understands that life in Winesburg "had become but a background on which to paint the dreams of his manhood" (pp. 302–303).

The effectiveness of *Winesburg, Ohio* is in part a result of the unity of its locale. The village, filled with lonely people disappointed in their ambitions, seems to offer a judgment on the nature of human existence. At the same time, the stories are just as much a part of Chicago as of Winesburg. Because they have become so committed to the theory of Anderson as the voice of the small town, many critics willingly discount Anderson's own view of his work. Yet, before he was victimized by critical opinions, Anderson made several cogent observations about *Winesburg, Ohio*. Speaking of the composition of his tales in the isolation of the Cass Street boarding house, Anderson later recalled their creation:

> It was as though I had little or nothing to do with the writing. It was as though the people of that house, all of them wanting so much, none of them really equipped to wrestle with life as it was, had, in this off way, used me as an instrument. They had got, I felt, through me, their stories told, and not in their own persons, but, in a much more real and satisfying way, through the lives of these queer small town people of the book.[20]

And in a letter to John Hall Wheelock of Charles Scribner's Sons, he was to claim, "when I wrote *Winesburg*, I had no social theories about the small town."[21]

By 1919 and the publication of *Winesburg, Ohio*, Anderson's all-inclusive view of urban life had taken shape. As he boards the train, George Willard is simply one more product of the magnetic pull of the city. At that moment of departure, he shares with Sam McPherson and Beaut McGregor the mythic dream of the city as a place of freedom, growth, and success. While the Midwest and its primary metropolis are historical entities with clearly defined geographical borders, they also are psychological and symbolic points of reference. What George Willard will find in the city, as Sam and Beaut as well as those who were not successful were to learn, will depend as much upon his own inner drive as upon a chaotic and disordered city that will do little to foster human endeavors. But whether George succeeds or fails, his story, like those of the thousands who made the same journey, also will be a partial chronicle of American civilization.

Irving Howe has raised an interesting question about Anderson's relationship to Chicago. He tries to assess the actual significance of "Anderson's dramatic exposure [during the] 1913–15 [period] to the Chicago literary world," and observes: "From Anderson's Elyria work to the achievement that is *Winesburg* there is so abrupt a creative ascent that one wonders what elements in his Chicago experience, whether in reading or personal relations might have served to release his talents." Howe attributes the city's "literary milieu" with convincing "Anderson that American writers need an indigenous style which, if only they were bold enough, they could then and there construct; it taught him that before language could be used creatively it might have to be crumbled into particles; and it made him conscious of the need for literary consciousness."[22]

While he certainly makes some valid points, even Howe did not recognize the importance Sherwood Anderson was to assume in the evolution of both a distinctive style in the Midwest and an acceptance of the notion that the human could coexist with the urban, thereby minimizing the naturalistic pull of the city. The earliest novelists already had discovered that the city needed a new language to express itself adequately. They received much of their inspiration from the city's journalists; and many of these storytellers, as well as the poets, had been so indoctrinated by the perceived linguistic standards of more established literatures that they were not always able to execute the need for a new language. The success of Anderson in this regard suggests that his role as a transitional writer within the sphere of Chicago literature included more than an approach to subject matter. His use of language permitted him also to move beyond photographic portraits of the reality of the city and begin the impressionistic details that were to become outstanding characteristics of urban literature.

Yet, before any of this evolved, he specifically had examined the actuality of the American city through Chicago in *Windy McPherson's Son* and *Marching Men*, explored the contrasting moods of the urban and the cornfields back of the city in *Mid-American Chants*, and suggested that a group of city dwellers could be presented through the town of Winesburg.

To an observing person . . . Bidwell
. . . might have seemed no longer a
quiet town filled with people who
lived quiet lives and thought quiet
thoughts, but a tiny section of some
giant modern city. . . . The thing that
was happening in Bidwell happened
in towns all over the Middle West. . . .

—*Poor White*

8

Out of a Town,
a City

T o view *Poor White* (1920) as a product of Anderson's interest in urbanism might appear, at least to some critics, to be a violation of interpretive license or an unconvincing theory. Certainly, when one speaks of an "urban" or "city novel," the implication clearly is suggested that the work deals with a well-defined locale. Cities that are merely *in the process of becoming* are seldom included under this literary rubric. While it records the dissolution of a small town, *Poor White* addresses the issue of urban development and is the narrative of those historic moments of flux. The novel focuses upon the changes that occur through the metamorphosis of a town by examining the effects of phenomenal growth on both the people and the place.

On one level, *Poor White* is the story of an aspect of Clyde, Ohio, thinly disguised as Bidwell. Using practically the same language as the novel, Anderson recalled the advent of industrialism in his home town when he wrote his *Memoirs*.[1] Accepting the novel as "Anderson's experience with the industrial revolution in Clyde," William Sutton indicated the novelist's brief stint as a worker in the local bicycle factory "started a train of reflection and investigation which was to last all his life." Certainly, there is no question that Anderson was indeed "particularly interested in the reaction of the factory worker to work in the factory";[2] however, *Poor White* goes beyond this limited view and explores the spirit as well as the actuality of industrialism. Urban history reveals that the nation has had many "boom towns," which literally exploded into existence. Chicago, for example, grew from a small town in an out-of-the-way location to a metropolis within a few years and became a popular illustration of what unbridled growth could do. As a result, the chronicle of Bidwell is not an isolated tale but is the story of the early days of a Chicago or any other prosperous city whose rise was accompanied by rapid expansion. Whether such communities fulfill their expected potential depends upon numerous factors, many of which are considerably different from those that occur in cities marked by gradual evolution.

Moving from the exactness of Chicago that prevailed in *Windy McPherson's Son* and *Marching Men*, Anderson told the general story of both the *how* and the *why* of certain American cities in *Poor White*. Although he had admitted earlier in his career that the American city existed as a powerful force in human life and provided the background for the realization of the American Dream, he now committed himself to a reexamination of this force. By the time of *Poor White's* action, Anderson tells the readers of his novel that "the huge commercial city at the foot of Lake Michigan, because of its commanding position in the very center of a vast farming empire, had already become gigantic . . . [with] thousands of people rushing about like disturbed insects . . . a whirling churning mass of humanity."[3]

Using what he saw as the pitfalls of thoughtless expansion to mirror what occurred in his fictional town of Bidwell and contemplating the relationships among technological advances, so-called modern business techniques, and human beings led Anderson to study the significance of the interaction among place, people, and events to suggest the association between material success and spiritual failure. Thus, *Poor White*, as a metaphoric statement, explains the development of the many cities whose phenomenal growth, like that of Chicago, was a marvel not only in the Midwest but also in the United States. Eventually, Anderson understood the universality of *Poor White* and remarked that it "has since become a sort of document of . . . change. It is used by a good many historians to give present day students a sense of the so-called 'industrial revolution,' brought down into a single American town."[4]

The novel, set in the Midwest, transcends region and is a pivotal work that summarizes and synthesizes the urban novel up to its time. Voicing a major premise of those novelists who insisted upon the importance of place, Anderson claimed "what happened" to the town was "more . . . important than what happened to the people."[5] Undoubtedly David Anderson was correct in taking issue with the illogical and simplistic notion that Bidwell is "really the hero" of the novel. He argued that it "is not the biography of a town" but rather "the biography of the people in the town whose lives have been warped by industrialism and its concomitant, greed." Yet, to assert the novelist's statement "must not be taken literally [because] he knew that he must focus on individuals"[6] is to minimize Sherwood Anderson's purpose and to miss a major point of *Poor White*. Of course, the novel has to have characters who act and interact; but in the final analysis, the work, which uses stock figures to transmit the narrative, records the death of the old order and the birth and life of the new in Bidwell. That the novelist's interpretation of the town's existence is conditioned by his view of the effects of industrialism is made clear by the characters chosen as examples of the town's growth and dubious progress.

As it catalogues the many social problems and economic issues that have interested modern novelists of American culture, the novel captures the American city in the process of becoming a chaotic place inhabited by strivers and dreamers, who have replaced the art and poetry of living with the spirit of acquisition. The working out of Anderson's views in this manner apparently was not as deliberate as they now appear but represented the creative use of his own evolving thoughts on the subject of urban life. In a single work, however, he included all of the themes generally associated with urbanization. *Poor White* aids in explaining the inevitability of the growing spirit of isolation that is so characteristic of modern life, at least in Anderson's view. As a result of his explorations, he became one of the few urban novelists to concern himself with that shadowy and seldom-defined period in the evolution of the modern American city by recording the changes within a community as it moves through unprecedented growth toward becoming a metropolitan center.

Consequently, the effectiveness of *Poor White*, one of his most provocative works, essentially lies in the drama of that moment of metastasis. And the reader legitimately can conclude that as the many Bidwells of the nation pass through such transitional periods, there will be a multitude of industrial cities from coast to coast. Therefore, Chicago, the mighty city victimized by mercantilism, and Bidwell, a town being swiftly transformed, simply are symptomatic of the pattern of urban American civilization. To condemn or praise what occurred is to ignore the central issue of the effects of the cataclysmic changes upon humanity. Even though ugliness, disorder, and chaos cannot be stopped by railing against conditions, Anderson seems to suggest there is a need to recognize the types of human alienation that can result from the rapid growth of cities.

Those who dealt with the city in fiction prior to Anderson were convinced that only strong men, titans who unconsciously exemplified the Darwinian principle of survival, understood urban power. Anderson, on the other hand, portrays the creators of the city simply as small, ordinary men and women, caught in the flow of life, who unwittingly make Judge Horace Hanby's prophecy of a "new war" come true. Unlike the Civil War, the new conflict will be bloodless. "At first it's going to be a war between individuals to see to what class a man must belong; then it is going to be a long, silent war between classes, between those who have and those who can't get. It'll be the worst war of all." Hanby reminds those gathered about him: "In eastern towns the change has already come. Factories are being built and every one is going to work in [them]. . . . Some of the men stand at one bench and do one thing not only for hours but for days and years" (pp. 51–52). It is such monotony that comes to signify Anderson's city just as it minimizes the human role.

|

Lest readers assume that *Poor White* is merely a plea for a return to the picture-postcard towns of the past, before the action of his novel begins, Anderson presents a tale of two villages. One certainly is not idyllic. Called Mudcat Landing, it is a poverty-stricken place where "the soil . . . was tilled . . . by a race of long gaunt men who seemed as exhausted and no-account as the land on which they lived." It is a place without hope and without dreams. Those who live there are "chronically discouraged" as are "the merchants and artisans." The "credit system" allows residents to get service and materials for which they must pay later. "Only the town's two saloons prospered [because their] . . . keepers sold their wares for cash and, as the men of the town and the farmers who drove into town felt that without drink life was unbearable, cash always could be found for the purpose of getting drunk" (p. 3).

Anderson's subsequent explanation for Mudcat Landing does little to mitigate the circumstances of the town although it offers one interesting aspect of the novelist's view of American history. Most of the people, he claims, are "of Southern origin." Then, in a long passage, he explains the effects of life in an area that had been dependent upon slave labor. But instead of describing the wealthy land owners, he focuses on the heirs of those who, "having no money to buy slaves of their own and being unwilling to compete with slave labor, had tried to live without labor." As a result, their "children grew up long and gaunt and yellow like badly nourished plants. Vague indefinite hungers took hold of them and they gave themselves over to dreams." Anderson continues: "The more energetic among them, sensing dimly the unfairness of their position in life, became vicious and dangerous. Feuds started among them and they killed each other to express their hatred of life." Moving North during the antebellum years, they were to influence their new homes. "In Southern Indiana and Illinois they were merged into the life about them and with the infusion of new blood they a little awoke. They have tempered the quality of the peoples of those regions, made them perhaps less harshly energetic than their forefathers, the pioneers " (pp. 18–19).

Anderson's interest in the Mudcat Landings of the nation modifies any notion of a romanticized view of American villages. On the surface it appears that the novelist is saddened by the loss of those values and ideals frequently related to the countryside as the later urbanization of Bidwell seems to destroy goodness and truth. But the loss is not merely one which can be reduced to the either/or of the country versus the city argument. There is nothing pleasing about Mudcat Landing, which has not as yet come into contact with urban forces.

Meanwhile, when Anderson introduces Bidwell, the reader recognizes the place has a surreal quality and seems suspended in time. Clearly, a more successful town than Mudcat Landing, it is on two railroad lines with a group of picturesque people. The surface idyllic life of the village includes descriptions of berry-picking season with happy folk riding in wagons and others contentedly lounging near the general store. The evenings are given to young lovers who stroll about the peaceful town. But significantly this portrait, which seems to be a prose rendition of a Norman Rockwell painting, is qualified by Anderson's observation:

> In all the towns of mid-western America it was a time of waiting. The country having been cleared and the Indians driven away into a vast distant place spoken of vaguely as the West, the Civil War having been fought and won, and there being no great national problems that touched closely their lives, the minds of men were turned in upon themselves.

The apparent contentment of a contented people is in the process
of being destroyed through a breakdown of previously accepted
ideas. In the town, Anderson notes:

> The soul and its destiny was spoken of openly on the streets. Robert
> Ingersoll came to Bidwell to speak in Terry's Hall, and after he had
> gone the question of the divinity of Christ for months occupied the
> minds of the citizens. The ministers preached sermons on the sub-
> ject and in the evening it was talked about in the stores. Every one
> had something to say. Even Charley Mook, who dug ditches, who
> stuttered so that not a half dozen people in town could understand
> him, expressed his opinion. (p. 46)

In setting forth the nature of Bidwell, Anderson (once again before the opening action of the novel) makes it clear that the town, unlike Mudcat Landing, is ready to respond to the growth of the new
order. Because they are to figure so prominently in the transformation
of the village, the novelist describes prevailing conditions in detail.
First of all, Anderson claims that the new way of life "met a need that
was universal. It was meant to seal men together, to wipe out national
lines, . . . to change the entire face of the world in which men lived."
Personifying the controlling force of the new order, he continues:

> Already the giant that was to be king in the place of old kings was
> calling his servants and his armies to serve him. He used the meth-
> ods of old kings and promised his followers booty and gain. Every-
> where he went unchallenged, surveying the land, raising a new
> class of men to positions of power. Railroads had already been
> pushed out across the plains; great coal fields from which was to be
> taken food to warm the blood in the body of the giant were being
> opened up; iron fields were being discovered; the roar and clatter of
> the breathing of the terrible new thing, half hideous, half beautiful
> in its possibilities, that was for so long to drown the voices and con-
> fuse the thinking of men, was heard not only in the towns but even
> in lonely farm houses, where its willing servants, the newspapers
> and magazines, had begun to circulate in ever increasing numbers.

Not only is expansion related to the new order but also the famous
entrepreneurs are products of it.

> At the town of Gibonsville, near Bidwell, Ohio, . . . oil and gas fields
> were discovered. At Cleveland, a precise, definite-minded man
> named Rockefeller bought and sold oil. From the first he served the

new thing well and he soon found others to serve with him. The
Morgans, Fricks, Goulds, Carnegies, Vanderbilts, servants of the new
king, princes of the new faith, merchants all, a new kind of rulers of
men, defied the world-old law of class that puts the merchant below
the craftsman, and added to the confusion of men by taking on the
air of creators. They were merchants glorifed and dealt in giant
things, in the lives of men and in mines, forests, oil and gas fields,
factories, and railroads.

Somewhere along the way, the good intentions of the builders
were forgotten in an attempt to satisfy human greed. The poetry of
life was rejected as people heard that loud cry of the new age. Thus
Anderson concludes his long analysis:

> And all over the country, in the towns, the farm houses, and the
> growing cities of the new country, people stirred and awakened.
> Thought and poetry died or passed as a heritage to feeble fawning
> men who also became servants of the new order. Serious young men
> in Bidwell and in other American towns, whose fathers had walked
> together on moonlight nights . . . to talk of God, went away to tech-
> nical schools. Their fathers had walked and talked and thoughts had
> grown up in them. The impulse had reached back to their father's
> fathers on moonlit roads of England, Germany, Ireland, France, and
> Italy, and back of these to the moonlit hills of Judea where shep-
> herds talked and serious young men, John and Matthew and Jesus,
> caught the drift of the talk and made poetry of it; but the serious-
> minded sons of these men in the new land were swept away from
> thinking and dreaming. From all sides the voice of the new age that
> was to do definite things shouted at them. Eagerly they took up the
> cry and ran with it. Millions of voices arose. The clamor became
> terrible, and confused the minds of all men. In making way for
> the newer, broader brotherhood into which men are some day to
> emerge, in extending the invisible roofs of the towns and the cities to
> cover the world, men cut and crushed their way through the bodies
> of men. (pp. 63–64)

In *Poor White*, the lessons of the new age and the nation are localized. And, lest one think such philosophical musings must be related
to heroic figures, through a portrait gallery of selected townspeople
who often meet at Birdie Spinks's drugstore (a gathering place for the
young and old), Sherwood Anderson makes certain that readers
understand the ordinary nature of the people of Bidwell. Many of
them are stereotypes to be sure, but their symbolic relationships to

the process of change aid in marking the shifts that occur as a city evolves from a town; hence, to isolate them from their meanings is to lose the basic power of the novel.

The characters, some of whom later play important roles in the novel, are a diverse and seemingly insignificant lot. Furthermore, in sentence sketches or by identifying people through their functions in the community, Anderson gives the reader a sense of the complacent nature of Bidwell. Allie Mulberry, the town's dimwit, has great artistic ability and is far more important than his intellectual development would suggest. Peter White, the tailor, has a talkative wife who is the bane of his existence. Ezra French is a tyrant who bullies his family. Jane Orange, widow of a wealthy landowner who was suspected of being less than honest in his dealings with others, is a petty thief and is caught (much to the delight of the townspeople) stealing eggs from the grocery store. Thomas Butterworth, a wealthy farmer, has a daughter, Clara, one of Anderson's liberated women. Her vague personal search for identity eventually leads her to marry Hugh McVey. Abraham Hunter, the jeweler, is a small-town businessman; but his son, Steve, perceives the great possibilities of the changing times. In varying degrees, so do the other young men of Bidwell.

For many readers, Joseph Wainsworth, harness maker and "a tradesman of the old school" (p. 53), is the most pathetic figure in the novel as he tries to instill his love of craftsmanship in his apprentice, Will Sellinger. For those who insist the major theme of the novel is concerned with the waning days of the artisans who have been victimized by a mechanized world, Wainsworth is the prime example of the individual producer lost in an industrial society predicated upon mass production. One sees the futility of his attempt to hold on to the old ways of doing things because a "new force that was being born into American life and into life everywhere all over the world was feeding on the old dying individualistic life. The new force stirred and aroused the people" (p. 62). But, given the nature of the character, the question arises: Would he have been able to survive in a world of the creative craftsmen?

Then there is Judge Horace Hanby, who recently has moved to Bidwell after his stint as "a carpet-bag Governor of a southern state in the reconstruction days after the Civil War and [who] had made some money" (p. 50). He is perceptive enough to understand the course of the development of American culture. After recounting the price that people in England and in the East have paid for the inevitable introduction of industrialism, he suggests "the thing is to get educated . . .

to get ready for what's coming. It's the only way. The younger generation has got to be sharper and shrewder" (p. 52). But he concludes
that freedom will be replaced by the enslavement of mankind by and
to the machine. The prophetic talk of Judge Hanby influences some of
the young men.

II

Hugh McVey, who connects Mudcat Landing and Bidwell, is nominally the protagonist of the novel. Born in the former town and forced
to scrounge for an existence by the shiftlessness of his father, the
motherless Hugh is saved from his father's fate when he is fourteen
years old. Henry and Sarah Shepard, the town's stationmaster and his
wife, take him in. Working in the railroad station brings a new way of
life to the young boy who has never been to school. Mrs. Shepard, a
firm believer in the American Dream, is convinced that the day will
come when her husband will be promoted to some higher position.
Not only does she read of success stories but also sees on occasion "of-
ficials of the railroad . . . [who pass] through the town riding private
cars hitched to the end of one of the through trains" (p. 15). She accepts
without question her repeated directive to her husband and to Hugh:
"Do little things well and big opportunities are bound to come"
(p. 16). For five years, she indeed is a "shepherd" who tries to "civi-
lize" and educate Hugh while awaiting her husband's "big chance."
Such an opportunity never arrives. Without comment, Anderson
simply records the fact. It is the reader who, in time, will probably
view Henry and Sarah Shepard as further statistical evidence of the
ineffectiveness of the American Dream itself.

After the Shepards leave Mudcat Landing, Hugh becomes the
stationmaster and tries to fulfill his mentor's admonition to "do everything neatly and carefully" in order to "show [himself] worthy of the
trust that [had] been given [to him]" (p. 15). But a year later, after the
death of his estranged father in a drunken brawl, Hugh decides to
move on because he has not been comfortable in the town. In a reversal of the "go-West-young-man-go-West" theory, Anderson observes
that Hugh, who is now twenty years old, understands "in a general
way that to reach the land and the people who were to show him by
their lives the better way to form his own life, he must go east" (p. 22).

At one point in his travels, Hugh "passed through the city of Chicago and spent two hours there, going in and out at the same railroad

station." The experience is the basis for some speculation, and "he never forgot the two hours . . . spent standing in the station in the heart of the city and walking in the street adjoining the station." Despite Chicago's legendary magnetism, "he was not tempted to become a city man" (p. 30). The chaos of the city differs markedly from the imagined peace of the prairie. Once in Chicago's terminal, Hugh is appalled by the unruly crowds and realizes there is no way to relate to these animal-like people. The characteristic urban hustle, accepted by most city dwellers as inevitable, frightens Hugh; but he ventures out to get "to the bridge to look at the river that flowed past the station." Instead of seeing a beautiful restful scene, he discovers a dirty river "narrow and filled with ships. . . . A pall of black smoke covered the sky." The noise is intrusive. "From all sides of him and even in the air above his head a great clatter of bells and whistles went on" (p. 31).

Hugh wanders from town to town "always seeking the place where happiness was to come to him and where he was to achieve companionship with men and women" (p. 32). This vague search for meaningful human relations was to be a goal of so many of Anderson's characters, both in his novels and short tales, but in a measure, Hugh's quest seems more pitiful than that of other Anderson figures. After three years of a nomadic life, in which he exists by doing odd jobs, Hugh, the silent migrant worker whose presence in various communities always puzzles townspeople without creating any real interest in him, settles in Bidwell, the small agricultural town like so many others on the Middle Border. Without realizing conditions in the place or the nature of the people who are in a state of expectancy, Hugh McVey—the tall, taciturn, lonely, twenty-three-year-old man—begins life in the town as the telegraph operator at the railroad station. Wanting to fill the empty hours of his life and remembering Mrs. Shepard's advice, he occupies his spare time with various mechanical experiments. This eventually leads to his developing some labor-saving devices for the farmers.

As an inventor, Hugh, who initially does not recognize the full impact of his experiments, is the catalyst that assures the shift of the sleepy town to a booming urban center. By being instrumental in bringing drastic changes to Bidwell, Hugh personifies the inevitability of industrialism with its attendant sense of dehumanization. Implicitly supporting the efficacy of modern technology, he thinks that his devices will give men and women more time for life and love. Because he is detached from the life of Bidwell, the townspeople assume that he is the emissary of an unidentified great force, rather than a lonely man who simply is trying to spend his leisure time wisely. The men of Bidwell who have been listening to Judge Hanby and who wish to imitate "the progress" being made elsewhere quickly seize the opportunity to organize themselves around the possible success of McVey's inventions. Hugh, on the other hand, mistakes their interest as he provides the machines designed "to industrialize" Bidwell. Instead, he has merely provided an outlet for human greed and the further enslavement of many. For each person swept into his projects, the reward is a great sense of alienation.

As he records the changes that occur in Bidwell, Sherwood Anderson makes several cogent observations. Significantly, the first attempts to render Hugh's design into a functioning model are done by Allie Mulberry, who impresses both the townspeople and visitors with his ability to whittle and carve realistic objects although his exercises with wood have produced essentially useless things. Inarticulate though he is, he understands what Hugh is trying to do and, on one occasion "when a part Hugh had fashioned would not work, the half-wit himself made the model of a part that worked perfectly. When Hugh incorporated it in the machine, [Allie] was so happy that he could not sit still, and walked up and down cooing with delight (p. 116).

Central to Anderson's analysis of the phenomenal development of Bidwell is the attempt to discover the nature of progress through the visible effects upon both the people and the region. Ben Peeler, the carpenter, is a practical prototype of success in Bidwell. He becomes a nervous entrepreneur involved in not only building but also in other, related activities. He used to work alone, happy in his craft and willing to help neighbors, now he employs "four gangs of six men each and had a foreman to watch the work and keep it moving." In the meantime, "his son, who in other times would also have been a carpenter, had become a salesman [who] wore fancy vests and lived in Chicago" (p. 204). Gordon Hart, a former bank cashier, joined Peeler. Together, they had formed Peeler and Hart with such an interest in lumber that they virtually controlled building construction in Bidwell.

Steven Hunter, the shrewdest of them all, decides to take Judge Hanby's advice. Caught up in the talk of "change" and "progress," he goes East to business school. Upon his return to Bidwell and after hearing tales about the activities of Hugh McVey, he gambles on the unknown inarticulate stranger about whom legends had developed.

"Steve [who] had in him the making of a live man of affairs . . . was impressed by the notion, then abroad in Bidwell, that Hugh had been sent to town by some one, perhaps a group of capitalists who intended to start factories there" (pp. 74–75).

Anderson, however, reminds the readers that "Steve had not been highly regarded in his home town." There was nothing in his early life that would have marked him for success except that as the owner of the first bicycle in town, he had always been a showoff. Now he decides "to become a manufacturer, the first one in Bidwell, to make himself a leader in the new movement that was sweeping over the country" (p. 86). In order to fulfill his plans, he gambles on the greed of such local businessmen as John Clark (the banker) and Tom Butterworth (wealthy farmer); he is not disappointed. After an interview in which Steve alludes to powers not yet his, he makes the older men believe in him. "Steve knew instinctively how to handle business men. One simply created the notion of money to be made without effort. He had done that to the two men in the bank and it had worked. After all he had succeeded in making them respect him. He had handled the situation. He wasn't such a fool at that kind of thing" (p. 94).

When success does come, as a result of his business liaison with Steve Hunter, Tom Butterworth, as struck by greed as the others in the town, assumes the role of Bidwell's aristocrat. His daughter listens to his "boast[ing] of his new position in the town." He has become more arrogant and unfeeling, and "like Steve Hunter he was beginning to grow fat" (p. 196). Although he sees himself as a power broker, Tom is perceptive enough to realize the great potential of Bidwell as he predicts "the town is going to be a city now and a mighty big city" (p. 350). Whatever the faults of Steve and Tom, Anderson recognizes that these "were solid business men, mentors of the new age, the kind of men who, in the future of America and perhaps of the whole world, were to be the makers of governments, the molders of public opinion, the owners of the press, the publishers of books, buyers of pictures, and in the goodness of their hearts, the feeders of an occasional starving and improvident poet, lost on other roads" (pp. 180–81).

Representing the old way of life, the harness-maker initially draws the reader's sympathy especially when he is harassed by his swaggering employee, Jim Gibson,[7] who not only laughs after forcing the old man to buy factory-made products but boasts about his power over his employer to the townspeople. "Some day you come in the shop casual-like and I'll boss him around for you. I'm telling you I don't know how it is that it came about, but I'm the boss of the shop as sure as the devil" (p. 213). In a strange reversal of roles, the laborer has become boss, and the owner is simply a pawn in the hands of his employee. Just as for Clara "the harness maker had come to stand for all the men and women in the world who were in secret revolt against the absorption of the age in the machine and its products" (p. 354), so Wainsworth evokes a certain air of pathos. Clara seems perceptive in accepting him "as a protesting figure against what her father had become and what she thought her husband had become" (p. 355).

Effectively recounting the changes taking place, Anderson lets readers view the people of Bidwell through the eyes of Tom Butterworth's daughter, who returns to town after an absence of three years. Clara sees "almost every man and woman in town had become something different in his nature from the man or woman bearing the same name she had known in her girlhood" (p. 203). Yet, when the harness-maker goes beserk toward the end of the novel, she understands that his attempt to hold to a dead past has gone beyond the realm of reason. But she also knows that men like Steve Hunter, Ezra French, or her father really were no better before the coming of industrialism; their present negative features simply are extensions of their former miserable selves. Unlike Fuller and Herrick, who insisted in the conflict between the old and the new ways of life that the former was good and the latter might be inevitable but evil, Sherwood Anderson offers no such clear-cut answer, and he dismisses violence as an instrument of change.

Even the inarticulate, simple Hugh is affected by the events around him. Partially in response to Judge Hanby and partially in response to his own interest in mechanical problems, Hugh "put himself into touch with the spirit of the age." Yet, "unlike [the other young men of Bidwell] he did not dream of suddenly acquired wealth" (p. 68). But his success story is spread by Steve Hunter, the principal beneficiary of Hugh's inventive genius. When a journalist arrives in Bidwell to write about Hugh, he discovers that the inventor is not inclined to talk. Steve, however, has no such trepidations. Talking to the reporter "for an hour," Steve creates a mythical Hugh. In the end, "the story made Hugh a strikingly romantic figure." Later "the advertising manager of the corn-cutter factory" designs a brochure with Hugh perched on top of a "mountain" of corn and with the created biography that had appeared in the newspaper (pp. 228–29). And so it is that Hugh is subjected to the advertising techniques of modern journalism.

Although Hugh's machine indeed does relieve farm workers,

Hugh soon becomes unnecessarily defensive and, like other entrepreneurs of his age, comes to the conclusion that all of his actions have been justified. "He spoke of the swift growth that had come to the town of Bidwell as though it were an unmixed blessing, the factories, the homes of happy, contented people, the coming of industrial development as something akin to a visit of the gods. Rising to the height of egotism he shouted, 'I have done it. I have done it.'" Anderson observes that Hugh, "having awakened to his own importance in the life about him, . . . wanted direct, human appreciation" (p. 257). In the wake of the changes in Bidwell and a doubtful urban progress, Hugh can convince himself: "What I have done here amounts to something." As he looks at the evidences of growth surrounding him, he does "not see the disorder or the ugliness of the buildings, [but] [t]he sight that lay before him strengthened his waning vanity" (p. 262). At the same time, he begins to realize that all is not well in the paradise he has created.

In the meantime, the homogeneous population of Bidwell is changing, and the flurry of industrial activity leads to an influx of others. As Bidwell undergoes a phenomenal growth, Anderson notes that the town is filled by foreigners from surrounding towns and from Europe, who crowd into the young city looking for success. Although one may have been more aware of various ethnic groups in large cities because they tended by design and necessity to live together in neighborhoods, Bidwell also has such an area. The Italians of *Poor White*, like many of their urban counterparts, are willing to live in hovels in anticipation of seeing their perceptions of the American Dream fulfilled. But for many of them, the promise of the nation means little. "In the new place they had not, as they had hoped, been received as brothers" (pp. 289–90). Furthermore, all of them soon discover that those who had been slaves to the land have become slaves to the machine. Customarily, the urban novel uses the immigrant to demonstrate the discrepancy between the real and the ideal. While many of the older writers such as Fuller, Herrick, and Payne used recently arrived immigrants to illustrate their beliefs that "foreigners" fostered labor unrest and discontent, Anderson understood the new settlers often were victimized by their faith in the American Dream.

Ultimately, Anderson presents the ambiguity of the urban experience. The rise of a complex commercial world and its evolving factory system will produce a corresponding decline in the humanness of people. This, in turn, leads to a deemphasis of truth and to its eventual loss. By implication, if a town can remain safe from these outside influences, one might assume that the idyllic village could exist; however, it would be out of step with the real world. Progress, improvements, and change (usually interrelated concepts) are inevitable, just as the rise of the modern businessman reveals that he is as much a victim of the system that has been created in order to bring freedom as is the worker who is hampered by it.

Because the efficacy of the Dream is dependent upon breaking the current system of growth, labor problems soon follow in the wake of the industrialization of Bidwell. Finally, an agitator appears who attacks "not the piece work prices at the corn-cutting machine plant, but the whole system that built and maintained factories when the wage scale of the workmen could be fixed by the whim or necessity of one man or a group of men." The workers are frightened, and some of them find there is the introduction of a puzzling philosophy. They do not mind striking against the townsmen whom they know, but they hesitate to condemn the government as the agitator suggests. "The Government was to them a sacred thing, and they did not fancy having their demands for a better wage scale confused by the talk of anarchists and socialists." Anderson explains their loyalty:

> Many of the laborers of Bidwell were sons and grandsons of pioneers who had opened up the country where the great sprawling towns were now growing into cities. They or their fathers had fought in the great Civil War. During boyhood they had breathed a reverence for government out of the very air of the towns. The great men of whom the school-books talked had all been connected with the Government. In Ohio there had been Garfield, Sherman, McPherson the fighter and others. From Illinois had come Lincoln and Grant. For a time the very ground of the mid-American country had seemed to spurt forth great men as now it was spurting forth gas and oil. Government had justified itself in the men it had produced. And now there had come among them men who had no reverence for government. (pp. 336–37)

As labor problems become more acute so, too, does the anti-immigrant spirit seem to grow. First brought in to facilitate the work in the factories, the foreigners are looked upon with suspicion. In time, "like the other people of Bidwell, Hugh did not like to see foreigners about" (p. 273). Furthermore, "the new men . . . coming from many lands had brought with them strange doctrines." Soon they begin to make sense to the workers of Bidwell as they observe "you've had great men here; . . . but you're getting a new kind of great men now." Making clear that there has developed a distinction between the old and new orders, they note:

> These new men are not born out of people. They're being born out of capital. What is a great man? He's one who has power. . . . [Y]ou fellows here have got to find out that nowadays power comes with the possession of money. Who are the big men of this town?—not some lawyer or politician who can make a good speech, but the men who own the factories where you have to work. Your Steve Hunter and Tom Butterworth are the great men of this town.

Among those who lecture to the workers is the Swedish socialist "who had come to speak on the streets of Bidwell" and who calls the town's elite "thieves who by a trick had robbed their fellows." Anderson observes that the socialist, standing "on the box beside his wife, and raising his fists shouted crude sentences condemning the capitalist class, [and] men who had gone away angry came back to listen." As the foreigner begins to make sense, the townspeople conclude: "Some of these days we got to break up the system" (pp. 337–38 *passim*).

Another manifestation of change occurs with various physical shifts that take place in Bidwell. "Big houses began to appear at the edge of the berry lands" (p. 102). It is "a time of hideous architecture, a time when thought and learning paused. Without music, without poetry, without beauty in their lives or impulses, a whole people, full of the native energy and strength of lives lived in a new land, rushed pell-mell into a new age" (p. 130). But a certain monotony also comes with *progress*. It finds expression "on the farms and in the houses of the town [where] the men and women worked together toward the same ends in life . . . [and] lived in small frame houses set on the plains like boxes, but very substantially built." In the old days "the carpenter who built a farmer's house differentiated it from the barn by putting what he called scroll work up under the eaves and by building at the front a porch with carved posts" (p. 131). Now, "the houses were cheaply constructed and ugly and in all directions there was a vast disorder" (p. 262). On the other hand,

> on the bluff and back of it on a sloping hillside many of the more pretentious new houses of the prosperous Bidwell citizens had been built. Facing the river were the largest houses, with grounds in which trees and shrubs had been planted and in the streets along the hill, less and less pretentious as they receded from the river,

were other houses built and being built, long rows of houses, long streets of houses, houses in brick, stone and wood. (p. 319)

In fact, "in the fast-growing town, men who were engaged in organizing companies representing a capital of millions lived in houses thrown hurriedly together by carpenters who, before the time of the great awakening, were engaged in building barns" (p. 130).

In addition to the turmoil of labor problems and the repeated construction of poorly planned buildings, industrialism brings with it other attendant signs of progress: new heroes, a flurry of excitement, over-subscribed stock companies, a revitalization of the American Dream, and a growing business elite, many of whom subscribe to Steve Hunter's overconfidence. As the town's leading entrepreneur, he cautions his associates against revealing the possibility of failure by reminding them: "It is a case of the survival of the fittest" (p. 124). The banker, John Clark, realizes that the new times will demand new people to be workers. He assumes:

> When the factories start coming to a town and it begins to grow as this town is growing, no man can stop it. The fellow who thinks of individual men, little fellows with their savings invested, who may be hurt by industrial failure, is just a weakling. Men have to face the duties life brings. The few men who see clearly have to think first of themselves. They have to save themselves in order that they may save others. (p. 127)

By personalizing the changes in Bidwell through his characters, Anderson creates a greater sense of immediacy. The ultimate merit of this technique can be viewed through Ezra French and his children. Opposed to the shifts taking place in Bidwell, Ezra believes neither God nor Nature meant for man to employ mechanical instruments in farming. Literally used as slaves by their father, the French boys escape from the farm. Musing over the events of his life, one of them realizes sadly

> in the country I worked like a dog a few weeks a year, but here I'll probably have to work like that all the time. . . . I thought it was mighty funny, all this talk about the factory work being so easy. I wish the old days were back. I don't see how that inventor or his inventions ever helped us workers. Dad was right about him. He said an inventor wouldn't do nothing for workers. (p. 263).

The transformation of Bidwell illustrates the power of the de-humanizing forces that are at work in the process of urbanization. This, in turn, leads to a growing sense of human inadequacy. Each character is caught in the web of enthusiasm that follows in the wake of the growing city. For some, it is an evolving feeling that they have lost control of their lives. And everywhere there are signs of "a vast disorder." Labor disputes, strikes, violence, lack of concern for others, ad infinitum suggest that the wheels of urban progress cannot be reversed. Yet, Anderson reminds the reader of the *romance of industry*. The town may have become disorganized, there may be a host of people speaking in "strange languages," the workers may be dissatis-fied, and the calm of the landscape may have been broken by the in-troduction of the ugly, black factories; yet, so many are convinced that good will result from all of the activity, as is Clara Butterworth who "like every other citizen of America . . . believe[s] in heroes." Anderson attributes her acceptance of the American Dream to the stories "she had read of heroic men who had come out of poverty by some strange alchemy to combine in their stout persons all of the vir-tues." And he continues: "The broad, rich land demanded gigantic figures, and the minds of men had created the figures. Lincoln, Grant, Garfield, Sherman, and a half dozen other men were some-thing more than human in the minds of the generation that came im-mediately after the days of their stirring performance." Significantly, "already industry was creating a new set of semi-mythical figures" (pp. 252–53). No matter how one might react to the newspaper ac-counts of Hugh, the tale being circulated in the advertising catalogue of the McVey Corn-Cutter machine emphasizes the legend of the in-ventor's rise in the world. Once again the "from rags-to-riches" story has been given human form.

While the chronicle of Bidwell is fastpaced and moving, the ac-tual story of Hugh McVey is not. Part of the problem undoubtedly is caused by Anderson's use of two midwestern figures who have be-come such integral parts of the mythology of the region that they nei-ther fit well into the urban milieu nor can their legends bear any al-teration. Both Abraham Lincoln and Huckleberry Finn result from such isolated specific historic moments that it is difficult to imagine Huck as a grown man or Lincoln after the Civil War. Furthermore, to move from the fictional Huck Finn to the reality of Abraham Lincoln results in mixed images and metaphors that cloud the effectiveness of Hugh McVey as a character and creates a major flaw in the novel. Even the similarity of names, Huck and Hugh, seems strangely sug-

gestive. Acknowledging Anderson's apparent indebtedness to Samuel
Clemens, Irving Howe asserted in "Sherwood Anderson and the
American Myth of Power" that not only had the novelist been "influenced by Twain" in his production of *Poor White* but also he "is best
when describing the hero's youth along the Mississippi."[8] Yet, somehow one does not expect a grown Huck Finn to become an Abe Lincoln even in physical appearance.

Furthermore, on a philosophical level there is the suggestion that
the well-meaning attempts of Hugh are misunderstood. This obviously raises the question concerning Anderson's view of Lincoln's
reluctant use of Emancipation and the irony of Lincoln becoming
known as the "great Liberator." Whether or not Hugh as Lincoln is
successful, Anderson's interest in Lincoln was real. Several years after
the publication of *Poor White*, he turned his attention to the idea of the
Lincoln figure again. He projected a dramatic rendition that would
have included a character such as McVey "who has something of a
Lincoln quality."[9] A few months later, he wrote to two friends of his
vision of "Lincoln, working now, not just to free the blacks, but to
free all labor, the heavy brutal labor that for ages has tied man to the
soil."[10] Then, in 1936 in still another letter, he spoke of the problems
of the modern world and concluded by saying: "A new Lincoln may
be the thing that is most needed."[11] That he was proud of the former
President is quite apparent from his message to Robert Sherwood
after the latter's play, *Abe Lincoln in Illinois*,[12] but his notions are not
pursued in *Poor White*, and the reader can do no more than speculate
on possible meanings or connections.

Another weakness of the novel is centered in its title. Although
one may understand the background of Hugh and the importance of
his early days in Mudcat Landing, semantically the title of the novel
does not seem to be all-encompassing and creates more problems
than it solves. Of course, one might hazard a number of possibilities
for the ultimate value of "poor white" per se; however, the limitations
of the term aid in masking some of the apparent concerns of the
novel. One may with some justification view both Huckleberry Finn
and Abraham Lincoln as examples of "poor whites" in American culture; yet, both have become part of the folklore of the nation for reasons that transcend their racial and economic backgrounds. On the
other hand, the Huck and Lincoln elements are so superficial that
they fail to deepen Anderson's portrayal of McVey. And instead of re-
lating to the similarities, the reader is constantly aware of the differences, even though the two figures are apparently used to establish

the regional basis for the novel.[13] If the comparison is to have any value, the irony of it is not lost on the reader. Thinking his inventions will free mankind, Hugh eventually discovers that he has created the means for the enslavement of thousands of workers. But, if he had not provided an instrument of change, someone else would have. It was a moment for agricultural inventions. The same argument could be used to explain Lincoln's role in history. In the meantime, like Lincoln whom he physically resembles, Hugh never loses his frontier characteristics although conditions force him into the company of far more sophisticated men and women.

Blanche Gelfant, in an interpretation of Hugh as "one of Anderson's grotesques," has suggested that the hero of Bidwell can be explained as "less a human being than a human equivalent to a state of social change." She continues: "His early stupor is hardly credible; yet his lethargic state of vague dreaming is evocative of America's slow sleepy towns. His complete isolation and fumbling inarticulateness are also unbelievable; yet they too become a satisfactory projection of man's inner dissociation in a world of machines." Within this context, Gelfant explains not only the evolution of the urban but also the presence in the novel of Mrs. Shepard who, with her husband, is Hugh's guardian for a few years.

> As Hugh changes from the lazy giant who slept by the mud-banks of the Mississippi to a busy inventor always making "definite" things, he embodies the *process* of urbanization. And it is significant that he is prodded out of his dreamy lethargy by a woman from New England. The driving practicality, enterprise, and shrewdness that overtake and transform the Midwest have come from the bustling centers of the East, where industrialism first took hold.[14]

In spite of Gelfant's assessment, the disappearance and shadowy role of Mrs. Shepard reveal another significant weakness of *Poor White*, which is filled with minor characters who momentarily have some interest but who do not contribute significantly to the overall narrative. Furthermore, the prolonged story of Clara Butterworth (especially her relationship with Kate Chancellor at the university, a relationship clearly designed to reinforce the notion of Clara as a free spirit) does not advance the story of Bidwell nor do the allusions to the *depth* of feeling between the two women make Clara's later "love" for Hugh more believable. As sympathetic as Anderson appeared to be to the plight of women and considering his apparent one-time

view of himself as something of a Lothario, he continually had difficulty, especially in his novels, with the portrayal of female characters.
They might be sex symbols, but ultimately it is the maternal instinct
that became dominant for him. Professional and business women,
who were certainly part of Anderson's world, have little place in his
fiction. Even the knowledge that Kate wants to be a doctor is not as
developed as it might have been.[15] Yet, sections of the novel demonstrate that Anderson understood some of the issues involved in an examination of the place of the so-called modern woman in an urban
world. That Hugh marries Clara, that she is a "strong" woman, that
she in essence becomes the mother-figure for Hugh who had spent
motherless days in Mudcat Landing seem to suggest another story
that might have been developed, unconnected to the biography of
Bidwell. In the final analysis, his difficulty in distinguishing between
love and *sex* are inconsequential because the real love story, if such
exists in *Poor White*, is the *romance of industry*.

Throughout his tale, Anderson never completely loses sight of
the specter that what occurs is inevitable in Bidwell, but the expected
sense of dread is absent. Instead, the novelist is ambivalent, and his
work ends on an ambiguous note. There is the promise of new life
symbolically represented by Hugh's unborn child, but there is also the
reality of the factory whistle that shrieks through the natural world
with its unnatural sound. There is the image of Hugh significantly fin-
gering the colored stones at the end of the novel as their "colors
blended and then separated again" when struck by a slant of light.

> The same light that had played over the stones in his hand began to
> play over his mind, and for a moment he became not an inventor but
> a poet. The revolution within had really begun. A new declaration of
> independence wrote itself within him. "The gods have thrown the
> towns like stones over the flat country, but the stones have no color.
> They do not burn and change in the light." (pp. 364–66 *passim*)

In the end, human destiny must rest with human beings.

And so it is that *Poor White* presents the story of change that, like
"the thing men call growth, was in the air. Perhaps, in its own way,
revolution was in the air, the silent, the real revolution that grew with
the growth of the towns" (p. 331). Is growth good or evil or simply
inevitable? Hugh begins to doubt the efficacy of some of the changes
that have occurred in Bidwell. "In the past he had seen towns and
factories grow and had accepted without question men's word that

growth was invariably good. Now his eyes looked at the towns, at Bidwell, Akron, Youngstown and all the great new towns scattered up and down mid-western America" (p. 369), and it is apparent that he is no longer sure. Yet, whatever one might think of Bidwell, it is just one example of

> the thing that was happening . . . all over the Middle West. . . . Over night, towns grew into cities. A madness took hold of the minds of the people. . . . To some of these places, so anxious were the people to get to them and to invest their money, excursion trains were run. Town lots that a few weeks before the discovery of oil or gas could have been bought for a few dollars sold for thousands. Wealth seemed to be spurting out of the very earth. (p. 129)

Quite central to Anderson's analysis of the phenomenal growth of Bidwell is the not-so-unique observation that change is in reality an integral part of nature. Briefly recounting an episode of Steve Hunter in a storm, the novelist describes the young man as equating the turmoil of the natural elements with events in Bidwell. Seeing people rushing about to seek shelter, "Steve Hunter's imagination [is] aroused. For some reason the black clouds of dust and the running people gave him a tremendous sense of power. . . . He and the storm were in a way akin to each other" (p. 112). As Steve ponders the possibilities of the future, "the hurrying black clouds in the sky were, he fancied, like clouds of smoke pouring out of the chimneys of factories owned by himself. In fancy he also saw his town become a city, bathed in the smoke of his enterprises. As he looked abroad over the fields swept by the storm of wind, he realized that the road along which he walked would in time become a city street." But lest the reader believe that Steve Hunter is in complete control of the elements, Anderson indicates that at a moment when Steve is declaring to the heavens "I'm a man," it is only after he has "lifted his tiny hands to the skies" (p. 113). And the reader knows that the work of change will not be the complete responsibility of those with "tiny hands" in the face of overwhelming natural forces.

One may mourn for the past and reject the coming of the new world as does Joe Wainsworth, but such actions are not consistent with reality. Clara, who has been most reluctant to accept the new way of life, comes to understand through the crazed actions of the harness-maker that the past indeed is dead. Thus, unlike Henry Adams who mourns for the old days of spiritual certainty, Anderson

recognizes the fated necessity of a "progress" that does not immediately utilize the old verities; indeed the new world has insisted
upon a *truth* of its own. The acceptance of the urban prison is one
such truth. Beneath the sense of sadness and ennui permeating parts
of the novel is a plea for a humanizing love that will make the new
world acceptable.

It is unfortunate, however, that Anderson's noble idea and version of the rise of a city are caught in a maze of details and undeveloped characters about whom the reader may care little. The
force of industrialism is portrayed graphically through such figures as
Joe Wainsworth, who becomes the first victim, and by the new breed
of capitalists that includes so diverse a group as Steve Hunter, Tom
Butterworth, Ben Peller, Ed Hall, and the reluctant Hugh McVey. As
it illustrates the evolution of cities, the novel presents those men who,
often by chance, become the captains of industry and the giants of
finance. By implication, beneath any John D. Rockefeller or Henry
Ford or Potter Palmer, one might find a Steve Hunter or Tom Butterworth or even Hugh McVey. At the same time, when all of them succumb to "the new ways," they make the fall from grace in the garden
far more graphic as they become victims of their own selfish greed.
Thus, the piercing of the calm of nature with the unnatural sound of
the factory whistle is significant at the end of the novel. If one considers the development of the city as representative of man triumphant,
then the inconsequential factory whistle has had an even greater
triumph.

In his attempt, however, to personify the creation of varying urban forces, Anderson sometimes has difficulty in maintaining the
level of seriousness demanded by his theme, and his characters often become caricatures who do not arouse strong feelings. Even the
search of Clara Butterworth for love, admirable though such a quest
may be, seems inconsequential. On a realistic level, the marriage of
Clara and Hugh taxes credibility. Only when the two are viewed as
representing a "new" spirit in the modern world do they seem to
make sense.

Yet, in spite of the weaknesses and serious flaws of *Poor White*,
the novel is more than a sociohistoric tract. It is Anderson's artistic
attempt to render the tale of urban growth. The reader is aware of a
strange sense of inevitability that pervades the novel. Despite Anderson's recital of the ills of urbanized life, *Poor White* is not an overt plea
for a return to a former day. One need not think the small town, by
virtue of its size, is a place of perfection. Mudcat Landing is horrible,

and Bidwell appears to be practically a time bomb simply waiting to explode. Furthermore, in spite of its large cast of characters, *Poor White* is not really a story about people. Perhaps it would have been stronger had it been. Rather, it is a record of the meaning of progress and the toll it exacts from both the place and the people.

Judge Hanby's early discourses in the novel make plain the ultimate necessity of all of the actions. Within this context Hugh McVey, whose desire to eliminate certain time-consuming chores but who inadvertently leads the townspeople into a slavery they never knew before, is a pawn "in the game of life." He has no way of knowing that the restrictions of the farm will become the restrictions of the factory. If Hugh's story begins as another midwestern version of the young man with the ne'er-do-well father, the narrative makes clear that the protagonist searches for an acceptable life by lighting out for "new territory." But *Poor White* is more than the story of Hugh McVey.

III

Perhaps it was the reception of *Winesburg, Ohio* that caused *Poor White* to be reviewed so widely. By now Anderson was considered a major— if also misunderstood—writer. As might be expected, critics were divided on the merits of the novel. There were many positive reviews, some of which praised Anderson and hailed his work as an excellent study in midwestern realism.[16] Heywood Broun, however, objected to the novel because he felt it was predicated upon a Midwest that had never existed,[17] and Elia W. Peattie, the genteel book reviewer for the Chicago *Tribune* who had literally become a one-woman institution, begrudgingly admitted that it was a work of "abortive power" but rued Anderson's unfair use of the region.[18] Robert Morss Lovett of the University of Chicago's English Department was impressed with the novelist's use of a realism that had been "enlarged and made significant by symbolism." While noting Anderson had recorded the state of the nation at a time of "industrial progress and spiritual impotence," Lovett was one of the few reviewers to focus upon Hugh McVey as "a distinct human type" and called him "a sort of subconscious Lincoln."[19]

Both John Cournos[20] and V. F. Calverton[21] felt *Poor White* came close to fulfilling the requirements for that nebulous "great American novel." There were others who claimed the book had no form and was philosophically unsound.[22] Ironically, it was Albert Bailly who early understood the full impact of the novel. Writing in *La Bataille Litteraire,* he saw the chronicle of Bidwell as a study of the growth and development of American civilization and concluded the town was simply symbolic of the mood and themes that had created the nation.[23] Bryllion Fagin suggested Anderson's novel exemplified a theory of the genre while displaying the artist' weaknesses.

> The true novelist needs great patience to weave all his threads into a unified design. Anderson is too hasty, too intense to command such patience. *Poor White* is more like a collection of short stories. There is the story of Hugh McVey and the story of Clara Butterworth; of Henry Shepard and Sarah Shepard; of Allie Mulberry . . . there are twenty-nine distinct stories. Sometimes they merge into the novel and sometimes they don't.[24]

Even while decrying the short-story characteristics of the novel, Fagin admits that the characters "merge into the life which gave them birth—the inner life of a changed and changing America."[25] Whether for good or ill, *Poor White* displays a panoramic sweep rather than the intense concentration of the short story.

Unfortunately, *Poor White* appeared in the same year as Sinclair Lewis's *Main Street,* and comparisons between the two novels were unavoidable. No one seemed to understand that the works, despite their small-town settings, had been motivated by totally different spirits. Both novels are considered as part of the "revolt-from-the-village" movement, but in reality Anderson's work was not only a "revolt" from those qualities or forces that had created ugly cities in the Midwest but also was a call for a renewed spirit of independence that actually went beyond any selfish protectionism of old craftsmen while trying to get at a workable truth. Despite Anderson's attempt to tell a story of the city in the process of becoming, *The Nation* declared that the novel "lack[ed] fire and edge, lucidity and fulness" when compared to Main Street,[26] but the *Manchester Guardian* felt that *Poor White* was the better of the two works although "the patterns of behavior" cited in the novel are "improbable."[27]

Throughout American history, the pioneers of American culture have been romanticized, especially those associated with the nation's various frontiers. As a result, the westward movement—epic though it was—frequently has been reduced to romantic vignettes describing a strong people surviving in the midst of hardships as they willingly try to create a more perfect society. Even the tales of the great rising urban centers are chronicles of the successful efforts of a diversified group of people to establish themselves on the frontier. *Poor White*, falling philosophically within the ideology of the revolt-from-the-village movement, does not concentrate only on the pettiness and the provincialism of small town folk but suggests that the greed and acquisitive nature of mankind, generally associated with the urban environment, are "people problems" rather than problems of locale.

Quite obviously, *Poor White* is not a Chicago novel in the traditional sense of the term. It can be argued, however, that, in his fictionalized explanation of the evolution of an urban area, his theory could be as applicable to Chicago as to any other metropolis. Certainly, before Chicago was Chicago with all that its name implies, it was like a Bidwell struggling to grow and be "progressive." One has only to look critically at the city's early entrepreneurs (Kinzie, Ogden, McCormick, Pullman, etc.) to realize that in the transition from town to city these men were not as noble as urban tales have suggested. Neither should one forget that these legends frequently are created deliberately by advertising men. In reality, then, the new men and women are often opportunistic liars who have more nerve than their small-town counterparts. Focusing on a theme that had already captured his attention in *Windy McPherson's Son*, Anderson continued to examine the extent to which greed, avarice, alienation, and a lack of meaningful communication marked modern life.

The study of the relationship of Sherwood Anderson to the city is hampered by the customary tendency to view a writer's work chronologically. Hence, *Poor White* becomes difficult to define. Coming as it does after *Windy McPherson's Son* and *Marching Men* and appearing the year after *Winesburg, Ohio*, the novel seems related primarily to the writer's concern for the small town rather than to his execution of the urban novel. As they follow Hugh McVey "from rags to riches," readers also follow the evolution of Bidwell from a sleepy midwestern farm hamlet to an industrial city where success is measured in materialistic terms. Bidwell may have been a Winesburg in the beginning, but at the end of the novel it is a Chicago. Perhaps Bidwell is not as large or as complicated, but one realizes that it is only a matter of time before it will be "teeming" with millions of souls. It is this period of transition, seldom recorded in American fiction, that Anderson has preserved in *Poor White*.

Accepting uncontrollable growth with its various manifestations does not change Anderson's view of the negative force of this growth when it takes a toll upon the human spirit. Joe Wainsworth cannot cope with the introduction of machine-made harnesses and becomes bitter. Utilizing a concept that Dunbar used in his 1901 naturalistic *The Sport of the Gods,* Anderson seems to base the development of Wainsworth's character upon the concept: "whom the gods wish to destroy, they first make mad." Joe commits murder in his madness and is incapable of finding meaning in his life. "Smokey Pete," journey blacksmith, becomes the town's conscience and is dismissed as being crazy. The French boys leave the farm for a more intense factory enslavement. Harley Parsons and Ed Hall are victims of the corrupting nature of the new way of life because they do not have the inner stamina to withstand temptation.

While it is generally assumed that the characters fall in moral grace as the city evolves, the weaknesses one finds in the people are not "caused" by the city but are simply "excused" by the nature of the urban environment. What one might think of as the "dignity of the common man" is nothing more than the absence of those forces that ultimately make the "madness, greed, and corruption" apparent. It is the triumph of the darker nature of mankind and, in the final analysis, may account for the success of the city. It is not, then, the innate goodness of humanity that strikes Sherwood Anderson but the natural proclivity for evil, a story as old as the legend of the Original Sin.

Anderson's created universe is not devoid of a recognition of the mystery and sacredness of life that frequently borders on the religious but he is often aware of human distortions. In the early days of his operations, Hugh McVey receives a lucrative contract for one of his proposed projects from Steve Hunter. Feeling "he had been in the presence of a kind of god," Hugh is determined to work out the problems associated with his plant-setting machine. He comes to understand that what he is doing is "of great and mysterious importance to . . . civilization. . . . There seemed to him something almost sacred in that fact" (p. 106). The "sacredness" of the new way of life is made even clearer through the actions of Joe Wainsworth and David Chapman both of whom, having invested heavily in the project upon the advice of Steve Hunter, resort to traditional rites to voice their concerns. Visiting the new plant at night, Wainsworth "knelt on the floor and put his hands about the heavy legs of the machine." Anderson observes that Joe "had an impulse to do something he knew would be foolish, to kiss the iron legs of the machine or to say a prayer as he knelt before it." But he did neither. Creeping home, he discovers his neighbor, David Chapman, "a devout Methodist . . . praying for Hugh McVey and for the success of his invention" (p. 137). One man wants to pray for the machine, the other prays for the inventor; and both have apparently missed the real message of religion. But neither does the answer rest with Ezra French who denies the importance of the new machinery by declaring it is "wicked and ungodly to try" to alter the plans of God (p. 122).

Like the prophets and storytellers of old, Anderson uses an exemplum to explain the theme of *Poor White*. The fable of the mice is the apparent sermon that presents the irrevocability of the continued growth of cities in spite of the recognition that they might hinder the development of the more enduring values of life.

> Modern men and women who live in industrial cities are like mice that have come out of the fields to live in houses that do not belong to them. They live within the dark walls of the houses where only a dim light penetrates, and so many have come that they grow thin and haggard with the constant toil of getting food and warmth. Behind the walls the mice scamper about in droves, and there is much squealing and chattering. Now and then a bold mouse stands upon his hind legs and addresses the others. He declares he will force his way through the walls and conquer the gods who have built the house. 'I will kill them,' he declares. 'The mice shall rule. You shall live in the light and warmth. There shall be food for all and no one shall go hungry.'
>
> The little mice, gathered in the darkness out of sight in the great houses, squeal with delight. After a time when nothing happens they become sad and depressed. Their minds go back to the time when they lived in the fields, but they do not go out of the walls of the houses, because long living in droves has made them afraid of the silence of long nights and the emptiness of skies. In the houses giant children are being reared. When the children fight and scream in the houses and in the streets, the dark spaces between the walls rumble with strange and appalling noises.
>
> The mice are terribly afraid. Now and then a single mouse for a moment escapes the general fear. A mood comes over such a one and a light comes into his eyes. When the noises run through the houses he makes up stories about them. . . . When he discovers a female mouse looking at him he runs away with a flip of his tail and the female follows. While other mice are repeating his saying and getting some little comfort from it, he and the female mouse find a warm dark corner and lie close together. It is because of them that mice continue to be born to dwell within the walls of the houses. (pp. 114–15)

Given its position early in the novel, the fable of the mice becomes the counterpoint to the story of the transformation of Bidwell. The prediction that "the town is going to be a city" is fulfilled by the end of the novel. The shrewd citizens realize that there are fortunes to be made in the rush of the town's growth; but only the perceptive will ever understand and learn to coexist with the forces of modern life. Those willing to break through the artificial and psychological barriers have the best chance for survival. Hugh may wonder about his role in the process of change, but the reality of life ultimately rests in the often futile search for love. Despite its frequent and obvious didactic posturings, *Poor White* does not really offer a simple resolution. Anderson, the storyteller, merely gives life to "the thing that was happening in Bidwell . . . [and] in towns all over the Middle West."

... the sea of silence into which people were always so intent on sinking themselves was in reality death.

—*Many Marriages*

Because moments are hard to come at, because everything fades quickly away, is that any reason for becoming second-rate, cheap, a cynic?

—*Dark Laughter*

9

The Metaphoric City

S HERWOOD ANDERSON'S departure from Chicago coincided with the artistic exodus from the city in the 1920s. Literary history has made much of the men and women from midwestern villages who moved into Chicago. It was believed that when they discovered the goals and commitments of the metropolis that had "nurtured" so many artists were antithetical to the artistic life, they fled from the city. Clearly, mercantile interests continued to occupy the civic center stage, and struggles for the fruits of success still seemed to motivate even those for whom success would never be more than a mirage.

Unlike many of his immediate associates, Sherwood Anderson did not leave Chicago because the East offered better opportunities for his literary development. Between the publication of *Poor White* in 1920 and *Many Marriages* in 1923, much had happened to him. He was growing restless in a boring job, his second marriage was failing, and he was taking trips to other places. He had made a pilgrimage to Europe in 1921 with his friend Paul Rosenfeld. Later that year, he again spent time in the South. After a longer than usual stay in Reno during 1923, in order to get a divorce, he lived in New Orleans, from his marriage to Elizabeth Prall in 1924 to the construction of Ripshin, his Virginia home, in 1926.

His apparent rejection of Chicago was a repetition of his general behavioral pattern. To escape from an unpleasant personal relationship, from an unworkable marriage, meant he had to leave Chicago, just as he had left Clyde and Elyria in the past to begin his life anew.

His inclination to start over again was of paramount importance to him and is indicative of an optimistic strain that he never completely lost. His tendency to run away whenever his life became unbearable and his ability to make himself satisfied in a variety of places can aid critics in understanding his personal ambivalence toward many subjects, just as it can lead to a misinterpretation of his actions. Be that as it may, on the surface, the Sherwood Anderson of Marion, Virginia, is distinctly different from the Sherwood Anderson of Chicago, Illinois; yet, the country man was made possible by the city man who, in his turn and at a specific moment, had been created from a midwestern villager.

During this period, New Orleans appealed to his sense of the exotic and primitive. Rooted in Spanish and French cultures, the city offered a romantic respite from the frankly commercial structure of Chicago. In letters to friends, written between 1924 and 1925, he often mentioned his fascination with the city; but Bruce Dudley's simple discovery in *Dark Laughter* that "New Orleans is not Chicago"[1] belonged to Anderson as well. The novelist had already been "scarred" by Chicago, and in time he came to view the city as one of his spiritual homes. He might leave the physical place, but Chicago would always remain with him. While he never again wrote a novel in the tradition of *Windy McPherson's Son* or *Marching Men*, neither did he ever again spend as much time trying to come to terms with methods of urbanization. Yet, the variety of his post-Chicago work should not conceal the observation that much of it can be read as a retrospective of his days "as a city man." Because industrialism continued to interest him and he was increasingly concerned about the effects of loneliness, he returned to various aspects of Chicago or Chicago-related incidents not only in *The Triumph of the Egg* (1921) but also in portions of *Horses and Men* (1923), *Many Marriages* (1923), and *Dark Laughter* (1925), in order to display some of the qualities that he found disturbing in modern life and to contemplate the city dispassionately after the excitement of the Renaissance had passed. Whereas there is nothing magical about the year 1925, by this time his urban vision had been developed not only from his period in Chicago but also from what Chicago meant to the sons and daughters of the Middle Border. Although he assumed the mantle as spokesman for small towns, urban elements remained part of his work; but they offered no new analyses and no new interpretations. Thus, the most creative elements of his association with Chicago were substantially over with the publication of *Dark Laughter*.

His subsequent references to the city, then, generally were as symbolic reference points from which he impressionistically and graphically portrayed urban influences in the United States. Furthermore, he discovered that the prevalent talk in Chicago of personal and artistic freedom was largely an illusion that had misled an entire generation. He was also concerned about the failure of Chicago's promise to those who gave themselves to the city in search of some elusive dream. At the same time, he saw that the small towns in trying to imitate the imagined urban life had become crude and greedy, as Sam McPherson, Beaut McGregor, and Sherwood Anderson were to learn. In fact, Sam's "heart was bitter at the thought of men throwing the glamour of romance over the sordid, ugly things he had been seeing in that city and in every city he had known."[2]

Idealistic though he was on some issues, Sherwood Anderson came to realize that, as currently practiced, reform also was out of the question as an immediate answer for change, because (at least in part) would-be reformers seldom knew what changes were really needed. Sam McPherson discovers the impossibility of reshaping people in his own image. Beaut comes to believe that the creative and productive aspects of life can be ignored, that workers marching "shoulder to shoulder" could change the city; but the reader realizes that life in Chicago remains unchanged despite McGregor and his marching men. Hugh McVey, the reluctant instrument of modernization in Bidwell, never fully recognizes his effect upon the town; but far more telling than his ignorance is the awareness that Hugh is merely a tool of the inevitability of change, which Judge Hanby and Steve Hunter so ably understand. The self-interest, blindness, and inability to communicate of both the reformer and the business establishment too frequently intrude, creating further chaos and rendering ineffective any substantive modification in patterns of living. Thus, after his physical departure from Chicago, there is evidence to suggest that psychologically he did not leave the city for a number of years.

Of course, it is important to remember that Anderson as a teller of tales was not always an Aristotelian logician. Neither was he a social scientist. Even though, at specific moments, he could present discerning views of American life, underlying contradictions appear in his work; but he never equivocated on his concern with the inability of humans to adjust to the demands of modern life. Thus, Chicago, as a representation of the disorder of American civilization, continued to plague him. Essentially, his fiction provided a forum for thinking through various situations as he attempted to grapple with the role of the individual in a world that generally had distorted the meaning of self-reliance by equating it with extreme selfishness or perverted notions of strength. Moreover, the formlessness and chaos of urban life provided no viable options. Yet, his observations ultimately must be evaluated in terms of their narrative frames.

I

Both *The Triumph of the Egg* and *Horses and Men* return to the genre of *Winesburg, Ohio;* but unlike his first collection of short stories, these do not have the unifying force of a George Willard. For example, *The Triumph of the Egg* is held together by the repetition of themes and ideas that he had examined in his urban fiction and that were increasingly of concern to him: the inability of men and women to communicate, the alienation that results from the lack of lasting human relationships, the importance of love as a humanizing force, the always-present possibility of being inundated by a sense of futility, and the ultimate sanctification of the human spirit. Even when they commit themselves to meaningful associations or try to communicate with others, Anderson's isolatoes are either thought to be insane as in "Brothers" or forced to withdraw into a still greater isolation as in "The Door of the Trap." Everywhere, the sense of impotence permeates life; and it is an ennui that seems to defy analysis.

The final tale, "Out of Nowhere into Nothing," utilizing a phrase that Anderson repeated on more than one occasion, is a long short story set in both Willow Springs (Iowa) and Chicago. It deals with Rosalind Wescott's return to her home town after a period in the big city. Like others, she has rejected her village for Chicago because she believes that one can find freedom from the binding restrictions of Willow Springs as well as greater chances for love and success. City life had much to recommend it. Even the "night noises" in their impersonality are not as terrifying as the "homely insistent noises of her father's house" partially because "certain terrible truths about life did not abide in them."[3] Life in the city, then, has certain advantages. Despite its size, noise, and ugliness, she recalls "there is something alive there. . . . In Chicago, in the midst of the twisting squirming millions of men and women there were voices. One occasionally saw men or at least heard of the existence of men who . . . had kept some precious thing alive in themselves" (p. 183).

As a relatively competent stenographer in the city, she had found a degree of success, but her life seems empty. Her work for Walter Sayers awakens new interests and desires, but he is a married man. Not understanding her own emotions, Rosalind spends much time in reflection; and Sherwood Anderson explains:

> [She] had gone away from the Wescott house and from Willow Springs, Iowa, feeling that life was essentially ugly. In a way she hated life and people. In Chicago sometimes it was unbelievable how ugly the world had become. She tried to shake off the feeling but it clung to her. She walked through the crowded streets and the buildings were ugly. A sea of faces floated up to her. They were the faces of dead people.

Incorporating his knowledge of the city with the combined impression of death and filth, Anderson continues:

> The dull death that was in them was in her also. They too could not break through the walls of themselves to the white wonder of life. After all, perhaps there was no such thing as the white wonder of life. It might be just a thing of the mind. There was something essentially dirty about life. The dirt was on her and in her. Once as she walked at evening over the Rush Street bridge to her room on the North Side she looked up suddenly and saw the chrysoprase river running inland from the lake. Near at hand stood a soap factory. The men of the city had turned the river about, made it flow inland from the lake. Someone had erected a great soap factory there near the river's entrance to the city, to the land of men. Rosalind stopped and stood looking along the river to the lake. Men and women, wagons, automobiles rushed past her. They were dirty. She was dirty. "The water of an entire sea and millions of cakes of soap will not wash me clean," she thought. The dirtiness of life seemed a part of her very being and an almost overwhelming desire to climb upon the railing of the bridge and leap down into the chrysoprase river swept over her. Her body trembled violently and putting down her head and staring at the flooring of the bridge she hurried away. (pp. 238–39)

Discovering the enforced isolation that had already frustrated many who had looked for the elusive American Dream in an equally elusive city, Rosalind realizes that much of life has to do with finding and understanding love. Rather than remaining in the urban environment simply to become another statistic, she returns home. But the futility of life is in no way mitigated. She subsequently escapes into the night's darkness, but

she had herself become something that within itself contained light.
She was a creator of light. At her approach the darkness grew afraid
and fled away into the distance. When that thought came she found
herself able to run without stopping to rest and half wished she
might run on forever, through the land, through towns and cities,
driving darkness away with her presence. (p. 267)

Despite the optimistic notion of Rosalind as "a creator of light," an
actual void exists and is symbolized by her unsuccessful longings.
She actually moves "out of nowhere into nothing." Whatever the
causes for Anderson's personal despair (and there are reasons to believe they were many), the almost passive presentation of the effects
of human isolation renders the final story of *The Triumph of the Egg* as
one of his outstanding statements on the ambiguity of modern life,
which presents both the limitations and hopes of that life.

It is perhaps significant that *Horses and Men,* his third collection
of short fiction, should have been dedicated to Dreiser, another writer
who "adopted" Chicago for a short period. The opening selection,
"Dreiser," commends the novelist who, through his sympathy and
understanding of Life, provides a pattern for younger writers. "Because of him, those who follow will never have to face the road
through the wilderness of Puritan denial, the road that Dreiser faced
alone."[4] The tales that follow are marked by the same sense of futility
that characterize those in *The Triumph of the Egg,* but there is a more
actively honest attempt to recognize, examine, and comprehend life.

Of particular interest is Anderson's growing understanding of
the meaning of the urban experience and of the Chicago Renaissance.
The small-town locale with which Anderson was associated once
again is shifted, and several of the tales in *Horses and Men* are set in
cities. David Anderson has quite correctly noted the parallel nature of
the tales, which are paired in an alternating fashion "between a rural
agricultural setting and an urban, commercial setting."[5] But place
does not determine action, rather it is a companion to action and
merely serves as a means by which one can reflect upon events. For
example, the fact that "Milk Bottles" occurs in Chicago is ultimately
unimportant, even though it does record a phenomenon associated
with urban life, with the city furnishing the necessary background to
make the story concrete. Thus, Chicago is the metaphor and symbol
for the ambiguity of life.

"Milk Bottles" concerns a young man who has visions of becoming a writer but who spends his days producing advertising copy for a

Chicago firm. During a particularly hot spell in the city, he is asked to stay overtime in order to write an advertisement for a condensed milk company. Wanting to get home, he grinds out what becomes a spectacular advertisement that proclaims "the health and freshness of a whole countryside is condensed into one can of Whitney-Wells Condensed Milk" (p. 238). When he finally gets to his hot North Side apartment, he ironically drinks some milk that has become sour from the heat. In fact, throughout the city, those people without the means for adequately cooling their food keep their milk bottles on their window sills with the inevitable results. Either they must drink sour milk or have no milk.

As Sherwood Anderson constructs the story, using a framework device, the reader meets Ed through a narrator who works for the same agency. Both men, bothered by the August heat, go for late-night walks. When they meet, Ed invites the narrator to go home with him. The two men talk about writing, and Ed admits that he has a "dream to write something stirring and big." He wants to present Chicago as "the capital and heart . . . of the whole Central West." Angrily, Ed remarks: "People come here from the East or from farms or from little holes of towns like I came from and they think it smart to run Chicago into the ground. . . . I thought I'd show 'em up." The narrator, however, discovers Ed's city is really "some mythical town" that does not exist.

> He called it Chicago, but in the same breath spoke of great streets flaming with color, ghostlike buildings flung up into night skies and a river, running down a path of gold into the boundless West. . . . The people of the city . . . were a cool-headed, brave people, marching forward to some spiritual triumph, the promise of which was inherent in the physical aspects of the town.

The narrator admits that he cannot "tell an author to his face that his work is rotten," so he lies to his friend. "You've knocked out a regular soc-dolager of a masterpiece here. Why you sound as good as Henry Mencken writing about Chicago as the literary centre of America, and you've lived in Chicago and he never did. The only thing I can see you've missed is a little something about the stockyards, and you can put that in later" (pp. 234–35).

In addition to his "masterpiece," Ed had also written of his city in a mood born out of his thwarted dreams and anger. Using the silent milk bottles, he had told of "a half-filled bottle of spoiled milk standing dim in the moonlight on a window sill" (p. 236). The discarded fragment impresses the narrator. It is "another bit of the kind of writing that is—for better or worse—really presenting the lives of the people of these towns and cities—sometimes in prose, sometimes in stirring colorful song. It was the kind of thing Mr. Sandburg or Mr. Masters might have done after an evening's walk on a hot night in . . . West Congress Street in Chicago" (p. 236). Unfortunately, Ed does not recognize the merit of his unfinished work. In the meantime, Sherwood Anderson juxtaposes the reality of Chicago with a mythical city, also called Chicago; but ultimately, the tale examines not only the lies that are used to create a sense of need but also the inability to distinguish between that which is true and that which is false.

"The Man's Story" also is set in the North Side of Chicago. It recounts the pitiful attempt of a Kansas housewife to find happiness by running away with another man. The couple lived in Chicago for three years

> in that section of old three- and four-story brick residences that were once the homes of what we call our nice people, but that had afterward gone to the bad. The section is having a kind of rebirth now but for a good many years it rather went to seed. There were these old residences, made into boarding-houses, and with unbelievably dirty lace curtains at the windows, and now and then an utterly disreputable old tumble-down frame house—in one of which Wilson lived with his woman.

Deliberately interrupting his story, Anderson comments:

> The place is a sight! Someone owns it, I suppose, who is shrewd enough to know that in a big city like Chicago no section gets neglected always. Such a fellow must have said to himself, "Well, I'll let the place go. The ground on which the house stands will some day be very valuable but the house is worth nothing. I'll let it go at a low rental and do nothing to fix it up. Perhaps I'll get enough out of it to pay my taxes until prices come up." . . . [It was on the second floor that the two people live in rooms that] were altogether cold and cheerless. (pp. 291–92)

The setting contributes to the sense of human isolation that is partially mitigated by the woman's silent understanding of the needs of her companion, who spends his time writing poetry. For a time, the anonymity of urban life provides a shield for them although their poverty is oppressive. While the central action occurs in a cold, detached city, for a moment the two people share a meaningful relationship that ends with her death. When she is killed, the man, Edgar Wilson, is accused but is freed because the real murderer confesses.

Although the specific incidents of "The Man's Story" may tax credibility, the tale is told through a narrator who is a newspaperman and who relates events as he perceives them. He is particularly impressed with Wilson's poetry, which deals with such ideas as "this notion, that men had erected walls about themselves and that all men were perhaps destined to stand forever behind the walls. . . . One couldn't quite make out whether there was just one great wall or many little individual walls. Sometimes Wilson put in one way, sometimes another." The poet also was concerned "about deep wells." People were

> everywhere constantly digging . . . themselves down deeper and deeper into deep wells. They not wanting to do it, you understand, and no one wanting them to do it, but all the time the thing going on just the same, that is to say the wells getting constantly deeper and deeper, and the voices growing dimmer and dimmer in the distance—and again the light and the warmth of life going away and going away, because of a kind of blind refusal of people to try to understand each other, I suppose. (pp. 294–95)

If "The Man's Story" seems to anticipate a theme explored more deeply in *Many Marriages*, "The Sad Horn Blowers" reexamines an idea that already had appeared in *Poor White*. Will Appleton escapes from Bidwell to Erie, Pennsylvania, when family misfortunes make it necessary for him to get a job in a factory town; but "all day long he stood at a machine and bored holes in pieces of iron." There is nothing creative about his work.

> A boy brought to him the little, short, meaningless pieces of iron in a box-like truck and, one by one, he picked them up and placed them under the point of a drill. He pulled a lever and the drill came down and bit into the piece of iron. . . . The hole was drilled and now the meaningless pieces of iron were thrown into another box-like truck. It had nothing to do with him. He had nothing to do with it. (p. 279)

One of the undercurrents of the story's sadness results from the observation "men were like the pieces of iron in which holes had been bored—one pitched them aside in a box-like truck. One had nothing

really to do with them. They had nothing to do with oneself. Life became a procession of days and perhaps all life was just like that—just
a procession of days" (pp. 279–80). The story articulates Anderson's
reflection upon what happens to a life conditioned by an industrialism where the machine produces jobs that seem to have no beginning and no end.

Despite the pathos of the tale in which he appears, at least Edgar
Wilson, if only briefly, "had come up out of the sea of doubt, had
grasped for a time the hand of the woman, and with her hand in his
had floated for a time upon the surface of life" (p. 311); however, the
central figure of "A Chicago Hamlet" is not as fortunate. Once again
using his favorite framework device, Anderson presents a rambling
account of a narrator's relationship with Tom, an acquaintance who
works in the same advertising office. The story begins as the two sit in
"a little combined saloon and restaurant in what is now Wells Street
in Chicago" (p. 139). While the city does not condition the outcome of
the tales told by Tom, it is the fall of the year, the season of "a kind of
weariness." And the reader is told:

> At times all Chicagoans grow weary of the almost universal ugliness
> of Chicago and everyone sags. One feels it in the streets, in the
> stores, in the homes. The bodies of the people sag and a cry seems to
> go up out of a million throats,—"we are set down here in this con-
> tinual noise, dirt, and ugliness. Why did you put us down here? . . .
> Millions of us live on the vast Chicago West Side, where all streets
> are equally ugly and where the streets go on and on forever, out of
> nowhere into nothing. . . . What is it all about? Why did you put us
> down here, mother of men?" (pp. 139–40)

The queries, based upon the lack of communication and the absence
of beauty that characterize modern life, use Chicago symbolically to
represent the effects of urban growth. The place, then, gives a sense
of concreteness to abstract questions.

"A Chicago Hamlet" tells of the various dreams that Tom had
had as a young man. Still committed to the promise of America, he
thought if he worked hard,

> after a time he would have an accumulation of money and would go
> into cities, study, read books, live. He had then a kind of illusion
> about American cities. "A city was a great gathering place of people
> who had grown tired of loneliness and isolation. They had come to
> realize that only by working together could they have the better

things of life. Many hands working together might build wonder-
fully, many minds working together might think clearly, many impulses working together might channel all lives into an expression of
something rather fine."

Anderson hastens to add that Tom's vision of urban life was not based
upon a real city but was "a feeling—of a sort" (p. 172).

On the other hand, the Wells Street saloon, standing near LaSalle
and Lake Streets where "about us surged the home-going crowds
while over our heads rattled the elevated trains" (p. 158) and walking
through city streets give Tom an opportunity to see an actual city as
he reflects upon his life. Later in the story, on "a spring evening,"
Tom and the narrator take a street car "for a walk in Jackson Park"
(p. 163). Always Tom talks and the narrator listens. The various episodes that Tom relates ultimately are inconsequential, as are the vignettes of the city, but there is a cogent observation about Tom's storytelling ability that addresses itself to the art itself.

> I do not know as to that but in telling this tale I have an advantage
> you who read cannot have. I heard the tale told, brokenly, by the
> man—who had the experience I am trying to describe. Story-tellers
> of old times, who went from place to place telling their wonder tales,
> had an advantage we, who have come in the age of the printed
> word, do not have. They were both story-tellers and actors. As they
> talked they modulated their voices, made gestures with their hands.
> Often they carried conviction simply by the power of their own con
> viction. All of our modern fussing with style in writing is an attempt
> to do the same thing.

Beyond being an indictment of phases of urban living, "A Chicago Hamlet" explores aspects of human communication. The city
may be a "horrible town," but in the final analysis, men and women
in it must rebel against constricting forces in order to fulfill themselves. The liberation movement still being highly praised in some
circles as an epoch that "freed" the artist to experiment and to use
subjects ordinarily banned by tradition was not, as Anderson had discovered, nearly as selfless as its historians had suggested. Even the
liberators and freedom-seekers were consumed by their own pettiness and adopted a certain self-righteousness that made life an empty
exercise.

"The Triumph of a Modern" partially deals with the issues of
contemporary art. Anderson sets forth a biting indictment of the

movement and its participants. Subtitled "Or Send for the Lawyer," the short tale presents, almost facetiously, a thirty-two-year-old man as the narrator. He has lived in Chicago for thirty of those years. In a moment of pique, he writes to his aunt in Madison, Wisconsin. The letter is a strange combination of truth, lies, distortions of language, and unsupported assertions. The dying aunt is so impressed by the "reality" of her nephew's work that she alters her will in order to leave her fortune to him. Inherent in the tale is an exposé of the deluding aspects of modern art, an art whose assumed fidelity to truth is itself a distortion of life. (Later in *Many Marriages* and *Dark Laughter,* he was to repeat his concern.) Certainly, Anderson had come far from his own optimistic call for "The New Note." He had discovered later that the philosophical statements of the Dell group of Fifty-seventh Street meant little; and a number of that circle had been co-opted, as had Anderson, by the glitter and glamour of it all. But far more damaging was the tendency to accept ideas and repeat them for their shock value rather than out of a profound belief. In "The Triumph of the Modern" the reader sees such duplicity in action. The story, simple and detached though it may seem, has added value when read in the light of the goals and statements that came out of the Chicago literary movement.

II

Thorough though some of Anderson's short stories are in exploring connections between his characters and the urban locale, it is in *Many Marriages*, dedicated to Paul Rosenfeld, that Anderson examines most fully the individual in a state of rebellion. Increasingly, this storyteller, the imagined voice of midwestern villagers, reveals himself as both the spokesman for the inarticulate and as an interrogator of the patterns of modern life. Both the title of the novel and the circumstances of Anderson's own divorce from Tennessee Mitchell may well have obscured the novel's significance. Since the city does not figure prominently as a setting, it is possible to overlook his references to it. But, given his previous work, the allusions assume a symbolic value and further demonstrate his urban vision.

Some of those who reviewed the book shortly after its publication were personally ambivalent toward the novel, although they understood its complexities. F. Scott Fitzgerald, for example, was supportive. In "Sherwood Anderson on the Marriage Question," he praised the work's apparent feeling of liberation. He saw the book as "transcendental naturalism" that was "violently antisocial" but "not immoral."[6] Ludwig Lewisohn saw it as "imperfect," "absurd," and "dull" but also found it "electrically alive [and] memorable."[7] Although he considered Anderson to be "a very gentle . . . and loving soul," Upton Sinclair was convinced that Anderson had been "caught in a trap" with the dire result that *Many Marriages* became "a sick book, written by a sick man about a sick world."[8]

Whether the novel really provided Anderson with a personal catharsis is open to speculation; however, it clearly asks the reader to explore once again those values of traditional society that have been accepted without question. Thus, as might be expected, the novel also evoked much negative criticism. Many readers and most critics saw it as merely a novel whose author was strangely and perversely preoccupied with sex and the ugliness of life in a disgusting way.[9] Among the more liberated critics of 1923, the novel was viewed as boring and tedious[10] or as a complete failure.[11] The work probably deserves more attention than Jane Heap was willing to give it. She dismissed Anderson's tale as inconsequential and maintained that there was a "whiskey school of prophecy and art" to which it belonged.[12] Unfortunately, the critics who found it wearisome and poorly-executed were at one time among the most important names in the American critical establishment.

While later critics have been willing to see the novel as more than just an obscene work,[13] many still emphasize the prominence of sexual matters.[14] Among such free spirits as Henry Miller and Theodore Dreiser, Anderson found some support,[15] which culminated in Charles Glicksberg's assertion that Anderson was the "anointed prophet" of the sexual revolution in American letters.[16] The variety and scope of critical commentary eventually included those who were willing to go beyond the elements of sensationalism and were impressed with the work's mysticism. Yet, the notion that the work is a garbled, aesthetic failure has continued through the years.

When the novel is considered at all, Cleveland Chase and Rex Burbank are fairly representative of current judgments about it. In his biography of Anderson, Chase announced that the storyteller "stretched out the material for a mediocre short story into a full length novel and . . . made the material worthless in the process." He observed: "The book rambles; repeats words, thoughts, symbols; were it not so thoroughly confused and meaningless, it would come close to being immoral."[17] Burbank, on the other hand, found the novel's obscurity a source of its failure. He asserted that such symbols as the Virgin Mary "are made to carry a greater rhetorical burden than they can bear." While one may agree with the assessment of the "rhetorical burden" imposed upon the novel's symbols, Burbank's harsh observation that the novel "is a thoroughly irresponsible work both artistically and intellectually" is open to serious consideration even though he tempers his judgment by claiming "we need not question Anderson's integrity of purpose."[18] What seems to be capricious and untrustworthy is the introspective examination of a life in which the protagonist and antagonistic forces are centered in John Webster. Through him and the disorder of the novel, Anderson reproduces the chaos of modern life. The problem is compounded when readers attempt to discover whether this aspect of the novel represents a conscious act or simply results from Anderson's powerful feeling, which in a Wordsworthian sense was recollected (perhaps not in tranquility) and then recorded.

If one assumes that the surface story concerning a middle-aged, small-town manufacturer's rejection of his life and marriage is of paramount importance, then it appears that Anderson took the most obscure way to tell such a tale and raises more questions than it could possibly answer. David Anderson has simplified the work by asserting that it is a protest against the empty relationships of all kinds "that have driven [Sherwood Anderson's] people to despair."[19] That it is as much a search for personal identity and individual meaning as an examination of the relative importance of communication and interpersonal alliances, as in *Windy McPherson's Son* or *Marching Men*, is not always apparent. Many years after the novel's publication, in a letter to Georgia O'Keeffe, Anderson said his work "was terribly misunderstood." After indicating the universal nature of "making marriages," he explained: "In my book I wanted to represent a man simply as struggling to escape that feel of dirt. To do it, he had, he felt, to go to rather extreme lengths. He wanted not only to free himself but his daughter. He knew his wife past freeing. He sacrificed her."[20]

Furthermore, at a time when advocates of urban life were finding the growth of cities to be a positive force because it increased opportunities and provided anonymity for those who wished it. Anderson questioned what these urban contacts were actually doing to people. The assumption seems to be that if this query can be answered on the most personal level, it can provide a response when large numbers of people are gathered together. While Anderson's urban vision initially had evolved out of his reaction to the external world, *Many Marriages* moves to the internal universe and emphasizes the importance of the self in any analysis of life.

The novel uses several ideas that Anderson continued to pursue throughout his career; and although his notions seem only tangentially related to his urban vision, the acceptance of them would obviously alter an individual's perception of the nature of the city. He extends his exploration into the efficacy and importance of love as a means of communication. He takes great pains, however, to separate "unasking love" from "animalism," which, as he declares, "one did not escape . . . so easily." And he muses that the prostitutes in the city may have had an important value. "Perhaps the very sins [John] had committed, his shamefaced running off sometimes to other women in the cities, had saved him." Webster is not certain about that observation but suspects "with a quick inner throb of satisfaction" that it "would be a pronouncement to throw into the teeth of the good pure people if it were true."[21] When he occasionally goes to Chicago to find a prostitute, he views the city as a place of escape and a place of freedom, but it is a freedom dictated by pleasure and circumscribed by the individual's limited perception. For example, when he becomes aware that his attraction for Natalie, one of his office workers, is going beyond the bounds of propriety, he imagines "it would be better if he did not go back to the office, but went off at once and took a train to Chicago or Milwaukee" (p. 30), repeating his belief that an urban community can be used as a means of escape even if such escapes do not solve any problems.

Eventually, "the notion of going off to Chicago or Milwaukee to walk through dirty streets hungering for the golden woman to come to him out of the filth of life was quite gone now" (p. 32). Much later, as John Webster contemplates leaving Natalie, he thinks he will "go to the city and get drunk and write her a letter telling her to go away to where he would not have to see her again" (p. 200). Instead the two of them escape together and plan to "take the train as far as Chicago and get off there. Perhaps they would get on another train at once. . . . [or] they would stay in Chicago for a day or two" (p. 221).

Anderson's view of communicative love is not as well defined as a reader might wish; yet it gives not only a sense of the encompassing scope of Anderson's understanding of the power of that type of love that could be achieved as "one . . . walk[s] through towns and cities" but also suggests an urban utopia. But in his dreams the author's persona envisions "new and marvelous cities" filled with a new race of people who are marked by their openness.

> He went along imagining such cities. For one thing the doors to all the houses were wide open. Everything was clean and neat. The sills

to the doors of the houses had been washed. He walked into one of
the houses. Well, the people had gone out, but on the chance some
such fellow as himself would wander in they had set out a little feast
on a table in one of the rooms downstairs. . . . There was a city,
wherein each house was a feasting place and this was one of the
houses and in its sweet depths things other than the belly could be
fed. (pp. 167–68)

Anderson, of course, was not the first to envision a utopian city,
but his voiced optimism displays his own idea of urban possibilities,
even if they could not be urban probabilities. These places that have
little relationship to the real world are beautiful and are peopled by
those "who had learned the secret and the beauty of bestowing unasking love." He explains:

Such a people would inevitably keep their own persons clean and
well arrayed. They would be colorful people with a certain deco-
rative sense, a certain awareness of themselves in relation to the
houses in which they lived and the streets in which they walked.
One could not love until one had cleansed and a little beautified
one's own body and mind, until one had opened the doors of one's
being and let in sun and air, until one had freed one's own mind and
fancy. (pp. 222–23)

Closely associated with the communicative powers of "unasking
love" are the distinctions John Webster is able to make between life
and death. He is convinced

Death was a thing, like life, that came to people suddenly, that
flashed in upon them. There were always the two figures walking
through towns and cities, going in and out of houses, in and out of
factories and stores, visiting lonely farmhouses at night, walking in
the light of day along gay city streets, getting on and off trains, always on the move, appearing before people at the most unexpected
moments. It might be somewhat difficult for a man to learn to go in
and out of other people but for the two gods, Life and Death, there
was no difficulty. (p. 216)

The pessimism of his view of death is tempered by the expression of
the importance of love to the life of mankind in the city and ultimately
to the abundance of love in the world.
      As he continues his musings on Life and Death, Webster con-

cludes: "There was a cleansing, a strange sort of renewal within the house of the man or woman when the god of Life had come in." On the other hand, Webster thinks Death is not so open and often "had many strange tricks to play on people. . . . Sometimes he let their bodies live for a long time. . . . It was as though he had said, 'Well, there is no great hurry about physical death. That will come as an inevitable thing in its time. There is a much more ironic and subtle game to be played against my opponent Life.'" As Death continues its soliloquy, urban communities become the obvious target. "'I will fill the cities with the damp fetid smell of death while the very dead think they are still alive'" (p. 217). As if to lessen the impact of his views of Life and Death, Anderson earlier cautions against attempts to articulate the meaning of life and asserts: "There was something wicked and ungodly in this business of defining life too sharply" (p. 152), but this does not mitigate the observation that cities are often inhabited by those who are already dead.

In many ways John Webster represents another aspect of the contradictory forces that had motivated Sam McPherson, Beaut McGregor, and Hugh McVey. Yet, his surname devoid of the *Mc* that the reader finds in the names of Anderson's earlier heroes suggests that not only is the implied rebellion against an ineffectual father to be unimportant but of greater significance is the absence of a sense of human continuity presumed by each character who is "the son of." Webster's rebellion, however, is directed toward those dated and dead notions that control so much of human life. Consequently, throughout the recital of Webster's thoughts, Anderson maintains that truth and communication are extremely important. Too frequently people are bogged down by the lies which they tell themselves, "a kind of furious passion of lying that, once started, couldn't be stopped" (p. 147); and this ultimately leads to "a kind of perpetual denial of life" (p. 113) that in turn, accounts for much misery.

The evolution of urban life is blamed for distinct changes in human existence. "It must have come about that as men and women went out of the fields and hills to live in cities, as factories grew and as the railroads and steamboats came to pass the fruits of the earth back and forth a kind of dreadful unawareness must have grown in people" (p. 43). In time, it becomes clear to Webster that

> as things are now, here in this town and in all the other towns and cities I have ever been in, thing are a good deal in a muddle. Everywhere lives are lived without purpose. Men and women either spend

their lives going in and out of the doors of houses and factories or
they own houses and factories and they live their lives and find
themselves at last facing death and the end of life without having
lived at all. (p. 88)

Central to John Webster's contemplative mood is an analysis of
the use of words in relationship to truth. "People everywhere told
things, talked of things they thought interested them, but no one told
truths" (p. 164). Even education, which provides "facts," could not
get to "truth." During most of the novel, John Webster is delivering a
monologue addressed to his unusually silent daughter, whose role in
the story is frequently as puzzling as Webster's actions. That she provides a passive and unquestioning audience is one device by which
Webster can "talk through" his ideas as he repeatedly returns to the
equation that relates the individual body to the complexity of the city.
He tries to explain the collapse of his marriage, a collapse based largely
upon the lack of communication and an inability to recognize truth as
Webster understands those concepts.

Lest one dismiss his imagination as inconsequential or perhaps
the ravings of a diseased mind, Webster is convinced, as was Sherwood Anderson, that a "man's fancy, the creative thing within him,
was in reality intended to be a healing thing, a supplementary and
healing influence to the working of the mind" (p. 200). On the other
hand, the creative impulse is constantly being thwarted by the various required trappings of society. In this regard, Webster's physical
nakedness before the statue of the Virgin might be considered not as
misplaced eroticism but rather as both an explanation of the role of
clothing in society and a revelation of the spiritual nakedness of modern man. "The clothes he habitually wore and that he had learned to
dislike because they had been made not for himself, but for some impersonal being, in some clothing factory" (p. 86) are very much like
the ideas and precepts of life adopted for convenience and comfort.

The formlessness of human existence and the general sense of
futility in *Many Marriages* are indicative of the presence of these forces
in modern life. Much of this is exacerbated by an optimistic feeling
which has pervaded American civilization. Webster is aware "all
through his life . . . there had been a notion to which he had clung."
He realizes that

it had been a kind of beacon that now he felt had from the first led
him into a false trail. He had in some way picked up the notion from

others about him. It was peculiarly an American notion, always being indirectly repeated in newspapers, magazines and books. Back of it was an insane, wishy-washy philosophy of life. "All things work together for good. God's in his Heaven, all's right with the world. All men are created free and equal" . . . [And he concludes:] What an ungodly lot of noisy meaningless sayings drummed into the ears of men and women trying to live their lives! (pp. 208–209)

But this sense of futility does not keep John Webster from embarking upon a quest that will give existence more meaning than the routine chores of business might suggest, just as it does not deter other men and women including Sherwood Anderson. In the process, there is an examination of the effects of modern life.

III

Bruce Dudley, the protagonist of *Dark Laughter* (1925), conducts a similar search and comes to a like conclusion. He views himself as a modern-day Huck Finn "setting out on a little voyage of discovery" and, after escaping from life in Chicago, travels down the Mississippi River. He settles in Old Harbor, Indiana, where he had spent part of his childhood. By this time, he has changed his name to John Stockton with the ease associated with the western frontier where the question What do you call yourself? had supplanted the query What is your name? Breaking one's ties with the past, considered by some to be a peculiarly American characteristic, also provides an opportunity for a new beginning unrestricted by a former time or place. His new identity, however, is partially an attempt to live incognito because he does not want to be remembered as the son of the man who at one time had been a school principal in Old Harbor. (This obviously raises a question about the selection of Old Harbor rather than a number of other possible choices inasmuch as his previous life in that town is not unduly significant in the novel.) Of greater importance than the name change is Bruce's attempt to understand his own identity. He has a "notion that Myself is a land few men know about. I thought I'd take a little trip into myself, [and] look around a little there" (p. 61). In so doing, he does go home again.

While in Chicago, his childless marriage is marked by the spirit of liberation; but characterized by a lack of communication and a wall of silence, it has increasingly become unbearable. Just as in previous works where the city serves either as an escape *to* or *from* for the characters, *Dark Laughter,* primarily an internalization of the thought processes of Bruce Dudley as he seeks freedom from the constricting forces of his life, presents a story of a man who goes to Chicago looking for the success promised by the dream of the city and who escapes when the illusion cannot be realized. Anderson, however, poses the question: "Had Bruce fled from his city, Chicago, hoping to find, in the soft nights of a river town, something to cure him?" (p. 122). While the question remains unanswered, Anderson utilizes the same technique he had used earlier in *Many Marriages* by fusing the past, present, and future as he travels back and forth in time. Anderson's use of the flashback technique, with the often confusing treatment of chronology, reveals that he had some difficulty with the psychological aspects of his work; but there is far more action in this novel than in *Many Marriages.*

Critical reactions frequently dismissed *Dark Laughter* as a poorly written obscene book, whose symbolism did not make sense and that relied too heavily on the notion of the degeneracy of mankind.[22] Archibald MacLeish, in his perceptive analysis of the novel, singled out Anderson's obvious indebtedness to Joyce as leading to the work's central problem, primarily because Anderson could not effect Joyce's approach to "internalization." There was such a confusion between the author and his characters that the internal action took place in Anderson's mind rather than in the minds of his characters.[23] Ernest Boyd, however, claimed that the novel was not only a plea for a concerted rejection of those forces that chained people to unworkable traditions but also a statement of the life of the alienated artist.[24] William Langfield also was convinced that the work was autobiographical.[25] Stuart P. Sherman agreed and assumed that the novel was simply an outgrowth of Anderson's life in New Orleans.[26] (Neither critic presented a particularly startling idea inasmuch as Anderson's entire canon can be read as an autobiographical statement.)

As might be expected, the negative judgments were balanced by those that claimed the novel was a "good" one.[27] In fact, apparently, there were many who thought that *Dark Laughter* was Anderson's best work up to that time.[28] Public reaction resulted in the good sales of the book, which ultimately provided the monetary freedom that allowed him to move to Virginia in order to begin a new life; hence, in some ways the escape of Bruce Dudley is prophetic of the freeing of Anderson.

One might correctly suspect that initially the popularity of the novel had little to do with the theme of the work. *Dark Laughter* appeared at a time when white writers were once again discovering the potential of Negro life in America. It was published during the heyday of the Harlem Renaissance and explored the imagined primitive aspects of Afro-American life that many found so fascinating. Yet the title, as in other works by Sherwood Anderson, seems misleading. The "dark laughter" does occur, and the novelist seems to let it intrude as an underlying auditory background for some of the action; but the stereotypical notion that Negro women are more sensuous and perceptive does not particularly advance the story of Bruce Dudley and Aline Grey, unless the reader is supposed to believe that Anderson is assuming that these two people would find true happiness if they would strip away their pretensions to "civilization" and become "more primitive."

However, if there had been no "dark laughter," the situations would have been the same in the novel or, at least, they would not have been altered appreciably. But many critics took Anderson's title seriously and concluded that he had written a profound tale of Negro life; however, his central premise regarding that life had obviously been conditioned by his time and place. Thus, he did little more than repeat the customary images. He set forth two diametrically opposed viewpoints: the *natural*, unfortunately often called *primitive*, and the *mechanistic* or ordered, often confused with culture, civilization, or sophistication. Apparently, the undercurrent of the laughter of the nameless Negro characters in New Orleans, up and down the Mississippi River, or in Old Harbor is supposed to suggest a comment on the natural when faced with the falsity of the sophisticated. It may well be that had Anderson really pursued his distinction between the "truth" of "dark laughter" and the "falsity" of the unsmiling "white smiles," he could have produced a major work explaining some of the peculiar dimensions of race in the United States. But this was not his concern nor that of his novel.

Dark Laughter continues Anderson's exploration into the ambiguity of repudiating one life and accepting another. In *Many Marriages*, this is demonstrated primarily through Webster's introspective and often disjointed commentary as well as through his symbolic actions. In *Dark Laughter*, there is more deliberate overt action, and two stories come together. One deals with Bruce Dudley, the other has Aline Grey as the chief figure. After moving to a small Indiana town from Chicago, Bruce Dudley (now John Stockton) finds a degree of peace after his disastrous marriage to a liberated woman. He meets the dissatisfied Aline Grey, whose businessman husband has little under-standing of her needs. The relationship between Aline and Bruce in-tensifies. Eventually they escape. Their individual stories provide the framework for Anderson's examination of several facets of modern life.

In dealing with Dudley's life in Chicago, which constitutes al-most one-third of the novel, Anderson takes the opportunity to probe several facets of urban life. He suggests the limitations of a universe composed of modern multiple-family dwellings. Without investigat-ing all possible details of that world, the novelist describes it in terms of the apartment building in which Bruce Dudley lives with his wife, Bernice. The reader learns it is "near a corner where men coming out from the downtown district got off north- and south-bound cars to take other cars going east or west" (p. 25). Anderson notes that the building "was one of the sort of places that are being fixed up nowa-days in American cities to house just such childless couples as [Bruce] and Bernice. . . . There were a lot of such places in New York City and in Chicago and they were fast coming into vogue in smaller cities like Detroit, Cleveland, and Des Moines. They were called studio apartments." Then, in a rare presentation of such urban living ar-rangements in American literature, Anderson observes:

> The one Bernice had found and had fixed up for herself and Bruce had a long room at the front with a fireplace, a piano, a couch on which Bruce slept at night—when he did not go to Bernice . . .—back of that was a bedroom and tiny kitchen. Bernice slept in the bed-room and wrote in the studio, and the bathroom was stuck in be-tween the studio and Bernice's bedroom. When the couple ate at home they brought in something, usually from a delicatessen store, for the occasion, and Bernice served it on a folding table that could afterwards be put away in a closet. In what was called Bernice's bed-room there was a chest of drawers where Bruce kept his shirts and underwear, and his clothes had to be hung up in Bernice's closet. (pp. 46–47)

Anderson continues: "The couple had no servant. Every morning a woman came in for two hours to clean up the place. That was the way such establishments were run" (p. 51). Chic though this life-style might be with its "take-out" form of dining, the novelist covertly em-phasizes its emptiness and disorder.

Bruce is fascinated by city people when he can observe them from the isolated security of his apartment window. He is intrigued by a sense of oneness that really reinforces the isolation of urban dwellers. As he views "men and women getting on and off street cars at the street intersection where the cross-town cars met the cars in and out of the Loop," he says to himself: "God, what a world of people in Chicago!" Struck by such crowds, he muses: "What a lot of people getting off one car and onto another. They had all been down-town working and now they were going to apartments much like the one in which he lived with his wife" (pp. 39–40 *passim*).

In a few sentences Anderson transmits the sense of isolation, in spite of the city crowds, and the futility of those lives that have settled into a routine with a debatable comfort. As Bruce continues to look out of his window, down at the spectacle of the rushing people, he wonders:

> Why did they all look so tired? What was the matter with them? What he had in his mind at the moment was not physical tiredness. In Chicago and in other cities he had visited the people were all in-clined to have that tired, bored look on their faces when you caught them off guard, when they were walking along through the streets or standing at a street corner waiting for a car and Bruce had a fear that he looked the same way. Sometimes at night when he went off by himself, when Bernice was going to some party he wanted to avoid, he saw people eating in some cafe or sitting together in the park who didn't look bored. Downtown, in the Loop, during the day, people went along thinking of getting across the next street crossing. The crossing policeman was about to blow his whistle. They ran, little herds of them, like flocks of quails, escaping with their lives . . . When they had got to the sidewalk on the other side a look of triumph. (p. 41)

The powerlessness and impotence of urban crowds had also struck Beaut McGregor when he had contemplated the people in the streets of Chicago. In his unusual way, he had attempted to overcome this and give city folks a sense of purpose. Bruce, however, has no such commitment to reform the city.

Anderson singles out several phases of life closely associated with urbanism in order to explain the modern mind. While he found, as have other observers, newspapers to be important in determining public opinion, he was convinced that through its inaccurate use of words and its ability to capture the minds of thousands of people, the world of urban journalism contributes to an understanding of the thwarted lives within the city itself. Thus, as they generate public opinions, the newspapers are also responsible for manufacturing private myths. Furthermore, he was equally confident that the "new way" of writing news stories separated journalists from the reality of life and created a class of "word slingers." Part of this tendency found further exploitation in the ascendancy of advertising. The novel also examines the activities of the Renaissance spirit with special focus upon the views of life, art, and creativity espoused by the "renaissance makers." The popularity of art colonies both here and abroad often had little to do with the true meaning of art. Consequently, in discussions of modern literature and modern art, Anderson addresses issues of "realism."

Bruce and Bernice work for a newspaper, but Bruce is never as confident about his work as his wife is about hers. In fact, he had "drifted into newspaper work [and] . . . had kept drifting for ten years." In the meantime, he has overlooked his own ambition. He had wanted to be a writer, but Anderson makes it clear that the newest journalistic procedures seem to be antithetical to writing. "There was a way to be a newspaper man . . . without writing at all. You phoned your stuff in, let someone else write it up. There were plenty of the scribbling kind of fellows about—word-slingers" (p. 20). While it helped him learn the city because "he had to do a lot of running about through Chicago streets," his job never increased his ability as a correspondent. After he had telephoned his stories into the office, "some fellow [there] dressed it up" (p. 40). He cannot share his feelings of misgivings about the entire matter, but he realizes that the "word-slingers [made] a mess at words, writing the newspaper jargon. Every year it got worse and worse."

These "word-slingers" disturb Bruce because "deep in him . . . [he] had always had buried away a kind of inner tenderness about words, ideas, moods. He had wanted to experiment, slowly, going carefully, handling words as you might precious stones, giving them a setting." He wrote "local stuff—murders, the capture of bootleggers, fires, labor rows, but all the time he got more and more bored, tired of it all." Eventually, he questions himself: "Had he but succeeded, after ten years, in building up within himself a contempt for life?" (pp. 20–21). In contrast to his own thoughtfulness and the popularity of his wife, "there was a young Jew in the office who could fairly make the words dance over the page. He did a lot of Bruce's stuff." It is unfortunate that Bruce never realizes his importance as a reporter.

> What they liked about [him] in the local room was that he was supposed to have a head. He had got a certain kind of reputation. His

own wife didn't think he was much of a newspaper man and the young Jew thought he wasn't worth anything, but he got a lot of important assignments that the others wanted. He had a kind of knack. What he did was to get at the heart of the matter—something of that sort. (p. 40)

His editor, Tom Wills, "was like all of the newspapermen Bruce had ever known. He really wanted to write a novel or a play" (p. 42), but he had sold out for the sake of comfort. Because he has respect for Bruce's ability and shares some of his misgivings, Tom Wills often talks with his young reporter. When he thinks of the weaknesses of modern life, Tom is convinced that newspapers do not fulfill their potential. Contemplating his own role as an editor, Tom seems to understand not only the extent of his personal compromise but also the lost opportunities of the world of journalism. Sharing his thoughts with Bruce, Tom says:

Think of it man . . . three hundred thousand readers. Think what that means. Three hundred thousand pairs of eyes fixed on the same page at practically the same hour every day, three hundred thousand minds supposed to be at work absorbing the contents of a page. And such a page, such stuff. If they were really minds what would happen? Great God! An explosion would shake the world, eh? If the eyes saw! If the fingers felt, if the ears heard! Man is dumb, blind, deaf.

Then he raises the essential question about the role of the newspaper world in the development of modern life. "Could Chicago or Cleveland, Pittsburgh, Youngstown or Akron—modern war, modern factory, the modern college, Reno, Los Angeles, movies, art schools, music-teachers, the radio governments—could such things go on blandly if the three hundred thousand, all the three hundred thousands, were not intellectual and emotional morons?" (p. 216). That newspapers with their tremendous circulations do not measurably alter the life-styles of the nation's cities is additional evidence, at least to Tom, of the impotence of life. Yet, whatever one might think of these journals, they "are a necessary part of modern life. They weave the loose ends of life into a pattern" (p. 65).

The city of Chicago is most significant in *Dark Laughter* as the center of the early twentieth-century Renaissance. It was quite apparent that shortly after his departure from Chicago, Anderson began to have serious doubts about the era and questioned the value of the satellite movements it spawned. Now he considered many characteristics of the period. For example, the dominant mood emphasizing free-dom and the spirit of liberation were manifested in lifestyles and art. There was a great desire to talk *about* life rather than to live it. In the novel, among those in the movement are "intellectual men, news-paper reporters who wanted to write novels, women feminists, illus-trators who drew pictures for the newspapers and for advertisements but who liked to have what they called a studio and to sit about talk-ing of art and life" (pp. 21–22). "The young illustrators and the writ-ers who gathered in the rooms in the evenings to talk . . . all worked in newspaper offices or in advertising offices just as Bruce did. They pretended to despise what they were doing but kept on doing it just the same. 'We have to eat,' they said. What a lot of talk there had been about the necessity of eating" (p. 35).

Much of the spirit of the era is portrayed through Bernice, one of the period's liberated women. In their warped interpretation of free-dom, she and her friends talk unashamedly of their personal lives "speaking openly of their loves. They compared notes. Perhaps they used every little emotion they had as materials for stories" (p. 36). They seem to fear silence. Clearly, much of the talk is in reality just chatter, as the freedom-seekers justify their lives. Anderson ques-tions the meaning of this freedom. "A woman might write short sto-ries, do Sunday special stuff, go about freely with men (modern women who had any sense did that a lot nowadays—it's the mood of the day) 'still and all,' as that Ring Lardner would say, 'it don't make no difference.' Women nowadays are putting up a great little fight to get something they want, something they think they want anyway" (p. 66). Bernice writes "special articles for the Sunday paper" and has "written a story that had been accepted by a magazine" (p. 24).

As his wife's reputation grows among her friends, Bruce (who is not convinced that this new movement is really faithful to life) is merely tolerated. "When they went together to one of the places where other newspaper men, illustrators, poets and young musicians gathered the people were inclined to look at Bernice, address their re-marks to her rather than to him. . . . Gradually she had come to have a following in Chicago and was already planning to move on to New York. A New York paper had made her an offer and she was consider-ing it." Her marriage is inconsequential, and she reminds Bruce: "You can get a job there as well as here" (p. 27).

In addition to the acceptance of some vague notion of freedom that seemed to enslave its believers and the constant tendency to dis-cuss everything in some detail, the period saw the rise of clubs and associations that also were taken quite seriously. When Bruce's wife begins to achieve some fame with her short stories, she "joined a writers' club in Chicago." Occasionally, "Bruce had gone along with her . . . to [its] meetings . . . going to studios where men and women sat talking." In a not-so-veiled reference to the activities of the Fifty-seventh Street colony, Anderson inserts the following description, which alters the facts simply by moving the location of the site ten blocks to the north but does little to change the spirit of the times:

> There was a place in Chicago, out near Forty-seventh Street near the park, where a lot of writers and painters lived, some low small buildings that had been put there during the World's Fair and Bernice had wanted him to go out there to live. She had wanted to associate more and more with people who wrote, made pictures, read books, talked of books and pictures . . . (p. 24)

The diversity of the participants in this artistic movement is not lost on Bruce. In addition to the writers and artists who consider themselves to be part of the vanguard, Bruce remembers "there was Mrs. Douglass, the rich woman who had a country home and one in town and who wrote poetry and plays. Her husband owned a lot of property and was a connoisseur of the arts. Then there was the crowd over on Bruce's own paper. When the paper was put down in the afternoon they sat about talking of Huysmans, Joyce, Ezra Pound, and Lawrence" (p. 39). There was a certain international spirit in the Renaissance, but as far as Bruce is concerned it does not lead to a broadening of life; rather it results in making "half acquaintances—half friendships. . . . The Middle Western intellectual circles along the edge of which Bruce had played—watching Bernice plunge more boldly in—were filled with men not American at all. There was a young Polish sculptor, an Italian sculptor, a French dilettante. Was there such a thing as an American?" (p. 74).

Anderson makes much of Bernice's latest unfinished story about "a very lonely man in the city who while walking one evening saw in a shop window the wax dummy of what in the darkness he took to be a very beautiful woman." In her tale, "something had happened to the street light at the corner where the shop stood and the man had for the moment thought the woman in the window alive. He had stood looking at her and she had looked back at him. It had been an exciting experience." Because the man is so "lonely," he continues to return to the window after he discovers "his absurd mistake."

Commenting "the whole thing was a whimsical notion [that] Bernice had been excited about" (p. 26), Anderson makes it clear that her husband is puzzled by the tale and does not think she has much ability to develop it. While he thinks that it would be nice to "have a sweet young girl, working in the store, step into the window some night . . . [and have] the beginning of a romance," Bruce knows his wife will have "to handle it in a more modern way" (p. 38). He wonders: "Did she . . . hate and fear all men and was making the hero of her story such a silly fellow because she wanted to make all men . . . small?" He speculates: "That would certainly make her, the female, loom larger. It might be that was what the whole feminist movement was about. Bernice had already written several stories and in all of them the men were like that chap in the book-shop" (p. 50).

Coupled with Anderson's presentation of Bernice as a writer, *Dark Laughter* displays a genuine concern for the issues raised by modern literature. Activities of the age proved "there was great pride in word-slinging. Such and such a man knew how to sling words. Little groups all over town talking of word men, sound men, color men, and Bruce's wife . . . knew them all." Despite the period's avowed commitment to the arts, Bruce raises the question: "What was it all about, this eternal fussing about painting, music, writing?" And he concludes: "There was something in it. People couldn't let the subject alone. A man might write something, just knocking the props out from under all the artists Bruce had ever heard about—it wouldn't be hard he thought—but after the job was done it wouldn't prove anything either" (p. 39).

Unlike many of the Renaissance makers, Anderson in *Dark Laughter* seems unable to accept any longer the covert idea "if it's new or young, it is good." Essentially, the main thrust of the Chicago Renaissance, at least the more popular aspects of it, called into question the old way of doing things. On the other hand, the novel addresses two philosophical principles upon which the Renaissance makers based their imagined uniqueness. They had or sponsored a prophetic vision that emphasized the coming affinity between humanity and art. That this relationship was never translated into actuality did not appear to bother some of the "artists" who were not always aware of their failures. In time, even they became as much "con" artists as businessmen. In a very brief episode as he recounts the life of the avant-garde artistic group after the First World War, Anderson portrays just such artists. Ostensibly serving as itinerant portrait painters, Joe and Esther Walker soon learn to give clients what they want to see especially if the right price can be established.

In some detail, Anderson describes the various art colonies in Chicago and in Europe. There is Aline, the daughter of a wealthy Chicago businessman, who is to marry Fred Grey of Old Harbor, Indiana. Her excursions into art consist of taking classes at the Art Institute and her friendship with such "professional" artists as the Walkers. Joe is "the painter who did the portrait of her dead brother from a photo. He also did one of Teddy Copeland for his father, then one of Aline's dead mother—getting five thousand dollars for each—and Aline had been the one who had told her father about the painter. She had seen a portrait of his at the Art Institute, where she was then a student" (p. 141). That Joe and Esther are charlatans who prey upon the wealthy escapes Aline at first. It is not until she reaches Europe that she begins to understand the Walkers. Traveling to the world's great museums, "of a sudden she, the American, began walking in the presence of men's work feeling really humble. Joe Walker, all of his type of men, the successful painters, writers, musicians, who were America's heroes, got smaller and smaller in her eyes. Her own clever little imitative art seemed in the presence of work by El Greco, Cezanne, Fra Angelico and other Latins but child's prattling" (p. 168). The narrative of Aline in France raises a very serious question concerning the war's relationship to art. Anderson seems to be of the opinion that many of the idealistic artists who had fled to France found themselves going "into the trenches instead" (p. 178). And the war designed to save the world had produced, instead, innumerable lost souls.

The fact that the Walkers can survive so well in a decadent world tells as much about them as about that universe. Clearly, the idea that the artist is a pioneer or has great principle is a traditional notion, but Anderson fears the artist is subject to the gross opportunism of the time. Modern art itself is taken too seriously by its advocates. And its appeal for "realism" and "truth" is often forsaken for the substituted *big lie*. Bruce is often fascinated by a portrait of Bernice that had been done by a young German artist. The painting is not Bernice but a deliberate misrepresentation. The artist

> had done Bernice in broad lines of color and had twisted her mouth a little to one side. One ear had been made twice the size of the other. That was for distortion's sake. Distortion often got effects you

couldn't get at all by straight painting. . . . Afterwards [Bruce] won-
dered about the portrait. He had wanted to ask Bernice about it but
hadn't dared. What he had wanted to ask was why she had stood for
it to be made to look as the portrait had made her look.

He concludes, not entirely convinced "it's for the sake of art, I guess"
(pp. 47–48).

In effect, Anderson's interest in modern art runs the gamut from
the Parisian scene to the pitiful Americans who try to imitate what
they think are the demands of art. Furthermore, it is perhaps in keeping with the catholicity of taste so frequently demonstrated during
the period that the novelist displays throughout *Dark Laughter* a general knowledge of world literature. There are many references to both
European and American authors. in some respects the "name-drop-
ping" tendency of the Walkers is repeated by Anderson, but ironically
toward the end of the novel Aline is discovered reading *The Rise of
Silas Lapham*. On a symbolic level, the grasping Walkers who "sell" art
to the highest bidder, Bernice's unfinished story about the lonely old
man, the distorted portrait of her that has a prominent place in her
Chicago apartment, and the world of urban journalism that minimizes the skill of writing are expressions of a dissatisfaction with the
tenets of the Chicago Renaissance. As he concludes *Dark Laughter*,
Anderson seems convinced that realism, so highly prized in art and
in life, in actuality is a distortion of the real world; and he began to
wrestle with the rationale behind such distortions. Earlier in *Many
Marriages* he had dealt with an aspect of this issue as "illusion" and
the creation of "unreality." He ascribed its development to the ineffectiveness of words to do what they should and the fear of people
to admit the inadequacy of language. This led to a further analysis of
a second issue that was often used to delineate the distinction of the
so-called Chicago Renaissance.

After some years on a Chicago newspaper with his wife, Bruce
decides to leave the city as well as his wife. His departure, though
selfishly motivated, gives him an opportunity to rethink his past life
and begin a new one. In the process, he begins to understand his inability to communicate with Bernice. Realizing that it is the medium
for one type of relationship, Anderson displays an intense interest in
language and talk. Simplistically aware that ideas are transmitted
through words, Anderson mourns the inefficiency of language usage.
Even Bruce is aware that "words are tender things, leading to poetry—or lies" (p. 60). As a child he had been impressed by the singing

Negroes working on the river but had been unable to understand
what they were saying. "The word, as meaning, [was] of no importance. Perhaps words were always unimportant" (p. 106). Central to
his meditation is the questioning of the meaning of life. He realizes
that "the strangeness and wonder of things—in nature—[which]
he had known as a boy . . . had somehow later [been] lost." He attributes this "sense" of loss to "living in a city and being married to
Bernice." He understands "there was the strangeness and wonder of
trees, skies, city streets, black men, white men—of buildings, words,
sounds, thoughts, fancies. Perhaps white men's getting on so fast in
life, having newspapers, advertising, great cities, smart clever minds,
ruling the world, had cost them more than they had gained. They
hadn't gained much" (p. 108).

Bruce's interest in "words" is whetted also by his reading. "Once
he had read a book by Zola, 'La Terre,'" but it was a book by James
Joyce that had impressed him (p. 120). Fred Grey, not nearly as per-
ceptively, understands the problems and importance of language
which he considers to be "like bullets. They hit you or missed and you
escaped" (p. 302). In examining the effectiveness of words, *Dark
Laughter* raises some issues that had so fascinated the Renaissance
makers that they had devoted an inordinate amount of time discussing language and its relationship to realism as well as to the other *isms*
of literature.

The role of "words" as a conditioning factor in modern life is further explored through the businessman's use of advertising. In fact,
the "advertising man from Chicago" came to represent the absence of
honesty as well as the tendency toward sham and pretense. Very
briefly, in *Many Marriages*, Anderson had alluded to the importance
of such a man who had attempted to convince John Webster of the
merits of "advertising his washing machine in the big national magazines." Webster knows "it would cost a great deal of money"; however, such a campaign would mean "that he could raise his selling
price and sell more machines." In the end, "it would make the business a big one, an institution of national prominence, and himself a
big figure in the industrial world. Other men had got into a position
like that through the power of advertising. Why shouldn't he do something of the sort?" The question raises a central point for Webster. In-
tuitively, he knows there is something wrong with the image of himself "as a man of national importance in the industrial world"; in fact,
he is aware "the advertising man from Chicago could use big words,
apparently without being in danger of suddenly beginning to laugh"

(pp. 48–49). Of primary significance is the ability of *advertising*, as based in places like Chicago, to create an unreal world to which all ultimately are subjected. And this is done with *language*, the central tool of communication.

Anderson pursues this subject further in *Dark Laughter*. The reader, for example, early discovers that Bruce's father, the former school principal, became "an advertising writer" in Chicago and was subjected to whatever current craze was sweeping the country or to whatever was "his latest enthusiasm." Uncomfortably, Bruce sees this as simply another form of "word-slinging" that is so detrimental to honest relationships. Toward the end of the novel, Fred Grey looks forward excitedly to the arrival of "an advertising man coming down from Chicago," who is bringing a proposal for "putting on a national advertising campaign" for Fred's firm in a magazine with a national circulation (p. 145). That Fred, Aline's ineffectual husband, is engaged in making wheels seems strangely fitting for this alternatingly elusive and pompous businessman whose "wheel factory had become the center of life" (p. 189). Yet, Anderson observes: "the factory was making a lot of money and if a man didn't spend some of it to build up good will for the future he would have to pay it all out in taxes. Advertising was an asset, a legitimate expenditure. Fred thought he would try advertising" (p. 146) and is aware that the "advertising man from Chicago" is "up to a game of his own," but Fred is convinced that the man is "smart" (p. 165) and reflects upon the matter after the man has "just made a contract for a national advertising campaign on Grey Automobile Wheels in the magazines." Fred knows "American people . . . read advertising." Soon "the name of the Grey Wheel Company [will be] spread over the pages of all the national magazines. People out in California, in Iowa, in New York City, up in little New England towns, reading about Grey Wheels." Even he realizes "what was wanted was just the right catch-line, something to stop the eye of the reader, make him think of Grey Wheels, want Grey Wheels" (p. 273).

Advertising would aid in the urbanization of Old Harbor. "Already [Fred] had helped more than any other man to make the little river town half a city and now he would do a lot more. Look what happened to Akron after they started making tires there, look what happened to Detroit because of Ford and a few others. As the Chicago man had pointed out, every car that ran had to have four wheels" (p. 274). Anderson's portrait of Fred as a businessman uses the traditional stereotype and agrees that there is a certain inevitable nature to much of what is accomplished by these entrepreneurs. From a hill, Fred looks at his town.

> Away down there was the factory. Then the Ohio River, flowing on and on. When you got a big thing started it did not stop. There are fortunes in this country that can't be hurt. Suppose a few bad years come and you lose two or three hundred thousand. What of it? You sit tight and wait. Your chance will come. The country is too big and rich for depression to last very long. What happens is that the little fellows get weeded out. The thing to do is to be one of the big fellows, to dominate in your own field. Already many of the things the Chicago man had said to Fred had become a part of his own thinking. In the past he had been Fred Grey, of the Grey Wheel Company, of Old Harbor, Indiana, but now he was to become something national. (pp. 274–75)

Fred realizes a "fellow had to take chances" (p. 280), but his confidence is not absolute. He thinks of common laborers and workers. "I'd like to know though, what would happen if there weren't other kinds of men too?" His sense of discomfort ends as he remembers "with satisfaction, what the Chicago advertising man had said. The men who wrote advertising, who wrote for newspapers, all that sort of fellows were really working-men, . . . and when it came right down to scratch, could they be depended upon? They could not." Fred concludes, still thinking to himself, "they hadn't judgment, that was the reason. No ship would ever get anywhere without a pilot. It would just flounder and drift around and after a while sink. Society was made like that. Certain men had always to keep their hands on the wheel, and [he] was one of that sort." In fact, "from the beginning he had been intended to be that sort" (p. 284).

IV

For those readers who require a tidy closure for any novel, both *Many Marriages* and *Dark Laughter* might prove to be a disappointment. Although they seem to indicate that their characters reject their current life-styles, they do not appear to offer clear alternatives nor options. In fact, their indecisiveness is perhaps best represented by Bruce Dudley, who arrived in Chicago with a sense of hope and $500. He quickly loses the former and promptly banks the latter as an insurance against the perils of the city. Even the final escape in both novels is inconclusive. For example, in *Many Marriages* one learns that John Webster and Natalie Scwarz will go to Chicago as at least the first stop in their running away from their old lives. Fred Grey assumes when Bruce and Aline leave Old Harbor they will seek anonymity in Chicago. That the city should figure as the possible destinations of the two couples and that it should serve as the locale of Sam McPherson's search for "humanizing love" as well as for the authoritarian discipline of Beaut McGregor are indications of the ambiguous views of the urban milieu.

The definition of the city, which had begun with Sherwood Anderson's first published novel in 1916, seemed to be complete by *Dark Laughter*. Certainly, his work up to 1925 reinforced his urban vision as he analyzed the current notions of the American city in general and the midwestern city in particular. Although he never has been known for a consistency of philosophical thought, in less than ten years, his fiction presented cogent and forceful arguments for and against the American city. Part of the appeal of his work undoubtedly rested in his belief that the human element still had the possibility of some control over its destiny. The major urban novelists of this era had repeatedly emphasized the force of the city as a naturalistic device determining the direction of humanity. Anderson did not deny the inevitability of this power, but he never lost sight of the ability of humans to effect changes or to alter what appeared to be fate. That they did not always do so said more about their weaknesses than about the power of their environment. In a pessimistic age, Anderson dared to voice his faith in life. By so doing, he took the American city that had been given "life" and "personality" by other novelists and reduced it to an accidental gathering of some grasping, greedy, selfish people who were as responsible for the outcome of urban life as the abstract city itself. In time, then, Anderson, who had been "tempted to become a city man," understood the worth of the individual in Emersonian terms and spent the remainder of his life trying to communicate this sense of freedom.

EPILOGUE
A Storyteller's Moment

I have come to think that the true
history of life is but a history of
moments.

—*A Story Teller's Story*

In the last fifty years a vast change has taken place in the lives of our people. A revolution has in fact taken place. The coming of industrialism attended by all the roar and rattle of affairs, the shrill cries of millions of new voices that have come among us from overseas, the going and coming of trains, the growth of cities, the building of the interurban car lines that weave in and out of towns and past farmhouses, and now in these later days the coming of the automobiles has worked a tremendous change in the lives and in the habits of thought of our people of Mid-America.

—*Winesburg, Ohio*

10

Sherwood Anderson's
Urban Cycle

F ROM 1896 to 1922, while Sherwood Anderson periodically was a
resident of Chicago, a civic metamorphosis took place. Circumstances in Chicago reflected events in a nation that had changed
in the years from the close of the Civil War to World War I. What had
been an agrarian nation became an urbanized, industrial one. The
years were short between the Chicago of Marshall Field and the city
of Al Capone, but both represented personifications of forces to be
found in the city. There was a need to accommodate preconceived notions of life not only to the dynamics of change but also to a different
sense of morality. Not to be overlooked, of course, were the phenomenal shifts occurring within the small villages. Although they realized
some of the effects of industrialism, residents of America's small towns
were not prepared for the cataclysmic upheavals in the city. Yet, almost without exception, they believed the tales told by traveling
salesmen, advertisers, urban historians, and others who had been to
the nearest metropolis.

As the nineteenth century came to a close and the twentieth century began, there were those who were still trying to define national
goals. The period was chaotic, and there was a need to determine the
meaning of it all. Clearly, the nation needed new voices. Henry Adams
raised a central issue as he recorded his reactions to the World's Columbian Exposition where "education ran riot." He argued that "Chicago asked in 1893 for the first time the question whether the American people knew where they were driving." Moreover, in the midst of

urban chaos, in that strangely beautiful White City set in the middle of the grim Black City, Adams expressed a position that others had tried to ignore and asserted "Chicago was the first expression of American thought as a unity; one must start there."[1]

Booker T. Washington and W. E. B. DuBois had come to grips with the significance of race in the United States. Perhaps neither man saw all of the ramifications of what became known in some circles as the "American dilemma," but their "controversy"—an early media event supported by inevitable recriminations and jealousies—has obscured the fact that both men believed the salvation of the country would be forthcoming when racial problems were solved. Washington was certain that the concept of rising by one's bootstraps, as he had done, was workable. He was defender of the faith in the American Dream and believed it could be fulfilled. DuBois, on the other hand, concluded that the twentieth century's advancement was dependent upon the education and integration of the "talented tenth" within American life. It was this group that would provide the leadership for Negro America, but he also was convinced the progress of the new century would be circumscribed by a concern with the "color line."

As William James reexamined the old doctrine of pragmatism and, like Benjamin Franklin and other Founding Fathers, found in it answers for the nature of the national character, historians were trying to record the facts of the country, and philosophers were offering various interpretations. Finally, a former professor of history from Princeton became the President of the United States. While the diversity of opinions and attempts to redefine the American experiment were taking place, Woodrow Wilson idealistically convinced a people that participation in what was thought of as a European war was necessary in order to save the world. Soldiers marched away in confidence and some returned in confusion. The American Dream came under close scrutiny, and there was the realization that this fairy tale could lead to frustrating problems.

A growing sense of pessimism reached its nadir in the Great Depression. The war had not made the world "safe for democracy." The belief in the American Dream was quickly being replaced by a reality that made clear that the predictions of reformers and paternalistic businessmen for a better world was not in the foreseeable future. Those who had supported the Emersonian doctrine of self-reliance had believed with Henley that man was indeed the "captain of his fate" and the "master of his soul," but the application of Darwinism to economic and industrial life made it apparent that technology with its machines would become both captain and master. There were protests; however, nothing was going to stop the "progress" of modern life. Sherwood Anderson and other writers could merely serve as interpreters.

For a brief period, it appeared that the Middle West, with Chicago as its capital, would become the setting for a new American literature—one rooted both in the reality of the land and the urban experience. Writers tried to find an artistic form that would best express what to them was a new civilization in the process of becoming. That the seeds for this "new" culture had been sown when the first New England Puritans made clear accommodations between their religion and their surroundings, then called it *covenant theology*, mattered little. As the cities of the nation were being transformed, like other urbanologists, Anderson showed an awareness of the meaning of this transitional period.

The era was marked not only by the rapid town-to-city shift but also by strong beliefs in the unlimited assets of the nation. Although modern conservationists often have difficulty understanding it, "the-land-of-plenty" concept was reinforced during a time of unexpected growth as natural resources formed the bases for many fortunes. Sherwood Anderson has graphically described this period in *Poor White*. "On farms in Indiana and Ohio giant gas wells blew the drilling machinery out of the ground, and the fuel so essential to modern industrial development rushed into the open. A wit, standing in the presence of one of the roaring gas wells, exclaimed, 'Papa, Earth has indigestion; he has gas on his stomach. His face will be covered with pimples.'" In a more serious vein, Anderson continues by noting: "Having, before the factories came, no market for the gas, the wells were lighted and at night great torches of flame lit the skies. Pipes were laid on the surface of the ground and by a day's work a laborer earned enough to heat his house at tropical heat through an entire winter."

Beneficiaries of such largesse felt they had to display their good fortune whenever possible.

> Farmers owning oil-producing land went to bed in the evening poor
> and owing money at the bank, and awoke in the morning rich. They
> moved into the towns and invested their money in the factories that
> sprang up everywhere. . . . A man in Ohio, who had been a dealer
> in horses, made a million dollars out of a patent . . . he had bought
> for the price of a farm horse, took his wife to visit Europe and in

Paris bought a painting for fifty thousand dollars. In another State of the Middle West, a man who sold patent medicine from door to door through the country began dealing in oil leases, became fabulously rich, bought himself three daily newspapers, and before he had reached the age of thirty-five succeeded in having himself elected Governor of his State. In the glorification of his energy his unfitness as a statesman was forgotten.

The immediate result of all of this was "a vast energy [that] seemed to come out of the breast of the earth and infect the people." It was an energy that found an outlet as "thousands of the most energetic men of the middle States wore themselves out in forming companies, and when the companies failed, immediately formed others."[2]

It was not long before ambitious men and women were convinced that prosperity was to be found in the city. Accounts of urban achievements were common, and the major cities became the destinations of many. Chicago was in a unique position. It was younger than the major urban centers of the East and of the South and was not hindered by any false fidelity to the past. Furthermore, the tales told about it were perhaps more true than those whispered about other communities, and the transformation of Anderson's Bidwell records a process that was fairly common on the Middle Border. Towns with agrarian orientations were transformed into industrialized cities within the life spans of the old settlers. In Chicago, the biographies of those who lived during this era recount the unbelievable changes that took place as the city moved from its establishment into its Civil War period, then to the rebuilding that occurred after the devastating Fire of 1871, and finally to the preparations for the World's Columbian Exposition. For many people, Chicago not only became illustrative of the speed with which a city could develop but symbolic of the modifications needed in the American Dream. Although they were convinced that Chicago was the place to be, many midwesterners, whose faith in themselves and in the Dream never wavered, overlooked the fact that failure in Chicago was common. Consequently, by 1896, when Sherwood Anderson first moved to Chicago, the city had become the acceptable indicator for the direction of urban development in America and had been explained in terms of its elusive force by historians and artists alike who were searching for those qualities that might explain the urban locale. Eventually, the specificity of the city became a metaphoric statement for the chaos and disorder of modern life.

Chicago, standing as the urban center of the Midwest and a symbolic expression of the evolution of modern America, became for Sherwood Anderson (especially in his earliest written fiction) representative of the urban milieu. And, throughout his life, certain aspects of Chicago in particular and of cities in general intrigued him. Whoever said "history tells us what happened, and fiction tells us how it felt" could have anticipated Anderson's urban cycle that turned historical data into literary material. As was the case with many Chicago novelists, he began his career by paying close attention to the geography and specificities of the region. Anderson deservedly has been praised for the creation of Winesburg; yet, his perceived nostalgia for the small town's past is not supported by the evidence of his early work. To read it as a rejection of the new way of life and a mournful longing for the old days of individual craftsmanship that no longer has a place in an urbanized society is a simplistic conclusion, no more justified than the emphasis upon him solely as a teller of short tales about the thwarted lives in a small town. Or, to explain Anderson's short stories and novels merely as a revolt from the village does not tell his complete story. Many of the residents of Winesburg have had or hope for a life in the city. Moreover, both Caxton and Coal Creek are places from which his protagonists escape in order to go to Chicago to seek their fortunes. Even Bidwell, his most idyllic village, is introduced to readers as an isolated area, suspended in time, and captured as one might record a beautiful scene on canvas. Nevertheless, when the novel's action begins, Bidwell is ready for change.

At a given moment in his career, then, Sherwood Anderson traced the transformation of American society from its agrarian roots to the acceptance of the urban as *the* way of life. That he later seemed to repudiate the distinctiveness of his early work by attributing it to his reading or by repeating what others said about his connections with the small town does not alter that period in his creative life when he wrestled with the meaning of the American city. He knew that increasingly those who had defined their happiness and contentment in terms of an association with the land were modifying their outlooks, and it was not long before the chimera of success was directly related to the American city. Convinced that "going to the city" and the fulfillment of the American Dream were related, he explored the rise and the effects of urbanism upon a series of figures created at a time when the writing of fiction itself was in a transitional state. Consequently, although he never overtly offered the defense used by those who apologized for their work by emphasizing "the truth" of it, *truth* became for Anderson a modus operandi rather than simply a series of moral directives. The conflict between romanticism and realism was partially an argument between a representation of life as it was imagined to be and life as it actually was. The resolution of this issue was rendered useless by the advent of the naturalists who not only agreed that people were sinners by nature but also that they were overpowered by external or internal forces.

On one level, Anderson's urban novels, despite some inherent protest elements resulting from his initial confrontation with the city, seem a restatement of the sentimental novels of the nineteenth century; and his short stories set in cities often appear to use locale as an afterthought rather than as an integral part of the action. But as his settings moved from the specificity of places like Chicago to the city in general, Anderson examined such qualities as the silence and the isolation that manifested themselves in those urban areas not usually associated with either silence nor loneliness. Many of his characters are psychological studies of the effects of modern urban life upon the nature of human beings. If he had made this the sole concern of his career, he undoubtedly would be considered a major city novelist; but he combined his interest in locale with a more generalized study of modern life and the illusions that motivated so much of it. Although much of what he wrote was rooted in the midwestern literary tradition, his characters ultimately transcend region and become symbolic of the alienation and communicative wasteland of modern life. Still, Anderson remained convinced that despair was not the only solution. His occasional naturalistic view of life was tempered by a belief in the power of the individual to alter the course of events. He was committed to the possibility that the individual—in spite of overwhelming odds, whether personal, environmental, social, or economic— could achieve moments of self-reliance.

To chart the influence of a particular place upon a particular person is one of the riskiest literary endeavors, just as determining with certainty the pressures that produce significant moments in any writer's life is tenuously subjective and axiomatic. Obviously, to talk of a storyteller and a city is to suggest that one had an influence over the other. Since Sherwood Anderson is generally viewed as the voice of the small, warped, midwestern village, it is significant to note that from his first published novel in 1916, he also was a distinctive urban voice displaying the tensions of the modern American and revealing his own ambivalence toward the inevitable development of the American city. At the same time, trying to establish a correlation between an artist's life and work can be a desultory exercise, especially when one relies heavily upon the words and assertions of a writer who deliberately erases the delicate line between what is real and what is fancy, between what has been, what might have been, and what is. In the final analysis, the outsider can only imagine what has taken place, and the writer, with the wisdom of hindsight, often singles out some force as having had great importance forgetting others of equal significance. If the writer is concerned with self-explanations and personal validations, as Anderson often was, these assertions can lead the producer to misunderstand the product. Ultimately, then, one of the roles of the literary historian is to construct, in light of certain possibilities, a speculative theory that appears to offer an illumination of a particular writer or literary era at a given time, bearing in mind always that writers can be unreliable when they attempt to merge their public and private persons.

Thus, to assume that Chicago alone contributed to Anderson's urban vision might seem to be begging the question, especially when it is remembered that Anderson lived in many places during varying stages of their urban development: Clyde, Cleveland, and Elyria in Ohio; Kansas City, Reno, New York City, and New Orleans; and Fairhope and Mobile, Alabama. He wandered through some towns in Kentucky and North Carolina, spent time on the West Coast, visited the literary and cultural capitals of Europe, and ended his career in Marion, Virginia. However, at least to some degree, it is necessary to regard the effects of his background upon his production. He was born into an era that witnessed the acceptance of the American Dream as a viable goal that still had converts and saw the urbanization of the Dream.

Much of the life of the nation has been informed by a persistent belief in the promise of success, with its emphasis upon the possibility of moving from a low position to one of greater significance. "From rags to riches," one version of the legend, stresses the importance of the individual, separated from the traditions and demands of the past, standing alone either in the Garden of Eden or in the boardroom of some highrise building devoted to commerce. Thus, whether conditioned by a romanticized version of agrarianism or a realistic view of the urban environment, over the years the American Dream has motivated untold thousands and has remained a popular myth despite the harsh realities of politics, social structure, and economics. American audiences and readers have been convinced that the "from-rags-to-riches" process is both highly desirable and possible. During the nineteenth century and into the twentieth, these dreamers accepted the premise that the promised land existed somewhere in the United States. Failing to find it in one place, they searched for it elsewhere and soon were convinced the Dream could be realized in the nation's cities. Capturing this mood, many of the mobile masses, alluding to the unfulfilled promises of urban life, eventually came to recognize the American Dream as *the* American tragedy. But, before this occurred, the era had made it clear that the businessman had already become the nation's cultural hero. It was an age that convinced many little boys and girls to believe the Horatio Alger stories.

Anderson first went to Chicago in the days when the city was the symbol for the consummation of the American spirit. What he saw there conflicted with what he had heard. And, although he eventually became moderately successful, he realized that the acquisitive urge had serious flaws. *Windy McPherson's Son* appeared when he was forty years old, and the theme of a man's search for himself was in reality his search just as the effects of the city were those he had observed. Of course, the study of the inevitability of cities and the transformation that the urban brought about in the human are presented, at best, in statistical studies that by their very nature must remain abstract. By translating the same material into the fictional realm, Sherwood Anderson made the story dramatic and immediate. This is not to suggest Anderson's unreliability as an observer but simply to suggest that the nature of storytelling itself and the limitations of human memory can create a new reality. Accepting the premise that people, at least in part, are a reflection of their experiences, then region undoubtedly plays a role in human development.

With varying degrees of intensity, Anderson portrayed the consequences of locale on both the willing and the reluctant urban dweller. Anderson's city does not reveal anything that is startling or new, but his imagined hatred of the industrial age is in reality a hatred for what people had become. He realized the city's power was so pervasive that the mirage of the place had even permeated the nation's small towns and hamlets. While T. K. Whipple's judgment that Anderson wrote "a sharp and bitter epitaph for the old world that was perishing" and cast "a curse [on] the new world being born"[3] certainly has validity—especially in light of such works as *Windy McPherson's Son, Marching Men,* and *Poor White,* Sherwood Anderson's work goes beyond mere protest. And, in his concern for the "new" America, he was not alone.

In those strange and chaotic groupings of people called cities, the artificiality of life was apparent to Anderson. Writing to Van Wyck Brooks in 1918, he concluded "our cities produce [a] . . . peculiarly shallow effect,"[4] but he never denied the reality of that life. Although he ceased to be "a city man," his interest in the urban centers of America did not wane, and Anderson's immediate interest in Chicago and what it represented, a love–hate relationship, did not end with his departure from the city in 1922. He remained a fascinated observer of urban life and maintained a correspondence with many of his close friends from his Chicago days. Yet, continually in his letters to friends, associates, and admirers, he returned to the subject and complained about the ugliness of cities. He was bothered by filthy streets, uninspired buildings, "hordes of unemployed," and the general air of depression that seemed to permeate every urban place and everybody within the city. He often spoke of the "distracted crowds in the midst of distracting things." In fact, the sense of disorder so prominently analyzed in *Marching Men* is one of his dominant impressions of Chicago.[5] Yet, the city held a peculiar fascination for him. In 1929 he wrote to Horace Liveright from Chicago. Speaking of *Beyond Desire* as "a Chicago novel of the present day," he said: "I may have made a mistake in coming out here. I came largely because I wanted to get the feel of Chicago back into me."[6] In 1930, Anderson again mentioned a belief in cities as places of the dead, an idea he introduced in *Many Marriages* without fully developing it. In a letter to Charles Bockler, he described a trip to Richmond where he had "lived in a middle-class hotel . . . there I saw dead faces about me. There is something about prosperity, the hunger for it, the pretense in all these middle-class Americans, that makes the soul sick."[7]

There was a fatal inevitability about cities that precluded the idea that their forces could be changed. Hence, modern urban literature, until Anderson, seemed to record the lives of doomed men and women. Rejecting the vast indifference of Chicago and the clatter of its life, Sam McPherson searched for a renewal of individual integrity and the dignity of human life. Like Anderson, he looked for the lost age of kindness, beauty, and love. Beaut McGregor deplored the disorder of modern life and tried to establish order through his marching men, forgetting that power without beauty carried with it the seeds of destruction and failure. John Webster, in his highly symbolic search for a communicative love, was probably going to escape to the city, whereas Bruce Dudley fled from the artificiality found there. In the meantime, Hugh McVey was the instrument that aided in changing a sleepy Bidwell into a growing hustling city. These are just a few of Anderson's characters who came to understand that modern life is beset by an alienation and isolation so frequently devoid of truth. But Anderson believed that love was the humanizing force.

One of his most telling critical judgments on the importance of love ironically appears in a letter to Van Wyck Brooks written from Reno in the summer of 1923. Speaking of his "solid weeks" of reading Henry James, Anderson came to the conclusion that here was "a man who never found anyone to love, who did not dare love." And he continued: "I really can't care much for any character after he gets through with it; he, in short, takes my love from me too." Anderson then raises a significant question about James: "Can it be true that he is the novelist of haters?"[8] Although he frequently accepted the presence of a gloomy world, Sherwood Anderson never abandoned his belief in the human potential. Thus, despite his commitment to tracing the effects of the city, he did not accept the power of the city as some final inviolate entity, as did many of his peers. Neither did he confuse storytelling with sociological treatises. Yet, his role as an urban historian cannot be overlooked.

Ordinarily one would suspect that little in Sherwood Anderson's background would have prepared him for his intense understanding of his fictional people; however, his ability as a successful advertising copywriter suggests that he gained important insights into human nature. Furthermore, through the examination of the lives of others, Sherwood Anderson sought answers to a never-ending stream of questions. So strongly did he apparently believe in the necessity of understanding others in order to comprehend one's own self that an underlying didacticism and incessant probing seem to undergird much of what he wrote. He admittedly acknowledged that his creative impulse was rooted in the transfer of the autobiographical to the fictional. But a thorough understanding of his life does not alter the creations of his imagination; however, Anderson's autobiographical statements and his many works on writing give a sense of what was important to him. Despite his claims against the novel as a genre, he obviously brought to it his view of storytelling which was highly dependent upon the use of the intrusive author as a device to give a sense of direction. Because traditional realists have eschewed this mechanism as being disruptive, old-fashioned, and not in keeping with "a scientific approach," Anderson may appear to be particularly discursive and narcissistic.

As he analyzed the struggles of a series of protagonists who search for fulfillment, he presented characters faced with psychological, spiritual, or environmental forces over which they appeared to have little immediate control. But he often concluded such obstacles could be overcome when individuals understand themselves in relationship to the surrounding universe. In the end, Anderson did not have the inclination to remain committed to those deterministic forces that generate a sense of despair primarily because he was convinced that human beings could make a difference. He was not content to accept the magnetic intensity of the-city-as-an-evil power, which had found proponents among many nineteenth-century writers, and he reintroduced moral judgments into an urban literature that traditionally had traced the impact of various forces upon those who succeed in the city and upon those who fail. As a result, the characters of other urban writers tend to be divided simplistically into the "haves" and the "have-nots," between those who live in the spacious elite neighborhoods and those who exist in overcrowded slums, between the power of urban institutions and the weakness of human beings caught by circumstances.

Whether he ever fully recognized that he had come at the end of one literary tradition and, in an appreciable way, had spawned a new generation of writers who quickly forgot their indebtedness to him is doubtful. There must have been moments of sadness for Anderson, however, as William Faulkner and Ernest Hemingway went on to achieve the accolades of their peers while he, sidelined by his personal search, never attained the unqualified acceptance of the literary establishment during his lifetime, in spite of the subsequent praise heaped upon *Winesburg, Ohio* as a new venture in the art of storytelling. His apparent lack of a consistent poetics of the novel may be disconcerting to some literary theoreticians. For a variety of reasons, he was unimpressed with many of the century's outstanding novelists and poets. Writers as diverse as Ezra Pound, James Joyce, Sinclair Lewis, and eventually Ernest Hemingway came under his close scrutiny and were found wanting. Obviously, some of his attitudes may be ascribed to a very human reaction about their fame and acceptability in relationship to his. On the other hand, his judgment on Hemingway exhibits a substantive concern for the younger man's tendency toward "romanticizing the real."[9]

Anderson's acknowledgment of the reality of Chicago obviously did not change appreciably the nature of the place; but at a significant moment in the life of each, the man and the city met. Perhaps, in the long run, Anderson himself best suggested the relationship between the storyteller and a city that symbolized the success formula with its attendant emphasis upon money, the nameless crowds seemingly moving without direction, and the disorder that ultimately permeated modern life itself.

> When you have been sick of [Chicago] to the very marrow and accepted it, then at last, walking hopeless, endless streets—hopeless yourself—you begin to feel its beauty, its half-wild beauty. The beauty of the loose and undisciplined, unfinished and unlimited. Something half-wild and very alive in yourself is there, too. The city you have dreaded is like your own soul.[10]

Although he never became known as a "Chicago novelist" despite his use of Chicago as the recognizable setting for a substantial portion of his fiction, Anderson probably did as much as any one to shift the use of Chicago in fiction from its sociological base to an aesthetic one. He used several rhetorical strategies and narrative techniques consistently enough to form an alteration of the typical pattern of the urban novel. For example, the fable of the fighting chickens, brief though the episode is, in *Windy McPherson's Son* and the fable of the mice in *Poor White* are thematic centers in each novel. Anderson's fondness for the exemplum and the intrusive statement might appear to be deviations from the well-made plot, but they contribute to the overall effectiveness of the storyteller in control of his narrative. Moreover, his epigrammatic style resulted in some memorable prose lines. Forerunner though he was to one phase of literary modernism, Anderson did not build an aesthetic upon the incomprehensible. Even the difficulty of *Many Marriages* reflects the chaos of the mental state being recorded; and it appears that he rejected his own experimental use of language in that novel when he returned to a simpler diction and syntax in *Dark Laughter*.

After his Chicago years, Anderson's novels, short stories, and essays never ceased to reflect aspects of his early work, and always there was that vague search for an even more vague *truth*. Increasingly, physical settings meant little for his stories, but he was determined to get at the meaning of America through a questioning of the relationship between machines and human life. At the same time he continued to examine the importance of communication and love as human endeavors most jeopardized by the "progress" of the modern world just as he reminded himself and others the cornfields west of

Chicago represented nature, order, and truth. As he left Chicago in the early 1920s, he had other dreams to pursue, and like Thoreau explaining his departure from Walden, Anderson also had other lives to lead. His later interest in the political nuances of the Franklin Roosevelt era, his concern for coal miners and the dispossessed of the nation, and his willingness to become a country editor in Virginia were some of those lives.

While much is made of Anderson's return to the small town, it is one of the ironies of his life that the man who had done much to reject his businessman's image should have reentered village life as the owner of two newspapers. It is worth noting that even though many writers have been associated with the journalistic world, most have primarily held staff positions and have not been integral parts of management. The fact that Anderson was one of the "haves" of his community is made clear by the tale of the building of Ripshin. Happy with his ability to hire townspeople for the construction of his large house, he was startled by the reality of the comment made by the old woman who liked the idea of such a splendid dwelling in their neighborhood, but she reminded him, "we were all poor together ... before you came." [11]

Whatever discomfort he felt did not preclude his purchase of the Marion *Democrat* and the *Smyth County News*, the former the voice of the Democratic party and the latter the Republican newspaper of the region. That this could have led to the type of thought control which had bothered him about Chicago journalism in *Dark Laughter* apparently did not occur to him. To his credit, he soon adopted the necessary techniques of accommodation to prevent hostility to his papers. Thus, it was that inadvertently Anderson brought some "city ways" to the community; but in so doing, despite whatever his personal turmoil might have been, he proved to the townspeople the efficacy of the American Dream that he had examined and rejected so carefully in earlier days.

His writing continued to mirror his varying interests in modern life as he considered the influences of commercialism upon the individual. Like many others, he was aware that the nation's increased reliance upon technology had decreased the ability of human beings to communicate with each other. He was not alone in his acceptance of the myth of Chicago. Neither was he the only novelist-poet who attempted to translate his life in the city into an aesthetic experience. Had he never lived in Chicago at an impressionable time in his life,

the process of urbanization probably would not have been as important to him. But he was both a believer and a victim. That he was concerned about what the urban experience could do to an individual,
especially to one who has faith in the myth, is clear; but to look to him
for solutions to the problems of a modern industrial culture and civilization is to expect more than a storyteller is obligated to give. Throughout his work his apparent answers often raise additional questions,
and many of his loosely constructed narratives seem to stop *in me-
dias res.*

To capture life's significant moments led him as a creative artist to
probe into those conditions, both internal and external, that affect the
human spirit. Unlike the practicing naturalists, who continually insisted that all details be catalogued in the belief that the importance of
a tale rested in the collective reporting done in a pseudo-scientific
manner, and unlike the popular realists, who viewed a faithful representation of life as the core of the art of writing, Sherwood Anderson
was convinced that such "reality to life" might "possibly be very good
journalism" but "bad art." In accepting his role as a storyteller he
blurred the lines between traditional romanticism, realism, and naturalism. He eventually assumed that a tale could be captured by a fidelity to his imagination as well as to his search for truth. Congruity and
incongruity came together in the artist. He saw his storytelling as a
means by which he could take those isolated significant moments of
human life as representative of some workable truth, and he willingly
accepted the city as a place of dreams where chaos and disorder
reigned, a place of death and misery.

Clearly the disorder of life was counterproductive; yet, there was
a hauntingly beautiful quality about the relationship between powerful people coming to terms with powerful places. But an urban aesthetic did not emerge because he could not agree where such a principle should be located; moreover, he was certain that it had little to
do with a transcription of reality. At the same time, the distortions of
the Cubists who were trying to define reality in purely personal terms
did not work either. And Dudley's questioning comment in *Dark
Laughter* ("For the sake of art, eh?") in part became Anderson's dismissal of certain theories based upon art as distortion.

By the end of his urban cycle, Sherwood Anderson was fully cog-
nizant of the city's ugliness but was convinced that its prospects for
beauty rested within the human potential. Despite the work of the
advertising men from Chicago, he affirmed the possible supremacy of

the human spirit that never forsakes its ability to seek a good life. As he charted the reality of urban life, a development in which millions of Americans participated during a phase of his productive period, Sherwood Anderson demonstrated that the validity of history was not at variance with the validity of narration. And at a specific moment his was an impressive urban voice.

Notes

1. THE LEGENDARY CHICAGO AND THE REAL CITY

1. *The Rise of the City, 1878–1898* (New York: Macmillan, 1933), p. xiv.

2. *Together* (New York: Macmillan, 1908), p. 208.

3. *The Autobiography of an Idea* (New York: American Institute of Architects, 1924), p. 325.

4. *The Education of Henry Adams* (Boston: The Massachusetts Historical Society, 1918), p. 339.

5. (New York: B. W. Huebsch, Inc., 1924), p. 228. Unless otherwise noted, all subsequent references to *A Story Teller's Story* are to this edition.

6. *Sherwood Anderson's Memoirs.* (New York: Harcourt, Brace and Company, 1942), p. 118. Cf. Ray Lewis White's *Sherwood Anderson's Memoirs: A Critical Edition* (Chapel Hill: The University of North Carolina Press, 1969), p. 155. Perhaps nowhere is the problem of using *Sherwood Anderson's Memoirs* more apparent than in these two editions. While Anderson had practically completed his work prior to his death, Mrs. Anderson and Paul Rosenfeld, with the aid of some friends, prepared the work for its 1942 publication. Through a study of the original manuscripts, Ray Lewis White discovered that the work had been subjected to such editing that it did not reflect Anderson's intention; hence, in 1969 his *Sherwood Anderson's Memoirs*, based upon the original notes, appeared. Where there are substantive differences between the two, I have tried to indicate them. In the present citation, however, the wording is the same. Furthermore, in subsequent references to the *Memoirs*, I will indicate the version being used by citing the date of the edition.

7. *Agricultural Advertising* 9 (February 1902):6–7. The articles Sherwood Anderson wrote for the trade journal *Agricultural Advertising* still provide a wealth of information about his early public writing career. His assignments included writing columns on business, and in these he glorified the philosophy and practitioners of a business ethic based upon the Franklin formula for achieving success. These columns now furnish significant background material for understanding his later work. Furthermore, they can be studied as the beginning of his evolution and transformation from an advertising writer to a creative literary artist. In retrospect, one can see the effects the city had upon

him as he absorbed scenes, concerns, and themes that were to provide a store-house of characters and incidents from which he was to draw later in his career.

Ray Lewis White has also observed, "Anderson's early enthusiasm for business and advertising can best be studied in his columns written for *Agricultural Advertising*." See his edition of *A Story Teller's Story: A Critical Text*. (Cleveland: The Press of Case Western Reserve University, 1968), p. 215. Cf. William Sutton, "Sherwood Anderson: The Advertising Years, 1900–1906." *Northwest Ohio Quarterly* 22 (Summer 1950):120–57.

8. While all biographers of Sherwood Anderson tend to give their theories of Anderson's illness, the most thorough account appears in William A. Sutton's, *Exit to Elsinore* (Muncie, Ind.: Ball State University, 1967). See also Sherwood Anderson, "When I Left Business for Literature," *Century* 113 (August 1924):489–96. In "Babbitt Strikes Out," Lloyd R. Morris refers to Anderson as undergoing "the experience of a Babbitt at odds with his environment" and claims when Anderson left the world of business he made his "most explicit criticism of his environment" (*Postscript to Yesterday* [New York: Random House, 1947], pp. 145–48.)

2. THE CITY "TRIUMPHANT": CHICAGO IN FICTION

1. (New York: Alfred A. Knopf, 1921), p. 394.
2. *Poor White* (New York: B. W. Huebsch, Inc., 1920), pp. 163–64.
3. (New York: Dodd Mead and Company, 1872), p. 106. All further references appear within the text.
4. (New York: Harper and Brothers, 1893), pp. 43–44.
5. *With the Procession* (New York: Harper and Brothers, 1895). All further references appear within the text.
6. *Heroines of Fiction* Vol. 2 (New York: Harper and Brothers, 1901), pp. 79–83.
7. (Chicago: Herbert S. Stone and Company).
8. (New York: Macmillan), pp. 101–104 *passim*.
9. (New York: Macmillan), p. 47.
10. (New York: Macmillan), p. 406.
11. *The New American Literature, 1890–1930* (New York: Century Company, 1930), p. 36.
12. "Chicago in Fiction," *The Bookman* (November 1913):270–72 *passim*.
13. *The Pit* (New York: Doubleday, Page & Co., 1903), p. 41.
14. (New York: John Lane, 1914), pp. 10–14 *passim*.
15. On March 10, 1921, Sherwood Anderson wrote to his friend, Paul Rosenfeld, "I am at various times grouped with [F. Scott] Fitzgerald . . ., [Henry Kitchell] Webster, William Allen White, [Floyd] Dell, [Sinclair] Lewis, E. P. Roe, and others." Quoted in Howard Mumford Jones and Walter B.

Rideout, *Letters of Sherwood Anderson* (Boston: Little, Brown and Company, 1953), p. 72.

16. *Memoirs,* (1942 ed.), p. 198.

3. SAM MCPHERSON: AN UNCOMMON PORTRAIT
OF A CHICAGO BUSINESSMAN

1. "Sherwood Anderson," *Double Dealer* 2 (July 1921):42–45.

2. *Letters on Contemporary Authors* (Boston: Four Seas Co., 1921), p. 15.

3. "Sherwood Anderson," *Friday Literary Review* (September 8, 1916):11.

4. "Windy McPherson's Son," *Little Review* 3 (November 1916):6–7. Many reviewers were apparently offended by what they deemed the repulsiveness of the novel. See "Fiction," *The Athenaeum* 4611 (November 1916):543.

5. *The Foreground of American Fiction* (New York: American Book Company, 1934), p. 113.

6. "Some Stories of the Month," *Bookman* 44 (December 1916):393–94.

7. "On Being Sherwood Anderson's Literary Father," *Newberry Library Bulletin* 5 (December 1961):315–21. Anderson also had referred earlier to Dell as one who "became a kind of literary father to me." See *Memoirs* (1942 ed.), p. 240.

8. "A New American Novelist," *Masses* 9 (November 1916):17. A month before Dell's review, the *New York Times Book Review* (8 October 1916) suggested a similarity between the Russian countryside of Dostoevsky and Sherwood Anderson's Midwest. Anderson's portrayal of "a most oppressive realism, the heavy, sordid atmosphere of a small town in the Middle West" was cited by the reviewer for *Spectator* 130 (28 April 1923):714–15, in an article entitled "The Mind of America."

9. "Some Outstanding Novels of the Year," *The Nation* 103 (30 November 1916):50.

10. (8 October 1916).

11. See H. W. Boynton, "Some Stories of the Month," *Bookman* 44 (December 1916):393–94. Cf. "The Mind of America," *Spectator* 30 (28 April 1923):714–15.

12. "A New Novelist," *Friday Literary Review* (8 September 1916):11.

13. "New Fiction," *Saturday Review* 135 (17 March 1923):375. Before the publication of *Winesburg, Ohio,* Gould wrote in "New Novels" for *New Statesman* (6 January 1917): "In *Windy McPherson's Son* Anderson first writes realistically and then melodramatically. Only in fragments of the story is there 'pathetic beauty'" (p. 330).

14. "The Creed of the Novelist," *Smart Set* 50 (October 1916):144. See also Ben Hecht, "A New Novelist," *Friday Literary Review* (8 September 1916):11.

15. "Between Book Ends: Sherwood Anderson's First Novel," St. Louis *Post-Dispatch* (21 December 1965):35.

16. "Three Not of a Kind," *Dial* 61 (21 September 1916):196–97. See also F.[rancis] H.[ackett], "A New Novelist," *New Republic* 9 (20 January 1917): 333–36 *passim*.

17. "Chronicle and Comment," *Bookman* 45 (May 1917):307.

18. "Windy McPherson's Son," (9 November 1916):536. Years later the novel was accused by the *Times Literary Supplement* of ignoring the beauty of life. See "New Novels" (8 March 1923):158.

19. "Emerging Greatness," *Seven Arts* 1 (November 1916):73–78. He called it "*made* and insincere." He continued: "I hope Mr. Anderson is ashamed of it. I hope he does not really believe that all man has to do, to find God, is to increase and multiply more helpless creatures like himself. This pretty surcease to trouble that comes from transferring the problems of life to the next generation is a biological fact. But it is not art" (76).

20. "Windy McPherson's Son," 204 (December 1916):942–43. See also "Current Fiction," *The Nation* 104 (11 January 1917):49–50; and Gerald Gould, "New Novels," *New Statesman* 8 (6 January 1917):330–31.

21. "From Newsboy Upward," Section 3, (25 November 1916):6.

22. "Some Outstanding Novels of the Year," *The Nation* 103 (30 November 1916):508. In some respects, it must be remembered, *Windy McPherson's Son* is a restatement of Maeterlinck's tale whose famous bluebird captivated readers and was a popular explanation for the futility of certain types of quests. Coincidentally, the dramatization of "The Bluebird" was frequently used by Chicago's elocutionists in their public programs.

23. *Sherwood Anderson* (Minneapolis: University of Minnesota Press, 1964), p. 16.

24. Howard Mumford Jones and Walter B. Rideout, eds., *Letters of Sherwood Anderson* (Boston: Little, Brown and Company, 1953), pp. 8 and 24. The second letter is dated November 2.

25. (New York: John Lane Company, 1916), p. 126. Analyses of *Windy McPherson's Son* sometimes create a problem because Anderson revised the novel in 1921. In 1922, the second edition appeared under the imprint of B. W. Huebsch, Inc. In 1965, as part of its "Chicago in Fiction" series, the University of Chicago Press reissued the novel, based upon Anderson's alteration of the original, with an introduction by Wright Morris. When references are made to the revised edition, that fact is made clear in the text; consequently, unless otherwise noted, references to Anderson's first-published novel are to the *first* unrevised edition of 1916, and the notations appear in the text.

26. Jones and Rideout, *Letters*, p. 82. In an unfinished letter to Ben Huebsch written during the latter part of 1921, Sherwood Anderson said: "I am afraid I had come to novel writing through novel reading. I could not leave Sam in my readers' hands having achieved nothing but money and weariness."

27. Ibid., pp. 81–82.

28. "Emerging Greatness," *The Seven Arts* 1 (November 1916):75.

4. BEAUT MCGREGOR: ANGRY ACTIVIST IN A DISORDERLY CITY

1. *Smart Set* 53 (December 1917):143.
2. *Sherwood Anderson's Memoirs* (New York: Harcourt, Brace and Company, 1942), pp. 283–85.
3. Ray Lewis White's critical edition of the *Memoirs* (Chapel Hill: University of North Carolina Press, 1969), pp. 186–87 *passim*.
4. See "For the People," *Nation* 105 (11 October 1917):403–404; "Dignifying Labor," New York *Tribune* (27 October 1917):9; and "Marching Men," *New York Times Book Review* (28 October 1917):442.
5. "To American Workingmen," *New Republic* 12 (29 September 1917): 249–50.
6. "Labor in Life," *Publishers Weekly* 52 (20 October 1917):1372.
7. *Intellectual America: Ideas on the March* (New York: Macmillan, 1941), p. 329.
8. "Discipline," *Dial* 113 (27 September 1917):274–75.
9. "Sherwood Anderson and the Power Urge: A Note on Populism in American Literature," *Commentary* 10 (July 1950):78–80.
10. *Sherwood Anderson* (New York: Holt, Rinehart, and Winston, 1967), p. 20.
11. "A Stroll Through the Fairs of Fiction," *Bookman* 46 (November 1917):338.
12. "For the People," 105 (11 October 1917):403.
13. "Dignifying Labor," (27 October 1917):9.
14. New York *Call* (11 November 1917):14.
15. (28 October 1917):442.
16. *The Achievement of Sherwood Anderson: Essays in Criticism* (Chapel Hill: University of North Carolina Press, 1966), p. 9.
17. Ibid., p. 25.
18. *Sherwood Anderson* (Minneapolis: University of Minnesota Press, 1964), pp. 17–20 *passim*.
19. (New York: John Lane Company, 1917), pp. 66–67. Although I am not unmindful of the very fine rendering of *Marching Men: A Critical Text* by Ray Lewis White (Cleveland: The Press of Case Western Reserve University, 1972), references to the novel are to the first-printed edition, and subsequent citations appear within the text. For those who wish to study the novel in greater detail, however, the White Introduction, Explanatory Notes, and Bibliography provide excellent materials.

5. "DISORDERLY" REALISM

1. "A Note on Realism," *Sherwood Anderson's Notebook* (New York: Boni and Liveright, 1926), pp. 72–76 *passim*.
2. *A Writer's Conception of Realism* (Olivet, Michigan: Olivet College, 1939), p. 26.

3. Anderson's essay first appeared in the November 8 issue of the *Dial* and was reprinted in *Sherwood Anderson's Notebook*, pp. 195–200.

4. *A Story Teller's Story* (New York: B. W. Huebsch, Inc., 1924), p. 360.

5. Quoted in Howard Mumford Jones and Walter B. Rideout, *Letters of Sherwood Anderson* (Boston: Little, Brown and Company, 1953), p. 78.

6. Augusto Centeno, ed., *The Intent of the Artist* (Princeton, N.J.: Princeton University Press, 1941), p. 64.

7. William Sutton, *The Road to Winesburg* (Metuchen, N.J.: The Scarecrow Press, Inc., 1972), pp. 191–92. In his critical editions of *A Story Teller's Story* (Cleveland: The Press of Case Western Reserve University, 1968); *Sherwood Anderson's Memoirs* (Chapel Hill: University of North Carolina Press, 1969); *Tar: A Midwest Childhood* (Cleveland: The Press of Case Western Reserve University, 1969); and *Marching Men* (Cleveland: The Press of Case Western Reserve University, 1972), Ray Lewis White consistently has pointed out the numerous times that Anderson, consciously or unconsciously, confuses and mixes fact and fiction, as does Martha Curry in her Introduction to the critical edition of *The "Writer's Book"* (Metuchen, N.J.: The Scarecrow Press, 1975); hence, there is no need to repeat nor recount instances of that tendency.

8. Letter written to Charles Bockler, dated circa November 12, 1930. Also quoted in Jones and Rideout, *Letters*, p. 226.

9. Centano, *The Intent of the Artist*, p. 47.

10. (Cambridge: Harvard University Press, 1949), pp. 159–60.

6. "SOMETHING BLOSSOMED IN CHICAGO": RENAISSANCE DAYS

1. *Memoirs* (1942 ed.), p. 241.

2. See Chapter X of *A History of Chicago* Vol. 2 (New York: Alfred A. Knopf, 1940), pp. 390–430.

3. For a detailed analysis of early literary efforts in Chicago, including a survey of the role of journalists and editors in the creation of a distinctive urban literature, see Kenny J. Williams, *Prairie Voices: A Literary History of Chicago from the Frontier to 1893* (Nashville: Townsend Press, 1981).

4. See James Stronks, "Lucy Monroe's 'Chicago Letter' to *The Critic*, 1893–1896," *MidAmerica* 5 (1978):30–38; and Kenny J. Williams, *In the City of Men: Another Story of Chicago*, (Nashville: Townsend Press, 1974), pp. 77–175.

5. See Bernard Duffey's *The Chicago Renaissance in American Letters* (East Lansing: Michigan State University Press, 1953); Hugh D. Duncan's *Rise of Chicago As a Literary Center: A Sociological Essay in American Culture* (Totowa, N.J.: Bedminster Press, 1964); and Dale Kramer's *Chicago Renaissance: The Literary Life in the Midwest, 1900–1930* (New York: Appleton-Century, 1966).

6. *Many Lives—One Love* (New York: Harper and Row, 1972), p. 64.

7. *Scofield Thayer and the* Dial (Carbondale, Ill.: Southern Illinois Press, 1964), pp. 102–103.

8. New York: Whittlesey House (McGraw-Hill Book Co.,) 1944, p. 75.

9. Butcher, *Many Lives*, p. 67.

10. Ibid., p. 66.

11. Ibid., p. 81.

12. *All Our Years* (New York: Viking Press, 1948), p. 122.

13. *Chicago's Left Bank* (Chicago: Henry Regnery, 1953), pp. 19–20.

14. Butcher, *Many Lives*, p. 77.

15. *Memoirs* (1942 ed.), p. 199.

16. 1 (March 1914), 23.

7. SONGS OF THE CITY AND SOME ROOMING HOUSE PEOPLE

1. "Book Reviews," *Yale Review*, New Series 8 (January 1918):437.

2. "Mid-America Awake," *Poetry* 12 (June 1918):155–58. See also Henderson's "The Soul of Man in Chicago," *New Republic* 17 (4 January 1919):288–89.

3. "A Novelist Turned Prophet," *Dial* 64 (23 May 1918):483–85.

4. "Nascent Poetry" (26 April 1918):10.

5. "Poetry and Drama" (14 April 1918):173.

6. "The Lutanist of Midsummer," Boston *Transcript* (5 June 1918), section 2:6.

7. "Poets, Rose Fever, and Other Seasonal Manifestations," *Bookman* 47 (August 1918):461–62.

8. (New York: Moffatt, Yard and Co., 1918), pp. 203–204.

9. *Mid-American Chants* (New York: B. W. Huebsch, Inc., 1918), pp. 16–18 *passim*. All further references to the poems in this work appear within the text.

10. "The Testament of Neuroses," *Bookman* 65 (August 1927):710–11.

11. "Sherwood Anderson," *The Nation* 126 (16 February 1928):189.

12. "From an Inner Fever," *Saturday Review of Literature* 4 (3 September 1927):85–86.

13. "An American Testament," New York *Sun* (22 June 1927).

14. *A New Testament* (New York: Liveright, 1927), p. 23. All further references to this work appear within the text.

15. See "A Gutter Would Be Spoon River," New York *Sun* (1 June 1919):3. (The review claims that Anderson moves "from human clay to plain dirt.") Cf. "Winesburg, Ohio," New York *World* (1 June 1919), section E: 6; William Allen White, "The Other Side of Main Street," *Collier's* 68 (30 July 1919):7, 18 (White attacks Anderson and claims that the tales are "the picture of a maggoty mind; a snap shot from a wapperjawed camera"); and Annie Russell Marble, "Sherwood Anderson," *A Study of the Modern Novel, British and American Since 1900* (New York: D. Appleton and Co., 1928), pp. 372–77 (she asserts that *Winesburg, Ohio* "shows the sordidness and sewerage of a village" that is displayed through the notions of "a prurient newspaper reporter").

16. Among the critics who cite *Winesburg's* realistic view of small-town life and the imposed restrictions created by such a life are: W.[illiam] S.[tan-

ley] B.[raithwaite], "Ohio Small Town Life," Boston *Transcript* (11 June 1919):
6. He also was one of the earliest critics to view Anderson as "an artist with
vision and sensibility, with comprehension and the capacity to test reality
with imagination." J. V. A. Weaver, in his "Sherwood Anderson" (Chicago
Daily News [11 June 1919]:12), compared Anderson to Gogol and Dostoevsky
and claimed he presented a "panorama with soul." Ernest Hemingway, who
was not always antagonistic toward Anderson, said in "Remembering Shoot-
ing-Flying: A Key West Letter" (*Esquire* 3 [February 1935]:21) that *Winesburg*
was among the "best of books" and that he "would rather read [it] again for
the first time . . . than have assured income of a million dollars a year." See
also John Nicholas Beffel, "Small Towns and Broken Lives," New York *Call* (21
September 1919):10; Llewellyn Jones, "The Uprooting of Winesburg," *Friday
Literary Review* (20 June 1919):9; M.[axwell] A.[nderson], "A Country Town,"
New Republic 19 (25 June 1919):257, 260; and H. L. Mencken, "Novels, Chiefly
Bad," *Smart Set* 59 (August 1919):140, 142. The last two citations also make
a point of identifying *Winesburg* in terms of its introduction of a new short
story form.

    17. There was a fairly widespread consensus that *Winesburg, Ohio* gener-
ally was a prose version of *Spoon River Anthology* and that the collection of
tales represented Anderson's rejection of the village life of Ohio. See "Books
of the Fortnight," *Dial* 66 (28 June 1919):666; Louis Wann, "The 'Revolt from
the Village' in American Fiction," *Overland Monthly and Out West Magazine* 83
(August 1926):299. Burton Rascoe, while implicitly comparing the two works,
felt that Anderson does not hate his characters as did Masters. See "Winesburg, Ohio," *Chicago Tribune* (7 June 1919):13.

    Interestingly, in a letter to Van Wyck Brooks dated May 31, 1918, Ander-
son wrote that he did not know Masters and had "no pull to him, lonely as I
sometimes am. I get the notion fixed in my mind that his successes have been
founded on hatred. A burning hatred arose in him and galvanized his lacka-
daisical talent into something sharp and real. Then the fire went away and left
the man empty. This is all theory. I do not know the fellow" (quoted in Jones
and Rideout, *Letters*, 39).

    C. Lewis Hind, on the other hand, saw *Winesburg* as a portent of the
future where *Spoon River* recorded what had been or what had occurred; consequently, he makes a distinction between the past and the future. See his
"Sherwood Anderson," *Authors and I* (New York: John Lane Company, 1921),
pp. 19–23. Carl Van Doren also felt that Anderson had a great affection for his
fictional people, which would separate him from Masters. See "Contemporary American Novelists—X: The Revolt from the Village: 1920," *Nation* 113 (12
October 1921):408–12 *passim*. John Hervey, however, was convinced that
Winesburg was inferior to *Spoon River* in his "Sherwood Anderson," *All's Well*
5 (March 1925):9.

    According to Ernest Ervin Leisy, *Winesburg* was a product of "more po-
etry and less wit that Lewis'" *Main Street*. See *American Literature: An Interpretive Study* (New York: Thomas Y. Crowell, 1929), pp. 216–17. James Gray

disagreed and felt that Anderson's work was substantially better than *Main Street*. In fact, he believed that the Nobel Prize for Literature should have been shared by the two men. When he compared *Winesburg* and *Main Street*, Bernard DeVoto noted that both works formed part of the "revolt from the village movement," which they basically started. At the same time they require "a suspension of critical intelligence." For further comments on the subject, see Mark Schorer's biography of Sinclair Lewis. Anderson himself was not unmindful of the comparisons, and there are numerous references to the matter in his *Memoirs* as well as in his letters.

18. *Winesburg, Ohio* (New York: B. W. Huebsch, Inc., 1919), p. 33. Unless otherwise noted, all references are to this edition and appear within the text.

19. The story of the Irish in Chicago is the story of a group of people who composed a large percentage of the nineteenth-century blue-collar workers. Settling primarily on the North Side and on the South Side in the now-famous Bridgeport area, they were early workers on the Canal and in the various packing houses. They were singularly characterized by a strong sense of nationalism that ultimately led to the formation of a number of Irish societies in the city. Protected by civil and ecclesiastical authority, these secret societies were not above mischief-making in the city. The Fenian Brotherhood, one such society committed to the independence of Ireland, was national; and by November of 1863 it had enough strength to hold a national convention in Chicago. A year after the close of the Civil War, the Fenians had collected enough money and recruits to form an army that proposed to invade Canada through Buffalo, New York, and only the vigilance of Andrew Johnson and the courts (using the mandates of the 1818 Neutrality Act) prevented this involvement of Americans in such an endeavor. Subsequently, the Irish who supported the Fenians felt the Democratic Party was no longer responsive to their needs nor sympathetic to the cause of Irish independence. The Republicans took advantage of this situation, and by the end of the 1860s supported its Irish members in varying verbal attacks directed toward England.

While the power of the Fenians waned, a strong Irish population in the city still was held together by political interests and religious commitments as well as the jobs in the work force that they controlled. By the 1880s, there were powerful secret organizations once again. Joining the Fenian Brotherhood were other such groups as the Clan-na-Gael. St. Patrick's Day celebrations and other religious and Irish holidays gave an opportunity for this strong spirit of nationalism to be displayed as well as the hatred for England.

To outsiders, groups such as the Clan-na-Gael seemed impenetrable, but in reality they were often rocked by great internal divisions. Ultimately, this problem brought the power of the Irish secret societies to more people. The Clan-na-Gael was divided into two strong factions, both of which struggled for the absolute power of the organization. Dr. Patrick Henry Cronin was the leader of one clique, and the discovery of his murder propelled the "Irish question" into the public press and into the public consciousness for months. According to the story, on or about May 4, 1889, Dr. Cronin went on a routine house call. He was not heard of until almost three weeks later when his body was discovered in the North Side community of Lake View on May 22. Subsequently, a number of suspects were arrested, and finally seven men were indicted for murder. The trial revealed the internal operations of the secret society and led to all kinds of charges of bribery, jury tampering, and duplicity. While the facts surrounding the murder were never proved to the complete satisfaction of all observers, there were some convictions and sentences passed. One of those indicted escaped from the city and was not brought to trial.

20. Ray Lewis White, ed., *Sherwood Anderson's Memoirs: A Critical Edition* (1969), p. 348.

21. Quoted in Jones and Rideout, *Letters*, p. 217.

22. *Sherwood Anderson* (New York: William Sloan Associates, 1951), pp. 91–96 *passim.*

8. OUT OF A TOWN, A CITY

1. (1942 ed.), pp. 79–80. See also Ray Lewis White's critical edition (1969), pp. 66–67, 116ff., and Sherwood Anderson, *A Story Teller's Story* (New York: B. W. Huebsch, Inc., 1924), pp. 64–65.

2. William Sutton, *The Road to Winesburg* (Metuchen, N.J.: Scarecrow Press, Inc., 1972), p. 34.

3. Sherwood Anderson, *Poor White* (New York: B. W. Huebsch, Inc., 1920), p. 30. All subsequent references to this novel, unless otherwise noted, are to this edition.

4. (1969 ed.), p. 354.

5. *Poor White*, Modern Library Edition (New York: Random House, 1925), p. vi. The novel initially appeared on November 1, 1920, and was issued by Ben Huebsch of New York. It was reprinted five years later in a Modern Library edition to which was added Anderson's prefatory explanation of his work. Then, in 1966, it was reissued by the Viking Press (New York) with an introduction by Professor Walter B. Rideout without the Anderson Preface.

6. *Sherwood Anderson: An Introduction and Interpretation* (New York: Holt, Rinehart, and Winston, Inc., 1967), p. 56.

7. *Poor White*, p. 213. See also the story of Jim Gibson in *A Story Teller's Story*, p. 155.

8. *Tomorrow* 8 (August 1949):52–54 *passim.*

9. In a letter to H. S. Kraft, dated March 18, 1933, Anderson considered the possibility of "a combination of the figures of Henry Ford and Abraham Lincoln" and thought "that the town of Bidwell . . . [could become] a place like Ford's Dearborn." See Jones and Rideout, *Letters*, 279.

10. Letter addressed to H. S. Kraft and Louis Gruenberg; quoted in ibid., 283.

11. Ibid., p. 342.

12. Ibid., pp. 424–25.

13. See David D. Anderson, "Sherwood Anderson's Use of the Lincoln Theme," *Lincoln Herald* 64 (Spring 1962):28–32.

14. *The American City Novel* (Norman: University of Oklahoma Press, 1954), pp. 100–101.

15. Cf. the development of Dr. Prance in Henry James' *The Bostonians* (1887) and Dr. Isabella Herrick in Hamlin Garland's *Rose of Dutcher's Coolly* (1895).

16. See "Latest Works of Fiction," *New York Times Book Review* (12 December 1920):20; "Feast of Unleavened Realism," New York *Sun* (24 December 1920); Eric Gershom, "The Factory Comes to Ohio," *Publishers Weekly* 98 (18 December 1920):1888; Harry Hansen, "The Book of the Week," Chicago *Daily News* (1 December 1920):12; and Constance M. Rourke, "A New Middle West," New York *Evening Post Literary Review* (4 December 1920):4. It is of some interest that Rourke relates Anderson's realism to a "flexible naturalism" and his sense of poetic prose not only to his reading but his understanding of Whitman. Other favorable reviews appear in the work of Robert C. Benchley (*Bookman* 52 [February 1921]:559–60); Francis Hackett (*New Republic* 24 [24 November 1920]: 330); Robert Morss Lovett (*Dial* 70 [January 1921]:77–79); and C. Kay Scott (*Freeman* 2 [5 January 1921]:403).

17. "Books," New York *Tribune* (13 December 1920):8.

18. "Sherwood Anderson's 'Poor White,'" *Chicago Tribune* (18 December 1920):10.

19. "Mr. Sherwood Anderson's America," *Dial* 70 (January 1921):77–79.

20. "A Welcome Guest," London *Daily Herald* (5 October 1921):7. Often foreign critics were more sympathetically disposed toward Anderson's work and were willing to see the totality of the novel's impact rather than concentrating upon some imperfect part of it. See Charles LeVerrier, "Dernières Publications," *L'Europe Nouvelle* (26 February 1921):287–88; Friedrich Schonemann in "Der Arme Weisse," *Das Literarische Echo* (28 April 1925):372–73, was ecstatic about the novel. John Hurley in "The Ambler of the Middle Western States" (Manitoba *Free Press* [5 April 1926]:1) felt that *Poor White* "discovers and understands America," and Victor Max Wullich in "*Pobre Blanco, Novela de Sherwood Anderson*" (*Nosotros* 66 [December 1929]:432–33), saw the novel as representing the growth of America. It is also important to note that at the time of Anderson's death, of all of his works, only *Poor White* had been translated into Dutch.

Anne M. Springer has reviewed the popularity of Anderson in German from the 1920s and has maintained that it represented a general interest in American literature. See her *The American novel in Germany: A Study of the Critical Reception of Eight Novelists Between the Two World Wars* (Hamburg: Cram de Gruyter, 1960), pp. 6–85 *passim*. Although Anderson's work began to appear in Russia in the mid-1920s, it was not until he was viewed as the coming voice of the proletariat in the 1930s that he became popular there. Fundamentally,

Russian disenchantment with him followed the perception that he did not deal harshly enough with the cause–effect results of the American political system as the primary problem in American life. This notion is partially explored by Deming Brown in *Soviet Attitudes Toward American Writing* (Princeton: Princeton University Press, 1962), pp. 23–319 *passim*.

21. "Sherwood Anderson: A Study in Sociological Criticism," *Modern Quarterly* 2 (Fall 1924):82–118. Although he did not like Anderson's later work, Calverton thought that the novelist was at his best when dealing with the effects of industrialism upon people and places.

22. See Edwin Francis Egett, "An American Zola of the Middle West," Boston *Transcript* (1 December 1920):8; F.[rancis] H.[ackett], "Poor White," *New Republic* 24 [24 November 1920]:330; G. H., "Out of the West," *World To-morrow* 4 (January 1921):29–30. The critic does allow, however, that the lack of form is balanced by the author's understanding of the issues he raises. Whereas both A. L. S. Wood ("Agates and Migs," Springfield [Mass.] *Union* [26 December 1920]) and C. Kay Scott ("Books," *Freeman* 2 [5 January 1921]) contend that the work is without structure and philosophically unsound, the latter critic asserts that Anderson displays a poetic vision.

23. "Sherwood Anderson: Romancier Americain" (25 September 1921): 182–85. In his overall praise, however, Bailly was not convinced that Anderson always exercised control over his structure and story.

24. *The Phenomenon of Sherwood Anderson* (Baltimore: Johns Hopkins University Press, 1927), pp. 40–41.

25. Ibid., p. 41. Cf. Irving Howe, *Sherwood Anderson* (New York: William Sloane Associates, 1951), p. 123; James Schevill, *Sherwood Anderson: His Life and Works* (Denver: University of Denver Press, 1951), p. 127ff; Brom Weber, *Sherwood Anderson* (Minneapolis: University of Minnesota Press, 1964), p. 32; and David D. Anderson, "Use of the Lincoln Theme," 60ff.

26. "The Epic of Dullness," 111 (10 November 1920):536–37.

27. A. E. C. [*"Poor White"*] (16 September 1921).

9. THE METAPHORIC CITY

1. (New York: Boni and Liveright, 1925), p. 76. All further references to the novel are from this edition and appear within the text.

2. *Windy McPherson's Son* (New York: John Lane, 1916), p. 317.

3. (New York: B. W. Huebsch, Inc., 1921), p. 179. Unless otherwise noted, subsequent references to *The Triumph of the Egg* are to this edition.

4. (New York: B. W. Huebsch, Inc., 1923), p. xii. Unless otherwise noted, subsequent references to *Horses and Men* are to this edition.

5. *Sherwood Anderson* (New York: Holt, Rinehart, and Winston, 1967), p. 74.

6. "Sherwood Anderson on the Marriage Question," New York *Herald* (4 March 1923), section 9: 5. This essay has been reprinted in Matthew J. Bruccoli

and Jackson R. Bryer, eds., *F. Scott Fitzgerald in His Own Time: A Miscellany* (Kent, Ohio: Kent State University Press, 1971), pp. 138–40. For similar positions on the relative merits of *Many Marriages*, see also Llewellyn Jones, "Sherwood Anderson's Biggest Achievement," Chicago *Evening Post Literary Review* (2 March 1923); Percy N. Stone, "Novels a la Carte," *Bookman* 57 (April 1923):210–11.

7. "Novelist and Prophet," *Nation* 116 (28 March 1923):368.

8. "Sick Novels of a Sick World," *Haldeman-Julius Weekly* (31 March 1923):4. See also Edmund Wilson's review "Many Marriages," *Dial* 74 (April 1923):399–400. Although he is convinced that Anderson demonstrated the ability to inspect life honestly and completely, Wilson thought the novelist had produced a tedious work in the process.

9. See "Anderson's 'Many Marriages,'" Springfield *Republican* (11 March 1923), section A: 8; "Advertising Bad Books," *New York Times* (15 March 1923):18; "'Many Marriages,'" *Times Literary Supplement* (2 August 1923):518; "An American Book in British Courts," *Literary Digest* 79 (24 November 1923):30; and Robert Littell, "Many Marriages," *New Republic* 37 (11 April 1923):6–8. In his "The Triumph of the Nut or Too Many Marriages" in *The Triumph of the Nut and Other Parodies* (New York: Henry Holt and Co., 1923), pp. 1–9, Christopher Ward bitterly satirizes Anderson's hero, John Webster, and concludes that he ends his life in a Wisconsin asylum after his diatribe on sex.

10. See F.[ranklin] P. A.[dams], "The Conning Tower: The Diary of Our Own Samuel Pepys," New York *World* (24 February 1923):11; "Latest Works of Fiction," *New York Times Book Review* (25 February 1923):10; "Many Marriages," Boston *Transcript* (7 March 1923): section 3: 6 (also called it a "crudely written story" recounting "the beastly amours of a married man"); H. W. Boynton, "Man the Blunderer," *Independent* 110 (31 March 1923):232 (in which the critic concludes that the novel's end result is a discussion of "the slavery of the marriage bond," which he sees as "a pretentious tract [on] a trite theme"); and H. L. Mencken, "H. L. Mencken Gives Meed of Praise to Anderson's Stories," Baltimore *Evening Sun* (8 December 1923). See also his "Some New Books," *Smart Set* 71 (July 1923):138–39, which also appears in William Nolte, ed., *H. L. Mencken's Smart Set Criticism* (Ithaca: Cornell University Press, 1968), pp. 272–78.

11. See Gerald Gould, "New Fiction," *Saturday Review* 136 (8 September 1923):281; [Ben Hecht,] "Anderson Soars on Phantom Wings, and, Alas! Flops," *Chicago Literary Times* (15 March 1923):2; and "Purging the Reading Public," *New York Times* (24 April 1923):20. Raymond Mortimer ("New Novels," *New Statesman* 21 [4 August 1923]:500–501) dismissed it as "a really silly book," and Burton Rascoe ("Psychology, Realism and Rhapsody," New York *Herald Tribune Book News and Reviews* [25 February 1923]:17) kindly attributed the failure of the novel to the fact that Anderson, in his judgment, could not execute the novel form.

12. "Books and Other Matters," *Little Review* 10 (Autumn–Winter [1924–1925]:19–21.

13. Henry Seidel Canby maintains that the novel presents the role of the artist in conflict with the materialistic world. See his *American Memoirs* (Boston: Houghton Mifflin, 1947), pp. 263–325 *passim*. Henry Steele Commager declares that it is part of the primitivist movement in American letters, a movement designed to celebrate the emotions to the exclusion of the intellect. See his *The American Mind: An Interpretation of American Thought and Character Since the 1880s* (New Haven: Yale University Press, 1950), pp. 125–27. And Irving Howe concludes that Anderson's primitivism in *Many Marriages*, as well as in *Dark Laughter*, is a poor attempt to render D. H. Lawrence's primitivism in an American setting. See his "Sherwood Anderson and D. H. Lawrence," *Furioso* 5 (Fall 1950):21–33.

14. See Wilbur L. Cross, *The Modern English Novel: An Address Before the American Academy of Arts and Letters* (New Haven: Yale University Press, 1928), pp. 28–40 *passim*; Stanley Thomas Williams, *The American Spirit in Letters* (New Haven: Yale University Press, 1926), pp. 293–99 *passim*; Morris L. Ernst and William Seagle, *To the Pure: A Study of Obscenity and the Censor* (New York: Viking Press, 1928); James Branch Cabell, *Some of Us* (New York: Robert M. McBride, 1930), pp. 77–85 *passim*; and Philip Rahv, *Image and Idea: Fourteen Essays on Literary Themes* (Norfolk, Conn.: New Directions, 1947), pp. 3ff. Anne Lyon Haight comments on the banning of *Many Marriages* in England in her note on Sherwood Anderson in *Banned Books: Informal Notes on Some Books Banned for Various Reasons at Various Times and in Various Places* (New York: R. R. Bowker, 1935), p. 69.

15. In *The Colossus of Maroussi* (Norfolk, Conn.: New Directions, 1941), Henry Miller maintained that Anderson was "the one [modern] American writer . . . who has walked the streets of our American cities as a genuine poet" (pp. 34–35). See also Miller's *Letters of Anias Nin*, edited by Gunther Stuhlmann (New York: G. P. Putnam's Sons, 1965), pp. 49, 213, 259; and his *The Books in My Life* (New York: New Directions, 1969), pp. 41, 217–19. Obviously Miller felt a great kinship with Anderson's introspective nature. Throughout the Robert H. Elias edition of *Letters of Theodore Dreiser*, 3 vols. (Philadelphia: University of Pennsylvania Press, 1959), pp. 279, 307, 310–11, 314, 347, 416–17, 422, 427, 586, 642, 645, 647, 653–56, 666–67, 753–55, 760–63, and 768–69, there are numerous references to Dreiser's fondness for *Many Marriages*. Perhaps it is not surprising that Dreiser liked the novel. See also Bernard Raymund, "The Grammar of Not-Reason in Sherwood Anderson," *Arizona Quarterly* 12 (Spring 1956):48–60 and (Summer 1956):136–48. Raymund holds that *Many Marriages* is the best of Anderson's novels.

16. *The Sexual Revolution in Modern American Literature* (The Hague: Martinus Nijhoff, 1971), pp. 47–57ff.

17. *Sherwood Anderson* (New York: R. M. McBride, 1927), p. 96.

18. *Sherwood Anderson* (New York: Twayne, 1964), pp. 83–85. Burbank saw the novel as one of many by Sherwood Anderson that attempted to

present "psychological and moral solutions [for] the problem of modern industrial society." Yet, Anderson was not really equipped to study life psychologically in a systematic way, and his attempt at psychological impressionism, often passed off as the scientifically real thing, weakens the novel.

19. *Sherwood Anderson*, p. 67.

20. Quoted in Jones and Rideout, *Letters*, p. 238.

21. *Many Marriages* (New York: B. W. Huebsch, Inc., 1923), p. 190. All further references to the novel are to this edition and appear within the text.

22. Many critics seem to have tacitly accepted I. A. Richards' notion that the novel did not make sense in its attempt to present "a record of disorder, not a new ordering of our responses." See "Reading Novels," *Forum* 76 (August 1926):319. See also "Sherwood Anderson Contemplates Life on the Levee," *New York Times Book Review* (20 September 1925):9; Fanny Butcher, "Reviewer Twins No Bay Wreath for Sherwood Anderson," *Chicago Tribune* (10 October 1925):14; Walter Haviland, "Fiddlededee, Fiddlesticks!" *American Parade* 1 (1 April 1926):186–88; and P. C. Kennedy, "New Novels," *New Statesman* 27 (5 June 1926):199.

23. "Bookshelf," *Atlantic Monthly* 136 (December 1925):14.

24. "Readers and Writers," *Independent* 115 (12 September 1925):302.

25. "Sherwood Anderson Pursues Elusive Emotions," *Literary Digest International Book Review* 3 (November 1925):805ff. See also Henry Seidel Canby, "The Woman Takes . . .," *Saturday Review of Literature* 2 (10 October 1925):191.

26. "Sherwood Anderson's Tales of the New Life," New York *Herald Tribune Books* (4 October 1925):1–2.

27. Obviously the distinction between a "good" novel and a writer's "best" novel will be highly dependent not only upon the subjective views of the evaluator but also upon the ultimate definition of such terms as *good* and *best*. Among those who viewed *Dark Laughter* as a "good" novel are H. L. Mencken ("Fiction Good and Bad," *American Mercury* 6 [November 1925]: 379–80) and Carl Van Doren ("Short Cuts," *Century* 111 [January 1926]:384). The reviewer of the novel in "Fiction" (*Booklist* 22 [January 1926]) saw it as an "intimate, rather wandering, but on the whole . . . a finely written story of a man and a woman" (p. 161).

28. See Robert Morss Lovett, "Dark Laughter," *New Republic* 44 (21 October 1925):233–34; Susan Wilbur, "What Mark Twain Left Out," *Chicago Evening Post Literary Review* (25 September 1925):1ff; Helen MacAfee, "Some Novelists in Mid-Stream," *Yale Review* 15 (January 1926):349–51; and C. Henry Warren, "Sherwood Anderson," [London] *Bookman* 74 (April 1928):22–24.

10. SHERWOOD ANDERSON'S URBAN CYCLE

1. See chapter 1, note 4.

2. *Poor White*, pp. 129–31 *passim*.

3. "Sherwood Anderson," *Saturday Review of Literature* 9 (10 December 1932):305. Quoted in Jones and Rideout, *Letters*, p. 102–103.

4. Quoted in Jones and Rideout, *Letters*, p. 38.

5. See many of Anderson's letters to Van Wyck Brooks and Karl Anderson. Cf. Michael Fanning, "New Orleans and Sherwood Anderson," *Southern Studies* 17 (1978):199–207.

6. Jones and Rideout, *Letters*, p. 200.

7. Ibid., p. 223.

8. Ibid., pp. 102–103.

9. In a letter to Jasper Deeter, Sherwood Anderson spoke of Hemingway's "super-realism" and continued his assessment of the younger writer: "The imaginative world, as I understood it, was to be more or less chucked but it seems to me that in trying for this he has only got into a kind of romanticization of the so-called real . . . a kind of ecstasy over elephant dung, killing, death, etc., etc." Quoted in Charles E. Modlin, *Sherwood Anderson: Selected Letters* (Knoxville: The University of Tennessee Press, 1984), p. 197. Cf. Anderson's letter to Ralph Church in Jones and Rideout, *Letters*, p. 345.

10. *Sherwood Anderson's Memoirs* (1942 ed.), p. 109.

11. Ibid., p. 372.

Bibliographic Essay

To write of a storyteller and a city is to bring together two dissimilar subjects; yet, out of a consideration of a man, a time, and a place, a synthesis will emerge. Of course, much has been written separately about the man and the city. Whether one considers Sherwood Anderson to be a major or minor writer, notices of him appear in most critical and historical studies of American literature. Although the present study is "biographical" in the sense that it utilizes certain "facts" of Sherwood Anderson's life, it is not a traditional biography that gives equal attention to all phases of the subject's life; however, there are works that provide excellent background material for *A Storyteller and a City*. In addition to the critical reviews and articles that followed the publications of Anderson's various works and articles, two major biographical studies appeared during his lifetime, issued in the 1920s: Cleveland B. Chase, *Sherwood Anderson* (New York: Robert M. McBride Company, Inc., 1927) and Bryllion N. Fagin, *The Phenomenon of Sherwood Anderson* (Baltimore: Johns Hopkins University Press, 1927).

Since 1941, the year of Anderson's death, several critical biographies have been published. Most of them include, in varying degrees, interpretations of his work. See David D. Anderson, *Sherwood Anderson: An Introduction and Interpretation* (New York: Holt, Rinehart, and Winston, Inc., 1967); Rex Burbank, *Sherwood Anderson* (New York: Twayne Publishers, Inc., 1964); Irving Howe, *Sherwood Anderson* (New York: William Sloan Associates, 1951); James Schevill, *Sherwood Anderson: His Life and Works* (Denver: University of Denver Press, 1951); William A. Sutton, *The Road to Winesburg: A Mosaic of the Imaginative Life of Sherwood Anderson* (Metuchen, N. J.: The Scarecrow Press, 1972); and Brom Weber, *Sherwood Anderson* (Minneapolis: University of Minnesota Press, 1964).

Despite Anderson's own tendency to combine fact and fancy, his autobiographies and theoretical studies provide an important basis for an analysis of his life and work. In order of publication, they are *A Story Teller's Story* (New York: B. W. Huebsch, 1924); *The Modern Writer* (San Francisco: Gelber, Lilienthal, Inc., 1925); *Tar: A Midwest Childhood* (New York: Liveright Publishing Corporation, 1926); *Sherwood Anderson's Notebook* (New York: Liveright Publishing Corporation, 1926); *Sherwood Anderson's Memoirs* (New York:

Harcourt, Brace, and World, 1942); and *Sherwood Anderson's Memoirs: A Critical Edition*, edited by Ray Lewis White (Chapel Hill: University of North Carolina Press, 1969).

Sherwood Anderson was a prolific letter writer, and his letters can be found in both likely and unlikely places. Among those published, four collections are of significance and also will prove helpful to those attempting to reconstruct phases of Anderson's life: Howard Mumford Jones and Walter B. Rideout, eds., *Letters of Sherwood Anderson* (Boston: Little, Brown and Company, 1953); Charles E. Modlin, ed, *Sherwood Anderson: Selected Letters* (Knoxville: The University of Tennessee Press, 1984); William A. Sutton, ed., *Letters to Bab: Sherwood Anderson to Marietta D. Finley, 1916–33* (Urbana: University of Illinois Press, 1985); and Ray Lewis White, ed., *Sherwood Anderson/Gertrude Stein: Correspondence and Personal Essays* (Chapel Hill: University of North Carolina Press, 1972).

With the exception of the "urban" elements of *Mid-American Chants*, two important aspects of Sherwood Anderson—seldom treated extensively elsewhere and not covered in my study—need to be considered. One deals with his poetry and the other with his relationship to Afro-American literature through *Dark Laughter*. Whereas much has been made of his short fiction, Anderson's poetry has not attracted a great deal of critical attention, and perhaps for good reasons; however, there are areas of it that need further study. His tendency to write poetry at turning points in his life is probably just coincidental, but one can use *Mid-American Chants* and *A New Testament* as works that mark the end of one literary period and the beginning of another. Before the publication of the latter volume, however, he wrote to Harry Hansen in 1922 and indicated his recognition of the transitional nature of his poetry:

> I wrote an unsuccessful book of poetry, called *Mid-American Chants*, but I myself believe that the writing of this broke me into a second period that might be covered by *Winesburg, Poor White* and *The Triumph [of the Egg]*. Then I wrote another long book of poetry which I have had the hardihood not to publish, and I believe this broke me into a third mood in writing, the first expression of which is the new novel, *Many Marriages*. (The entire letter appears in Charles E. Modlin, ed., *Sherwood Anderson: Selected Letters* [Knoxville: The University of Tennessee Press, 1984], pp. 40–42.)

The obvious Whitmanesque elements of Anderson's work have been treated in Viva Elizabeth Haught's "The Influence of Whitman on Sherwood Anderson" (Unpublished M.A. Thesis, Duke University, 1936). In 1961, Winfield Scott Lenox attempted to establish the importance of Anderson's verse in "The Significance of Sherwood Anderson's Poetry" (Unpublished M.A. Thesis, Loyola University). It is well to note that even when they do not go into detail, all of the major critical studies of Anderson not only make at least a passing reference to *Mid-American Chants* and *A New Testament* but also stress the "poetic" elements in his fiction.

The appearance of Jean Toomer's *Cane* in 1923, two years before *Dark Laughter*, is obviously a coincidence. It is known, however, from Anderson's correspondence that he wrote to Toomer praising *Cane*. Toomer, on the other hand, had been struck by the versatility displayed by *Winesburg, Ohio*. There is a slight chance that *Cane* influenced *Dark Laughter*. Various aspects of this possibility have been treated by the following: Mary Jane Dickerson, "Sherwood Anderson and Jean Toomer: A Literary Relationship." *Studies in American Fiction* 1 (Autumn 1973):163–65 (she posits the theory that *Winesburg* . . . and *Cane* [are] similar in structure, theme, narrator-observer, emphasis on inner life, and rural setting); Darrell W. McNeely, "Jean Toomer's *Cane* and Sherwood Anderson's *Winesburg, Ohio:* A Black Reaction to the Literary Conventions of the Twenties" (Unpublished Ph.D. Dissertation, University of Nebraska, 1974); and Darwin T. Turner, "An Intersection of Paths: Correspondence Between Jean Toomer and Sherwood Anderson," *CLA Journal* 17 (June 1975):455–67.

In many ways the history of Chicago also has been subjected to a combination of fact and fancy. Certainly, that history has provided a fascinating chapter in urban development and has been the basis for innumerable studies. For many, the city represents America in microcosm. This is especially true of the period from the 1870s to the 1920s. The histories themselves range from the very objective scientifically presented works to the personal reactions and gossipy anecdotal surveys that give a sense of the city even when they are not always faithful to the facts. Nineteenth-century historians, often apologetic for the crudeness of the Midwest, were generally dedicated and intent upon proving the city's worth. Their productions range from the work of Joseph Balestier in the 1840s to that of William Bross in the 1870s. Probably the first stage of historic writing culminated with the detailed survey of Captain A. T. Andreas, which still provides a base for a study of the ante-fire period. Unfortunately, the three-volumed work ends with 1885 and is difficult to find today. Joseph Kirkland's *The History of Chicago*, 3 vols. (Chicago: Dibble Publishing Co., 1892–1894) covers much of the same material as the Andreas, but it is shorter and ends with 1893.

During the months preceding the World's Columbian Exposition, many histories appeared, designed to acquaint visitors with Chicago; however, most of them simply repeat the legends and unchecked materials of earlier volumes. The postfair period also produced a number of books, monographs, and articles dealing with the effect of the fair upon American civilization, an importance that cannot be overestimated. For example, in the "Letter from an Altrurian Traveller," dated September 28, 1893, from Chicago, Aristides Homos believed that the beauty and plan of the fair would become the pattern for urban development. He said: "An immortal principle higher than use, higher even than beauty, is expressed in [the fair], and the time will

come when they will look back upon it, and recognize in it, the first embodi-
ment of the Altrurian idea among them, and will cherish it forever in their
history as the earliest achievement of a real civic life." Homos saw the White
City as an example of the beauty that results from cooperation rather than
competition. See the reissue of William Dean Howells, *The Altrurian Romances*
(Bloomington: Indiana University Press, 1968), p. 218. Other works have dealt
with specific areas of interest; however, Hubert Howe Bancroft's *The Book of
the Fair* (1894) is still the most comprehensive study of the exhibition itself.
Despite the many excellent studies of the fair, there still needs to be a detailed
examination of the issues raised by Henry Adams.

To view Chicago as a significant example of those forces that contributed
to the development of the nation is not as chauvinistic as it might appear. A
survey of the writings of foreign visitors to the World's Columbian Exposition
will reveal the number of times they emphasized the city as probably a microcosm of the nation. And several general historians have made a similar point.
See the following: Daniel Boorstin, *The Americans: The National Experience*
(New York: Random House, 1965); Constance Green, *American Cities in the
Growth of the Nation* (New York: Harper and Row, 1957); Howard Mumford
Jones, *The Age of Energy: Varieties of American Experience, 1865–1915* (New York:
Viking, 1970); Zane L. Miller, *The Urbanization of Modern America: A Brief His-
tory* (New York: Macmillan, 1973); Arthur M. Schlesinger, Sr. *The Rise of the
City: 1878–1898* (New York: Macmillan, 1933); and Sam Bass Warner, *The Urban
Wilderness: A History of the American City* (New York: Harper and Row, 1972).

The most outstanding history written in the twentieth century remains
Bessie Pierce's *A History of Chicago*, 3 vols. (New York: Alfred A. Knopf,
1937–57). This work also ends with 1893, and the other, projected volumes
were never written. Among the twentieth-century works that provide an adequate historic background, some well known ones are Wayne Andrews,
Battle for Chicago (New York: Harcourt Brace, 1946); Emmett Dedmon, *Fabu-
lous Chicago* (New York: Random House, 1953); Finis Farr, *Chicago: Personal
History of America's Most American City* (New Rochelle, N.Y.: Arlington House,
1973); Lloyd Lewis, and Henry Justin Smith, *Chicago: The History of a Reputation* (New York: Harcourt Brace, 1929); Stephen Longstreet, *Chicago: 1860–1919*
(New York: McKay, 1973); Edgar Lee Masters, *The Tale of Chicago* (New York:
G. P. Putnam's Sons, 1933); Harold Mayer and Richard Wade, *Chicago: Growth
of a Metropolis* (Chicago: University of Chicago Press, 1966); and Edward
Wagenknecht, *Chicago* (Norman: University of Oklahoma Press, 1964).

There have been many detailed studies of the city's political life. They
often focus upon the significance of boss-ward politics (a situation frequently
deplored by the city's novelists) or upon the varying contributions of ethnic
groups to the urban political system. To study the city's structure, then, at
least in part, is to survey the immigrant groups (whether from western or
eastern Europe or the American East, South, or West) who supported the
"boss" system. There were also periodic calls for social reform, movements
designed to counteract "dirty" politics. For those interested in reform organi-

zations, the papers of such groups as the Municipal Voters' League, Civic Federation, and Union League Club might prove helpful. While they are obviously limited by subjects and by the viewpoints of their authors, the following present Chicago's political system, the ethnic groups involved in it, and attempts to institute reforms: John Allswang, *A House for All Peoples* (Lexington: University of Kentucky Press, 1971); Ulf Beijorn, *Swedes in Chicago . . .* (Stockholm: Laromedelsforlaget, 1971); Philip B. Bregstone, *Chicago and Its Jews: A Cultural History* (Chicago: Privately printed, 1933); Chicago Race Relations Commission, *The Negro in Chicago, A Study of Race Relations and a Race Riot* (Chicago: Commission on Race Relations, 1919); St. Clair Drake and Horace Cayton, *Black Metropolis* (New York: Harcourt Brace, 1945); Harold F. Gosnell, *Negro Politicians: The Rise of Negro Politics in Chicago* (Chicago: University of Chicago Press, 1935); Harold F. Gosnell, *Machine Politics: The Chicago Model* (Chicago: University of Chicago Press, 1947); Alex Gottfried, *Boss Cermak of Chicago: A Study of Political Leadership* (Seattle: University of Washington Press, 1962); Claudius O. Johnson, *Carter Henry Harrison I: Political Leader* (Chicago: University of Chicago Press, 1928); Edward W. Levine, *The Irish and Irish Politicians: A Study of Cultural and Social Alienation* (South Bend, Ind.: Notre Dame University Press, 1966); Charles Merriam, *Chicago: A More Intimate View of Politics* (New York: Macmillan, 1929); Humbert S. Nelli, *The Italians in Chicago, 1880–1930: A Study in Ethnic Mobility* (New York: Oxford University Press, 1970); Milton Rakove, *Don't Make No Waves—Don't Back No Losers* (Bloomington: Indiana University Press, 1975); Milton Rakove, *We Don't Want Nobody Nobody Sent* (Bloomington: Indiana University Press, 1979); Mike Royko, *Boss: Richard J. Daley of Chicago* (New York: E. P. Dutton, 1971); Carl Sandburg, *The Chicago Race Riots, July, 1919* (New York: Harcourt Brace, 1919); Vernon Simpson and David Scott, *Chicago's Politics and Society: A Selected Bibliography* (DeKalb: Northern Illinois University Center for Government Studies, 1972); Allan H. Spear, *Black Chicago: The Making of a Negro Ghetto, 1890–1920* (Chicago: University of Chicago Press, 1967); William T. Stead, *If Christ Came to Chicago* (Chicago: Laird and Lee, 1894); Andrew Townsend, *The Germans of Chicago* (Chicago: University of Chicago Press, 1932); William Tuttle, *Race Riot: Chicago in the Red Summer of 1919* (New York: Atheneum Press, 1970); Louise C. Wade, *Graham Taylor, Pioneer of Social Justice, 1851–1938* (Chicago: University of Chicago Press, 1964); as well as Lloyd Wendt and Herman Kogan, *Lords of the Levee: The Story of Bathhouse John and Hinky Dink* (Indianapolis: Bobbs-Merrill, 1943).

Among the reformers who often wrote of their personal efforts to change the course of events in the city, it is interesting to note how frequently women and women's groups were involved. For example, Dr. Alice Hamilton studied the diseases of factory workers and made a significant contribution to what now is called industrial medicine. The evolution of the settlement house idea in the work of Jane Addams, who founded Hull House in 1889 accompanied by Ellen Gates Starr, is still one of the significant accomplishments of nineteenth-century Chicago. They were aided by a group of women convinced

that the problems of society required not only reform legislation but also a
sense of humanism in order to reach viable solutions. Such society ladies as
Mrs. John Glessner, Bertha Honore Palmer, Harriet Pullman, and her daughter Florence Pullman Lowden also tried to effect changes in the city. Many of
the "social queens" demonstrated a real concern for the downtrodden, and
their charitable works became an integral part of the civic uplift movement.
Edith and Grace Abbott were interested specifically in the life-styles of immigrant women forced to labor under inhuman factory conditions, and Florence
Kelley was opposed to child labor. She understood its implications in deter-
ring the development of sound family relationships. Such women were joined
by others who might more comfortably have settled into "the ways of society." Would-be arbiters of elite tastes such as Julia Lathrop, Mary Kenny
O'Sullivan, Louise DeKoven Bowen, and Mary McDowell worked untiringly
to raise the standards of living among the city's laborers, as did Dr. Alice
Hamilton, already mentioned in connection with the development of industrial medicine. All of these women were further aided by Lucy Parsons and
Emma Goldman, well-known radicals, who operated in a different sphere
and social circle and whose political philosophies and loyalties eventually
called into question traditional beliefs.

The nineteenth and twentieth centuries also saw the development of
some "strong" women in the arts. There was, of course, Anna Morgan whose
work and studio became the forerunner of the Little Theatre Movement, for
which Maurice Browne has frequently received the credit. Her avant garde
work included early presentations and readings of Ibsen and Shaw, both of
whom were considered "advanced" in their day. And no history of Chicago
literature—and ultimately the literature of the United States—is complete
without an understanding of the contributions of Harriet Monroe and her *Poetry: A Magazine of Verse*, as well as of Margaret Anderson with her *Little Review*. Perhaps, an equally interesting sidelight to these works is to be found in
the fact that Chicago provided a background for the reinterpretations of the
roles of women. This should not be surprising because, long before the feminist issue became one of national scope, women in Chicago had proved their
strength could produce some outstanding results, many of which have not
been surpassed even in this day of mass communications and media exposure. If Fuller's Mrs. Bates and Garland's Rose seem unusual to the average
reader today, it must be remembered that they were simply reproductions of
a type of woman who came to power and influence in nineteenth-century
Chicago. Closely allied to the reform movement and some of the works of the
city's women were many of the participants in the Chicago School of Sociology, who produced classic studies based upon their observations.

Of importance are the following selected works: Edith Abbott, *Tenements
of Chicago* (Chicago: University of Chicago Press, 1936); Jane Addams, *Twenty
Years at Hull House* (New York: Macmillan, 1910); Nels Anderson, *The Hobo:
The Sociology of the Homeless Man* (Chicago: University of Chicago Press, 1923);
Louise DeKoven Bowen, *Growing Up with a City* (New York: Macmillan, 1926);

Louise DeKoven Bowen, *Speeches, Addresses, and Letters of . . . , Reflecting Social Movements in Chicago*, 2 vols. (Ann Arbor, Mich.: Edwards Brothers, 1937); Clarence Darrow, *The Story of My Life* (New York: Scribners, 1932); Eugene V. Debs, *Walls and Bars* (Chicago: Socialist Party of America, 1927); Alice Hamilton, *Exploring the Dangerous Trades* (Boston: Little, Brown, 1943); Homer Hoyt, *One Hundred Years of Land Values in Chicago: The Relationship of the Growth of Chicago to the Rise in its Land Values, 1830–1933* (Chicago: University of Chicago Press, 1933); Florence Kelley, *Some Ethical Gains Through Legislation* (New York: Macmillan, 1905); Graham Taylor, *Chicago Commons Through Forty Years* (Chicago: Chicago Commons Association, 1936); Frances E. Willard, *Glimpses of Fifty Years: The Autobiography of an American Woman* (Chicago: H. J. Smith, 1889); Louis Wirth, *The Ghetto* (Chicago: University of Chicago Press, 1928); and Harvey Zorbaugh, *The Gold Coast and the Slum: A Sociological Study of Chicago's Near North Side* (Chicago: University of Chicago Press, 1929).

No matter what the subject, all of the books mentioned so far share a common theme, because it was generally believed that the phenomenal growth of the city and of its problems in some way represented certain forces in American civilization. The same story has been told through the chronicles of various types of urban entrepreneurs. In many ways, the fictional businessmen created by Anderson are composites of the men who actually created the city. The following may be of particular interest: Dorsha Hayes, *Chicago: Crossroads of American Enterprise* (New York: Julian Messner, 1944); Harper Leech and John Carroll, *Armour and His Times* (New York: Appleton-Century, 1938); Forrest MacDonald, *Insull* (Chicago: University of Chicago Press, 1962); Ernest Poole, *Giants Gone: Men Who Made Chicago* (New York: McGraw-Hill Book Company, 1943); Louise Swift, *The Yankee of the Yards: The Biography of Gustavus Franklin Swift* (Chicago: A. W. Shaw Company, 1927); John Tebbel, *An American Dynasty: The Story of the McCormicks, Medills, and Pattersons* (Garden City, N.Y.: Doubleday, 1947); John Tebbel, *The Marshall Fields: A Study in Wealth* (New York: E. P. Dutton, 1947); and Morris Werner, *Julius Rosenwald: The Life of a Practical Humanitarian* (New York: Harper Brothers, 1939).

There have been some attempts to show the interrelationship among the historic, political, economic, social, literary, and artistic forces in Chicago. These attempts have been successful in establishing a single construct from which to view the city. Two, for example, use Louis Sullivan as a focal point around which a chronicle of the city is told. See Hugh D. Duncan, *Culture and Democracy: The Struggle for Form in Society and Architecture in Chicago and the Middle West During the Life and Times of Louis Sullivan* (Totowa, N.J.: Bedminster Press, 1965) and Kenny J. Williams, *In the City of Men: Another Story of Chicago* (Nashville: Townsend Press, 1974).

Traditionally, the Chicago Renaissance has occasioned more discussion than other literary eras of the city. Although it is generally assumed that the major work of the period essentially was done in the twentieth century by a group of transient writers, it is my contention that the period had a much broader time frame and that instead of representing a single movement located within the Fifty-seventh Street group, there were in reality several movements that involved the entire city. For this reason, it is important to survey the entire city to point out the various "cultural centers" that contributed to the ferment taking place in the city as I have done in Chapter 6. In detailing the impact of institutions on the cultural life of the city, one such center was, and still is to some extent, the University of Chicago. Although an important (though often ignored) force in the city, it made considerable inroads and changes in the disciplines of higher education in both national and international circles with especial interest in graduate and professional training. For example, the university's emphasis upon the social and behavioral sciences has been studied by Robert Farris, *Chicago Sociology, 1920–1930* (San Francisco: Chandler Publishing Company, 1967); James Short, Jr., *The Social Fabric of the Metropolis: Contributions of the Chicago School of Urban Sociology* (Chicago: University of Chicago Press, 1971); and by Thomas V. Smith and Leonard White in *Chicago: An Experiment in Social Science Research* (Chicago: University of Chicago Press, 1929). Among the scholars "called to Chicago" the following have been studied for their contributions to American thought. The sources cited are intended to be representative and not definitive: John Dewey, who used the Laboratory School he founded to gather data for his famous *The School and Society* of 1889, is analyzed in Ida B. DePeniser's *The History of the Laboratory School, The University of Chicago, 1896–1965* (Chicago: Quadrangle Books, 1967). See also Lawrence Cremin, *The Transformation of the School: Progressivism in American Education, 1876–1957* (New York: Alfred A. Knopf, 1961). For a study of George Herbert Mead in philosophy, see R. M. Barry's "A Man and A City: George Herbert Mead in Chicago" in *American Philosophy and the Future: Essays for a New Generation* edited by Michael Novak (New York: Scribner's, 1968). For a study of Albion Small in sociology, see L. L. Bernard and J. Bernard, *Origins of American Sociology: The Social Science Movement in the United States* (New York: Crowell, 1943) and George Christakes, *Albion Small* (Boston: G. K. Hall and Co., 1978). Jacques Loeb's work in behavioral psychology is considered in Donald Flemming's *The Mechanistic Conception of Life* (Cambridge: Belknap Press of Harvard University, 1964). For information on the liberal theologian Shailer Mathews, see Lloyd J. Averill, *American Theology in the Liberal Tradition* (Philadelphia: Westminster Press, 1967). Thorstein Veblen is studied within the context of general economic theory in America by Joseph Dorfman in his *Thorstein Veblen and His America* (New York: Viking Press, 1961). See also Veblen's *The Higher Learning in the United States* (Stanford, Calif.: Academic Reprints, first published in 1919).

Perhaps, nowhere has the artistic contribution of the city been more manifest than in the various studies of its architecture. It can be argued convincingly that the Monadnock building served as a model for Fuller's Clifton, but by 1893 there were enough commercial buildings (called *business blocks*) in Chicago to suggest that the Clifton was a type rather than a specific structure. Despite the fame of many of the city's buildings, the city's novelists often shared Sherwood Anderson's attitude about the "tall begrimed" structures.

Fuller, the most antagonistic, said in "The Upward Movement in Chicago," which appeared in *The Atlantic Monthly* 80 (July 1897):

> The associated architecture of the city becomes more hideous and more preposterous with every year, as we continue to straggle farther and farther from anything like the slightest artistic understanding. Nowhere is the naif belief that a man may do as he likes with his own held more contentiously than in our astounding and repelling region of "skyscrapers," where the abuse of private initiative, the peculiar evil of the place and the time, has reached its most monumental development. (541)

For many of the city's novelists the buildings had become the symbol for what Barr Ferree found so exciting in his "Chicago Architecture," which appeared in *Lippincott's Magazine* 52 (July 1893):

> Chicago may well pride herself on her architectural achievements. Placed upon a soil scarcely stable enough to support the weight of an ordinary dwelling, she has produced the largest office-buildings in America, developed a characteristic type of structure, carried to a high degree of perfection a new system of construction, and begun an architectural revolution that will powerfully affect the art in this country. No other American city can claim such a record . . . Chicago buildings are not palaces, they are not highly ornamental edifices, they are not wonders of decorative skill nor miracles of gingerbread appendages. They are calm business structures, designed for business, used for business, and admirable because the business motive is so evident. (94)

The entire subject of architecture in Chicago fiction gains added significance because almost without exception the architect is frequently cast as a character and plays a relatively important role in the lives of the elite. It is also of some interest that Maitland's *Dictionary of American Slang*, issued during the 1890s, defined a skyscraper as "a very tall building such as now being built in Chicago."

Whereas there have not been many studies of the role of the architect or architecture in Chicago fiction (see *In the City of Men*, pp. 40–53, 207–338, 378–418 *passim*), there are many studies of architectural developments in the city. Whether written for the specialist or the generalist, these works emphasize that the art and practice of architecture in the city affected national and international trends. Often the emergence of Chicago as an artistic center is dated from the days after the Fire of 1871 when Jenney developed the true principles of the skyscraper with the skeleton frame construction of the Home Insurance Building (1884–1885). At least, there can be little doubt that it was in architecture that one discovers the first overt artistic reaction to the commercial way of life. This development has been traced by a number of outstanding architectural historians. Among the valuable sources are several by Carl Condit: *American Building Art: The Nineteenth Century* (New York: Oxford University Press, 1960); *American Building Art: The Twentieth Century* (New York: Oxford University Press, 1961); *The Chicago School of Architecture: A History of Commercial and Public Buildings in the Chicago Area, 1875–1925* (Chicago: University of Chicago Press, 1964); *Chicago, 1910–1920: Building, Planning, and Urban Technology* (Chicago: University of Chicago Press, 1973); and *Chicago, 1930–1970: Building, Planning and Urban Technology* (Chicago: University of Chicago Press, 1974). Additional studies have been made by Siegfried Giedion, *Space, Time, and Architecture: The Growth of a New Tradition*, 5th ed. (Cambridge: Harvard University Press, 1967); William Jordy, *American Buildings and Their Architects: Academic and Progressive Ideals at the Turn of the Century* (Garden City, N.Y.: Doubleday, 1972); William Jordy, *The Rise of American Architecture* (New York: Praeger, 1970); Lewis Mumford, *The Brown Decades, a Study of the Arts in America, 1865–1895* (New York: Harcourt Brace, 1931); and Mark Peisch, *The Chicago School of Architecture: Early Followers of Sullivan and Wright* (New York: Random House, 1964). The work of the architectural historians has been complemented by works on and by individual architects.

After the completion of a thorough study of Chicago's landmark buildings, the U.S. Department of Interior's Office of Archeology and Historic Preservation concluded:

> The developments in Chicago in the late nineteenth century were as consequential in world cultural history as the developments in twelfth century France that produced Gothic architecture and in fifteenth century Italy that produced Renaissance architecture. Of these three equally significant modal points in the history of western man, only the consequences of the Chicago School were truly global in scope. (See Hugh C. Miller, *The Chicago School of Architecture* [Washington, D.C.: U.S. Department of the Interior, 1973], p. 1)

Most studies that deal with the cultural Chicago, however, have focused upon the Fifty-seventh Street group and the influence of those who lived in that neighborhood. Like Henry May's *The End of Innocence: A Study of the First Years of Our Times, 1912–1917* (New York: Alfred A. Knopf, 1959), these studies have tended to locate the period of greatest literary activity between the World's Columbian Exposition with Hamlin Garland's assertion that Chicago was to become the nation's literary capital (see Garland's *Crumbling Idols* of 1894) and the departure of many writers, including Sherwood Anderson, by the early 1920s. In addition to Bernard Duffey's classic study (*The Chicago Renaissance in American Letters*) and Dale Kramer's *Chicago Renaissance: The Literary Life in the Midwest, 1900–1930*, a popular journalistic rendition of the period that is limited to the major figures, there also is Hugh Duncan's *Rise of Chicago as a Literary Center from 1885 to 1920* (Totowa, N.J.: The Bedminster Press, 1964), which contains some excellent material but use of it is hampered by a lack of an index, inadequate development of some ideas, and the poor reproduction of the typescript.

Among the literary histories of the latter part of the nineteenth century and the opening years of the twentieth, the following take cognizance of the role of Chicago and its writers within the framework of American literature: Warner Berthoff, *The Ferment of Realism: American Literature, 1884–1919* (New York: Free Press, 1965); Jay Martin, *Harvests of Change: American Literature, 1865–1914* (Englewood Cliffs, N.J.: Prentice-Hall, 1967); Louis Untermeyer, *The New Era in American Poetry* (New York: Holt, 1919); and Larzer Ziff, *The American 1890s: Life and Times of a Lost Generation* (New York: Viking Press, 1966).

In the meantime, for a detailed study of various facets of the Chicago novel, see Clarence Andrews, *Chicago in Story* (Iowa City: Midwest Heritage Publishing Company, 1983); Hugh D. Duncan, *The Rise of Chicago as a Literary Center from 1885 to 1920*; and Kenny J. Williams, *In the City of Men: Another Story of Chicago* (Nashville: Townsend Press, 1974) as well as Kenny J. Williams, *Prairie Voices: A Literary History of Chicago from the Frontier to 1893* (Nashville: Townsend Press, 1981). While it offers nothing that is substantially new and is essentially derivative, Carl Smith's *Chicago and the Literary Imagination: 1880–1920* (Chicago: University of Chicago Press, 1984) demonstrates the ongoing interest in the subject. With the exception of the Duncan and Smith volumes, these sources include relatively complete bibliographies of Chicago fiction. Also, both William Dean Howells ("Certain of the Chicago School of Fiction," *North American Reviews* 126 [May 1903]:734–46) and Floyd Dell ("Chicago in Fiction," *The Bookman* 38 [November 1913]:270–77; [December 1913]:375–79) deal briefly but comprehensively with some of the major novelists of the city. Howells, for example, praised the democratic element in the literary productions of Chicago as "the really valuable contributions of the West, and of Chicago in which the West has come to consciousness." Noting the work of Henry B. Fuller, Edith Wyatt, George Ade, and Finley Peter Dunne, essentially pre-Renaissance writers, Howells observed that "the democracy which was the faith of New England became the life of the West and now is the Western voice in our literary art."

Of special interest are the following autobiographies, some of which are by participants in the so-called Chicago Renaissance. These works provide further insight into the intersection of the city's commercial and cultural lives: Margaret Anderson, *My Thirty Years' War* (New York: Covici-Friede, 1930); Sherwood Anderson, *Memoirs* (New York: Harcourt Brace, 1942); Maurice Browne, *Too Late to Lament* (Bloomington: Indiana University Press, 1956); Fanny Butcher, *Many Lives—One Love* (New York: Harper and Row, 1972); Floyd Dell, *Homecoming* (New York: Farrar and Rinehart, 1933); Theodore Dreiser, *A Book About Myself* (New York: Boni and Liveright, 1922); Theodore

Dreiser, *Dawn* (New York: Boni and Liveright, 1931); Ben Hecht, *A Child of the Century* (New York: Simon and Schuster, 1954); Hamlin Garland, *Companions on the Trail* (New York: Macmillan, 1931); Hamlin Garland, *My Friendly Contemporaries: A Literary Log* (New York: Macmillan, 1932); Hamlin Garland, *Roadside Meetings* (New York: Macmillan, 1930); Vachel Lindsay, *Adventures While Preaching the Gospel of Beauty* (New York: Michael Kennerly, 1931); Robert Morss Lovett, *All Our Years* (New York: Viking, 1948); Edgar Lee Masters, *Across Spoon River* (New York: Farrar and Rinehart, 1936); Arthur Meeker, Jr., *Chicago With Love* (New York: Alfred A. Knopf, 1955); Harriet Monroe, *A Poet's Life: Seventy Years in a Changing World* (New York: Macmillan, 1938); Anna Morgan, *My Chicago* (Chicago: Ralph Fletcher Seymour, 1929); Burton Rascoe, *Before I Forget* (Garden City, N.Y.: Doubleday, 1937); Opie Read, *I Remember* (New York: Richard R. Smith, 1930); Carl Sandburg, *Always the Young Strangers* (New York: Harcourt Brace, 1953); Melville Stone, *Fifty Years a Journalist* (Garden City, N.Y.: Doubleday, 1921); and Eunice Tietjens, *The World at My Shoulders* (New York: Macmillan, 1938).

These by no means represent an exhaustive survey of background materials, but they should provide a point of beginning for those interested in the myth and reality of Chicago.

Index

Abe Lincoln in Illinois (Sherwood), 212
Adams, Henry, 13, 214, 259–60
Addams, Jane, 160
Ade, George, 42, 147, 160, 301
Adventures of Huckleberry Finn, 210, 211
Advertising, 272–73; SA in, 17–18, 19, 21, 23, 151, 175; in *Dark Laughter*, 254–55; in *Many Marriages*, 253–54; in urbanization, 218, 246, 254–55, 259; in *Windy McPherson's Son*, 70, 71–72, 73
Afro-Americans, 154–55, 260, 292; stereotypes of, 243
Agricultural Advertising, v, 17, 18, 275–76
Aldis, Dorothy, 154, 160
Alger, Horatio, 21, 51; stories of, 8, 266
Algren, Nelson, 27, 40, 44, 96, 129, 154, 161, 164
Allerton, Samuel W., 9
America, 147
American Dream, the, 29, 30, 40, 51, 53, 100, 123, 127, 129, 130, 133, 149, 169, 194, 260, 265–66, 271; SA and, 18, 73, 98, 263, 266; Chicago and, 7, 8, 262; efficacy of, 10, 207, 271; in *Marching Men*, 99, 104; in "Out of Nowhere Into Nothing," 227; in *Poor White*, 201, 206, 209, 210; pursuit of, 13;

in *Windy McPherson's Son*, 52, 59, 74, 85–86, 133
Anderson, David D., 92, 194, 228, 236
Anderson, Eleanor Copenhaver, 275
Anderson, Karl, 19
Anderson, Margaret, 149, 151, 156, 157, 162, 163, 164, 301
Anderson, Sherwood:
—business career of, vi, 18, 19, 21, 23, 85, 87, 107, 151. *See also* Advertising
—Chicago novel and, 83–85, 86
—divorces of, 151, 223, 234
—early life of, v, 7, 85, 130, 193
—editorship of, 271
—idealism of, 41, 87, 121, 169, 172, 173, 234, 265–66, 272–73
—illness of, 1912, vi, 18–19, 22
—literary realism and, 47–48, 83, 124–25, 131–32, 134, 189, 216, 217, 246, 251, 252, 253, 264, 285
—marriages of, vi, vii, viii, 18, 151, 223
—military service of, v, 16–17
—travels of: Alabama, 151, 265; Chicago, vi, vii, 7, 14–18, 19–20, 21–22, 145, 150–52, 165–67, 259, 262, 266, 267; Europe, vii, viii, 18, 151, 223; New Orleans, 151, 224, 242, 265; New York City, 171, 265; Virginia, vii, 181, 242, 265, 271

—urban vision of, 23, 49, 77, 98–
99, 103, 106, 119, 123, 127, 128–31,
132, 133–34, 152, 163, 166, 171,
172, 173, 177, 182, 189, 219, 224–
26, 228, 234, 236–37, 239–40,
256, 263–66, 267, 269–70,
271–72
—work of (*see also* specific work):
autobiographical nature of, 43,
50, 85, 93, 124, 126–27, 171–72,
174, 193, 268, 280; critical evalua-
tions of, 49–51, 90, 91–93, 170–
71, 182–83, 216–17, 234–36, 242,
282, 285–86, 287–89; writing
style of, 43, 50, 93, 124–25, 126–
27, 130, 132–33, 134, 152, 169, 171,
190, 200, 210–11, 217, 220, 226,
229, 231, 232, 233, 235–36, 240,
242, 264, 266, 268, 269, 270, 272,
292. *See also* Intrusive author
device
Anderson Manufacturing Company, vi, 18
Antigone, 121
Apartment buildings, 15, 229, 230,
244, 252
"Apology for Crudity," 125
Architecture, 10, 11, 14, 26–27, 38,
52, 64, 95, 100–101, 102, 103, 148,
155, 157, 158, 182, 208–9, 298–
300
Architecture and the Spirit of Man
(Hudnut), 131
Art, therapeutic nature of, 126–27
Art colonies, 155, 246, 251
Art Institute of Chicago, 11, 251
Astor Street, 159
Austen, Jane, 160
Autobiography (Franklin), 7
Autobiography of an Idea, The (Sul-
livan), 12

Bailly, Albert, 216–17
Balzac, 57

Barnes, Margaret Ayer, 27, 160,
161, 164
Barriers Burned Away (Roe), 31,
32–33, 42
Baum, Frank, 155
Beffel, John Nicholas, 92
*Beginning: Romance of Chicago As It
Might Be, The*, 40
Bellow, Saul, 161
Beman, Solon S., 155
Beyond Desire, viii, 267
Biblical literature, 51, 54, 79, 86,
180, 181
Blake, Tiffany, 161
Board of Trade Building, 38
Bockler, Charles, 127, 267, 280
Bodenheim, Maxwell, 157, 158–59
Bomb, The (Harris), 40
Bookman, The, 50, 148
Borghese, G. A., 161
Boston *Evening Transcript*, 50
Bostonians, The (James), 36, 285
Boyd, Ernest, 242
Boynton, H. W., 49, 50, 92
Boynton, Percy, 154, 161
Bradley, Mary Hastings, 160
Braithwaite, William Stanley, 171,
282–83
Brashler, William, 26
Brewer, Kate, 154
Bromfield, Louis, 160
Brooks, Van Wyck, 267, 268, 282
"Brothers," 226
Broun, Heywood, 216
Browne, Francis Fisher, 149, 156,
157
Browne, Maurice, 155, 163, 301
Burnham and Root, 157
Business, the game of, 29–30, 58,
61, 71, 106
Businessmen, 26, 29, 31, 35, 51–52,
53, 54–55, 65–66, 71, 199; com-
plexity of, as fictional characters,
83–84; as fictional types, 33, 34,
36–39, 40–41, 53, 63–66. *See also*

Anderson, Sherwood, business career of; *Marching Men; Poor White; Windy McPherson's Son*
Burbank, Rex, 235–36, 288–89
Burnham, Daniel, 159
Butcher, Fanny, 153, 154, 158–60, 162, 163, 289, 301

Calverton, Vernon F., 216, 286
Campbell, Gladys, 161
Canal Street, 108
Canby, Henry Seidel, 288, 289
Cane (Toomer), 293
Capone, Al, 21, 259
Cargill, Oscar, 92
Carlyle, Thomas, 60
Carson, Samuel, 10
Cass Street (North Wabash Avenue), vi, 159, 182, 189
"Certain of the Chicago School of Fiction" (Howells), 41, 301
Chapman, John Jay, 93, 121
Chase, Cleveland, 235
Chatfield-Taylor, Hobart C., 25, 30, 39, 73, 160
Chicago: culture in early, 11, 145–47, 152; growth of, 5–7, 8–11, 21, 26, 145–46, 149, 194, 218, 293–301; as legend, 7–9, 14, 20, 21, 23, 25, 26, 27, 31, 34, 47, 52, 57, 98, 105, 124, 149, 230, 271; as literary center, 41–42, 229, 261; Loop of, 52, 95, 101, 102, 245; North Side of, v, vi, 15, 27, 52, 95, 101, 102, 159, 182, 227, 229, 230, 283, 284; South Side of, 18, 19, 27, 52, 97, 102, 153, 154, 283; symbolic nature of, 52, 162, 163, 225, 232, 259, 263; West Side of, v, 16, 27, 52, 60–61, 67, 97, 103, 106, 129, 232. *See also* Chicago Renaissance and specific Chicago street
"Chicago" (SA), 144, 174

"Chicago" (Sandburg), 159, 166
Chicago Book and Art Auction, 155
Chicago *Daily News*, 148, 149, 159, 161
Chicago Flag, 153
"Chicago Hamlet, A," 232–33
"Chicago in Fiction" (Dell), 148–49, 301
"Chicago Letters" (Monroe), 148
Chicago Literary Club, 146
Chicago Literary Times, 159
Chicago novel, 26–27, 30–44, 48, 51, 63, 70–71, 86, 98, 124, 127, 131, 133, 145, 154, 160, 161–62, 164–65, 198, 206, 218, 263, 301; SA and, 83–85, 86
Chicago Poems (Sandburg), 172
Chicago Renaissance, 12, 30, 44, 49, 93, 144, 146–51, 152–60, 163, 169, 170, 186, 190, 223, 224, 225, 228, 234, 246, 247, 248, 250, 252, 297–98, 300–301; SA's attitude toward, 233, 234, 247–48, 250, 252; nineteenth-century roots of, 146–49. *See also Dark Laughter*
Chicago River, 27, 52, 63, 107, 159, 173, 174–75, 202, 227
Chicago School of Architecture, 12, 146, 159
Chicago Symphony Orchestra, 11, 157
Chicago *Times*, The, 147
Chicago Tribune, 41, 147, 153, 155, 161, 216
Chicago: With Love (Meeker), 154
Chimes (Herrick), 154
Christianity, 42, 81–82, 119, 198, 199
City planning, 11–12
"Civil Disobedience" (Thoreau), 93
Civil War, 59, 64, 146, 187, 196, 197, 200, 207, 210, 259, 262
Clark Street, 101–2
Clemens, Samuel, 83, 125, 131, 211
Clergy, 73–74, 79, 80, 129

Cleveland, Ohio, vi, 18, 185, 265
Cliff-Dwellers, The (Fuller), 31, 33–
34, 38, 42–43, 158, 298
Cliff-Dwellers Club, 157
Clyde, Ohio, v, 149, 183, 193, 223,
265
Coliseum, 52
Colossus, The (Read), 36
Commager, Henry Steele, 288
Common Lot, The (Herrick), 37–38
Communication, 44, 66, 75, 108,
111, 112–13, 175–76, 186, 218, 233,
237, 239, 241, 250, 253, 271. *See
also* Language
Communicative love, 237–38, 256,
267, 268, 270
Communism, 93
Compton, Arthur, 160
"Congo, The" (Lindsay), 159
Congress Street, 230
Conkling, Grace Hazard, 170
Cook, Howard W., 171
Cook County Jail, 101
Cooke, George Cram, 149
Cooper, James Fenimore, 26
Cornfields, 98, 132–33, 172, 174,
177, 191, 270–71. *See also* Nature;
Order
Cournos, John, 216
Covenant theology, 261
Covici, Pascal, 159
Covici-McGee Bookshop, 158
Cowdrey, Robert, 40
Crane, Hart, 49, 157
Creon, law of, 121
Critic, The, 148
Cronin murder case of 1889, 185,
283–84
Crowell Co., 17
Crumbling Idols, 148
Cuba, v, 17
Currey, Margery, 150, 153

D. H. Burnham Company, 157
Dark Laughter, vii, 23, 222, 224, 234,

241–55, 267, 270, 271, 272, 292,
293
Darrow, Clarence, 40, 44, 96, 160
Darwinism, 14, 89, 196, 209, 260
Dearborn Street, 52
Death-and-resurrection theme, 130
Dell, Floyd, 19, 25, 38, 41, 44, 49,
147, 148, 151, 153, 162, 163, 164,
165, 176, 234, 277, 301
Denslow, Frank, 155
Determinism, 87, 132. *See also*
Naturalism
Dial, vii, 147, 149, 150, 151, 152, 156,
170
Dictionary of American Slang, 158,
299
Dillon, George, 160, 161
Disorder, 44, 90, 98, 99, 117, 119–
20, 123, 128, 129, 167, 172, 239–
40, 262, 272
Division Street, vi, 27
"Doctrine of Non-Resistance, The"
(Chapman), 93
Donlin, George B., 92
"Door of the Trap, The," 226
Dostoevsky, Fyodor, 49, 277, 282
Douglas, Stephen, 153, 155
Dreiser, Theodore, 20, 22, 26, 30,
49, 51, 73, 98, 125, 129, 147, 148,
149, 162, 163, 164, 180, 228, 235,
288, 301–2. *See also* specific work
"Dreiser" (SA), 228
Drexel Boulevard, 103
DuBois, W. E. B., 260
Dunbar, Paul Laurence, 219
Dunne, Finley Peter, 147, 301
Dynasty novels, 39, 164–65

East, the, 6, 11, 22, 23, 25, 42, 43,
63, 82, 146, 151, 156, 171, 179, 200,
201, 212, 223, 229, 262
Eberhart, Mignon G., 160
Economic depressions, 13, 14, 15,
96–97, 260
Eddy, Arthur J., 30, 39

Education of Henry Adams, The, 13, 259–60
Eggleston, Edward, 183
Eliot, T. S., 157, 159
Ellis Avenue, 155
Elmer Gantry (Lewis), 79
Elyria, Ohio, vi, 18, 92, 149, 190, 223, 265
Emancipation Proclamation, 212
Emerson, Ralph Waldo, 4, 5, 6, 7, 8, 21, 23, 94, 150, 260
Erie Canal, 6
Erie Street, 159
Europe, vii, 7, 25, 151, 223, 251, 261, 262, 265
"Evening Song," 177
Everette, Henry, 40
Exemplum, SA's use of, 200, 270
Eye for an Eye, An (Darrow), 40, 96

Factories, 4, 16, 28, 99, 126, 193, 196, 255, 261. *See also* Industrialism
Fadiman, Clifton, 180
Fagin, Bryllion, 217
Fair, Ronald, 161
Fairbanks, Janet Ayer, 27, 160, 161, 164
Fairhope, Alabama, vii, 151, 265
"Farmer Wears Clothes, The," 17
Farrell, James T., 27, 40, 44, 96, 129, 154, 161, 164, 180
Fascism, 91, 92
Faulkner, William, 269
Ferber, Edna, 160
Ficke, Arthur Davison, 160
Field, Eugene, 147, 148, 158
Field, Marshall, 9–10, 110, 154, 164, 259
Fifty-seventh Street, vi, 12, 19, 150, 151, 152, 165, 166, 234, 249, 300
Financier, The (Dreiser), 40, 61
Fine Arts Building, 155–56, 157, 159
Finn, Huck, 212, 241

Fire of 1871, 7, 10–11, 32, 34, 35, 53, 212, 241, 262, 299
First Ward, 101, 109
Fitzgerald, F. Scott, 234–35, 276
Ford, Ford Madox, 157
Ford, Henry, 215, 254, 284
Fort Dearborn, 6
Fortnightly Club, 146
Frank, Waldo, 50, 51, 86
Frank B. White Co., v, 17
Franklin, Benjamin, 4, 5, 7, 8, 21, 51, 260
Frederick, John Y., 158
Free verse movement, 151, 167, 169, 170, 171, 179–80
Freitag-Loringhaven, Baroness Else von, 157
Friday Literary Review, The, 153, 170, 277
Friedman, I. K., 30
Front Page (MacArthur and Hecht), 160
Fuller, Henry Blake, 5, 22, 26, 30, 36, 39, 41, 73, 98, 125, 147, 148, 153, 164, 205, 206, 298–99, 301. *See also* specific works

Gage, Lyman, 10
Galantiere, Lewis, 159
Gale, Zona, 160
Ganton and Co. (Eddy), 39
Garland, Hamlin, 30, 35–36, 39, 125, 148, 157, 160, 161, 162, 163, 285, 300, 302
Gelfant, Blanche, 212
"General William Booth Enters Into Heaven" (Lindsay), 159
Genteel tradition, 39, 146, 170
Glicksberg, Charles, 235
Goodspeed, Dr. Edgar J., 160
Gospel of Freedom, The (Herrick), 10, 36–37
Gould, Gerald, 49
Graceland Cemetery, 10
Grant Park, 52, 77, 78, 118

Greenwich Village, 150
Grotesques, 130, 167, 212
Groveland Park, 155
Gunther, John, 159

Hackett, Francis, 16, 92, 151, 285, 286
Halsted Street, 98, 116
Hamilton, David, 154
Hansen, Harry, 159, 292
Harlem Renaissance, 243
Harper, William Rainey, 153, 154
Harris, Charles, 147, 148
Harris, Frank, 40
Harrison Street Police Station, 101
Harte, Bret, 183
Hartwick, Henry, 49
Hawthorne, Nathaniel, 23, 183
Haymarket Affair of 1886, 13, 40
Heap, Jane, 49, 157, 235
Hecht, Ben, 44, 49, 147, 149, 153, 158, 159, 162, 163, 164, 277, 302
Hemingway, Ernest, 157, 269, 282, 290
Henderson, Alice Corbin, 170
Heroines of Fiction (Howells), 35
Herrick, Robert, 6, 26, 30, 39, 41, 51, 73, 98, 148, 153, 154, 205, 206. *See also* specific work
Holy Grail, legend of, 86
Hoosier Schoolmaster, The (Eggleston), 183
Horses and Men, vii, 23, 181, 224, 226, 228
Howe, Edgar W., 181
Howe, Irving, 92, 190, 211, 288
Howells, William Dean, 22, 28, 35, 41, 83, 125, 131, 147, 160, 293–94, 301
"Howells or James?" (Fuller), 125
Hudnut, Joseph, 131
Huebsch, B. W., vi, vii, 278, 284
Hutchinson, Benjamin P., 9

Ibsen, Henrik, 155
If Christ Came to Chicago (Stead), 14, 102
Illinois Central Railroad, 6
Illinois Central Station, 101
Illinois Institute of Technology, 16
Immigrants, 6, 9, 10, 40, 98, 116, 187, 206, 210
Industrialism, 23, 30, 90, 104–5, 142, 170, 179, 187, 188, 193, 194–95, 196, 200–210, 212, 213, 215, 220, 224, 232, 258, 259, 260, 261, 266. *See also* Factories
Inland Steel Company, 9
Ingersoll, Robert, 198
Insull, Samuel, 20–21
Internalization, 242, 270. *See also* Anderson, writing style of
International Harvester Company, 9
Intrusive author device, SA's use of, 59, 64, 68, 70, 84, 99–100, 103, 120, 130, 131–32, 188, 198, 199, 207, 214, 227, 230, 232, 268, 270, 286. *See also* Anderson, writing style of
Irving, Washington, 23

"J'Accuse," 110
Jackson Park, 52, 78, 95, 233
James, Henry, 36, 83, 125, 131, 268, 285
James, William, 93, 260
Jones, Llewellyn, 49, 50, 170
Joost, Nicholas, 156
Journalism, 70–71, 73, 113, 147, 148, 161, 205, 271. *See also* Newspapers
Joyce, James, vii, 157, 242, 249, 253, 269
Jungle, The (Sinclair), 96

Kerfoot, Samuel, 11
Kinzie, John, 6, 218
Kraft, H. S., 284

La Baitaille Litteraire, 217
La Terre, 253
Labor and laborers, 7, 29, 91, 93, 94, 99, 114, 118, 119, 207, 210; exploitation of, 7, 13, 123, 209, 271. *See also Marching Men*
Lake Michigan, 5, 15, 52, 77–78, 102, 118, 182, 194
Lake Shore Drive, 27
Lake Street, 9, 108, 233
Lane, Cornelia, vi, 18, 151
Langfield, William, 242
Language, 72, 105, 111–13, 117, 119, 125, 132–33, 167, 170, 171, 181, 190, 232, 240, 243, 245–46, 250, 252, 253, 270. *See also* Communication
Lardner, Ring, 147, 248
LaSalle Street, 11, 38, 52, 62, 63, 101, 233
Laughlin, Clara, 161
Lawrence, D. H., 249, 288
"Letters from an Altrurian Traveller" (Howells), 293–94
Levin, Meyer, 27
Lewis, Janet, 161
Lewis, Lloyd, 159, 160
Lewis, Sinclair, 79, 169, 176, 182–83, 217
Lewis, Wyndham, 157
Lewis Institute, v, 16
Lewissohn, Ludwig, 234
Life for a Life, A (Herrick), 23
Lincoln, Abraham, 91, 97, 207, 210, 211, 212, 216, 284
Lindsay, Vachel, 159, 160, 163, 164, 170, 178, 302
Linn, James Weber, 30, 154
"Literary Capital of the United States, The" (Mencken), 41–42
Little Review, vii, 49, 149, 156–57, 165–66
Liveright, Horace, vii, viii, 267
Long-Critchfield Co., v, 17
Lorimer, George, 30

"Love Song of J. Alfred Prufrock, The" (Eliot), 159
Lovett, Robert Morss, 154, 161, 163, 216, 285, 289, 302
Lowell, Amy, 157

MacArthur, Charles, 147, 159
McClurg's Bookstore, 147, 158
McCormick, Cyrus, 9, 218
McCutcheon, George Barr, 160
McCutcheon, John T., 155, 160
MacLeish, Archibald, 242
Madison Street, 10, 97
Main Street (Lewis), 183, 217, 282–83
Malloch, Douglas, 160
"Man and His Imagination," 126
"Man's Story, The," 230–31, 232
Manchester Guardian, 217
Mandel Brothers, 10
Mann, Thomas, 161
Many Marriages, vii, 23, 181, 222, 223, 224, 231, 234–41, 252, 253, 255–56, 267, 270, 292
Marching Men, vi, 22, 26, 27, 31, 41, 44, 47, 48, 88, 89–121, 123, 124, 126, 128, 129, 130, 131, 132, 133, 145, 166, 167, 169, 171, 172, 181, 190, 191, 194, 218, 224, 225, 236, 239, 256, 266, 267; businessman in, 94, 108, 114–15, 118–19, 123, 129; critical judgments of, 90, 91–93; portrait of Chicago in, 89, 90, 95–103, 106–8, 112–13, 114–16, 120; village life in, 95, 104–5, 112, 116; women in, 95, 108–9, 115, 119
Marion, Virginia, vii, 224, 265
Marion *Democrat*, vii, 271
Master of the Inn, The (Herrick), 83
Masters, Edgar Lee, 42, 49, 149, 151, 163, 164, 170, 183, 230, 282, 302
Mayer, Oscar, 10
Medill, Joseph, 10
Meeker, Arthur, Jr., 154, 163, 302

Meine, Franklin J., 155
Memoirs of an American Citizen
    (Herrick), 31, 37, 53–54, 61
Mencken, H. L., 22, 41–42, 50, 90,
    162, 229, 282, 287, 289
Michigan Avenue, 16, 52, 77, 157
Mid-American Chants, vi, 23, 24,
    127, 166, 168, 169, 172–81, 191,
    292, 293; autobiographical ele-
    ments in, 171–72; critical recep-
    tion of, 170–71
"Mid-American Songs," 170
Middle West, 15, 42, 101, 125, 143,
    144, 145, 146, 154, 169, 171, 174,
    182, 190, 192, 194, 197, 214, 216,
    229, 249; symbol for modern
    America, 146; towns and villages
    of, 149, 165, 223, 234. *See also*
    Small Towns
Midland, The, 158
Midway, 12
Midway Gardens, 102
Miles, Hamish, 180
"Milk Bottles," 228–30
Miller, Henry, 235, 288
Mississippi River, 243
Mitchell, Tennessee, vi, vii, 151,
    223, 243
Mobile, Alabama, vii, 151, 265
Modern art, 233–34, 251–52, 272
Modernism, 148, 250
Monadnock Building, 101, 157
Money Captain, The (Payne), 36
Monroe, Harriet, 148, 153, 157, 159,
    160, 161, 163, 164, 170, 302
Monroe, Lucy, 148
Monroe Street, 52
Moody, William Vaughn, 149, 153,
    154
Moody, Mrs. William Vaughn: the
    salon of, 155
Moon-Calf (Dell), 25
Moore, Marianne, 157
Morgan, Anna, 153, 163, 302
Morgan Park, 153

Morton Salt Co., 10
Mowrer, Paul Scott, 161
Muckrakers, 14

Nation, The, 92, 217
Native Son (Wright), 28
Naturalism, 23, 26, 31, 48, 49, 51,
    66, 86, 87, 92, 106, 127, 130–31,
    132, 166, 172, 179, 180, 219, 231–
    32, 235, 256, 264, 266, 272
Nature, 8, 27–28, 77, 78, 214. *See
    also* Cornfields
Nazis, 93, 94
Neighborhoods. *See* Chicago,
    "sides" of
New England, 7, 15, 21, 33, 63, 301
New France, 6
"New Note, A," 87, 165–66, 234
New Orleans, vii, 151, 223, 224,
    242, 243, 265
New Testament, A, vii, 160, 180, 182,
    292, 293
New York City, vi, vii, 25, 57, 150,
    151, 152, 156, 162, 170, 171, 184,
    186, 244, 248, 265
New York Times Book Review, 49,
    92–93
New York *Tribune*, 92
Newspapers, 109–10, 198, 245–47,
    252. *See also* Journalism
Non-violent civil disobedience, 93,
    94–95, 113–14, 117, 120, 121
Norris, Frank, 26, 30, 36, 38–39,
    41, 85, 148
North, Sterling and Jessica, 161
North American Review, 50
Northwest Territory, 6

Ohio, 90, 107, 184, 207, 261
Ohio Street, 159
O'Keeffe, Georgia, 236
Olivet Baptist Church, 154–55
O'Neill, Eugene, 155

One Hundred and Eleventh Street, 153
Ontario Street, 159
Orchestra Hall, 157
Order, 98, 117, 120, 271. *See also* Disorder; Cornfields
Our Poets Today, 171
"Out of Nowhere Into Nothing," 226–28
Out of the Midwest, 158

Palmer, Bertha Honore, 148
Palmer, Potter, 9, 215
Parliament of Religions, 12
Pattee, Fred Lewis, 38
Payne, Will, 30, 36, 39, 73, 206
Payne, William, 147
P.E.N., 160, 163
Peattie, Donald Culross, 161
Peattie, Elia, 161, 216
People's Program, The (Everett), 40
Phelps, Willion Lyon, 50
Philanthropy, 28, 34–35, 67, 76, 109
Pierce, Bessie, 146
Pirle, John T., 10
Pit, The (Norris), 31, 36, 38–39, 85
Poe, Edgar Allan, 183
Poetic prose, 169, 172, 285, 293
Poetry: A Magazine of Verse, 149, 151, 153, 159, 161, 164, 170, 182
Poetry Club, 161
Political bosses, 14, 109
Polk Street, 109, 110
Poor White, vii, 29–30, 166, 183, 193–221, 223, 225, 231, 239, 261–62, 266, 267–68, 270; Bidwell's transformation in, 197–201, 205–10; Chicago in, 201–2; critical reception of, 216–17; Nature in, 214; symbolism in, 213; women in, 201, 212–13
Porter, Gene Stratton, 160
Pound, Ezra, vii, 157, 249, 269

"Practical agitation," theory of, 121
Pragmatism, 260
Prairie Avenue (Meeker), 159
Prall, Elizabeth, vii, 223
Press Club, 161, 163
Preston, Keith, 159
Protest novels, 28, 40, 96
"Protestant ethic," 21
Provincetown Players, 155
Pullman, George M., 9, 104, 218
Pullman Strike of 1894, 13
Puritans, 7, 21, 33, 228, 261

Race, significance of, in the United States, 260
"Rags-to-riches" theory, 7–8, 10, 53, 70, 89, 198, 199, 201–2, 210, 218, 265–66
Rasoe, Burton, 159, 163, 282, 287, 302
Read, Opie, 30, 36, 163, 302
Realism, doctrine of, viii, 48, 49, 50, 83, 123–24, 216, 246, 251, 253, 263–64, 271
Reform movements, 14, 111, 112; efforts of, 109–10; limitations of, 76, 94, 120, 123, 128, 225
Religion, 29, 32, 42, 73–74, 78–80, 86, 219–20; organized, 79, 81, 129
Reno, Nevada, vii, 223, 265, 268
"Revolt-from-the-village" movement, 31, 164, 184, 188–89, 217, 218, 263, 282–83
Revolutionary War, 6, 178
Richards, I. A., 289
Riley, James Whitcomb, 160
Ripshin, vii, 182, 223, 271
Rise of Silas Lapham, The (Howells), 252
Rise of the City, 1878–1898, The (Schlesinger), 8
Roberts, Elizabeth Madox, 161
Rockefeller, John D., 154, 198, 215
Roe, E. P., 26, 30, 31, 32–33, 35, 39, 42–43, 44, 73

Romanticism, doctrine of, 77, 132, 169, 217, 264, 272
Rookery, 52, 101
Roosevelt, Franklin, 271
Root, John, 159
Rosalie Court (Harper Avenue), vi, 18
Rose of Dutcher's Coolly (Garland), 35–36, 285
Rosenfeld, Paul, vii, 125, 126, 223, 243, 275, 276
Rourke, Constance, 285
Rush Street Bridge, 227
Russia, 93, 114, 285–86
Ryerson, Joseph and Martin, 9

"Sad Horn Blowers, The," 231
Saints and Sinners Corner, 147
Sandburg, Carl, 22, 42, 49, 147, 149, 159, 160, 162–63, 164, 166, 170, 172, 230, 302
Saturday Evening Post, The, 156
Schlesinger, Arthur M., Sr., 8
Schlogl's Restaurant, 159
Schlueter, Paul, 50
Schmitt, Dr. Bernadotte, 160
Scott, Robert, 10
Self-reliance, 4, 5, 6, 7, 28, 29, 94, 120, 130, 150, 226, 260, 264
Seligman, Herbert, 180, 181
Sell, Henry, 159
Shaw, George Bernard, 155
Sheean, Vincent, 161
Sherman, Stuart P., 242
Sherwood, Robert, 212
"Sherwood Anderson and the American Myth of Power," 211
"Sherwood Anderson on the Marriage Question," 234–35
Sherwood Anderson's Memoirs, viii, 3, 15–16, 19, 45, 85, 91, 145, 152, 165, 182, 193, 275
Sherwood Anderson's Notebook, vii, 122, 124, 125, 182

Sinclair, Upton, 40, 96, 162, 235
Sister Carrie (Dreiser), 31, 129
Sixty-third Street, 102
Skyscrapers, 52, 53, 58, 61, 64, 148, 180, 299. *See also* Architecture
Small towns, 31, 74–77, 83, 90, 133, 149, 164, 167, 178, 182, 183–84, 188, 189, 217, 218, 224, 225, 228, 259, 263, 271, 281–82
—SA's theory of, 189
—descriptions of: Bidwell, 194–95, 197–201, 202, 203, 204, 205–10, 213–14, 216, 218, 263; Caxton, 54, 55–56, 57, 58; Coal Creek, 104–5, 112, 116; Mudcat Landing, 196–97, 198, 201, 215; Winesburg, 183, 184, 185, 186, 187, 189, 218, 263
—imitate cities, 74–75, 225
—romanticized view of, 197
Smith, Alson J., 162
Smith, Henry Justin, 153, 159
Smith, John, 51
Smith, Rev. Justin, 153
Smith, Mark, 26
Smith, Sydney, 179
Smiths, The (Fairbanks), 161
Smyth County News, vii, 271
Socialism, 66–67, 92, 93
Society of Midland Authors, 160
Sommers, Lillian, 30
"Song of Industrial America," 24, 174
"Song of Myself" (Whitman), 172
"Song of Theodore," 176
"Song of the Soul of Chicago," 173, 174
"Song to New Song," 168, 172, 177
South, the, vii, 6, 17, 23, 196, 223, 262; compared to the North, 197
South Water Street, 52, 62, 63, 64, 77
South Water Street Market, 62–63
Spanish-American War, 16
Spiritual nature of life, 28, 30, 31, 36, 81, 127, 214

Spoon River Anthology (Masters), 49, 159, 183, 282
Sport of the Gods, The (Dunbar), 219
"Spring Song," 171
Starrett, Vincent, 159
State Street, 9, 10, 52, 97, 101
Stead, William T., 14, 102
Stein, Gertrude, vii, 133, 151, 157
Stevens, Charles, 10
Stevens, Wallace, 157
Stockyards, 9, 40, 42, 96, 229
Stone, Melville, 147, 163, 302
Storey, Wilbur, 147
Story of a Country Town, The (Howe), 183
Story Teller's Story, A, vii, 4, 14–15, 16, 19, 85, 125, 257
Strindberg, August, 155
Strobel, Marion, 154, 160
Studebaker Building, 155
Success, emphasis upon, 20, 25, 28–29, 38, 51, 53, 69, 70, 73, 74, 85, 87, 89, 105, 128, 129, 204, 223
Sullivan, Louis, 12, 123, 148, 157, 169, 297
Sutton, 126, 193
Swift, Gustavus, 9, 164

Taft, Lorado, 159
Tait, Samuel, Jr., 49
"Talented Tenth," 260
Tender Buttons (Stein), 133
Thirty-fifth Street, 153
Thirty-ninth Street, 102
Thomas, Theodore, 11, 157
Thoreau, Henry David, 93, 94, 120, 121, 271
Thornton Wilder's Writing Class, 154
Tietjens, Eunice, 163, 302
Titan, The (Dreiser), 31, 40–41, 61, 85, 90
Together (Herrick), 10
Toomer, Jean, 293

Tramp in Society, A (Cowdrey), 40
Transcendentalists, 93–94
Transportation, 25–26, 91, 101, 120, 177, 233, 244, 245
Tree Studios, 159
"Triumph of a Modern, The," 233–34
Triumph of the Egg, The, vii, 23, 224, 226, 227, 228
Truth, search for, 54, 72–77, 79, 80, 81–82, 86, 87, 147, 149. *See also Windy McPherson's Son*
Twelfth Street, 101
Twenty-third Street, 102
Twenty-fourth Street, 97

Ulysses (Joyce), 156
United Factories Co., vi, 18
University of Chicago, 12, 97, 102–3, 111, 150, 153–54, 155, 161, 216
Untermeyer, Louis, 170
Upton, George P., 147
Urban judicial system, 40, 96, 185
Urban novel, 25, 89, 106–7, 134, 193, 194, 256. *See also* Chicago novel
Urban politics, 109
Urbanization, 8, 9, 13, 23, 27, 28–29, 30, 40, 42, 84, 128, 193, 195, 207–9, 224, 236, 239, 244, 245–47, 262, 264–65, 271. *See also* Reform movements
Urbs in Horto, 95
Utopia, 39–40, 238

Van Buren Street, 52, 101, 110
Van Doren, Carl, 289
Veblen, Thorstein, 21, 93
Volkenburg, Ellen von, 155

Wabash Avenue, 52, 102
"Waiting for Ben Huebsch," 91

Walden, 94, 120, 171
Wall Street, 11
Walsh, Thomas, 171
Ward, Christopher, 187
Ward, Montgomery, 10
Washington, Booker T., 260
Washington Boulevard, v, 15
Washington Square, 186
Washington Square Players, 155
Web of Life, The (Herrick), 37–38
Webb, Doris, 92
Weber, Brom, 50–51, 90, 93
Webster, Henry Kitchell, 276
Wells Street, 232, 233
Wescott, Glenway, 161
West, the, 6, 25, 75, 171, 174, 177, 217, 229, 265
Wheelock, John Hall, 189
Whipple, T. K., 266
White, Horace, 147
White, Ray Lewis, 93, 275, 276
White, William Allen, 160, 276
White City. *See* World's Columbian Exposition
Whitman, Walt, 49, 125, 172, 285, 292
Wieboldt, William, 10
Wilder, Thornton, 154
Wilkie, Franc. B., 147
Williams, William Carlos, 57
Wilson, Edmund, 287
Wilson, Woodrow, 260
Winds Over the Campus (Linn), 154
Windy McPherson's Son, vi, 22, 26, 27, 31, 37, 41, 44, 48–87, 89, 90, 91–92, 95, 97, 100, 123, 124, 126, 127, 128, 129, 130, 131, 132, 133, 145, 166, 172, 190, 191, 194, 218, 224, 225, 236, 239, 256, 264, 266, 267, 270; Chicago in, 52–53, 54, 55, 57–58, 60–69; clergymen in, 73–74, 79, 80, 81; critical judgments of, 49–52; father-son rela-

tionship in, 58–59; journalism in, 70–71, 72; moral sense in, 69–70, 81; revised edition of, 69–70, 82–83, 278; Sam's search in, 50, 53–54, 72–77, 81–82, 84–85, 86, 91; small towns imitate cities, 74–75; use of nature in, 77–78; women in, 62, 66–68, 87
Winesburg, Ohio, vi, 23, 48, 93, 127, 130, 132, 133, 157, 166, 167, 171, 180, 182, 183–90, 216, 218, 226, 258, 266, 269, 293
Winters, Yvor, 161
With the Procession (Fuller), 34–35, 65
Wittenburg Academy, v, 17
Wizard of Oz, The (Baum), 155
Women, 34–36, 62, 66–68, 108–9, 115, 151, 212–13, 248, 295–97
World War I, 94, 250–51, 259, 260
World War II, 163
World's Columbian Exposition, 5, 11–13, 16, 34, 96, 102, 147, 148, 150, 156, 162, 259–60, 262, 293, 294, 300
Wright, Frank Lloyd, 93, 155, 156
Wright, Richard, 27, 28, 40, 44, 96, 129, 154, 161, 164, 180
Writer's Conception of Realism, A, 124
Wyatt, Edith Franklin, 39, 160, 301

Years of Grace (Barnes), 161
Yeats, William Butler, 157
Yerkes, Charles, 20–21, 36, 40
Young Men's Club, 146

Zabel, Morton D., 161
Zola, Émile, 253

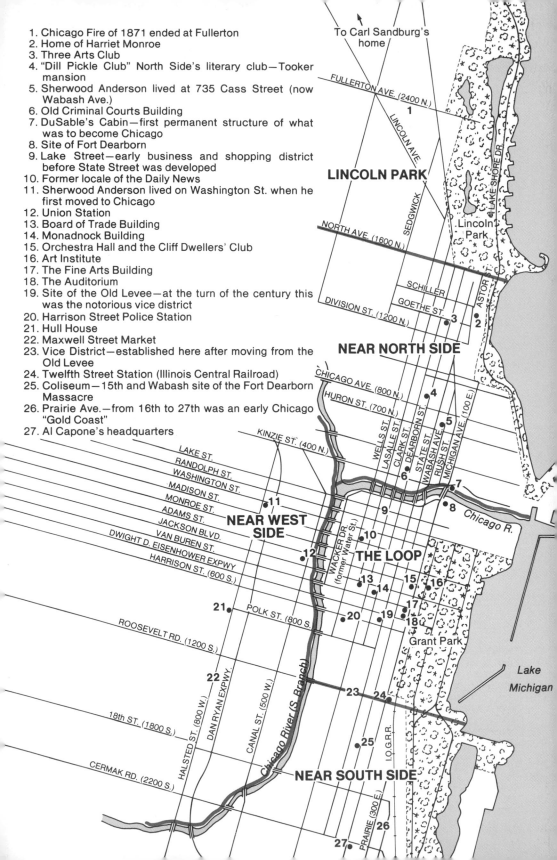

1. Chicago Fire of 1871 ended at Fullerton
2. Home of Harriet Monroe
3. Three Arts Club
4. "Dill Pickle Club" North Side's literary club—Tooker mansion
5. Sherwood Anderson lived at 735 Cass Street (now Wabash Ave.)
6. Old Criminal Courts Building
7. DuSable's Cabin—first permanent structure of what was to become Chicago
8. Site of Fort Dearborn
9. Lake Street—early business and shopping district before State Street was developed
10. Former locale of the Daily News
11. Sherwood Anderson lived on Washington St. when he first moved to Chicago
12. Union Station
13. Board of Trade Building
14. Monadnock Building
15. Orchestra Hall and the Cliff Dwellers' Club
16. Art Institute
17. The Fine Arts Building
18. The Auditorium
19. Site of the Old Levee—at the turn of the century this was the notorious vice district
20. Harrison Street Police Station
21. Hull House
22. Maxwell Street Market
23. Vice District—established here after moving from the Old Levee
24. Twelfth Street Station (Illinois Central Railroad)
25. Coliseum—15th and Wabash site of the Fort Dearborn Massacre
26. Prairie Ave.—from 16th to 27th was an early Chicago "Gold Coast"
27. Al Capone's headquarters

To Carl Sandburg's home

FULLERTON AVE. (2400 N.)

LINCOLN AVE.

LAKE SHORE DR.

LINCOLN PARK

Lincoln Park

NORTH AVE. (1600 N.)

SEDGWICK

SCHILLER

GOETHE ST.

ASTOR ST.

DIVISION ST. (1200 N.)

NEAR NORTH SIDE

CHICAGO AVE. (800 N.)

HURON ST. (700 N.)

WELLS ST.

LASALLE ST.

CLARK ST.

DEARBORN ST.

STATE ST.

WABASH AVE.

RUSH ST.

MICHIGAN AVE. (100 E.)

KINZIE ST. (400 N.)

LAKE ST.

RANDOLPH ST.

WASHINGTON ST.

MADISON ST.

MONROE ST.

ADAMS ST.

JACKSON BLVD.

VAN BUREN ST.

DWIGHT D. EISENHOWER EXPWY

HARRISON ST. (600 S.)

NEAR WEST SIDE

THE LOOP

WACKER DR. (former Water St.)

Chicago R.

POLK ST. (800 S.)

ROOSEVELT RD. (1200 S.)

Grant Park

DAN RYAN EXPWY.

CANAL ST. (500 W.)

HALSTED ST. (800 W.)

Chicago River (S. Branch)

I.C.G.R.R.

Lake Michigan

18th ST. (1800 S.)

CERMAK RD. (2200 S.)

NEAR SOUTH SIDE

PRAIRIE (300 E.)